MARXIST GOVERNMENTS

A World Survey

Volume 3   Mozambique – Yugoslavia

MARXIST GOVERNMENTS

A World Survey

Volume 3   Mozambique – Yugoslavia

Edited by

BOGDAN SZAJKOWSKI
Lecturer in Politics and Comparative Communism
University College, Cardiff

St. Martin's Press   New York

St. Martin's Press, Inc., 175 Fifth Avenue, New York, N.Y. 10010
Printed in Hong Kong
First published in the United States of America in 1981

Volume 1   Albania – The Congo   ISBN 0–312–51857–9
Volume 2   Cuba – Mongolia   ISBN 0–312–51858–7
Volume 3   Mozambique – Yugoslavia   ISBN 0–312–51859–5

Library of Congress Cataloging in Publication Data

Main entry under title:

Marxist governments.

Includes indexes.
CONTENTS: v. 1.   Albania – The Congo.
– v. 2.   Cuba – Mongolia. – v. 3.   Mozambique – Yugoslavia.
1.   Communist state.   2.   Communist countries –
Politics and government.   I.   Szajkowski, Bogdan.
JC474.M3512   1980   320.9′171′7   79–25471

MY 6 '82

086880

FOR SOPHIE

Contents

List of Maps

List of Figures

List of Tables

Preface

The growth in the number, global significance and ideological and political impact of countries ruled by parties which subscribe to the principles of Marxism-Leninism has presented students of politics with an increasing challenge. In meeting this challenge, Western commentators have put forward a dazzling profusion of terms, models, programmes and varieties of interpretation. It is against the background of this profusion that the present comprehensive survey of the Marxist-Leninist regimes is offered.

This collection, in three volumes, is envisaged as a textbook and to some extent reference book on the governments and politics of these states. Each of the monographs in these volumes was prepared by a specialist on the country concerned. Thus, twenty-five scholars from all over the world have contributed monographs which are based on first-hand knowledge. The geographical diversity of the authors, combined with the fact that as a group they represent many disciplines of social science, gives their individual analyses, and the collection as a whole, an additional and unique dimension. Each volume contains short biographical notes on the relevant authors.

The collection, which is organised alphabetically by country, is preceded by two theoretical chapters. The first, 'The Communist Movement: from Monolith to Polymorph', by outlining the history and development of the study of the Marxist-Leninist regimes, suggests that a radically new approach be taken to the study of the politics of communism. The second chapter, on the meaning of a Marxist regime, examines the theoretical parameters of the collection.

Three regimes have had to be omitted. In the case of the Democratic Republic of Afghanistan and the Democratic Republic of Madagascar, this was more for reasons of insufficient data than because their Marxist-Leninist orthodoxy was in dispute. Also excluded from the analysis is the communist government of San Marino, which was voted into office when the preparation of this collection was in its final stages.

It is hoped in subsequent editions to include chapters on the communist-led state governments in India, the communist parties' experiences in post-war West European governments, and the communist-led local councils in Italy, France, the Federal Republic of Germany and Portugal.

Each of the twenty-five scholars who contributed to this collection was asked to analyse such topics as the governmental structure, including the constitutional framework, the system of elections, the ruling party – variously called communist, labour, socialist or workers' – other mass organisations, party–state relations, the economy, domestic policies and foreign relations, as well as any features peculiar to the country and/or party under discussion. The exceptions to the pattern are the chapters on the USSR and China, where the wealth of material available could not be satisfactorily presented within the available space, and the article on Ethiopia, where the Marxist-Leninist experiment is still very new and does not yet permit extensive analysis.

Every effort has been made by the contributors to compile and present data on party and mass-organisation membership, electoral returns and multiple office-holding, except in the few cases where no such data exist.

In the preparation of this collection I have been given help by many people, some of whom should be singled out for special acknowledgement.

I am most grateful for the help afforded me by the Hon. Dr Abdulai Conteh, Minister for Foreign Affairs, Sierra Leone; Dr Thomas G. Hart of the Swedish Institute of International Affairs; Dr Tom Keenoy of University College, Cardiff; Dr Gary Troeller of the United Nations High Commission for Refugees; and Mr Richard Hodder-Williams of the University of Bristol.

I am grateful to all the contributors. Special thanks are due to Mr Michael Waller, Dr Ronald Hill, Ms Laura Summers, Professor Peter Schwab, Mr Fred Singleton and Dr Leslie Holmes.

Very special thanks are also due to Mrs Val Dobie for her help with the manuscripts, to Mr Tom Dawkes for his help in compiling the indexes, and to Mr Michael Breaks, the Social Science Librarian at University College, Cardiff, for his advice. I would also like to thank Miss Valery Brooks and her colleagues at Macmillan for their help in seeing these books through the press.

I am also very grateful to Mrs Jeanne Moorsom, whose house, The Coppice, proved to be the perfect place in which to write and was a most welcome refuge from the noise of my otherwise lovable children.

All the maps in this collection have been superbly drawn by Mrs Margaret Millen of the Department of Geology of University College,

Cardiff; her patience and endeavour were very much appreciated.

Above all, my very special gratitude goes to my wife, Martha, whose encouragement and help have been invaluable throughout the many months of work on these volumes.

4 January 1979   Bogdan Szajkowski
Dinas Powis

List of Abbreviations

Note: owing to their great familiarity, abbreviations such as km., vol., EEC, US and USSR are omitted from this list.

AK	[Home Army] (Poland)
AL	[People's Army] (Poland)
ASEAN	Association of South-East Asian States
AVNOJ	[Anti-Fascist Council for National Liberation] (Yugoslavia)
BOAL	Basic Organisation of Associated Labour (Yugoslavia)
COAL	Complex Organisation of Associated Labour (Yugoslavia)
Comecon	Council for Mutual Economic Assistance
Comintern	Communist International
COSVN	[Central Office for South Vietnam]
CPSU	Communist Party of the Soviet Union
CPY	Communist Party of Yugoslavia
DP	Democratic Party (Poland)
DRV	Democratic Republic of Vietnam
FAES	Federation of Arab Emirates of the South
FLOSY	Front for the Liberation of South Yemen
FNU	Front of National Unity (Poland)
FPLM	[People's Forces for the Liberation of Mozambique]
Frelimo	[Front for the Liberation of Mozambique]
FRG	Federal Republic of Germany
GCSTU	General Confederation of Somali Trade Unions
GDR	German Democratic Republic
GFTU	[General Confederation of Labour] (Vietnam)
GL	[People's Guards] (Poland)
GNA	Grand National Assembly (Romania)
Gosplan	[State Planning Commission] (USSR)
GUKPiW	[Main Department for the Control of the Press, Publications and Entertainments] (Poland)
GVP	[People's Vigilance Group] (Mozambique)

ICP	Indochinese Communist Party
Komsomol	[Young Communist League] (USSR)
KOR	[Workers' Defence Committee] (Poland)
KPP	[Polish Communist Party]
KPRP	[Polish Communist Workers' Party]
KRN	[National Council] (Poland)
KSS	[Committee for Social Self-Defence] (Poland)
LCY	League of Communists of Yugoslavia
LDP	Lao-Dong Party [Vietnam Workers' Party]
LIFEMO	[League of Mozambican Women]
MPLA	Movimento Popular de Libertação de Angola (Popular Movement for the Liberation of Angola)
NFLOS	National Front for the Liberation of the Occupied South (Yemen)
NLF	National Liberation Front (Yemen)
OAU	Organisation of African Unity
OLOS	Organisation for the Liberation of the Occupied South (Yemen)
OMM	[Organisation of Mozambican Women]
PAX	[State–encouraged Catholic organisation] (Poland)
PCP	Portuguese Communist Party
PCR	Partidul Comunist Român [Romanian Communist Party]
PDRY	People's Democratic Republic of Yemen
PFLO	Popular Front for the Liberation of Oman
PKWN	[Polish Committee of National Liberation]
PPR	Polish Workers' Party
PPS	[Polish Socialist Party]
PROSY	People's Republic of South Yemen
PRP	People's Revolutionary Party (Vietnam)
PSC	People's Supreme Council (Yemen)
PUWP	Polish United Workers' Party
PWP	Polish Workers' Party
RCP	Romanian Communist Party
RSFSR	Russian Soviet Federative Socialist Republic
RWP	Romanian Workers' Party
SAWPY	Socialist Alliance of the Working People of Yugoslavia
SDKPiL	[Social Democratic Party of the Kingdom of Poland and Lithuania]
SDR	Special drawing right (International Monetary Fund)
SDWO	Somali Democratic Women's Organisation

SEATO	South-East Asia Treaty Organisation
SFRY	Socialist Federative Republic of Yugoslavia
SRC	Supreme Revolutionary Council (Somalia)
SRV	Socialist Republic of Vietnam
SRYU	Somali Revolutionary Youth Union
SSR	Soviet Socialist Republic
SSRP	Somali Socialist Revolutionary Party
SUF	Socialist Unity Front (Romania)
UCY	Union of Communist Youth (Romania)
UPO–NF	Unified Political Organisation – National Front (Yemen)
UPP	United Peasant Party (Poland)
VCP	Vietnam Communist Party
VNQDD	Viet-Nam Quoc-Dan Dang (Vietnam Nationalist Party)
VWP	Vietnam Workers' Party
WSLF	Western Somali Liberation Front
WTO	Warsaw Treaty Organisation
ZBoWID	[War Veterans' Organisation] (Poland)

Notes on the Editor and Contributors

BOGDAN SZAJKOWSKI was educated in Eastern Europe and the Centre for Russian and East European Studies at Birmingham University. He conducted his postgraduate research at King's College, Cambridge, and St Antony's College, Oxford. Subsequently he was appointed to a lectureship in Comparative Communism at the Australian National University in Canberra. He has also taught at University College, Dublin, and is now Lecturer in Politics and Comparative Communism at University College, Cardiff. His writings on contemporary communist affairs have appeared in professional journals and the press, and he has extensive broadcasting experience. He is the editor of the annual volume *Documents in Communist Affairs*.

DAVID ELLIOTT received his BA from Yale and his Ph.D from Cornell University. He spent a total of six years in Vietnam with the US Army, with the Rand Corporation, and as a private scholar. His research interests have been centred on the Vietnamese revolutionary movement in South Vietnam and the problems of political integration in North Vietnam. In addition to his Ph.D dissertation titled 'Revolutionary Reintegration: the Foundation of the Post-liberation State in China and Vietnam', he has written several articles on contemporary Vietnamese politics, including 'North Vietnam since Ho', in *Problems of Communism*, and 'Political Integration in North Vietnam: the Co-operativization Period', in J. Zasloff and McAlister Brown (eds), *Communism in Indochina: New Perspectives* (Lexington, Mass.: D. C. Heath, 1975).

THOMAS H. HENRIKSEN is Associate Professor of History at the State University of New York, Plattsburgh. He is the author of *Mozambique: A History* (London: Rex Collings, 1978) and is co-editing *Chinese and Soviet Aid to Africa* (New York: Praeger, forthcoming). A graduate of Michigan State University, he has written numerous articles appearing in the *Journal of Modern African Studies, African Affairs, African*

Studies Review and *Phylon*. He served as Chairman of the New York African Studies Association in 1976–7.

RONALD J. HILL trained in Russian studies at Leeds University (1961–5) and in political science at University of Essex (MA, 1968; Ph.D, 1974). He was appointed in 1969 to his present post as Lecturer in Political Science at Trinity College, Dublin, where he was elected a Fellow in 1978. He specialises in Soviet politics and society, and has several times visited the USSR and Eastern Europe, including extended visits to Kishinev and Moscow. He is the author of *Soviet Political Elites: The Case of Tiraspol* (London: Martin Robertson, 1977), and has contributed articles and reviews to a number of scholarly journals. He is at present completing a book on political science and political reform in the Soviet Union.

TAREQ Y. ISMAEL is Professor of Political Science at the University of Calgary. He was educated at the Universities of Baghdad and Indiana and received his Ph.D at George Washington University in 1967. He is the author of several books on contemporary Middle East politics, including *Governments and Politics of the Contemporary Middle East* (Homewood, Ill.: Dorsey, 1970); *The Middle East in World Politics: A Study in Contemporary International Relations* (Syracuse, NY: Syracuse University Press, 1974); *The Arab Left: A Study in Contemporary Ideology* (Syracuse, NY: Syracuse University Press, 1976). He has contributed to several collections and written numerous articles, some of which have been translated.

IOAN LEWIS is Professor of Anthropology at the London School of Economics and Political Science. He was educated at the Universities of Glasgow and Oxford, where in 1957 he received his D.Phil. Professor Lewis has conducted field research in the Somali Democratic Republic (former British and Italian Somalilands) and French Somaliland in 1955–7, 1962, 1965, 1974 and 1978. He has also made several visits to Ethiopia. His many publications include *Peoples of the Horn of Africa [The Somali, Afar (Danakil), and Saho]* (London: International African Institute, 1955; rev. ed., 1969); *A Pastoral Democracy: Pastoralism and Politics among the Northern Somali of the Horn of Africa* (London: Oxford University Press, 1961; 4th ed., 1970); *The Modern History of Somaliland: From Nation to State* (London, Weidenfeld and Nicolson, 1965; new ed., 1979); and *Social Anthropology in Perspective* (Harmondsworth: Penguin, 1976).

GEORGE SANFORD was educated at the Universities of Bristol and

London, where he received his Ph.D. He is at present Lecturer in Eastern European Studies in the Department of Politics at Bristol University. Dr Sanford is the author of numerous articles in *Polish Review, Slavonic and Eastern European Review, Historical Journal, British Journal of Political Science* and *Przeglad historyczny.* He is a regular visitor to Poland, where during the past twelve years he carried out research at various Polish academic institutions.

MICHAEL SHAFIR is a Fellow of the Centre for the Study of the USSR and Eastern Europe, at the Hebrew University of Jerusalem. He taught political science and Russian studies at the same university and is currently completing his Ph.D on contemporary Romanian affairs. He is the author of *Bibliography on the Study of the Communist World* and several articles on Romanian and communist affairs (in *Wissenschaftlicher Dienst Südost Europa, Südost-Forschungen, Cahiers de l'Est, Index on Censorship* and other periodicals).

FRED B. SINGLETON was educated at the Universities of Leeds and Helsinki. His first visit to Yugoslavia was in 1945, whilst serving in the Royal Navy. In 1948 he took part in the building of the Zagreb–Belgrade highway as a member of a youth brigade. He has visited Yugoslavia since then, as a mountaineer, a director of WEA summer schools, organiser of a British student work brigade to assist in the reconstruction of Skopje after the 1963 earthquake, and as a lecturer and academic researcher. He is now Reader in Yugoslav Studies and Chairman of the Post-graduate School of Yugoslav Studies, Bradford University. He has written many books and articles on East European, and particularly Yugoslav, topics, including *Background to Eastern Europe* (Oxford: Pergamon, 1965) and *Twentieth Century Yugoslavia* (London: Macmillan, 1976). He is Chairman of the British National Association for Soviet and East European Studies.

19 People's Republic of Mozambique

THOMAS H. HENRIKSEN

Mozambique is one of the most recent countries to adopt a Marxist form of government. Mozambican Marxism represents the culmination of a ten-year war of independence (1964–74) waged against Portuguese colonialism by the Front for the Liberation of Mozambique (Frelimo). Its victory severed a 400-year political connection with Portugal.

Situated in south-east Africa athwart the oil lanes from the Persian Gulf to the West and amid the growing racial storm engulfing Zimbabwe and the Republic of South Africa, Mozambique has gained international strategic recognition. Its geographical location in the white-dominated southern quarter of the continent influenced its colonial past and war of liberation and impinges on its current quest for economic development and political stability within a Marxist framework.

Mozambique is bordered by Tanzania, Malawi, Zambia, Zimbabwe, Swaziland and the Republic of South Africa. Its Indian Ocean coast is 2380 km. long. Topographically, the country can be divided into four main regions: coastal plain (45 per cent), low plateaux (20 per cent), high plateaux (25 per cent), and mountains (10 per cent), with the highest peak 2600 metres. Mozambique is criss-crossed by several rivers, the most important of which is the Zambesi, one of the most significant water-courses in Africa.[1] Although the terrain has not been especially conducive to north–south communication, it alone cannot be singled out as hampering modernisation and development of a national consciousness. Portugal's poverty and neglect, along with the underdevelopment of Africa as a whole, account for much of the lack of progress. As elsewhere, the ethnic factor retarded nationalism and economic development.

Mozambique is composed of several indigenous ethno-linguistic

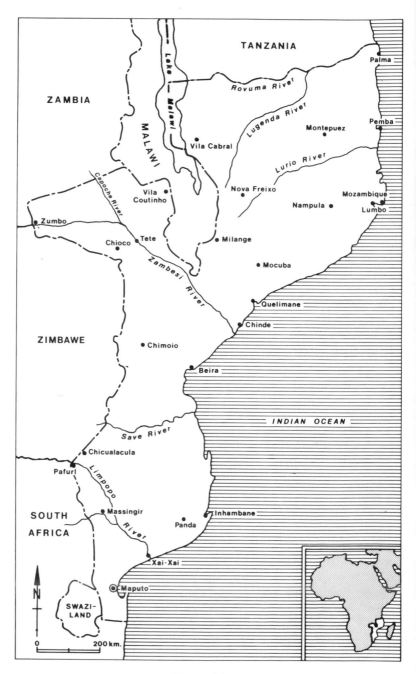

Mozambique

communities, whose diversification resulted from migrations and conquests. The last major incursion took place with the Ngoni invasion of the 1820s. In the north-east live the Makonde people, who figured predominantly in the initial stages of the independence struggle. To the west are the Nyasa and Yao. The Yao bear an Islamic imprint, as do coastal sections of the country's largest ethnic group, the Makua-Lomwe people, whose long contact with Moslem traders, and slavers explains their religious and cultural inclinations. North of the Zambesi and above the town of Sena are the peoples lumped together under the blanket term of Maravi or Malawi – the Nyanja, Chewa and Nsenga. Down the Zambesi valley proper are a mixture of Shona-related inhabitants, some of the principal communities being those of the Barue, Korekore, Tawara and Tonga. The proliferation of various peoples along the axis of the river reflects the historical movement of war and commerce on the vital water route.[2] Below them are other sub-groups of the Shona (Manyka, Teve and Ndau). Southern Mozambique is inhabited by the Chopi and Thonga and their sub-groupings. Since the mining of gold in the Transvaal during the late 1880s, large numbers of Thonga have gone to South Africa to dig the yellow metal. Another small but significant community in the south are the Ngoni, who also have population pockets in the north. Until the April 1974 army coup in Lisbon, which ended Portugal's colonial wars, the East African colony had some 230,000 European residents, the vast bulk of them Portuguese immigrants. There were also a few thousand British and German settlers, who owned plantations and businesses. An Indian population of 17,000 (1960) and 2000 Chinese traders and shopkeepers made up the rest of the non-African population. Only about 20,000 Portuguese remain of the former settlers.[3]

RESISTANCE AND NATIONALISM TILL WORLD WAR II

Mozambican Marxism is closely bound up with African opposition to Portuguese inroads.[4] Portugal's initial military and economic penetration up the Zambesi in the early 1500s waned in succeeding centuries to a shadow of a presence.[5] But, in the late nineteenth century, driven by fear of losing to other European powers, Lisbon embarked on protracted pacification campaigns. Pitched traditional resistance thwarted an easy conquest.[6] Even before they were militarily subdued by modern weapons, a handful of Mozambican intellectuals and journalists fired, in the 1890s, angry salvos of criticism at the gap between Lisbon's promises of colonial benefits and its practices of forced labour and injustices.[7] The Portuguese Republic (1910–26) tolerated some criticism, but the authoritarian regime of the Estado Novo (New State) of António de Oliveira Salazar clamped down hard on African and settler dissent.[8]

This repression through the late 1920s and the 1930s choked newspaper censure and transformed critical associations into regime-sponsored organisations. Up to this time, the protesters had espoused no genuine Marxism; their shrill message sprang from outraged liberalism, familiar to Western democracies, and was conveyed in a fiery polemical style. One minor and relatively unknown exception involved the uncovering of 'Bolshevist propaganda' in the capital. Mozambican mine workers on the Rand reportedly came in contact with the International Communist Union. One of its European agents allegedly circulated in southern Mozambique in 1924 communist literature printed in local dialects.[9] The impact of this incident on the evolution of Marxist consciousness was nil. At this juncture, Mozambican political thought among the tiny educated stratum focused on redress of colonial wrongs, achievement of racial dignity and individual advancement within the colonial system.[10]

NATIONALISM FROM THE SECOND WORLD WAR TO THE INDEPENDENCE WAR

Little information on Mozambican nationalism before the Second World War has come to light, because Lisbon keeps a secure lock on the archives housing twentieth-century materials. Periodic references to Mozambican discontent in the form of strikes, disturbances or the murder of a *patrão* (master or boss) crept into the occasional journalist article or consular report. After 1945, a ripple of the nationalist tide sweeping British and French colonies passed through Mozambique. Dock strikes with political overtones occurred, a student organisation took root in the capital, and African associations again became vocal about grievances. But no national movements like those elsewhere in the continent surfaced. Instead, the fledgling expressions of proto-nationalism induced the colonial authorities to suppress once again the embryonic signs of rebellion. Because of police surveillance, nationalist formation and political consciousness developed beyond Mozambique's borders. In Portugal a favoured few African students encountered Marxist ideas from underground contacts with the Portuguese Communist Party (PCP) in the universities at Lisbon and

Coimbra.[11] The most prominent Mozambican to study in Portugal before completing his degree in the United States was Eduardo Mondlane, later President of Frelimo until his assassination. Another future nationalist leader, Marcelino dos Santos, journeyed to Portugal for education before fleeing to Paris, where he lived among left-wing intellectuals and discovered Marxism.

Across Mozambique's frontiers in South Africa, Rhodesia and particularly Tanzania, Mozambican workers and exiled activists coalesced into political groups. Unlike in Angola, Mozambique's sister colony, there appear to have been no links between the PCP and underground organisations. Three of the exiled factions, which reflected regional and ethnic aspirations as much as nationalism, joined together in the newly independent Tanzanian capital of Dar es Salaam and formed Frelimo in June 1962. Mondlane was chosen as President and plans were laid for a congress.[12]

EVOLUTIONARY MARXISM AND GUERRILLA WARFARE

Frelimo held its First Congress in September 1962. Far from Marxist, the aims of the initial platform listed consolidation and promotion of a mass movement to achieve independence by peaceful or warlike means rather than an integrated ideology for a planned economy, scientific revolution or proletarian internationalism.[13] The overall composition of the movement was nationalist and reformist. Beyond goals of improved educational and health services for Mozambicans, there were hardly any statements concerning post-independence objectives.

Frelimo's path to Marxism was an evolutionary one. Aside from dos Santos and a tiny minority of the founding members, the preponderance of the membership had no systematic exposure to the philosophy of the German thinker or his followers in the Soviet Union and China. With no industrial work force to speak of, Mozambique did not meet classic Marxian preconditions for revolution. But it had other potent ingredients for revolution, which were recognised by Frelimo – harsh colonial rule, impoverished rural population and no legal or open channel for political opposition. So, as had happened in the case of the Chinese Communist Party, cadres went into the countryside to mobilise a mass movement.

Soon after the First Congress, Frelimo began preparation for armed struggle and began the search for international assistance. Both the Soviet Union and China responded. Upon returning from a visit to

China, Mondlane wrote in 1963, a year before the war broke out, that he was 'convinced that the historical struggle of the Chinese peoples has great relevance to the present struggle of the peoples of Africa'.[14] Mozambique's political circumstances, rugged terrain and economic conditions predisposed Frelimo's strategy towards popular insurgence along the lines of Mao Tse-tung's maxims as adapted to suit an African environment.[15] Steadily increasing amounts of Soviet-bloc and Chinese equipment and instruction furthered the development of a Marxist orientation by a movement seeking a blueprint for power and social justice. The radicalisation of elements of the leadership brought the adoption in 1968, by the Second Congress, of standard communist-party form, including a cell structure, democratic centralism, self-criticism sessions and a pervasive Marxist idiom. This revolutionising chemistry also spawned internecine quarrels, which the Portuguese secret police helped aggravate.[16] Mondlane's bomb death in February 1969 was the most notable of many assassinations. With the elimination of Mondlane, who some believed held moderate views, the radicalisation of Frelimo continued apace. After the collapse of six months of triumvirate leadership by dos Santos (in charge of foreign affairs), Samora Machel (who commanded the guerrilla army) and Uria Simango (who had been Vice-president), Frelimo returned to rule by a single man, with Machel assuming the presidency. Simango was expelled and after the war was tried for treason.

Aid from communist states expanded under Machel's presidency and Frelimo held the distinction of being the only African liberation movement to receive sustained assistance from both Moscow and Peking. It also obtained non-military support from Scandinavian governments and Western humanitarian organisations. The multiple sources of aid enabled Frelimo to strike an independent posture in the Moscow–Peking feud and to strengthen a stubborn nationalist streak while adopting Marxism. Frelimo's radicalisation therefore took place amidst competing ideologies, which points to the existence of various interpretations on the correct model to socialist development.[17]

Frelimo's extension of guerrilla warfare into central Mozambique greatly contributed to the deterioration of Lisbon's military standing in its three colonial wars. In the wake of its seeming breakthrough in the 'waist' of the country, Portuguese officers overthrew the Marcelo Caetano government in Lisbon on 25 April 1974 and terminated the wars. Following a nine-month transitional period, an independent People's Republic of Mozambique was proclaimed on 25 June 1975.[18]

THE FRONT FOR THE LIBERATION OF MOZAMBIQUE

Organisation

The evolution of Frelimo from a national front waging guerrilla warfare was advanced by the Third Congress in February 1977. At the congress, the first since independence, 379 delegates approved transformation to a 'Marxist-Leninist vanguard party'. As such the Party is 'the leading force of society and state' and 'must guide, mobilise and organise the broad masses in the task of building a People's Democracy'.[19] Opposition movements are illegal.

Because of this recent change in Frelimo's status and, more importantly, its short time in power, many of the conventional structures of a Marxist party are still rudimentary.[20] At present, Frelimo relies on the 'dynamising group' (*grupo dinamizador*) at the lowest level of the political structure. It established the groups to spread propaganda and politicise the population, especially in the non-liberated zones, once the fighting had stopped. A dynamising group usually has between six and eight members and works with a 'constituency' of a few hundred people. In towns the groups have been organised into 'circles' (*Circulos*) and further sub-divided into 'cells' focusing on a defined residential area. They are responsible to the Party. Originally, plans called for the universal elevation of *grupos* to the status of party committees (*comités de partido*), the first of which were formed in the guerrilla army in 1973. Being hastily formed to fill the vacuum of the withdrawing Portuguese administration after the Lisbon coup, the *grupos* functioned often without model or direction. Their membership was formed from many misinformed Mozambicans and not a few opportunists who used newfound status for individual gain. The groups have been purged while still serving Frelimo goals. Now party committees are to be made up from only the politically most committed members of the *grupos* or other organisations.

Admission to the Front is selective; figures on membership are not yet available, but after screening applications the Central Committee announced that between 3 February 1977 and 25 September 1978 (Mozambique's 'Revolution Day') 'tens of thousands of Mozambique workers will be admitted as Frelimo members'.[21] Party committees of Frelimo members are being formed at three levels: provinces (ten), districts (112) and *Circulos* or circles. The party committees in the *Circulos*, which represent the base of Frelimo, are defined as representing places where people work or live.[22]

At the top of Frelimo's organisation is the Congress, which has been convened three times since the formation of the national front. At the Third Party Congress, 40 per cent of the delegates were classified[23] as working class, 27 per cent as peasants and 33 per cent as belonging to other sectors (white-collar, the army, and so on).

The Front's Central Committee, elected during the last session of Congress, implements and guides the policy adopted by the Congress. The Third Congress voted to expand the membership of the Central Committee to sixty-seven members. Eight Central Committee meetings have taken place since the founding of Frelimo. Between the meetings it relies on a sort of political bureau, called (similarly to in the GDR) the Permanent Political Committee: this has ten members, and its composition also was decided in the last session of Congress. The Committee possesses wide powers, since it is the policy-making body of Frelimo. Most of its members (see Table 19.1) hold portfolios of specific ministries in the government and sit on the Council of Ministers, which is considered the highest administrative body of the government.

TABLE 19.1 Members of the Mozambican Permanent Political Committee and their governmental positions

Samora Moises Machel	President of Frelimo and President of the People's Republic of Mozambique
Marcelino dos Santos	Minister of the National Commission of the Plan
Joaquim Alberto Chissano	Minister for Foreign Affairs
Alberto Joaquim Chipande	Minister of Defence
Armando Emilo Guebuza	Political Commissar of the People's Forces for the Liberation of Mozambique
Jorge Rebelo	Minister of Ideological Affairs
Mariano Matsinha	Minister of Labour
Sebatiaso João Marcos Mabote	Vice Minister for Defence
Jacinto Soares Veloso	
Mario de Graca Machungo	Minister for Industry and Commerce

GOVERNMENT

Constitution

The precise relationship between Party and State has been the subject of recent Frelimo meetings which have been reported in the Mozambican weekly magazine *Tempo*. Yet the Constitution accords Frelimo the status of a State institution on its own, since 'the People's Republic of Mozambique is guided by the political line laid down by Frelimo'.[24] To date, it has been the case in Mozambique as in other Marxist States that the most prominent party members have held important posts in the government as well. There is no constitution carved in stone, and the Central Committee in late 1977 recommended the formation of a thirty-member committee to adapt it to conditions in Mozambique.[25]

The Constitution which was approved by the Central Committee on 20 June 1975 provided that the President of Frelimo is also President of the People's Republic of Mozambique. The term 'President of the Party', not 'First Secretary', is used. By the Constitution, the President has power to make many appointments, provincial governors and members of the Council of Ministers (among others) are named by him, and he can annul decisions of the provincial assemblies. The Third Congress scrapped the position of Vice-president. Each of the country's ten provinces has a governor responsible to the Party and the Council of Ministers.

The Constitution asserts that power belongs to the workers and peasants united and led by Frelimo. Although obligations are attached to private property, it is allowed in Mozambique. Income and property taxes are progressive. Religious institutions must conform to the State's laws. In foreign policy, the Constitution defends the principle of turning the Indian Ocean into a non-nuclear zone.

People's assemblies

According to the Constitution, the People's National Assembly is the highest legislative organ. Elections to it were to be held within a year of the Third Congress, and Frelimo complied with the stipulation: elections began on 25 September 1977 and finished on 4 December 1977. Party committees or dynamising groups presented a list of candidates to the voters, who could publicly question them. Some former collaborators with Portuguese colonialism were discovered and dismissed as candidates. Instead of directly electing representatives to a central assembly, Mozambicans over eighteen years voted publicly (because of illiteracy) on the composition of locality, *localidade*, assemblies, which in turn chose from among their membership delegates to a district electoral conference, which elected the district-assembly deputies. Deputies for the ten city assemblies (one for each of the provinces' major cities) were selected in similar fashion to members of the locality assemblies, and delegates from the district and city assemblies met to elect deputies for the provincial assemblies. These, finally, voted on membership of the People's National Assembly, a list of candidates being proposed by the Central Committee. Members of the Council of Ministers and the provincial governors are *ex officio* members of the People's National Assembly. (See Table 19.2 for a summary of the assembly structures.)

TABLE 19.2 Number of assemblies and deputies in Mozambique

Assembly type	No. of assemblies	No. of deputies
People's National Assembly	1	226
Provincial assemblies	10	734
City assemblies	10	460
District assemblies	112	3,390
Locality assemblies	894	22,230

Source: People's Power in Mozambique, Angola and Guinea-Bissau, no. 11 (Jan–Mar 1978) 24.

Between the two sessions each year of the People's National Assembly (for its composition, see Table 19.3), a Permanent Commission of fifteen of its members, proposed by the Central Committee, assumes the duties of the larger body and submits legislative acts for the approval of the People's National Assembly at its regular meetings.

TABLE 19.3 Composition of the Mozambican People's National Assembly

Group	No.	%
Men	198	87
Women	28	12
Workers	71	31
Peasants	65	28
People's Forces for the Liberation of Mozambique	35	15
State workers (i.e. anyone working for the State or municipality)	25	11
Representatives of mass organisations	13	5
Others	17	7

Source: Tempo (Mozambique), 1 Jan 1978.

The Council of Ministers

Pursuant to the Constitution, the Council of Ministers consists of ministers and, where appropriate, vice-ministers, in the manner of a parliamentary cabinet. At independence it had eighteen members. The President of the Republic makes the appointments or dismissals and presides over the Council. The Council's specific tasks include formulation and, after approval, implementation of the budget, the enactment of legislative decrees, and the drafting of laws and decrees for submission to the President of the Republic, the People's National Assembly or the Permanent Commission. In its work, the Council of Ministers is to comply with the resolutions of the Congress and People's National Assembly.

Local government

Local government is implemented by the local administrators, some of whom were appointed soon after independence and others more recently. They represent the Council of Ministers at the grass-roots level and oversee its programmes of health, education and public works. The local administrators also chair monthly meetings of the locality assemblies. Their 'nine tasks' include increasing production, improving living standards and maintaining vigilance. Two deputies together with the local administrator form an executive council responsible for carrying out the locality assembly's decisions and those of higher State bodies.

Mass organisations

A full range of professional, cultural and mass organisations have not yet appeared in Mozambique, but the Third Congress gave a strong impetus to their formation. During the liberation war, Frelimo advanced projects to involve the rural population in the struggle. It made a significant appeal to women. As such, the League for Mozambican Women (LIFEMO) appeared early in the war. Later the name was changed to the Organisation of Mozambican Women (OMM), which held its first conference in Tanzania in 1973 and its second in Mozambique in November 1976. In the course of the fighting, Frelimo formed a Women's Detachment, which saw some combat mostly in the role of militia. The Women's organisation's goals today are to achieve liberation from traditional and colonial views on the role of women, and to implement the party line. Women have already secured various political positions and the opportunity to enter all professions.

A distinct youth movement was established for students who studied abroad, but Frelimo suspended this formation when students refused to return to participate in the war effort and openly criticised the leadership. As a consequence of the Third Congress, the Mozambique Youth Organisation was formally set up on 29 November 1977, with emphasis on an international education for youth, literacy campaigns and construction projects. All Mozambicans between the ages of fourteen and thirty are eligible for memberships.[26]

A hundred Workers' production councils have been organised in work places to mobilise workers and to raise productivity. Recently a National Organisation for Journalists was set up.[27] Organisations for artists and co-operative peasants are in the planning stage. So as 'to detect and neutralise enemy activity', provincial governments are setting up people's vigilance groups, which will co-operate with the people's militia.

Mozambique's army, the People's Forces for the Liberation of Mozambique (FPLM), is seen as both a defence force and a mobilising movement. Frelimo's guerrilla army numbered about 12,000 fighters, with about 10,000 more in the militia or various phases of training by the end of the war. Since independence the FPLM has been moved in the direction of a conventional army, but with emphasis on political training and on making itself self-sufficient in food through collective production. On 28 March 1978 the Permanent Commission approved a law introducing two-year compulsory military service for all Mozambicans, women as well as men, of over eighteen years. After completion of military service, men will remain in the Reserves until the age of forty-five and women till the age of forty.

INTERNAL AFFAIRS

Health

Improvement in the health of the inhabitants has been given a high priority. Since independence the government has launched and completed a country-wide programme of inoculation against smallpox. Wells have been dug in some villages. Campaigns to dig and use latrines and to have every person kill thirty flies a day have been undertaken. In 1977 the Ministry of Health initiated a six-month training course for village health workers (resembling the Chinese 'barefoot doctors'), whose functions are mainly preventive care and first-aid. Emphasis is being placed on locating doctors and medical facilities out of the large cities where Portuguese rule concentrated them. The nationalisation of health services, funeral directors and the teaching and legal professions resulted in the departure of most Portuguese professionals. While native replacements are being trained abroad, Mozambique relies on foreign medical and other skilled practitioners, mainly from the Soviet bloc, China and Cuba.

Education

Another item of considerable importance to the new government is literacy. Next to defence expenditures, education, particularly secondary schools and teacher-training, received the highest allocation of funds, at 17 per cent of the 1976–7 budget.[28] Education and health were second only to defence, at $83 million in 1978.[29] Literacy carries a special meaning in Mozambique's ethnically diverse society, for education in the Portuguese language works to unify the separate communities.

Many of the *grupos* figured prominently in the effort to reduce the 85 per cent illiteracy rate.[30] To make up for the dearth of teachers, advanced secondary students have, since 1976, been released from school to instruct younger pupils, as well as staff sections of the ministries. Short preparatory instructor courses have claimed to turn out 1500 teachers a year.[31] Using these methods, school attendance jumped from 700,000 in 1973 to 2·2 million in 1976.[32]

Church relations

Taking over missionary schools resulted in the withdrawal of some religious groups and controversy with others. The Frelimo leadership regards religion with scepticism, for many of the churches tacitly approved or actively supported colonial rule. For this reason Frelimo, while guaranteeing freedom of religious worship, declared a separation of Church and State, banned infant baptism and warned the churches to stop 'mobilising' among the people. Collisions have occurred with two fundamentalist sects. The Church of the Nazarene was accused of obtaining funds from the United States to undermine the government. Frelimo imprisoned its pastor, Armand Doll, for a little over a year, releasing him in September 1976.[33] The Jehovah's Witnesses received stern government warnings to mend their ways or suffer 'the same fate as Portuguese colonialism',[34] and Maputo ordered home over 8000 Witnesses who had fled from Malawi into Mozambique.

Despite the fact that Catholic priests were harassed and five expelled from the country in late 1975, one Catholic order returned from self-imposed exile. Having left in 1971 as part of a public protest at the Portuguese army's widespread atrocities, the White Fathers now proceeded to re-establish some of their missionary activities. In August 1975 the Spanish Burgos Order, which had run foul of the colonial authorities for reporting the atrocities (later internationally publicised) at the village of Wiriyamu, welcomed the Frelimo government during an annual meeting.[35] Now severe friction exists between the Catholic Church and the government.

The economy

The improvements achieved in health care and literacy rates have not had their counterparts in the economic sector, where an acute crisis has persisted since independence. The new administration inherited from the old an unwanted burden of £400 million in foreign debts. Decolonisation brought a host of ills, natural and political. The major setbacks to the economy have been the 1976 border closure with Rhodesia and the inadequacy of international compensation; the abandonment and destruction of businesses, farms and machinery by fleeing settlers; the flight of skilled workers and managers; the disadvantageous international economic conditions facing most underdeveloped countries; and a spate of natural calamities, including droughts in the north, and in the Zambesi and Limpopo valleys the worst floods in a generation.

Export-crop production has tumbled to near-disastrous levels and in 1977 only the tea harvest approached the peak 1973 output.[36] Cashews, sugar, sisal, tea and cotton netted over 60 per cent of export revenues in 1973. Subsistence foods similarly declined. As a result, precious foreign currency has been expended on importing staple foods in order to avert famine. $75 million were spent in this way during 1977,[37] and the trade deficit for that year stood at $280 million.[38]

At the Third Congress, the Report on Economic and Social Guidelines outlined a four-year programme to restore agricultural and industrial production to 1973 levels by the end of 1980. The Congress also ratified the proposal of 'making the building of heavy industry the decisive factor in the battle to break with misery and imperialist domination'.[39] Specifically, the objective is to come as close as possible to industrial self-sufficiency, with Mozambique manufacturing its own tractors by the end of the century. The pre-independence manufacturing sector accounted for just 10 per cent of the gross national product and was limited to plants packaging goods for local consumption, firms processing export crops, and one oil refinery.

The precarious economic situation caused Frelimo not to be too hasty in breaking with capitalism – especially as regards the country's reliance, shaped under colonial conditions, on South Africa. By and large, only some 2000 abandoned large farms and a relatively few industries were nationalised and run by Frelimo-appointed committees. The activities, magnified by rumour, of a lawless element in the society were as responsible for the flight of white settlers as were Frelimo's projected plans of socialism and nationalisation. True, Frelimo abolished private rent collection and moved homeless families into housing abandoned by settlers. The new occupants pay the State rents according to their income. Yet Portuguese and Mozambican families were guaranteed not only possession of their own home but also the right to own an additional house or apartment in the country or by the seaside.

In some spheres there exists, however temporary, an accommodation with capitalism. While on the one hand private firms report 'healthy profits',[40] on the other the government extols the announcement of 200 additional 'people's shops', providing essential commodities at moderate prices 'in the struggle against speculation by private companies'.[41] The desperate agricultural plight made it necessary to tolerate private firms. Consequently, State and collective farms exist alongside private cultivation, which formerly produced all the export crops.

But the collectivisation of agriculture into communal villages (*aldeias communais*), co-operative cultivation or State farms embodies Frelimo's vision of a reorganised countryside. Coercion and intimidation have not formed a part of the plans. Nor have there been reports of waves of refugees streaming across the borders, as in the forced evacuation of Kampuchean cities. Local socio-economic realities have furthered some collectivisation. Unlike China or Europe, Mozambique lacked a traditional landlord class. Thus, redistribution of estates to a land-hungry peasantry played no significant role in the liberation war or afterwards. But, since over 90 per cent of the population is rurally based, no large-scale relocations have been deemed necessary by a regime that considers towns 'the fortress of the bourgeoisie'. The drift to urban centres, so much a part of contemporary Africa, does, however, require reversal. War in the north caused the resettlement of nearly 1 million villagers in *aldeamentos* (fortified villages like the strategic hamlets in

Vietnam) by the colonial army. As Frelimo utilised the better built *aldeamentos* for communal villages, the heaviest concentration of the latter is in the north-easternmost province of Caba Delgado, the scene of prolonged guerrilla warfare.[42] The new government in Maputo has also taken advantage of floods to resettle scattered villagers in central locations. Ideally, the communal villages are each to comprise about 1250 families, or about 6000 to 7000 inhabitants. In reality there are, of course, variances, and some villages are at a 'pre-co-operative' stage. Although party guidelines call for the expansion of co-operative farming, villagers are allowed to work their own plots or *shambas*, for personal consumption or for sale to others.

Mozambique's pressing economic difficulties led the government to introduce tight austerity measures and to launch propaganda campaigns to urge workers to step up production. Demands on worker production councils were another manifestation of the deepening anxiety. Partly in consequence of the authoritarian methods adopted, such as issuing production targets as orders, during the first year of independence angry workers resorted to strikes and go-slows. In response, Frelimo initiated drives aimed at worker education and participation in decision-making so as to boost enthusiasm for the goals set by the party.

The hiatus in nationalisation which followed the initial spate of it was broken in late 1977 by government take-overs of the Sonap oil company and Sonarep refinery and the remaining private banks.[43] There is, however, no categorical opposition to foreign investment in Mozambique. According to article 14 of the Constitution, 'foreign capital shall be authorised to operate within the framework of the State's economic policy'. In fact, Sweden – a stout backer of Frelimo in the war years – secured several concessions to exploit resources.[44] Frelimo officials stated that enterprises were taken over for reasons of corruption or, in the case of coal mines, because such industries were deemed 'strategic to the economy'.[45] It is still too early to form a balanced view of the overall results of Frelimo's economic policy. Development of the retarded economy is certainly a long-term problem. The continuing balance-of-trade deficit prompted in April 1978 a major reorganisation of the Council of Ministers, with the Ministry of Industry and Commerce being subdivided into the Ministries of External and Internal Trade.[46]

Frelimo's Marxist programmes have not excluded limited economic incentives, which are recognised in the Constitution as a criterion for distribution of wealth. Recalcitrant individuals whom Frelimo labels as guilty of individualism, prostitution, theft, profiteering or corruption are dispatched to mental decolonisation centres, *centros de descolonização mental)* for what is described as rehabilitation or re-education. One source reported 12,000 inhabitants in the camps, including a few former Central Committee members.[47]

EXTERNAL AFFAIRS

Frelimo has consistently professed non-alignment. As in the case of many other Third World nations, a non-alignment posture implies a quest for wide-ranging international relations bringing aid and trade, and clearly Mozambique must look beyond the narrow circle of Portugal and its friends. President Machel at the Third Congress made clear, however, that Mozambique regards as its 'natural allies the socialist countries and the Marxist-Leninist Parties'.[48] Throughout the war, Frelimo depended exclusively on Marxist countries for significant military assistance.[49] Some limited aid initially came from North African states and non-military aid emanated from Scandinavian countries and humanitarian organisations. While being the only sub-Saharan liberation movement to receive sustained help from both communist super-powers, Frelimo kept itself aloof in the Moscow–Peking controversy. But, because Chinese cadres were present in southern Tanzania training many Frelimo recruits in Mao's politics as well as military tactics, most observers concluded that China enjoyed the inspirational edge over the Soviet Union, whose historical and political conditions seemed so remote from Mozambique's. Two factors worked to reverse the ranking. First, during the Angolan civil war, Peking backed the faction which obtained South African support against the Popular Movement for the Liberation of Angola (MPLA) – a long-term companion movement of Frelimo. Even an indirect association with South Africa, whose apartheid policy is anathema in Black Africa, could not but severely tarnish China's image in Africa. Secondly, Mozambique's development needs received greater industrial and technical assistance from the redoubled exertions of the Soviet bloc and Cuba. On 31 March 1977, Maputo signed a twenty-year co-operation and friendship treaty with Moscow[50] – one of the four such agreements in Africa. In autumn 1977, Frelimo's policy of seemingly exclusive friendship with the USSR reverted to its former posture of an even-handed approach to the two principal Marxist states. High-level delegations visited China and one signed an accord outlining economic and technical co-operation with China.[51] Frelimo has not allowed any country military or naval facilities on Mozambican territory.

Much expertise and aid comes from the Warsaw Pact countries. The Cuban presence has also expanded, although it is much smaller than in either Angola or Ethiopia. About 12,000 Mozambican schoolchildren are at present being educated in Cuba. Maputo has in fact strengthened relationships with the smaller, non-European Marxist countries – Cuba and Vietnam, in particular. It is felt that their experience is closer to that of Mozambique.

Frelimo's ideological hostility to the racial policies of the Pretoria government has not led to a rupture of relations with its southern neighbour, which ships nearly 18 per cent of its total exports through the Maputo docks, which it helps operate. Proceeds from South African freight have at times accounted for as much as 30 per cent of total foreign-exchange earnings. South Africa also employs between 30,000 and 60,000 Mozambican workers in its mines and pays Maputo their salaries in gold; Mozambique pays the returning workers in local currency. A third source of invisible trade revenue was the spendings of thousands of Rhodesian tourists on Mozambique's winter beaches. Together the three sources of foreign-exchange earnings nearly offset the trade deficit. Now all three foreign-revenue providers are down, but South Africa stands to be the largest purchaser of electricity generated at the giant Cabora Bassa dam when full production begins in 1979.

Whereas coexistence characterises relations with South Africa, relations between Mozambique and the minority government in Rhodesia are marked by border warfare. Like Angola, Botswana, Tanzania and Zambia, the People's Republic of Mozambique is one of the front-line states opposed to the remaining forms of colonialism in Rhodesia. Mozambique serves as a rear base and sanctuary to 12,000 Zimbabwean guerrillas (Africans from Rhodesia opposed to white rule and privileges). Guerrilla attacks from independent Mozambique in 1975 and then border closure in 1976 have put Mozambique in the forefront of the struggle, as a result of which it has suffered scores of small retaliatory raids and half a dozen massive punitive strikes. President Machel reported that by July 1977 the war had caused 1432 civilian deaths (875 of the victims were Zimbabwean refugees) and property damage to the tune of $100 million in Mozambique. Lost income from the frontier closure was put at $106 to $132 million annually by UN sources in 1977.[52]

The African countries with which Mozambique is on the closest terms are Zambia and, especially, Tanzania. A regional economic grouping with these three states is a real possibility. In the case of Tanzania, a permanent commission with eight ministers from each country was established in 1976 to formulate plans on how the countries' economies may be made more complementary. This agreement included plans for each country's diplomatic missions to represent the other. Later it was announced that the two countries' diplomats are being instructed jointly at the Mozambique Institute in Dar es Salaam, where Frelimo trained its cadres in the liberation war. Plans are under way to build a 'Unity Bridge' across the Rovuma River, thereby linking Mozambique and Tanzania by road. The early openness at the border was curtailed in late 1977, owing to what Maputo termed as the passage of imperialist spies and smugglers.[53] Zambia and Mozambique signed the Maputo Agreement in April 1978. Among other things, it expressed the intent to construct a direct railway link between the two countries and established a commission of co-operation.

Aid from the West has been sought and obtained, mostly for flood victims or for the 60,000 refugees from the fighting in Zimbabwe. In 1976 the United States contributed $1·46 million to United Nations High Commission for Refugees (UNHCR) to assist the return home, after the war, of Mozambican refugees in neighbouring countries.[54] In late 1977 the United States provided for $6 million worth of surplus food under the Food for Peace Programme. But Congressional foes of Mozambique as well as other Marxist countries placed an amendment in the main foreign-aid bill prohibiting assistance. Britain in 1976 advanced a £15 million aid programme. The FRG, Canada, Japan, New Zealand and Australia have provided help. Aid from the Scandinavian countries has been particularly significant. Sweden, Finland, Denmark, Norway and Iceland have signed a $50 million agreement for agricultural development, which is possibly the largest package to date.[55]

BIOGRAPHIES

Samora Moises Machel, President of both Frelimo and the People's Republic of Mozambique, was born in 1933, of African parentage, in Gaza province, southern Mozambique. Machel had some Western-style education before working as a male nurse in the capital, and although he has less formal education than some university-trained members of the Council of Ministers, his academic progress was not without distinction in colonial Mozambique, where schooling was a rarity. When Mondlane visited Mozambique in 1961, Machel was one of those who urged him to form a nationalist movement. Machel was among the 250 recruits sent to Algeria for military training in early 1963. Later he succeeded to the positions of Secretary of Defence and Commander-in-chief of the FPLM, after the death of Filipe Magaia in 1966. From this power base Machel assumed the presidency of Frelimo when the triumvirate that had ruled since Mondlane's death, nine months earlier, collapsed in November 1969. The Central Committee formally conferred the presidency on Machel in May 1970. He was invested as President of the People's Republic of Mozambique in June 1975.

He has several times visited China and the USSR, where he received the Lenin Centenary Medal in 1971. He enjoys a charismatic appeal among ordinary Mozambicans, who call him by his first name.

Marcelino dos Santos, Minister of the National Commission of the Plan, was born of mixed parentage in the coastal town of Lumbo, opposite Mozambique Island. Before actively entering nationalist politics, he wrote anti-Portuguese poetry under the African name of Kalungano.[56] After studying briefly in Portugal, he moved to Paris, where he moved in left-wing circles and became exposed to Marxism. In the early 1960s he was Secretary-general of the Conference of Nationalist Organisations of the Portuguese Colonies (CONCP) which was formed by a few African nationalists from Portugal's colonies to co-ordinate their activities. Dos Santos took an active role in encouraging the merger of three Mozambican nationalist movements into Frelimo, in which he held the office of Secretary of External Affairs during the war years. With Machel and Vice-president Uria Simango, who was expelled in November 1969, he was a member of the triumvirate that led the Party following Mondlane's murder. His lack of a power base precluded his advancement into the presidency. He was Vice-president prior to the scrapping of that office by the Third Congress. His previous title, Minister of Planning and Economic Development, was changed in April 1978 to the present one.[57]

Eduardo Chivambo Mondlane. Despite Mondlane's death on 3 February 1969, his name still exercises a certain nostalgic, inspirational hold on Mozambicans, and even on some Portuguese opponents, who perceived him as a product of Portuguese civilisation and as a man with whom they could have worked. Born in 1920 in Gaza province, he attended missionary schools in Mozambique and South Africa before being expelled in 1948 as a 'foreign native'. He received some university training in Portugal after a light brush with the colonial authorities for embryonic nationalist tendencies. He finished his education in the United States, where he graduated from Oberlin College with a BA and was awarded a Ph.D by Northwestern University. He worked first at the United Nations and then taught at Syracuse University before being elected to the presidency of Frelimo in June 1962. His white American wife and education led some falsely to conclude that he was a moderate. One of his greatest achievements was in obtaining aid from both East and West. His death, whether it was Portuguese police collaborating with dissidents, or solely elements of Frelimo, that were responsible, is still something of a mystery. He, however, retains the rank of hero-martyr in Frelimo's pantheon of fallen comrades, and in consequence the Frelimo government has renamed the University of Lourenço Marques after him.[58]

BASIC FACTS ABOUT MOZAMBIQUE

Official name: People's Republic of Mozambique (República Popular de Moçambique).

Area: 783,140 sq.km (297,746 sq. miles).

Population (1978 est.): 11,000,000.

Population density: approx. 14 per sq. km.

Population distribution: 10 per cent urban, 90 per cent rural.

Administrative division: 10 provinces.

Major ethnic nationalities (1970)[59]: Makua-Lomwe, 3,000,000; Thonga, 1,850,000; Zambesi peoples, 900,000; Shona sub-groups, 765,000; Chopi and Tonga, 450,000; Maravi (or Malawi) group, 250,000; Makonde, 180,000; Yao, 170,000; Ngoni, 35,000.

Major towns: Maputo (the capital, formerly known as Lourenço Marques; 400,000 inhabitants, 1974, Beira (150,000 inhabitants, 1974), Inhambane, Nacala, Nampula, Quelimane.

National income by sector (1973): agriculture, 25 per cent; transportation and communications, 35 per cent; foreign-earned wages, 10 per cent; industry, 10 per cent; mineral export, 12 per cent; others, 8 per cent.

Main natural resources: coal, tantalite, beryl, iron, fluorite, copper and natural gas.

Foreign trade (1974): exports, $302 million; imports, $470 million; total, $772 million.

Main trading partners: South Africa, Rhodesia (Zimbabwe) (not since 1976), USA, Portugal, Romania, Japan, USSR, FRG.
Rail network: 3144 km.
Road network: 21,000 km.
Universities: 1, Eduardo Mondlane University (with 2500 students in 1973).
Foreign relations: diplomatic relations with over 64 countries; 18 diplomatic missions residing in Maputo; member of the UN since 1975.

NOTES

1. Herrick, *Area Handbook for Mozambique* (1969) pp. 5–23.
2. For historical studies, see M. D. D. Newitt, *Portuguese Settlement on the Zambesi* (1973) pp. 1–32; and A. F. Isaacman, *Mozambique: The Africanization of a European Institution* (1973) pp. 3–16.
3. Herrick, *Area Handbook*, pp. 67–9.
4. An introduction to Mozambique's history can be found in T. H. Henriksen, *Mozambique: A History* (1978).
5. For studies of Portuguese exploration and early imperialism, see E. Axelson, *Portuguese in South-east Africa, 1488–1600* (1973); and C. R. Boxer, *The Portuguese Seaborne Empire: 1415–1825* (1969).
6. A. F. Isaacman, *The Tradition of Resistance in Mozambique* (1976) ch. 5 and 6.
7. Henriksen, *Mozambique: A History*, pp. 155–60.
8. The finest exposition of Salazar's political policies remains J. Duffy, *Portuguese Africa* (1959) chs 11 and 12.
9. J. P. Moffitt (US Consul, Lourenço Marques) to Secretary of State, 19 Oct 1927, 853N 00/7, Consular Dispatches, Mozambique.
10. R. N. Dias, *A Imprensa Periódica em Moçambique, 1854–1954* (1956) pp. 66–7.
11. Interview with member of the International Centre, PCP, Lisbon, 10 Oct 1977.
12. For details, see E. Mondlane, *The Struggle for Mozambique* (1969) pp. 116–21.
13. Ibid., pp. 122–4.
14. *Mozambique Revolution* (Dar es Salaam), no. 1 (Dec 1963) 2.
15. T. H. Henriksen, 'People's War in Angola, Mozambique and Guinea-Bissau', *Journal of Modern African Studies*, XIV, no. 3 (1976) 377–99.
16. W. C. Opello, 'Pluralism and Elite Conflict in an Independence Movement: FRELIMO in the 1960s', *Journal of Southern African Studies*, II, 1 (1975) 66–82.
17. T. H. Henriksen, 'Angola, Mozambique and the Soviet Union: Liberation and the Quest for Influence', in W. Weinstein and T. H. Henriksen (eds), *Soviet and Chinese Aid to African Nations* (forthcoming).
18. T. H. Henriksen, 'Portugal in Africa: Comparative Notes on Counter-

insurgency', *ORBIS: A Journal of World Affairs*, XXI, no. 2 (1977) 395–412.
19. Fourth Thesis; see *Frelimo Central Committee: Report to the Third Congress*, pp. 43–52.
20. Elaboration of this and other points on Mozambique's Marxism can be found in T. H. Henriksen, 'Marxism and Mozambique', *African Affairs*, LXXVII, no. 309 (1978) 161–82.
21. 'FRELIMO Announces Party Development', in Foreign Broadcast Information Service, *Daily Report*, VIII, no. 249 (28 Dec 1977) E2.
22. 'Estatutos e Programa', *25 de Setembro Dia da Revolução Moçambicana* (1975) pp. 49–75.
23. *Notícias*, (Mozambique), 6 Feb 1977.
24. Constitution, Article 3.
25. 'Mozambique Constitution', *Daily News* (Tanzania), 22 May 1978.
26. 'President Gives Guidelines to Youth Organization', in Foreign Broadcast Information Service, in *Daily Report*, VIII, no. 230 (30 Nov 1977) E5.
27. Mozambique Information Agency, 12 Apr 1978, reported in *Facts and Reports* (Netherlands), VIII, no. 12 (19 Apr 1978) 16.
28. *Notícias*, 8 Feb 1977.
29. Defence appropriations in 1978 were $91 million (*Marchés Tropicaux*, 3 Mar 1978).
30. Only 14 per cent of the population had attended part of a six-year primary-education programme; another 0·9 per cent received secondary or vocational schooling and 0·1 per cent were attending the University at the end of the war (*Africa*, 8 June 1975).
31. Collins, 'Education for the People', *Southern Africa*, X, no. 5 (June–July 1977) 23.
32. *Notícias*, 16 Dec 1976.
33. A. Doll, *The Toothpaste Express: Letters from Prison* (1976).
34. 'Mozambique', in *Africa Contemporary Record, 1975–1976* (1976) B279.
35. For one source of information on the Wiriyamu massacre, see A. Hastings, *Wiriyamu* (1974).
36. *Notícias*, 4 Feb 1977.
37. 'Mozambique', in *Africa Contemporary Record, 1976–1977* (1977) B303.
38. *Africa Research Bulletin*, Apr 1978, p. 4812.
39. Fifth Thesis; See *Frelimo Central Committee: Report to the Third Congress*, pp. 52–9.
40. *Africa*, 31 May 1977; cited in *Facts and Reports* (Netherlands) VII, no. 13 (29 June 1977) 16.
41. *Tempo* (Mozambique), 15 May 1977.
42. I. Christie, 'Mozambique's Three Years of Independence', *Africa*, 14 June 1978.
43. 'Mozambique Takes Over Private Banks', *Daily News* (Tanzania), 4 Jan 1978.
44. T. Hodges, 'Mozambique: The Politics of Liberation', in G. M. Carter and P. O'Meara (eds), *Southern Africa in Crisis* (1977) 73.
45. *Notícias*, 22 Jan 1978; and Radio Maputo, 12 May 1978, in *Facts and Reports* (Netherlands) VIII, no. 11 (2 June 1978) 10.
46. 'Mozambique Reshuffle Puts Emphasis on Economic Policy', *Financial Times*, 25 Apr 1978.

47. D. Lamb, 'Mozambique Makes Progress', *International Herald Tribune*, 4 July 1978.
48. 'Mozambique', in *Africa Contemporary Record, 1976–1977*, B297.
49. Stockholm International Peace Research Institute. *The Arms Trade with the Third World* (1971) pp. 668–74.
50. 'Podgorny Visits Zambia, Mozambique', *Current Digest of the Soviet Press*, XXIX, 13 (22 Apr 1977) pp. 11–12.
51. *Marchés Tropicaux*, 15 Sep 1977.
52. UN Document E/5812, 30 Apr 1976, p. 24.
53. *Africa Research Bulletin*, Dec 1977, p. 4663.
54. 'Mozambique', *Africa Contemporary Record, 1976–1977*, B307.
55. *Daily News* (Tanzania), 8 Nov 1977.
56. R. A. Preto-Rodas, *Negritude as a Theme in the Poetry of the Portuguese-Speaking World* (1970) p. 70.
57. *Africa Research Bulletin*, Apr 1978, p. 4812.
58. For more information on Mondlane, see T. H. Henriksen, 'The Revolutionary Thought of Eduard Mondlane', *Génève-Afrique*, XII, no. 1 (1973) 37–52.
59. After 1960 the Portuguese conducted no published census by ethnic group, officially viewing all Mozambicans as Portuguese. These figures are derived from an official in the Centre for Tourism and Culture – see A. Rita-Ferreira, 'The Ethno-History and the Ethnic Grouping of the Peoples of Mozambique', *South African Journal of African Affairs*, III, no. 1 (1973) 56–76. Mozambique's Health Ministry found during the vaccination campaign that the overall population was closer to 11 million than to the previously estimated 9·5 million.

BIBLIOGRAPHY

Books

Abshire, D. M. and Samuels, M. A., *Portuguese Africa: A Handbook* (New York: Praeger, 1969).
Axelson, Eric, *Portuguese in South-east Africa, 1488–1600* (Cape Town: C. Struik, 1973).
Boxer, Charles R., *The Portuguese Seaborne Empire: 1415–1825* (New York: Alfred A. Knopf, 1969)
——, *Race Relations in the Portuguese Colonial Empire, 1415–1825* (Oxford: Clarendon Press, 1963).
Chilcote, Ronald H., *Portuguese Africa* (Englewood-Cliffs, N.J.: Prentice-Hall, 1967).
——, 'Mozambique: The African Nationalist Response to Portuguese Imperialism and Underdevelopment', in Christian P. Potholm and Richard Dale (eds), *Southern Africa in Perspective* (New York: Free Press, 1972) pp. 183–95.
Cornwall, Barbara, *The Bush Rebels* (New York: Holt, Rinehart and Winston, 1972).
Dias, Raul Neves, *A Imprensa Periódica em Moçambique, 1854–1954* (Lourenço

Marques: Imprensa Nacional de Moçambique, 1956).

Doll, Armand, *The Toothpaste Express: Letters from Prison* (Kansas City, Miss.: Beacon Hill Press, 1976).

Duffy, James, *Portuguese Africa* (Cambridge, Mass.: Harvard University Press, 1959).

'Estatuos e Programa', *25 de Setembro Dia da Revolução Moçambicana* (Maputo: no publisher listed, 1975).

Hamilton, Russell G., *Voices from an Empire: A History of Afro-Portuguese Literature* (Minneapolis: University of Minnesota Press, 1975).

Hastings, Adrian, *Wiriyamu* (London: Search Press, 1974).

Henriksen, Thomas H., *Mozambique: A History* (London: Rex Collings, 1978).

——, 'Angola, Mozambique and the Soviet Union: Liberation and the Quest for Influence', in Warren Weinstein and Thomas H. Henriksen (eds)., *Soviet and Chinese Aid to African Nations* (New York: Praeger, forthcoming).

Herrick, Allison Butler, *Area Handbook for Mozambique* (Washington, DC: US Government Printing Office, 1969).

Hodges, Tony, 'Mozambique: The Politics of Liberation', in Gwendolen M. Carter and Patrick O'Meara (eds), *Southern Africa in Crisis* (Bloomington: Indiana University Press, 1977) 48–88.

Isaacman, Allen F., *Mozambique: The Africanization of A European Institution; the Zambezi Prazos, 1750–1902* (Madison: University of Wisconsin Press, 1972).

——, *The Tradition of Resistance in Mozambique: Anti-Colonial Activity in the Zambesi Valley, 1850–1921* (Berkeley, Calif.: University of California Press, 1976).

Machel, Samora Moises, *Mozambique: Sowing the Seeds of Revolution* (London: Committee for Freedom in Mozambique, Angola and Guiné, 1974).

——, *The Tasks Ahead: Selected Speeches of Samora Machel* (New York: Afro-American Information Service, 1975).

Middlemas, Keith, *Cabora Bassa: Engineering and Politics in Southern Africa* (London: Weidenfeld and Nicolson, 1975).

Minter, William, *Portuguese Africa and the West* (New York: Monthly Review Press, 1972).

Mondlane, Eduardo, *The Struggle for Mozambique* (Baltimore: Penguin, 1969).

'Mozambique', in *Africa Contemporary Record*, ed. Colin Legum (London: Rex Collings, annual).

Newitt, M. D. D., *Portuguese Settlement on the Zambesi* (New York: Africana, 1973).

Paul, John, *Mozambique: Memoirs of a Revolution* (Harmondsworth: Penguin, 1975).

Preto-Rodas, Richard A., *Negritude as a Theme in the Poetry of the Portuguese-Speaking World* (Gainsville: University of Florida Press, 1970).

Stockholm International Peace Research Institute, *The Arms Trade with the Third World* (New York: Humanities Press, 1971).

Articles in periodicals (excluding unsigned news articles).

Alpers, Edward A., 'Ethnicity, Politics and History in Mozambique', *Africa Today*, XXI, 4 (1974) 39–53.

Christie, Iain, 'Mozambique's Three Years of Independence', *Africa*, 14 June 1968.

Collins, Carol, 'Education for the People', *Southern Africa*, x, no. 5 (June–July 1977) 23.

Hastings, Adrian, 'Some Reflections Upon the War in Mozambique', *African Affairs*, LXXIII, no. 292 (1974) 263–75.

Henriksen, Thomas H., 'Marxism and Mozambique', *African Affairs*, LXXVII, no. 309 (1978) 161–82.

——, 'People's War in Angola, Mozambique, and Guinea-Bissau', *Journal of Modern African Studies*, XIV, no. 3 (1976) 377–99.

——, 'Portugal in Africa: Comparative Notes on Counterinsurgency', *ORBIS: A Journal of World Affairs*, XXI, no. 2 (1977) 395–412.

——, 'The Revolutionary Thought of Eduardo Mondlane', *Genève-Afrique*, XII, no. 1 (1973) 37–52.

Lamb, David, 'Mozambique Makes Progress', *International Herald Tribune*, 4 July 1978.

Machel, Samora, 'Consolidating People's Power in Moçambique', *African Communist*, LXXII (1978) 32–50.

——, 'Women's Liberation is Essential for the Revolution', *African Communist*, LXI (1975) 37–51.

Oppello, Watler C., 'Pluralism and Elite Conflict in an Independence Movement: FRELIMO in the 1960s', *Journal of Southern African Studies*, II, no. 1 (1975) 66–82.

Rita-Ferreira, Antonio, 'The Ethno-History and the Ethnic Grouping of the Peoples of Mozambique', *Southern African Journal of African Affairs*, III, no. 1 (1973) 56–76.

Santos, Marcelino dos, 'The Revolutionary Perspective in Mozambique', *World Marxist Review*, XI, no. 1 (1968) 91–5.

Saul, John S., 'FRELIMO and the Mozambique Revolution', *Monthly Review*, XXIV, no. 10 (1973) 22–52.

——, 'Free Mozambique', *Monthly Review*, XXVII, no. 7 (1975) 8–22.

Slovo, Joe, 'FRELIMO Faces the Future', *African Communist*, LV (1973) 23–53.

20 Polish People's Republic

GEORGE SANFORD

Poland is both in area and in population the largest and the most important of the eight European people's democracies. She suffered massive population and economic losses as a result of the Second World War, and emerged from the war diminished in size but territorially more compact than she had been in the interwar period. The cession of territories in the east to the USSR was counterbalanced by Poland's new *de facto* frontier on the Odra (Oder) and Nysa (Neisse) rivers and the acquisition of most of East Prussia, although this was not legally accepted by the Federal Republic of Germany (FRG) until 1970. On balance Poland gained in terms of national resources and ethnic homogeneity. By 1978, ethnic and largely Roman Catholic Poles made up 98 per cent of the population. Processes of industrialisation and urbanisation and associated social and demographic transformations have changed Poland dramatically since communist rule was set up at the end of the Second World War.

Poland's population has increased to 35 million (1978), from the 1945 level of 24 million, as a result of a very high birth-rate, which, although it has recently levelled off, is still above the European average. As the death rate has also declined, the population is still rising steadily and is officially expected to be 41·2 million by 2000 AD. The population is also very young, as over half have been born since 1945. People's Poland has the demographic basis for a young and vigorous society, with an increasing percentage of the population now entering the work force and younger people thrusting themselves into responsible positions from the late 1960s onwards.

Poland lies very close to the geographical centre of Europe, and is strategically placed across important communication routes between Western and Eastern Europe and between the countries of Central Europe and the Baltic Sea.[1] Situated on the North European Plain, about 90 per cent of the country's terrain is rolling lowland with an

Poland: provincial boundaries

altitude of less than 1000 feet (300 metres), just under half of which is arable and over a quarter of which is forested. The country becomes more hilly on the southern frontier, which is formed by the touristically attractive and heavily forested Sudeten and Carpathian mountains. Perhaps no other country's history has been so dominated by its geographical position as has Poland's. The absence of natural boundaries to the east and west can be over-emphasised, though, in explaining the fluctuations in Poland's frontiers and fortunes during the thousand years of her statehood, which are usually reckoned from 966 AD, when Mieszko I of the Piast dynasty accepted Roman Catholicism. Certainly in mediaeval and early modern times the abilities of her kings were always an important factor, and the open frontiers, besides laying Poland open to attack, also allowed her to expand dramatically. One can also argue that it was the internal political weakness of the Polish commonwealth more than geographical factors which enabled Russia, Prussia and the Austro-Habsburgs to partition Poland off the map of Europe at the end of the eighteenth century. The Poles thus became a nation without a state for over a century.[2]

During the nineteenth century the earlier tradition of Polish national greatness was overlaid by a heroic struggle for the preservation of national values, traditions and independence.[3] Polish revolutionaries therefore became primarily concerned with the struggle for national liberation. It was then that the Roman Catholic Church cemented its identification with the Polish national tradition in the struggle against Russification and Germanisation. The Polish cause was also promoted by the European Left. It is worth remembering that the inaugural meeting of Karl Marx's First International was originally called to muster support for Poland.

Polish independence in 1918 was, however, mainly made possible by the simultaneous defeat of Russia and Germany and by the collapse of the Habsburg Empire. The new state started off as a parliamentary republic. After the army coup of May 1926 it was transformed into an authoritarian system dominated by Marshal Piłsudski until his death in 1935, and by his quarrelling successors until the destruction of the Polish state in September 1939.

One can now see the extent to which Poland's modern history has been dominated by her security problem, a theme which has been brilliantly developed by Adam Bromke.[4] He argues that the Poles have oscillated between periods of 'political idealism', as in the 1831 and 1863 insurrections, and in interwar Poland, and periods of 'political realism', as during the second half of the nineteenth century and after 1944. This provides an interesting key to the interplay between Poland's domestic and international politics and her dilemma as a medium-sized state which is too large to accept client status comfortably and yet too small to establish itself securely as a great power.

THE POLITICAL HISTORY OF POLISH COMMUNISM

Revolutionary socialism before the Second World War

The original divergence between Polish socialists, in their formative two decades before 1914, was caused by differing reactions to Poland's nineteenth-century experience as an oppressed and partitioned nation. This provides a continuing theme throughout the history of Polish Marxism, right up to the present day. The majority supported the Polish Socialist Party (PPS) founded in 1892.[5] They accepted Józef Piłsudski's argument that the struggle for national independence should have priority over social revolution. The contrary, and minority, view was that the Polish proletariat could only be liberated by social revolution at the same time as their Russian brothers and that incorporation in the new and more extensive socialist state would bring great economic benefits. The Socialist Democracy of the Kingdom of Poland and Lithuania (SDKPiL), led by Julian Marchlewski, Roża Luxemburg and Feliks Dzierżyński, embodied this internationalist Marxist tradition. In December 1918 they united with a left-wing socialist faction to form the Polish Communist (Workers') Party (KPRP later KPP) which affiliated itself to the Third International.[6]

The interwar Polish Communist Party believed that the reborn Polish state would soon collapse as the Bolshevik revolution spread into Central Europe. Its defeatist attitude during the Russo-Polish War of 1920, when it was banned, identified it with Soviet Russia, which was then widely hated in Poland for both national and social reasons. The Party was also weakened by the quarrelsome factionalism of its leaders, many of whom supported Trotsky against Stalin; by its mistaken support of the 1926 coup d'état; and by increasing Comintern control, which, however, did not become fully effective until the late 1920s. Given these factors, an unfavourable environment in an intensely nationalist, peasant and Roman Catholic country and increased repression after 1926, it is hardly surprising that the Communist Party never became a major political force. At its peak it had perhaps some 25,000 members, mainly industrial workers and ethnic minorities, and pockets of electoral support, which in 1928 enabled it to run ahead of the Socialist Party in the Warsaw, Łodz and Silesian industrial areas.[7] The evidence suggests that, although it was by no means a negligible force, it could never have carried out a revolution on the strength of its domestic resources alone. More important though, historical continuity was broken. Stalin wound up the Party completely in 1938. He had earlier executed almost all its major leaders, while much of the remaining interwar Polish Communist Party membership was eliminated by the Nazi occupiers after 1939.

The Polish Workers' Party (PPR) and the establishment of Communist Power, 1942–8

The PPR was set up clandestinely in Nazi-occupied Warsaw in January 1942. Its first two Russian-approved leaders, Nowotko and Finder, were shot, and the then-obscure Władysław Gomułka became its Secretary-General in, it appears, 1943, when radio contact with Moscow had broken down. Unlike the case with Tito's partisans in Yugoslavia, the PPR and its armed formations, the People's Army and the People's Guards, were a relatively minor force in the Polish resistance as compared with the Home Army. The latter was loyal to the government-in-exile in London, but was weakened by the tragedy of the Warsaw uprising of August–September 1944. The military occupation of Poland by the Red Army during 1944 and early 1945 enabled Stalin at Yalta and Potsdam to gain Western approval for Poland's new *de facto* western frontiers on the Odra-Nysa, to compensate for the incorporation into the USSR of Poland's eastern territories.[8] The Western allies also recognised the communist-dominated provisional government, in exchange for a promise of free elections and a widening of the 'Lublin' coalition of the PPR and the Socialist, Democratic and Peasant Parties by the inclusion of Sikorski's successor, by now ex-Premier of the government-in-exile, the Peasant leader Stanisław Mikołajczyk.

There were two main tendencies in Polish communism in 1944 which were to provide the basis for future divisions until well into the 1960s. The first was composed of those elements, led by Gomułka, who had joined the PPR and its military organisations in Poland and who had developed a more open and national approach, dictated by their wartime circumstances. The second were those communists and their associates who joined Soviet-sponsored political and military organisations established on Russian soil from 1943 onwards. A Polish army in the USSR was set up under General Zygmunt Berling. In December

1943 a National Council of Poland (KRN) was established by the domestic communists, but it soon became dominated by those communists, later to be known as Muscovites, who had spent the war in the USSR. This body provided the basis for the subsequent Polish Committee of National Liberation (PKWN) set up in Lublin in July 1944, which was transformed into the coalition provisional government at the end of 1944. The Muscovites, although already holding key political posts, allowed themselves to be overshadowed by the native element until 1948. The latter were better at rallying support from those increasingly large sections of Polish society which regarded the PPR as the party of real and long-delayed social revolution and which accepted the need for postwar friendship with the USSR.

Towards the end of the war, communism became the dominant political force in Poland, but its monopoly of political power was established gradually, between 1945 and 1948.[9] Although, in the final analysis, its victory was heavily dependent upon the conditions brought about by the USSR's victory over Nazi Germany, its postwar military control of Eastern Europe and the inability of the Western powers to oppose this situation, it would be wrong to dismiss the communist assumption of power as merely being the installation of a 'baggage-train' government by the Red Army. Much genuine support existed. The political struggle gained more from the intellectual and professional classes radicalised by the war and from workers and peasants attracted by the programme of social liberation and land reform. PPR membership thus increased dramatically from about 30,000 in January 1945 to 364,000 in July 1946, 820,000 in December 1947, and its pre-unification peak of over a million in November 1948.

The great social reforms of this period – the nationalisation of large and medium-sized industries, land reform, and such social and educational measures as could be effected given the horrific destruction wrought by the war – were, however, overshadowed by the political struggle.[10] This took place against the back-cloth of a very real civil war as Home Army elements continued armed resistance into the late 1940s. The opposition rallied around Mikołajczyk's Peasant Party, while the PPR used its control of crucial ministries, such as those of the Interior and Western Territories, to build up support and to intimidate opposition. The PPR gradually sliced off support from its nominal liberal, peasant and socialist allies. It outmanoeuvred Mikołajczyk over such issues as the referendum on the western frontier, the economic reforms and the abolition of the Senate in June 1946. By the time elections were held, in January 1947, the PPR by dint of its politically entrenched position and electoral sharp practice was able to gain an outright victory for its government Bloc. The denoucement followed rapidly. The communist leader Bolesław Bierut was elected President in February 1947, and the pro-communist socialist Józef Cyrankiewicz became Premier. Mikołajczyk fled the country, while remaining opponents were arrested and their organisations banned. The communist monopoly of power was completed by the somewhat delayed fusion of the PPR with the left wing of the Polish Socialist Party in the Polish United Workers' Party (PUWP) in December 1948. A variety of left-wing socialist and radical peasant trends then became incorporated, which contributed to producing a more diverse and faction-ridden party after the Stalinisation period had run its course.

From Stalinism to 'October'

1948 to 1953 was the period during which the Russian Stalinist form of communism was asserted over the more home-grown variety which had initially characterised the PPR.[11] 'Home communists' such as Władysław Gomułka, Zenon Kliszko and Marian Spychalski were removed from power during 1948 as the result of an internal power struggle promoted by Soviet pressure. They were replaced by the Muscovites, who, completely dependent upon Stalin, could be trusted to carry out his post-1947 hard-line policies. Their leader, President and First Party Secretary Bolesław Bierut, now became Poland's mini-Stalin, forming a leadership troika with Hilary Minc, the economic boss, and Jakub Berman, the ideological specialist. The most feared individual, however, became Stanisław Radkiewicz, the Minister of Public Security. Purges of the newly constituted PUWP were carried out. Police terror was unleashed against both the population at large and Party members, though on a lesser scale than elsewhere in Eastern Europe. Most significantly for the country's political development, no major 'show trials' took place. Gomułka and his friends thus survived to play their vitally important roles in 1956. Again, the limited collectivisation of agriculture and the conflict with the Roman Catholic Church were perhaps a degree less vicious than other contemporary East European developments; but the rest of the Stalinist process, remoulding the country's political and economic life, continued as frenziedly as elsewhere. This applied in particular to the massive development of heavy industry and the holding down of living standards in order to ensure a huge investment rate. Soviet control over the political and economic apparatus, the security police and the armed forces, headed by

Konstantin Rokossovsky, a Russianised Pole, was fully effective by March 1953, when Stalin died, as was the severing of Polish contacts with the West.

The short-lived Stalinist attempt to set Polish society in a totalitarian mould was, however, unsuccessful. It produced a reaction which transformed the communist regime and culminated in Gomułka's recall to power in October 1956.[12] The curtailment of the police terror and the slackening of the economic pressure during 1954–5 was insufficient to allay the increasingly vocal expression of discontent by writers and students. These intellectual currents were paralleled by workers' dissatisfaction with their low standard of living, which discontent burst out in the Poznań uprising in June 1956. Popular discontent was matched by a power struggle within the PUWP which paralysed its leading role.[13] The pressure of events during 1956 caused demands for reform to be made by a wing of the PUWP called the 'Puławy' faction, and, eventually, in a more moderate form, by a centrist group led by Edward Ochab, who took over as First Party Secretary following Bierut's death in Moscow in March 1956. This alignment facilitated a peaceful resolution to the dramatic confrontation in October 1956, during the Eighth PUWP Plenum, between, on the one hand, the hard-line 'Natolin' faction and their Soviet supporters, who, led by Khrushchev, had flown in from Moscow, and, on the other hand, the frenzied and pent-up Polish population. This deal was symbolised by Gomułka's return to power to effect popular demands for the readjustment of Polish–Soviet relations, better living standards, more open relations with the West, socialist democracy and the abolition of the reign of terror in domestic political life – high hopes which under the prevailing conditions in Eastern Europe could be only partially realised.

The Gomułka period, 1956–70

The very real aims of 'October' were maintained, even though Gomułka's Poland increasingly marked time politically and economically as the 1960s wore on.[14] Poland's relationship with the USSR was transformed from that of an obsequious satellite to that of a faithful senior ally which could be trusted to make its own domestic decisions. The dismantled police-terror apparatus was only partially revived in the late 1960s. The abandoning of collectivisation, the allowance of, by communist standards, a fair degree of intellectual freedom, and a grudging co-existence with the Roman Catholic Church, punctuated by periodic but controlled confrontations, such as the dispute between

Church and State in 1966 over the celebration of Poland's millennium, were one side of the coin. The essential hard core of Gomułkaism was the adaptation of communism to Polish conditions and the development of a national road to socialism. Initially this meant an emphasis on the improvement of living standards, boosted by private agriculture, but unfortunately this was not maintained into the 1960s. Gomułka's achievement, in spite of his tortuous political zigzags, marked by the recall of hard-line personalities after 1959 and his simplistic exercise of the PUWP's hegemony in Polish politics, was to reintegrate whole sectors of the population and Polish historical tradition which had been condemned during the Stalinist period. He produced a tolerable accommodation between the authoritarian PUWP and plural Polish society, but this volatile relationship was increasingly strained by generational and other conflicts.

The hopes and reforming enthusiasm of 1956–8 were followed by a consolidation period, the 'small stabilisation' lasting until around 1964. Then ensued a process of degeneration and relative economic stagnation, which led up to the 1968 crisis and the outbursts of December 1970. Much of the blame for this must be ascribed to Gomułka's style and policies. He was a decent, scrupulous and unostentatious man. But he held a simple dogmatic view of communism and lacked the intelligence and education to transcend the limitations of his Galician peasant background. In the 1960s he became increasingly authoritarian, irascible and opinionated.

Gomułka's poor grasp of reality is indicated by the fact that he came close to losing control of the PUWP. Nationalist hard-liners, called the Partisans because of their wartime resistance background, grouped themselves around Mieczysław Moczar, the Minister of the Interior. He expanded the security police and built up the standing of the War Veterans Organisation (ZBoWiD) from 1964 onwards. The Arab-Israeli War of 1967 allowed him to initiate an anti-Zionist campaign, directed in the first instance against Party members of Jewish origins, but really aimed at the remaining liberal communists, residual unreformed Stalinists, critical intellectuals and eventually Gomulka himself. All three groups suffered in the massive shake-up of Party, State, economic and above all academic cadres which followed the Warsaw student demonstrations of March 1968.[13] Gomułka, however, saved himself by promoting new men, by ceding power to provincial Party bosses, most prominent among whom was Edward Gierek, the Party leader in industrial Silesia (1957–70), and by holding on until the Soviet occupation of Czechoslovakia. At the Fifth PUWP Congress, in

November 1968, Gomułka was resoundingly endorsed by Brezhnev, who distrusted Moczar's 'Romanian'-type alternative.

The power struggle and associated events of 1968 thus eliminated the remaining communists of 1956 vintage and cowed the Polish intelligentsia, although the steam went out of Moczar's drive for power. Unlike in 1956, the workers remained largely passive. Poland thus was not to have its Dubček as the students had demanded. But a younger and more pragmatic generation, less affected by wartime and Stalinist traumas, now broke through into the highest spheres of political life. Important policy initiatives followed. A positive response was offered to Brandt's *Ostpolitik*. The FRG recognised Poland's frontiers in December 1970, opening up new hopes for *détente* and trade. A new economic reform was mooted to encourage material incentives and to increase decision-making powers of industrial enterprises as a means of revitalising the economy. Unfortunately it continued the emphasis on manufacturing at the expense of consumption and involved a 15 to 30 per cent increase in the price of foodstuffs, most maladroitly announced on 14 December 1970, just before the traditionally festive Christmas season. There followed five days of rioting, especially by shipyard workers, in the Baltic towns Gdańsk, Gdynia and Szczecin, and, although this was suppressed, at the cost of many lives, it persuaded the PUWP central *aktyw* to resort to political measures to calm the situation. Gomułka and his closest Political Bureau colleagues were replaced by Edward Gierek on 19 December 1970.[16]

Gierek's Poland

The social outburst which brought about the change of leadership in 1970 also demonstrated the growing role of the working class in Polish politics. Gierek initially faced a twofold task.[17] First, he stabilised the political situation by pacifying social groups, freezing food prices, scrapping the unpopular economic reform and, above all, by committing himself wholeheartedly to an economic policy designed to raise living standards. Secondly, he gradually extended his control over the Party and State and, like most new communist leaders, promised new policies, blamed his predecessor for the country's problems and promoted supporters at all levels within the Party and political organisations. Provincial PUWP secretaries were replaced, PUWP members were thoroughly screened and over 100,000 of them removed during 1971–3, the Sixth PUWP Congress in December 1971 rejuvenated the Central Committee (two-thirds of its full members were thus replaced since Gierek's take-over of power), and the March 1972 Sejm (National Assembly) election brought in a clear majority of new deputies. However, the circumstances of Gierek's accession to power, allied to his temperament and inclinations, caused him to re-establish confidence in his leadership by what he called a 'frank direct dialogue with the nation'.[18] The early period of 'liveliness' witnessed an interesting public discussion carried out by the mass media and public meetings but one that was largely restricted to practical problems of economic priorities and possibilities, as well as a whole host of complaints and suggestions about the improvement of specific inadequacies. Gierek's programme of economic prosperity and consumerism and reforms designed to improve the political, economic, educational and local-government structures within the existing framework of PUWP hegemony produced a mood of cautious and realistic optimism. This was strengthened by a four-year economic boom and by Gierek's personal popularity, justly gained in this period, as a result of his direct, man-to-man approach and efficiency as a political leader.[19]

Aspects of contemporary Polish government and society and Gierek's economic and foreign policies are dealt with separately in the sections which follow. One cannot hope to do justice to ongoing political processes or to come to definitive judgements about them. It is already clear, however, that Gierek's initial period of political and economic success was halted by the economic factors which provoked the attempt to raise food prices in June 1976 and which has since then ushered in a period of incipient political crisis and economic dissatisfaction.

This overview of the political history of Polish communism illustrates the following themes. Firstly, one of the continually recurring divisions has been between those revolutionary socialists who have emphasised the need for the preservation of the Polish national state and traditions and those who have been more preoccupied with an internationalist orientation, which from the 1920s onwards came to mean a pro-Soviet attitude. The Polish Socialist Party and the Socialist Democracy of Poland and Lithuania, Nativists and Muscovites, Puławy and Natolin, Partisans and Stalinists – the dichotomy continued at least until 1968. Secondly, in the Gierek period this conflict has become overlain by problems of modernisation and crisis management. Thirdly, Polish society was never turned successfully into a Soviet, let alone totalitarian, system. National traditions, links with the West, religious, peasant and intellectual values allied to a new social pluralism brought about by industrialisation have produced a society potentially at loggerheads with the authoritarian political system monopolised by the PUWP.

These stresses and strains burst out in three great crises, which transformed the political system (1956) and produced dramatic changes in leadership personnel as well as significant reorientations in economic, although not political, aims (1968 and 1970).

THE POLISH UNITED WORKERS' PARTY

Membership and social composition

Unlike its Czechoslovak or GDR counterparts, the PUWP has counted within its ranks a fairly low percentage of the population (see Table 20.1).[20] Fluctuations in its membership have also been caused by massive scrutiny and expulsions, as in the Stalinist period (1949–52), the 'March events' (1967–8) and Gierek's early years (1971–3), or by a dramatic flight from Party membership, as in 1955 to 1957. The general trend, though, has been for PUWP membership to rise steadily since 1958, when it was at a very low percentage for a ruling communist party. After almost three decades of political consolidation, it totalled 7·7 per cent of the entire population or 16 per cent of the work force. The PUWP leadership has always faced particularly difficult problems in recruiting and socialising a reliable membership. Its historical traditions and awareness of its relative political weakness within Polish society has been a key factor in encouraging a more flexible and less dogmatic approach since 1956. Thus, although its leaders promoted orthodox Marxism-Leninism of a Soviet type, they also, from the 1960s onwards, encouraged traditional national and military values. Polish communism has been marked by much factional activity, especially during the mid 1950s and late 1960s. The second main characteristic of PUWP membership, a consequence of the great upheavals and leadership changes in 1955–7 and 1968–70 as much as of subsequent policy, has therefore been a rapid and marked turn-over of members. In 1968, for example, over half the PUWP (1·2 million out of 2·1 million members) had joined since 1959. Thirdly, the influence of prewar Polish communists is now negligible. Even in 1968 the hard core of pre-1948 communists only totalled 390,000.

Gierek in his early years of power scrutinised Party membership intensively. He expelled many whom he considered politically or personally unsound and partially rejuvenated the Party. Gierek, however, could only maintain working-class and peasant membership at around their post-1960 proportions of 40 and 10 per cent respectively.

TABLE 20.1 Membership and social composition of the PUWP, 1948–75

	1948	1952	1955	1958	1960	1966	1970	1973	1975
Membership (incl. candidates)									
Millions	1·50	1·147	1·343	1·023	1·155	1·894	2·319	2·298	2·359
As percentage of the total population	6·26	4·47	4·9	3·55	3·9	5·6	7·13	6·89	6·94
Social composition (percentage of PUWP members)									
Manual workers	53·6	60·0	45·1	41·7	40·3	40·1	40·3	39·6	40·8
Peasants	26·5	17·0	13·0	12·2	11·8	11·9	11·5	10·1	9·6
Non-manual	17·6	20·0	39·2	42·1	42·9	42·6	42·3	43·9	44·5
Others	2·3	3·0	2·6	3·9	5·0	5·5	5·9	6·4	6·2

This is because the number of white-collar and professional members has been continuously on the increase. It has been greater than the manual-worker element since 1958. The pressure of some sections of the new professional elite to enter the Party has been a persistent feature since then. Party membership is semi-obligatory in many walks of professional life. It is unquestionably helpful in all of them. This generalisation can be modified in Poland because of traditional intelligentsia values and the social autonomy conferred by the possession of specialist skills, but this does not affect the statistical picture. The PUWP doubled in size between 1960 and 1975, but its number of white-collar workers more than trebled. The PUWP in 1975 was composed of 965,000 industrial workers and 225,000 agricultural workers, plus 478,000 white-collar professionals.[21] The remainder were, presumably, army members and the whole range of Party, State and other types of apparatchiks. Although some of the first-generation communists, referred to at the end of the preceding paragraph, still hold key positions, Gierek's PUWP is now overwhelmingly composed of individuals who have been brought up in People's Poland. The evidence suggests that, compared with their predecessors, they are better educated and less ideologically motivated, and, like Gierek himself, more concerned with the pragmatic resolution of practical problems.

Party organisation and processes

The PUWP, like all Leninist parties, is organised and functions on principles of democratic centralism, which are clearly set out in its Party statute. Gierek has been very active in keeping the Party's internal processes working. He has scrutinised membership regularly and has held frequent electoral-report conferences at every level. The PUWP was much reorganised in 1975, when its 300-odd county committees were abolished and its twenty-two provincial committees were replaced by forty-nine new ones. It then had 75,200 basic Party cells, 23,000 sections and 61,000 Party groups.

The Political Bureau usually meets weekly, but *ad hoc* meetings between key Political Bureau members, the Secretariat and heads of Central Committee departments occur as need arises. The highest policy decisions are discussed and taken within the Political Bureau and Secretariat, which are undoubtedly the main seats of political power within the PUWP. The Central Committee usually meets to discuss carefully prepared topics at about three or four plena every year. It is a large body which has tended to increase in size as extra interests and groups press for recognition by inclusion within it. The 1975 Congress elected 139 full and 111 candidate members, seventy-three of the former being new, while about three-quarters of the full members had been promoted by Gierek. The overwhelming bulk of Central Committee members are Party organisers and representatives of other political and social organs. Although the PUWP Central Committee played a crucial role at its Eighth Plenum, in October 1956, it is not normally a decision-making body. It has the potential to become so if the top leadership is divided. Normally it is significant mainly as a channel of direct influence on the leadership as regards both policy and personnel.

Political leadership

The PUWP has had only four first secretaries. Three, Bierut (1948–56), Gomułka (1956–70) and Gierek (since December 1970) have been undoubted leaders. They stamped their styles and policies on the country. Edward Ochab (March to October 1956) was a temporary compromise who gracefully made way for Gomułka.

Gierek, having first entered the Political Bureau in 1956, has over a decade of seniority over most of his colleagues, who are mainly post-1970 entrants. The Political Bureau elected by the Seventh Congress in 1975 had fourteen full and three candidate members. Gierek was assisted by nine Central Committee secretaries. As can be seen from Table 20.2, about half the Political Bureau have State responsibilities. Gierek's closest colleagues in 1978, who were also in the Secretariat, and hence dominant with him in running the Party and setting the general lines of policy, were Stanisław Kania, Jerzy Łukaszewicz, Edward Babiuch (originally his chief lieutenant) and Stefan Olszowski, whom many observers consider to be his main rival for the leadership. Relatively few demotions from the Political Bureau took place once Gomułka's supporters had been replaced and Moczar demoted.[22] Gierek's leadership has therefore so far been fairly stable in terms of personnel.

The political processes at this level are kept highly secret, although the Party newspaper publishes bland communiqués about Political Bureau meetings.[23] Most of the hard evidence is usually of a Kremlinological nature, relating to individuals rather than to particular decisions and how they were arrived at. There is a general consensus that the Political Bureau is the institutional locale where all the big political decisions are taken. One must remember, though, that these decisions are not taken in

TABLE 20.2 PUWP Political Bureau elected by the Seventh Congress, December 1975

Name	Date of birth	Date entered Political Bureau (as full member)	Main position (1978)	Previous major function
Edward Gierek	1913	1956	First Secretary, PUWP (1970–)	First Secretary, PUWP Katowice Province (1957– Dec 1970)
Edward Babiuch	1927	1970	Secretary of Central Committee, PUWP	Head, Central Committee Organisation Dept (1965–70)
Zdzisław Grudzien	1924	1975 (cand. 1971)	First Secretary, PUWP Katowice province	Secretary, PUWP Katowice province (1960–70)
Henryk Jabłoński	1909	1971 (cand. 1970)	Chairman, Council of State (1972–)	Minister of Education (1966–72)
Mieczysław Jagielski	1924	1971 (cand. 1964)	Deputy Chairman, Council of Ministers	Minister of Agriculture (1959–70); Chairman, Planning Commission (1971–5)
Piotr Jaroszewicz	1909	1970 (cand. 1964)	Chairman, Council of Ministers (1970–)	Deputy Chairman, Council of Ministers (1952–70)
Wojciech Jaruzelski	1923	1971 (cand. 1970)	Minister of Defence (1968–)	
Stanisław Kania	1927	1975 (cand. 1971)	Secretary of Central Committee, PUWP	Head, Central Committee Admin. Dept (1968–71)
Józef Kępa	1928	1975 (cand. 1970)	Deputy Chairman, Council of Ministers	First Secretary, PUWP Warsaw City (1968–76)

Name	Year	(cand.)	Position	Position
Stanisław Kowalczyk	1924	(cand. 1973)	Minister of Interior (1973–)	
Władysław Kruczek	1910	1968	Chairman, Central Council, Trade Unions	First Secretary, PUWP Rzeszów province (1956–71)
Stefan Olszowski	1931	1970	Secretary of Central Committee, PUWP (1976–)	Minister of Foreign Affairs (1971–6)
Jan Szydlak	1925	1970	(Left Political Bureau 1976)	Secretary of Central Committee, PUWP (1968–76)
Józef Tejchma	1927	1968	Deputy Chairman, Council of Ministers	Minister of Culture (1974–8)
Kazimierz Barcikowski	1927	(cand. 1971)	First Secretary, PUWP Kraków province	Minister of Agriculture (1974–8)
Jerzy Łukaszewicz	1931	(cand. 1975)	Secretary of Central Committee, PUWP (1971–)	Head of Central Committee, Propaganda Dept (1962–4)
Tadeusz Wrzaszczyk	1932	(cand. 1975)	Chairman, Planning Commission; Deputy Chairman, Council of Ministers	Minister of Machine Engineering (1970–4)

a vacuum but result from a wide variety of political, social and institutional pressures.

THE STATE SYSTEM AND POLITICAL ORGANISATIONS

The constitution

The Constitution is the basic or fundamental law. Its function is 'to give expression to and to consolidate the new political, social and economic system which had emerged as a result of revolution.'[24] The constitution of July 1952 remained in force with only minor changes until it was substantially amended in February 1976.[25] The PUWP's leading role was then written in for the first time (article 3 i). So was the requirement of friendship with the USSR (article 6 ii) and a section (ch. 8) outlining citizen's duties as well as rights. The latter innovations occasioned strong public protests, especially an open letter by fifty-nine prominent intellectuals, which led to some changes in their formulation.[26]

Although the Polish People's Republic is now declared to be a socialist state (article 1 i), its name, unlike those of the other East European states, remains the same. The theory of State power also remains unchanged. Sovereignty reposes with the working people of town and country. It is exercised by their elected representatives to both the unicameral National Assembly (Sejm) and the local or people's councils, to which the unified State administration (whose functions and powers are enumerated in great detail in the Constitution) is completely subordinated.

The National Unity Front and the party system

The PUWP attempts to limit organised political activity to a Front of National Unity (FNU). This provides the framework for a party system led and directed by the PUWP, but also including the United Peasant Party, the Democratic Party and three minor Catholic groups, as well as trade-union, youth and other approved organisations.[27] The FNU has no individual life or membership of its own. It is largely an umbrella body under whose banner single electoral lists are produced and electoral programmes publicised. Gierek revitalised the FNU in his early years of power, using it as a bridge enabling non-communists to participate in public life.

The PUWP's leading role is accepted unquestioningly by its junior partners within the FNU. Gierek declared that the PUWP 'is above all a party of the working-class, but we are also a party of all the working-people of the entire socialist building nation'.[28] The PUWP therefore recruits its members right across the whole of Polish society. The United Peasant Party, three-quarters of whose membership are peasants, is largely restricted to the countryside, while the Democratic Party is kept to the towns (for their membership, see Table 20.3).[29] Both these sectional parties seem to function more like pressure groups. They are consulted by the PUWP on matters such as agriculture and handicrafts which primarily concern their members.

TABLE 20.3 Membership of Poland's United Peasant and Democratic Parties

	1965	*1970*	*1977*
United Peasant Party	358,000	413,000	428,000
Democratic Party	69,000	88,000	96,000

The Roman Catholic Church and politics

Poland is an overwhelmingly Roman Catholic nation. The Church's great political weight continues in spite of the increasing secularisation of Polish life. It is still most marked in the countryside, where an important role is played by village priests. A 1973 survey also indicated that the old are significantly more religious than the young and that in general terms, at least, half the population are still decidedly practising believers, while only a quarter or so have lapsed in their belief.[30] The PUWP has recognised this reality by accepting the need for co-existence with the Church. It also licences religious groups which play minor but interesting roles. Two of these, Pax and the Christian Social Union, are considered pro-regime and are therefore disavowed by the Roman Catholic hierarchy, led by Cardinal Stefan Wyszyński. More significantly, a progressive Catholic group called **Znak** ('The Sign') is allowed, and not only produces its own publications but also usually sends five deputies to the Sejm.[31] Its existence supports Wiatr's thesis that the Polish political system is marked by a sufficient degree of pluralism to warrant its description as what he terms a hegemonic party system.[32]

Gierek's policy towards the Church has largely been one of accommodation, as evidenced by the 1971 agreement, his meetings with

Wyszyński in order to stabilise the situation after Radom, and his audience with Pope Paul VI in the Vatican in December 1976. Conflict is, however, built into the relationship between the Church and the Party, as both believe that they best represent the real interests of the nation. Disputes have cropped up continuously over such issues as religious education, the building of new churches, or demonstrations, such as the celebration of Poland's millennium in 1966. Both sides, though, realise that they have to live together. They therefore limit and control their recurrent confrontations, although a totally new dimension was opened up by the election of Cardinal Karol Wojtyła of Kraków as Pope John Paul II in October 1978. Whether the Church is a progressive force and whether the Poles support it for national rather than spiritual reasons are debatable matters. What is undeniable is that its mere continued existence produces a formidable check on the political power of the communist party in Poland.

The Sejm and elections

The Sejm is constitutionally the highest organ of State power in Poland. It exercises control over the Council of Ministers and other State bodies. All legislation, including the budget and economic plans, has to be either passed or confirmed by it. It also appoints a seventeen-strong Council of State from among its members. This acts as a collective presidency, its Chairman becoming in effect the head of State. There were indications during the mid 1970s that Gierek might take over this post or set up a new presidential office, but nothing then came of this. The Sejm itself meets for about ten days of plenary sessions per year, as all but a few of the deputies have other, full-time occupations. Here it performs what a leading American authority has called 'a legitimating, supporting function "by ratifying" the programme and policies of the regime (as spelled out in detail by the central party and governmental apparatus)'.[33] The originality and distinguishing characteristic of the Sejm among communist parliaments is the lively control and debating activity of its twenty-two specialist committees, which perform many useful parliamentary tasks.[34]

The 460 Sejm deputies are elected by direct and universal suffrage in multi-member constituencies, normally at fixed four-year intervals. In practice, the PUWP allocates the number of Sejm seats to go to its FNU partners and has always kept a small majority for itself.[35] The Polish voter may abstain or vote against the official list. However, turnout has increased from its (communist) low of 94·14 per cent in 1957 to 98·27 per cent in 1976, while the FNU vote has never been lower than 98·33 per cent. By 1976 it was up to 99·43 per cent. The notable characteristic of the Polish electoral system is that the voter also has the opportunity of choosing from a list which has up to half as many candidates more than there are seats. Although the officially favoured candidates have, with a single exception in 1957, been invariably elected, they obtain differing individual percentages of the poll, as voters often cross them off in favour of less well known candidates who are placed at the bottom of the electoral list.[36] Although communist elections are viewed with scepticism in the West, because of the absence of competing parties and programmes, they nevertheless serve a number of purposes in Poland, which I have discussed elsewhere.[37]

The Council of Ministers

Constitutionally the Council of Ministers is defined as the supreme executive and administrative organ of State power, directing the whole range of State activity by supervising the work of ministries, State committees and people's councils. It is a large body which works within the framework of laws and resolutions passed by the Sejm, which formally appoints and dismisses it.[38]

The chairmanship (premiership) is an important office held by the senior Political Bureau member in charge of the State administration. In Poland he now has a dominant position in this sphere, since he appoints and dismisses ministers and deputy chairmen, allocates their fields of responsibility, arbitrates matters in contention between them and generally co-ordinates and organises the work of the Council. These questions are clearly settled in continuous consultation with the First Secretary of the Party and his closest colleagues in the Political Bureau and Secretariat. The Chairman is assisted by deputy chairmen, who together with him compose the Presidium of the Council of Ministers.

Before November 1956 the Planning Commission was an independent body. Since then it has been attached to the Council of Ministers. The majority of ministries are concerned with economic questions, often of a specialised nature. Every ministry is run on collegial lines by the minister, assisted by a number of vice-ministers or under-secretaries of State. Together they supervise the work of their various departmental directors and field services.[39] There are also seventeen State committees. The most noteworthy ones are perhaps the recently strengthened State Prices Commission and the Main Department for the Control of the

Press, Publications and Entertainments (i.e. the body in charge of censorship).[40]

Ministries and other State bodies are in continuous consultation with their 'shadow' Central Committee departments. The theoretical division of labour between policy-making by the latter and policy preparation and implementation by the former is a very hazy one and so far has not been illustrated by policy case studies. One may suggest that the relationship has become a symbiotic one. Party bodies always have a tendency to get drawn into excessive detail, while State institutions, through control of information and the preparation of policy options, naturally become involved in most ongoing decisions. In the present state of our knowledge, one can only hazard an informed guess that the Political Bureau and the Secretariat, aided by the Central Committee departments, monopolise new or big decisions, while the ministries continually strive to maintain their autonomy on day-to-day matters.

Local government

From 1954 to 1975, a three-tier structure composed of twenty-two provinces, over 300 counties and a large number of rural districts and settlements prevailed. Each territorial division had an elected people's council, whose activities were formally supervised by the Council of State. Detailed control was, however, exercised by the Council of Ministers over the presidia and by ministries over departments of the provincial people's councils, which in turn controlled the lower-level ones.[41] In practice, the Party bodies, which paralleled the territorial divisions, dominated their local politics. The people's council plenum was also very much controlled by its PUWP-led presidium.[42]

This system was radically reformed in three main stages between 1972 and 1975.[43] First, the 4313 lower-level councils were replaced by 2367 larger and economically more self-sufficient communes (*gminy*), whose activities are now directed by full-time managers. Secondly, the chairman of each people's council became the appropriate local PUWP first secretary. Thirdly, the counties were abolished in May 1975 and the provinces were reorganised into forty-nine new ones.

SOCIAL CHANGE AND THE SOCIO-ECONOMIC STRUCTURE

The main characteristics of postwar social change in Poland may be summarised as follows.[44] First, the percentage of manual workers increased from 29 per cent in 1938 to 50 per cent in 1970, the white-collar stratum increased from 5·5 per cent to 25 per cent, the peasant sector decreased from 52 to 25 per cent, while the prewar bourgeois and large landowning class was eliminated completely.[45] Secondly, Poland has become a mainly urban country, with 28 per cent of its population living in towns of over 100,000 and 23 per cent in towns of between 10,000 and 100,000 inhabitants, while the rural population had by 1977 fallen to below 43 per cent. Thirdly, there has been a high rate of postwar social mobility, a widespread proliferation of educational qualifications of all types and a high level of occupational diversification, not only within the working class but also, more particularly, within the white-collar and intelligentsia groups. The latter can loosely be defined as the 800,000 individuals who have completed higher education. Fourthly, social diversification has perhaps allowed social groups and mass organisations to play a relatively active role. A convincing study has shown that Poland can fairly be described as 'a consultative but authoritarian political system'. The PUWP acts, in one respect, as a political broker maintaining itself in power by balancing social groups and lobbies against each other.[46] The result of all these developments, of which only the main ones are touched on here, is that Polish political culture resembles Polish society in being a highly original and often volatile synthesis of modernising, revolutionary trends promoted by the communist regime and the traditional and varied values of pre-communist Poland.[47]

Poland's great oddity among the communist countries is that since 1956 it has abandoned the direct collectivisation of agriculture and has promoted voluntary co-operatives called agricultural circles.[48] It also has a significant privately owned small-business sector, run by 287,000 Poles and their families, who employ a further 183,000. All told, the State and copoperative sector employs 11·63 million, as against 4·74 million in the private sector. The former, though, produces 86 per cent of the gross national product. In this respect Poland has not followed the Soviet path to the bitter end. She has developed her own, more gradual and nationally distinctive, form of building socialism.

THE ECONOMY: ACHIEVEMENTS AND DILEMMAS

By 1977 Poland figured among the world's top dozen industrial nations. Her production figures and world rankings for coal (186 million tons, fourth position), sulphur (third position) and steel and copper (ninth positions) were particularly impressive. Whole new industries, such as chemicals, shipbuilding, electronics, electrical-machine engineering and motor vehicles, had been built up from scratch. Poland still remained an important agricultural producer, even though agriculture's share in her gross national product had fallen to 11·8 per cent. These achievements had been brought about by fairly orthodox communist economic planning methods, marked by a high investment rate, much of it going into heavy industry for most of the postwar period. Many economic-reform ideas were generated during the Polish 'October', but no fundamental innovations in economic management followed from this, the reforms of 1964 and 1969–70 being partial ones.[49]

The economic situation during the 1970s became the key to political stability. Gierek's policy since 1970 has been to build a 'second Poland'. He claims to have carried out a second industrialisation by his programmes of economic expansion and modernisation. The 1971–5 Plan for Socio-economic Development outlined the strategy of stimulating the economy by raising the standard of living. It set very high housing, motor-car, consumer-goods and educational goals.[50] Secondly, Gierek wanted to modernise the economy by importing Western technology and to increase labour productivity by applying new techniques, as well as by raising the qualifications of the work force. These policies initially produced an economic boom in which consumption figured prominently and real earnings rose at twice the planned rate. According to official statistics, between 1971 and 1975 gross national product increased by 60 per cent (9·9 per cent per annum), industrial production by 73 per cent and agricultural production by 19 per cent, and Poland's foreign trade also expanded dramatically.

By 1976 Poland seemed to be undergoing the transition from a Stalinist command economy, which paid no heed to the consumer, to a domestic mass market characterised by a degree of consumer choice, albeit one that suffers from grave periodic shortages.[51] Gierek was unlucky in that his dash for growth was adversely affected by the 1973 oil crisis and its repercussions on the cost of raw materials and Western trade and credit.[52] He was, however, committed to increases of 16–18 per cent in real earnings and 35 per cent in the food supply for the 1975–80 period.[53]

The Achilles' heel of the Polish economy continues to be agriculture. The doubling of fodder imports produced a 29 per cent increase in livestock over the 1971–5 period, but this was halted by the post-1973 increase in world grain prices.[54] Gierek had abolished compulsory prices paid to the farmers in order to stimulate production. Food prices had largely remained frozen since 1971. The need therefore arose to raise consumer prices in order to decrease the subsidy on food. The leadership, however, postponed any general increase in food prices until June 1976, when they seem to have gambled everything on Gierek's prestige. However, it was Premier Jaroszewicz who announced the increases, ranging from 30 per cent for eggs, flour and butter to 69 per cent for meat and 100 per cent for sugar. They were to be compensated for by some wholly inadequate increases in wages and pensions.[55] Faced by spontaneous and nationwide resistance, which included riots at Radom and work stoppages, Jaroszewicz withdrew the price increases the following day, thus preventing the crisis from escalating. Gierek then moved to stabilise the political situation.[56] Various categories had their prices raised subsequently on a one-off basis, and phased sectoral increases seems to be the policy now favoured by the leadership. It is safe to predict that popular dissatisfaction with the supply and quality of food, especially meat, will continue as a major factor in Polish politics.[57]

Gierek's policy of buying Western technology and consumer goods increased Poland's foreign-trade indebtedness to Western countries dramatically. During 1977, measures were taken to curtail it, by restricting imports and living standards. Two additional trends in Polish foreign trade are worth noting. First, although the USSR is still her largest trading partner, Poland's trade within Comecon had by 1977 fallen to 50 per cent from the 60–70 per cent range in Gomułka's time, while her trade with the West was up to 40 per cent. Secondly, the structure of Poland's exports has changed completely from her earlier dependence on coal and agricultural products. In 1977, mechanical engineering and electrical products made up 41·3 per cent of her imports and 46·2 per cent of her exports.

Much of Polish trade is increasingly tied in with complicated loan and credit arrangements. This does not necessarily place her at a disadvantage. The £115 million shipbuilding agreement with Britain in 1977, for example, was reported as being heavily in Poland's favour. Most Western prognoses of Poland's economic future are gloomy ones. The great unknown, though, is not the underlying strength of the economy, which is often under-estimated, but the political repercussions of a strained and uncertain economic situation.

EXTERNAL RELATIONS

The main reality in postwar Polish foreign policy has been Poland's relationship with the USSR. She was transformed in 1956 from a subservient satellite into a close and loyal senior ally, and through both Comecon and the Warsaw Pact, institutions in which she has played her full part, has been closely linked with, in particular, the USSR, Hungary, Bulgaria, Czechoslovakia and the GDR.[58] She has followed the Soviet line closely in the quarrels with Albania and China from 1961 onwards. Her top governing circles have never been particularly attracted by Romania. Relations with Yugoslavia and the West European communist parties were excellent in the late 1950s, but have on occasions been rather cooler since then. Gierek supports but does not get too involved in the harder Soviet line on Eurocommunism. Like Gomułka in the 1960s, he continually reiterates the theme of Polish loyalty to the USSR, both on communist-bloc matters and on wider issues, such as the Middle East. He has been more skilful than his predecessor, though, in protecting Polish interests, especially her economy and foreign trade, within this framework.

It is difficult to over-estimate the significance of the German problem for postwar Polish politics. The fear of FRG revanchism was made one of the key justifications of the Soviet alliance by Gomułka. In 1972 Gierek completed the normalisation of relations with the FRG – initiated by the treaty of 7 December 1970, by which Bonn recognised Poland's postwar frontiers and renounced the use of force against her – by exchanging diplomatic representatives.[59] Irritations, such as the repatriation of Polish citizens of German origin and Bonn's slowness in bringing Nazi war criminals to justice, still bedevil Polish–FRG relations, but the weakening of the quarrel decreased the tension and insecurity felt by the Poles. With the fading of wartime memories, this encouraged Poland to concentrate on her social and economic problems. But this was coupled with a further expansion of Poland's tourist and cultural-exchange links with the West.

Gierek took advantage of the Soviet–American detente to visit Washington and most of the major European capitals. Innumerable Western and Third World statesmen visited Warsaw in return during the 1970s. This increased diplomatic activity on the part of Gierek, Premier Jaroszewicz and the two foreign ministers of the period, Stefan Olszowski and Emil Wojtaszek, was primarily designed to raise Poland's international standing and to further economic, cultural and technological links.[60] It was thus aimed especially at the advanced Western and Scandinavian countries. The Poles played a constructive role in the Conference on Peace and Security in Europe, which culminated in the 1975 Helsinki Agreement. They hoped that it would produce their desired form of detente, confirming the political and territorial *status quo* and facilitating the flow of Western credits and economic collaboration.[61] These aims were partly fulfilled. The unforeseen price was that the so-called 'Third Basket' on human rights agreed at the Helsinki Conference encouraged the various dissident groups which developed in Poland from mid 1976 onwards.

PROSPECTS

The following points may act as signposts to Polish developments in the late 1970s.

1. One should note the continuing vitality and dynamism of Polish society, as demonstrated by the 'social veto' of the 1976 price rises. An interesting development since then has been the growth of dissident movements and the appearance of samizdat literature. Organisations such as the Workers' Defence Committee (since October 1977 the Committee for Social Self-Defence), the Students' Solidarity Committee, the Movement for the Defence of Human and Civil Rights and, above all, the 'Flying University' (TKN) vary considerably in their aims and composition.[62] They are best viewed as pressure groups in favour of civil rights rather than as outright opponents of the present leadership, let alone the communist system. Gierek has used intelligent and restrained political methods in handling these groups. He knows that the cost of their suppression, both at home and abroad, would be high. It would also drive opponents underground and make it difficult to keep them under surveillance. Although a harder line has prevailed within the PUWP from mid 1977 onwards, the policy of 'safety valves' was continued. This included easier travel, to the West and within Eastern Europe, and the screening of controversial films.[63]

2. The massive structural problems of the Polish economy may well take a long time to resolve. One cannot foretell whether radical economic reforms will be introduced in order to resolve them. It is safer simply to state (a) that collectivisation does not seem to be a serious alternative to the present gradualist agricultural policies, and (b) that the foreign-trade indebtedness is undoubtedly a heavy millstone. The Gierek leadership have, though, accepted that the economic benefits of carrying it preclude too-drastic attempts to diminish it, which would mean slowing down the Polish economy and thus placing even greater strains on the population.

3. The balance of political forces within the top echelons of the PUWP is neither clear nor certain. But Gierek has Brezhnev's support and is very experienced and skilled in controlling the Party. The main threat to him remains the possibility of another social outburst. One can presume,

though, that Gierek has assimilated the lessons of 1976. The limited economic and domestic policy options open to him render his task more difficult, but no obvious successor or political alternative was apparent late in 1978.

4. A steely nationalism and pro-Western intellectual and political traditions have set the PUWP acute problems in its attempts to build socialism in Poland. Industrialisation, which elsewhere has often produced new elites and social strata loyal to the regime, has done so only partially in Poland and has fanned increasing demands for higher living standards. Since 1956 the PUWP has accepted that it is not fully in control of Polish society and that it has to reckon with an autonomous Roman Catholic Church, independent peasants, and social groups who possess either indispensable skills or organised power (as witness the shipyard workers in 1970–1). Relations between State and society have been marked by sharp cyclical swings from relative harmony to conflict, as in 1956, 1968, 1970 and 1976. This unstable *modus vivendi* has produced a system of communist rule marked by national characteristics which has been termed 'a popular or everyday version of socialism'.[64] This is accepted by most Poles not only because of the USSR's domination of Eastern Europe but also because the PUWP has succeeded in anchoring itself in Polish society in its own right.

AFTER-NOTE

The political crisis of the summer of 1980, again sparked-off by popular discontent with food shortages and price increases, started with a wave of sporadic strikes from early June onwards, most of which were resolved by economic concessions. Once again the discontented workers on the Baltic seacoast demonstrated their strength. The workers' occupation of the Lenin Shipyard in Gdańsk and the unexpected emergence of inter-factory strike committees (MKSs), maintaining liaison and support between it and similar bodies elsewhere, forced the authorities into a tense and protracted negotiation on their political demands. Held in the full glare of world publicity, these culminated in late August in the unparalleled concession by the PZPR of 'Free trade unions' and of the right to strike. Babiuch, Premier since March, was now replaced by the economist Józef Pińkowski (b. 1929). Gierek's closest supporters (Babiuch, Szydlak, Łukaszewicz and Wrzaszczyk) were sacked. An erstwhile critic, and likely successor to Gierek, Stefan Olszowski (b. 1931), was recalled to run the economy. The evolution of the economic reform-programme and the fate of individuals was uncertain as the PZPR entered into yet another period of *sturm und drang*.

Edward Gierek, First Secretary of the PUWP, was born 6 January 1913 in Porąbka in Katowice province. On the death of his father in a mining accident, he emigrated with his mother to France in 1923, where from the age of thirteen onwards he worked as a miner. He became a trade unionist, joined the French Communist Party in 1931 and in 1934 was arrested and expelled from France to Poland because of his participation in a miners' strike. In 1937, after compulsory military service, Gierek emigrated to Belgium, joined the Communist Party there and during the war helped to organise a communist resistance movement against the German occupiers. In 1948 he returned to Poland to work as an official, first in the PPR Central Committee and then in the PUWP Provincial Committee in Katowice. He completed extra-mural studies at the Kraków Academy of Mining and Metallurgy, graduating as an engineer in 1954. That year, at the PUWP's Second Congress, he became a member of its Central Committee, and for the next two years was head of the Central Committee's Heavy Industry Department. In 1956 he became a Secretary of the PUWP Central Committee and a member of the Political Bureau.

From 1957 to December 1970 Gierek was First Secretary of Poland's largest and most industrial province, Katowice. He built up a reputation as an efficient administrator who knew how to pamper the miners, to foster local pride by keeping Silesia as the richest part of Poland and to maintain an open and approachable political style. Many commentators marked him out as Gomułka's likely successor as early as the Fourth Congress in 1964, and considered that he was the spokesman for the technocratic element in the PUWP. This was only partly true, as he showed real political skill in helping Gomułka to hold Moczar in check in 1968, in making a political deal with the latter in order to come to power in December 1970, and then in subsquently taking over his clientele and, in a less strident form, parts of his political programme as well.

Since 1970 Gierek has dominated Polish communism. At the time of writing the indications were that his health was good and that no serious political challenger could be expected for the foreseeable future.

Piotr Jaroszewicz, Chairman of the Council of Ministers, was born on 8 October 1909 in Nieświez, Warsaw province. Like his father, he became a teacher, and from 1934 to the outbreak of war was headmaster of a secondary school in Garwolin. From September 1939 he worked as a teacher in the USSR, and in 1943 he volunteered to join the Polish army in the USSR. He completed an officer's course and, in the First army, fought the whole way from Lenino to Berlin, being promoted to Colonel and becoming the army's Deputy Commander for Political Education. In 1944 he joined the PPR and the following year he was a delegate at its First Congress. Late in 1945 he advanced from being Deputy Head of the Main Political Education Bureau of the Polish army to Deputy Minister of Defence and was promoted to Brigadier-general. In 1950 he became a General of Division and Deputy Chairman of the State Economic Planning Commission. From 1952 until 1970 he was a deputy chairman of the Council of Ministers, a post he held simultaneously with being Minister of the Coal Industry (1954–6) and Permanent Polish Representative to Comecon and member of its Executive Committee (1955–70).

Jaroszewicz has been a full member of the PUWP's Central Committee from its foundation in December 1948 and also a Sejm deputy from 1947 onwards. He became a candidate member of the PUWP Political Bureau in 1964 and a full member at the Seventh Plenum, on 20 December 1970, which replaced Gomułka by Gierek. Three days later he became Chairman of the Council of Ministers, a choice perhaps decided by Soviet support, his long experience in the State and economic machines and by the fact that he had not associated himself with any political faction. Since 1970 he has emerged as a strong Premier, working closely with Gierek, who used him to announce the unpopular food-price increases of 1976 but who stood by him afterwards.

J. F. Brown, *The New Eastern Europe* (New York: Praeger, 1966) contains biographies of Władysław Gomułka (pp. 273–9) and Józef Cyrankiewicz (pp. 279–9). See also *Who's Who in the Socialist Countries* (New York: Saur, 1978) for biographical detail on Babiuch (pp. 35–6), Jabłoński (p. 246), Jaruzelski (p. 251), Kania (p. 264), Olszowski (p. 448) and Wrzaszczyk (p. 686).

BASIC FACTS ABOUT POLAND[65]

Official name: Polska Rzeczpospolita Ludowa (Polish People's Republic).
Area: 312,683 sq. km. (120,300 sq. miles).
Population (July 1978): 35,000,000.
Population density: 112 per sq. km.
Population distribution: 57·4 per cent urban, 42·6 per cent rural.

Membership of political parties (including candidate members):
PUWP (Polska Zjednoczona Partia Robotnicza), 2,718,400 (7·7 per cent of the population); United Peasant Party (Zjednoczone Stronnictwo Ludowe), 428,100; Democratic Party (Stronnictwo Demokratyczne), 96,500.

Administrative divisions: 49 provinces (*województwa*), 803 municipalities and 2070 communes (*gminy*).

Ethnic nationalities: Poles, 98·7 per cent; plus 180,000 Ukrainians, 165,000 White Russians and 12,000 Jews (est.).

Population of major towns: Warsaw (Warszawa, the capital), 1,532,100; Łodz, 818,400; Kraków, 712,600; Wrocław, 592,500; Poznań, 534,400; Gdańsk, 443,800; Szczecin, 381,400; Katowice, 350,400. (There are 33 cities with a population of over 100,000.)

National income by sector: industry, 52·3 per cent; construction, 12·9 per cent; agriculture and forestry, 11·8 per cent; transport, domestic trade and others, 22·4 per cent.

Main natural resources: coal, copper, sulphur, zinc, rock-salt, potassium, natural gas and timber, plus lesser deposits of iron and oil.

Foreign trade: *(foreign exchange złoties)* exports, 48,600 million ($ 14,507 million); imports, 40,800 million ($12,179 million); total, 89,400 million ($26,686 million).

Main trading partners: USSR, GDR, FRG, USA, Czechoslovakia, France, UK, Hungary and Sweden.

Railnetwork: 26,734 km.

Road network: 257,206 km.

Higher education: 10 universities and 79 other higher education institutions; 151,500 students in university sector (29,500 graduates) and 338,500 in other forms of tertiary education (51,600 graduates).

Foreign relations: diplomatic relations with 119 countries; 57 diplomatic missions in Warsaw; member of the UN since 1945.

NOTES

1. A useful historical and geographical survey is V. L. Benes and N. J. Pounds, *Poland* (London: Benn, 1970).
2. For a general history see S. Kieniewicz *et al., History of Poland*, 2nd ed. (Warsaw: Państwowe Wydawnictwo Naukowe, 1979).
3. This period is covered in two classic studies by R. F. Leslie: *Polish Politics and the Revolution of November 1830* (London: Athlone Press, 1956), and *Reform and Insurrection in Russian Poland 1856–65* (London: Athlone Press, 1963).
4. A. Bromke, *Poland's Politics: Idealism vs. Realism* (Cambridge, Mass.: Harvard University Press, 1967).

5. J. Holzer, *PPS Szkic dziejów* (Warsaw: Wiedza Powszechna, 1977) p. 21.
6. The only easily available overview of Polish Communism is M. K. Dziewanowski, *The Communist Party of Poland: An Outline of History*, 2nd ed. (Cambridge, Mass.: Harvard University Press, 1976).
7. A. Polonsky, *Politics in Independent Poland 1921–39* (Oxford: Clarendon Press, 1972) p. 250.
8. Contrast the versions by E. Rozek, *Allied Wartime Diplomacy: A Pattern in Poland* (New York: Wiley, 1958), and W. T. Kowalski, *Walka Dyplomatyczna o miejsce Polski w Europie 1939–45* (Warsaw: Książka i Wiedza, 1967).
9. A considerable and well documented literature has appeared in Poland since 1970 on this period. Two interesting examples are N. Kołomejczyk and B. Syzdek, *Polska w latach 1944–49. Zarys historii polityczny* (Warsaw: Państwowe Zakłady Wydawnictw Szkolnych., 1971) and F. Ryszka (ed.), *Polska Ludowa 1944–50. Przemiany społeezne* (Warsaw: Ossolineum, 1974).
10. B. Ireland, 'Poland', in R. R. Betts (ed.), *Central and South-East Europe 1945–48* (London: Royal Institute of International Affairs, 1950); and S. Lotarski, 'The Communist Takeover in Poland', in T. Hammond (ed.), *The Anatomy of Communist Takeovers* (New Haven: Yale University Press, 1975).
11. R. F. Staar, *Poland 1944–62: The Sovietization of a Captive People* (Baton Rouge: Louisiana University Press, 1962), although couched in quaint cold-war terminology, contains useful, although not always fully accurate, material.
12. K. Syrop, *Spring in October: The Story of the Polish Revolution 1956* (London: Weidenfeld and Nicholson, 1957).
13. G. Sakwa (Sanford), 'The Polish October: A Reappraisal through Historiography', *Polish Review*, XXIII, no. 3 (1978) 62–78.
14. There is as yet no full-scale overall study of the Gomułka period. Excellent material is contained in the following: Bromke, *Poland's Politics*; R. Hiscocks, *Poland: Bridge for the Abyss?* (London: Oxford University Press, 1963); and H. J. Stehle, *Poland: The Independent Satellite* (London: Pall Mall, 1965). The biography by N. Bethell, *Gomulka: His Poland and His Communism* (London: Longmans, 1969), is particularly slight and basic on his years of power.
15. A. Ross Johnson, 'Poland: The End of the Post-October Period', *Survey*, XIV (July 1968) 87–98.
16. The political background to these events is discussed in A. Ross Johnson, 'Polish Perspectives: Past and Present', *Problems of Communism*, XX (July–Aug 1971) 59–72.
17. The symposium of Polish and Western views A. Bromke and J. Strong (eds), *Gierek's Poland* (New York: Praeger, 1973), throws much light on the early years of Gierek's rule.
18. A. Bromke, 'Poland under Gierek: A New Political Style', *Problems of Communism*, XXI (Autumn 1972) 25.
19. Contrast the Polish interpretation by J. Maziarski *et al.*, *The Polish Upswing 1971–75* (Warsaw: Interpress, 1975), with R. W. Dean, 'Gierek's Three Years: Retrenchment and Reform', *Survey*, XX (1974) 59–75.

20. H. G. Skilling, *The Governments of Communist Eastern Europe* (New York: Crowell, 1966) p. 108.

21. *VII Zjazd Polskiej Zjednoczonej Partii Robotniczej, 8–12 grudnia 1975r. Stenogram z obrad plenarnych* (Warsaw: Książka i Wiedza, 1976). Gierek's report also revealed (p. 61) that only 264 remaining PUWP members had belonged to the Social Democracy of Poland and Lithuania, 22,000 to the interwar communist party, and 24,000 to the wartime PPR and its military organisations.

22. There has been a gradual turn-over though. Coming men such as Tadeusz Wrzaszczyk (Chairman of the Planning Commission), Aloizy Karkoszka (Warsaw City Party chief) and Party secretaries still outside the Political Bureau, such as Zdzisław Zandarowski, Józef Pińkowski and Jerzy Łukaszewicz, replaced in influence personalities such as Szydlak, Szlachcic, Kępa, Tejchma and Barcikowski, who had fallen out of favour.

23. The lid was only partially lifted on Gomułka by his interpreter, who published some low-quality and not wholly reliable recollections in the West – E. Weit, *Eyewitness: The Autobiography of Gomułka's Interpreter* (London: André Deutsch, 1973). For a typical report of a Political Bureau meeting, see *Trybuna Ludu*, 30 Aug 1978, p. 1.

24. S. Rozmaryn, *Konstytucja jako ustawa zasadnicza PRL* (Warsaw: Państwowe Wydawnictwo Naukowe, 1976) p. 9.

25. *Konstytucja PRL* (Warsaw: Książka i Wiedza, 1976). An authoritative Polish analysis is W. Sokolewicz, *Konstytucja PRL po zmianach z 1976r* (Warsaw: Państwowe Wydawnictwo Naukowe, 1978).

26. Protests of this sort, such as one by thirty-four leading intellectuals in 1964, have been an ongoing feature of Polish political life since 1956. The 1976 constitutional conflict, however, presaged the growth of new types of more organised dissident movements. See A. Bromke, 'A New Juncture in Poland', *Problems of Communism*, xxv (Sep–Oct 1976) 12–13.

27. M. Sadowski, *System partyjny PRL* (Warsaw: Książka i Wiedza, 1971).

28. *VIII plenum KC PZPR. 6–7 lutego 1971r* (Warsaw: Książka i Wiedza, 1971) p. 50.

29. On the UPP consult O. Narkiewicz, *The Green Flag: Polish Populist Politics 1867–1970* (London: Croom Helm, 1976). For the Democratic Party, see P. Winczorek, *Miejsce i rola SD w strukturze politycznej PRL* (Warsaw: Epoka, 1975).

30. S. Nowak, 'Niedaleko od Jabłoni', *Polityka*, 10 Apr 1976.

31. See Bromke, *Poland's Politics*, ch. 12.

32. J. J. Wiatr, 'The Hegemonic Party-System in Poland', in *Studies in Polish Political System (sic)* (Wrocław: Ossolineum, 1967) p. 118.

33. R. C. Gripp, *The Political System of Communism* (London: Nelson, 1973) p. 58. Contrast this view with W. Sokolewicz, 'Changes in the Structure and Functions of the Polish Sejm', *East-central Europe*, II (1975) 78–91.

34. G. Sakwa, *The Organisation and Work of the Polish Sejm 1952–72* Centre for Russian and East European Studies Discussion Paper, series RC/C, no. 12 (Birmingham: Birmingham University, 1976) pp. 27–34.

35. The Sejm elected in 1976 was composed of 261 PUWP, 113 United Peasant Party, 37 Democratic Party and 49 non-party and Catholic deputies.

36. Z. Jarosz, *System wyborczy PRL* (Warsaw: Państwowe Wydawnictwo

Naukowe, 1969). For possibly the most comprehensive examination of any communist election see Z. Pełczynski, 'Poland', in D. Butler (ed), *Elections Abroad* (London: Macmillan, 1959).

37. G. Sakwa and M. Crouch, 'Sejm Elections in Poland: An Overview and a Reappraisal', *British Journal of Political Science*, VIII (1978) 403–24.
38. The Council in 1974 totalled thirty-seven members. It was composed of Premier Jaroszewicz, seven deputy chairmen, twenty-eight departmental ministers and the Chairman of the Supreme Control Chamber (Moczar).
39. Cf. J. Wiatr, 'The Functional Equivalents of Top Civil Servants in the Socialist State', in M. Dogan (ed.), *The Mandarins of Western Europe* (London: Wiley, 1975).
40. See *Czarna księga cenzury PRL*, vol. I (London: Aneks, 1977).
41. W. Sokolewicz, *Rząd a prezydia rad narodowych* (Warsaw: Państwowe Wydawnictwo Naukowe, 1964).
42. W. Sokolewicz, *Przedstawicielstwo i administracji w systemie rad narodowych* (Warsaw: Państwowe Wydawnictwo Naukowe, 1968), and J. Piekalkiewicz, *Communist Local Government: A Study of Poland* (Athens, Ohio: Ohio University Press, 1975) are the most comprehensive examinations of the old system.
43. R. Taras, 'Democratic Centralism and Polish Local Government Reforms', *Public Administration*, LIII (Winter 1975) 403–26.
44. See J. Szczepański, *Polish Society* (New York: Random House, 1970).
45. These aspects are discussed more fully by M. Vaughan, 'A Multidimensional Approach to Contemporary Polish Stratification', *Survey*, XX (Winter 1974) 62–74.
46. D. Lane and G. Kolankiewicz (eds), *Social Groups in Polish Society* (London: Macmillan, 1973) p. 322.
47. J. R. Fiszman, *Revolution and Tradition in People's Poland* (Princeton, N.J.: Princeton University Press, 1972), is a study which demonstrates the tension between these two strands.
48. 81 per cent of the arable and 76 per cent of all agricultural land in 1975 belonged to 3·1 million private plots (three-fifths being less than five hectares in size), on which worked 4·26 million peasants. The reader is reminded that these figures, like most statistics in this chapter are drawn from *Maly rocznik statystyczny 1978* (Warsaw: GUS, 1978) and *Rocznik statystyczny 1976* (Warsaw: Główny Urząd Statystyczny, 1976).
49. See J. Zielinski, *Economic Reforms in Polish Industry* (London: Oxford University Press, 1973).
50. *6th Congress of the Polish United Workers Party: Basic Documents* (Warsaw: Książka i Wiedza, 1972) pp. 241–332.
51. Lydia Beskid, 'Ekonomiczne i społeczne czynniki kształtowania konsumpcji', *Zycie gospodarcze*, 30 May 1976.
52. See Bromke, in *Problems in Communism*, XXV; and R. Davy, 'Can Mr Gierek Stop Poland's Powder Keg from Exploding?', *The Times*, 26 Nov 1976.
53. Cf. R. Zabrzewski, 'Kierunki zmian struktury konsumcji w Polsce', *Nowe drogi*, no. 325 (June 1975) 63–9.
54. M. Makowiecki, 'Produkcji zwierzięcie w latach 1971–75', *Zycie gospodarcze*, 27 June 1976.

55. *Trybuna ludu*, 25 June 1976.
56. Most notably in a speech at Katowice in his Silesian power base – *Trybuna ludu*, 3–4 July 1976.
57. B. Mieczkowski has discerned a cyclical pattern in communist Poland according to which personal consumption increases most during periods of regime weakness – 'The Relationship between Changes in Consumption and Politics in Poland', *Soviet Studies*, XXX (Apr 1978) 262–9.
58. For an authoritative Polish presentation, see M. F. Rakowski, 'Trzydziestolecie polskiej polityki zagranicznej', *Nowe drogi*, no. 301 (June 1974) 20–38.
59. Cf. A. Bromke and H. von Riekhoff, 'The West German-Polish Treaty', *World Today*, XXVII (1971) 124–31.
60. See A. Bromke, 'Polish Foreign Policy in the 1970s', in Bromke and Strong, *Gierek's Poland*.
61. These themes are apparent in Foreign Minister Olszowski's comments 'Polish Foreign Policy in an Age of Detente', *Polish Perspectives*, XVIII (Mar 1974) 3–12.
62. *The Times*, 17 Apr 1978 and 28 July 1978. There were also similar stirrings among peasants discontented at the cost of their new pension scheme. For documents relating to the formation of these groups and their aims, see B. Szajkowski (ed.), *Documents in Communist Affairs – 1977* and *Documents in Communist Affairs – 1979* (Cardiff: University College Cardiff Press, 1978 and 1979).
63. Most notably Andrzej Wajda's *Marble Man*, during 1977.
64. G. Kołankiewicz and R. Taras, 'Poland: Socialism for Everyman' in A. Brown and J. Gray (eds), *Political Culture and Political Change in Communist States* (London: Macmillan, 1977) p. 124.
65. Figures cited are those for 1977 unless otherwise stated. Most are drawn from *Mały rocznik statystyczny 1978* (Warsaw: Główny Urząd Statystyczny, 1978) and *Rocznik statystyczny 1976* (Warsaw: Główny Urząd Statystyczny, 1976).

BIBLIOGRAPHY

See also references in the Notes.

Benes, V. L. and Pounds, N. J., *Poland* (London: Benn, 1970).
Bromke, Adam, *Poland's Politics: Idealism vs. Realism* (Cambridge, Mass.: Harvard University Press, 1967).
Bromke, Adam and Strong, John (eds), *Gierek's Poland* (New York: Praeger, 1973).
Cieplak, Tadeusz, *Poland since 1956: Readings and Essays on Polish Government and Politics* (New York: Twayne, 1972).
Concise Statistical Yearbook of Poland (Warsaw: Central Statistical Office, annual [since 1958]).
Dziewanowski, Marian, K., *The Communist Party of Poland: An Outline of History*, 2nd (revised) ed., (Cambridge, Mass.: Harvard University Press, 1976).

Heine, Marc. E., *The Poles: How They Live and Work* (London: David and Charles, 1976).

Hiscocks, Richard, *Poland: Bridge for the Abyss? An Interpretation of Developments in Post-War Poland* (London: Oxford University Press, 1963).

Kieniewicz, S. *et al., The History of Poland*, 2nd ed. (Warsaw: Państwowe Wydawnictwo Naukowe, 1979).

Lane, David and Kolankiewicz, George (eds), *Social Groups in Polish Society* (London: Macmillan, 1973).

Matejko, Alexander, *Social Change and Stratification in Eastern Europe: An Interpretative Analysis of Poland and Her Neighbours* (New York: Praeger, 1974).

Maziarski, Jacek, *et al., The Polish Upswing 1971–1975* (Warsaw: Interpress, 1975).

Morrison, John F., *The Polish People's Republic* (Baltimore: Johns Hopkins University Press, 1968).

Narkiewicz, Olga A., *The Green Flag: Polish Populist Politics 1867–1970* (London: Croom Helm, 1976).

Pirages, Dennis, *Modernisation and Political Tension Management – A Socialist Society in Perspective: Case Study of Poland* (New York: Praeger, 1972).

Polska informator (Warsaw: Interpress, 1977).

Rocznik polityczny i gospodarczy (Warsaw: Państwowe Wydawnictwo Ekonomiczne, annual [since 1968]).

Sanford (Sakwa), George, *The Organisation and Work of the Polish Sejm 1952–1972*, Centre for Russian and East European Studies Discussion Paper, series RC/C no. 12 (Birmingham: Birmingham University, 1976).

Staar, Richard, F., *Poland 1944–62: The Sovietisation of a Captive People* (Baton Rouge: Louisiana State University Press, 1962).

Stehle, Hansjakob, *Poland: The Independent Satellite* (London: Pall Mall, 1965).

Szajkowski, Bogdan (ed.) *Documents in Communist Affairs – 1977* (Cardiff: University College Cardiff Press, 1978) (annual).

——, *Documents in Communist Affairs – 1979* (Cardiff: University College Cardiff Press, 1979) (annual).

Szczepański, Jan, *Polish Society* (New York: Random House, 1970).

Szeliga, Zygmunt, *Polska dziś i Jutro* (Warsaw: Książka i Wiedza, 1978).

21 Socialist Republic of Romania

MICHAEL SHAFIR

Romania is the second largest state in South-east Europe. It is bordered on the east and north by the Soviet Union, which occupied Bessarabia (historically a Romanian territory between the rivers Prut and Dniestr) and northern Bukovina in 1940. On the south, the country is bordered by Bulgaria, to which the territory of southern Dobrogea (annexed in 1913 as a result of the Second Balkan War) was ceded in the same year. In the west, Romania is bordered by both Hungary (to the north) and Yugoslavia (to the south). The Hungarian border has also been the subject of dispute. The present border was established in 1945, returning the territory of northern Transylvania, ceded to Hungary as a result of the August 1940 Vienna award, to Romanian sovereignty.

The birth of the modern Romanian state may be traced back to the mid nineteenth century – more precisely, to the 1859 unification of the Romanian principalities of Moldavia and Wallachia under .Prince Alexandru Ioan Cuza. Skilfully manoeuvring in favourable international circumstances, and driven by surprisingly intensive (considering their relatively recent vintage[1] nationalist motivations, the local political circles of the time thereby managed to lay the basis of the process of 'state-building' in the Romanian lands.

As in many other divided European national entities, the 'state-building' process had been preceded by the 'nation-building' process, by which we in this case specifically understand awareness of a common bond uniting the then politically divided Romanian inhabitants of the three traditional provinces, Moldavia, Wallachia and Transylvania. According to the official line now employed (or, rather, re-employed) in Romanian historiography, nation-building was a 'historically long process', and developed 'as a consequence of the struggle for the defence of national being waged along centuries . . . by the Rumanians on both

Romania: provincial boundaries

slopes of the Carpathian mountains'. These, it is held, were 'the descendants of the Romanised Dacian population that has been uninterruptedly living in the Carpathian Danubian territory, a population with its centre in Transylvania, and lying at the basis of the formation of the Rumanian people.'[2] Challenged by historians in neighbouring countries – mainly Hungary – this interpretation is of old-new vintage in Romania itself. Prevalent among Romanian historians before the Second World War, it was partially rejected by Stalinist historiography, which used to paint the Romans in black colours. In the 1950s the Roman forefathers were turned into 'conquerors' and 'exploiters' of the native Dacians, in striking juxtaposition with the alleged benevolent influence later exercised by the neighbouring Slavs.[3] Even the official name of the state, up to 1965, was 'Rominia',[4] attempting to diminish the association with historical Rome and with the west in general.

The evidence concerning the birth and formation of the Romanian nation is still controversial and somewhat obscure. The Daco-Roman entity vanished from recorded history for one thousand years, then reappeared in the thirteenth and fourteenth centuries in the form of the voivodates of Wallachia and Moldavia. Transylvania, the third historical province of Romania, was by that time part of the kingdom of Hungary. Turkish suzerainty over the voivodates was established in the fifteenth century.

The United Principalities won formal independence from Turkey as a result of the Russo-Turkish war of 1877–8. At the end of the war, however, the country found itself territorially smaller than it had been at its outset. For, in spite of the considerable contribution of the Romanian army to the war effort, the Russians recompensed their allies by reannexing Bessarabia.[5]

The foreign policy of the 'Old Kingdom' in the immediate post-independence period was above all aimed at the establishment of 'România Mare' (Greater Romania), comprising all the territories inhabited by the Romanian population and, if possible, their *hinterland* as well. The dream became reality as a result of the First World War and of the October revolution in Russia. As one of the victorious powers, Romania was awarded Transylvania and formerly Austrian northern Bukovina. In Bessarabia, the 'Sfatul Ţării' (the Bessarabia Assembly), a more or less representative body, proclaimed the territory's reunification with Romania. Territorially, the country more than doubled its area, while the population doubled. About a quarter of the total population, however, was made up of national minorities.[6]

However, Greater Romania was sacrificed on the altar of the Soviet-German pact of August 1939. In June 1940 Moscow presented the Romanian government with a twenty-four hour ultimatum, demanding the return of Bessarabia and the incorporation of northern Bukovina into the Soviet Union. In August 1940 southern Dobrogea was ceded to Bulgaria and northern Transylvania to Hungary. When Germany launched its attack against the Soviet Union, Romania joined the war on the side of the Axis.

With the Red Army advancing towards Romanian territory in 1944, a number of politicians attempted to approach the Western powers, urging General Antonescu, Romania's arch-conservative leader, to surrender to them in the hope of avoiding Soviet occupation. The British-Soviet design for postwar Eastern Europe, however, prevented any such arrangement. Meanwhile, Lucreţiu Pătrăşcanu, one of the leaders of the minuscule Romanian Communist Party (RCP), negotiated the establishment of a United Workers' Front with the Social Democrats in April 1944; the Front allied itself with the two 'historical parties' – the Liberals and the National Peasant Party – in June, becoming the National Democratic Bloc. The current official Romanian version of the August 1944 events notwithstanding, it was not the Bloc, and even less the leadership provided by the RCP, that sealed the fate of the Antonescu regime. The coup of 23 August was largely a palace coup, engineered by the young King Mihai and his immediate entourage. Its purpose was to topple Antonescu's regime before the Russian troops had entered Bucharest, and to turn arms against the Germans, thus avoiding occupation as a defeated Nazi ally.

The design, aimed at avoiding an immediate communist take-over as well, proved feasible as a short-run tactic only.[7] Communist representatives were included in three successive governments between August 1944 and February 1945. On 6 March 1945, threatened with an ultimatum delivered by Soviet Deputy Foreign Minister, A. Vyshinsky, that Romania might cease to exist as an independent state, the king entrusted Dr Petru Groza, a 'fellow traveller', with the formation of a new cabinet. The immediate pay-off for pliancy was Soviet recognition of Romanian sovereignty over all Transylvania, the future of which had deliberately been kept uncertain. At the end of December 1947, Mihai was forced to abdicate. Romania became one of Eastern Europe's people's republics.

MARXISM IN ROMANIA: THE EARLY STAGES

Despite several Party resolutions providing for the publication of an official history of the RCP,[8] no such work has yet been published in Romania. One of the main reasons for this seems to be the difficulty of producing a convincing explanation for the Party's failure to attract more than a handful of activists before 1944. Western estimates concerning the size of the Party at the time of its emergence from illegality put its membership at from a few hundred to less than 1000 members,[9] with an unknown number of unregistered sympathisers.[10] According to an article printed in the Soviet publication *Bolshevik* in 1950, on 23 August 1944 the Romanian party had fewer than 1000 members. In proportion to the population it was, according to the same source, the smallest communist party in Eastern Europe, while in absolute numbers its membership equalled that of the Albanian party.[11]

The rise and development of socialist thought in Romania had been hindered by three main factors: the socio-economic structure of the society, which was predominantly agricultural; the ethnic origin (Jewish, Hungarian) of many of the original or later exponents of socialist and communist ideas; and, last but by no means least, the disregard displayed by the RCP towards the traditional national aspirations, as a result of its absolute subservience to Moscow.

Founded in 1893, the Romanian Social Democratic Party soon hit a crisis of identity, as a result of the lack of any meaningful following.[12] The Party's narrow appeal, the socialist leader G. Diamandi admitted at the Sixth Congress in 1899, was the unavoidable outcome of a situation in which 'socialism did not start from bottom to top, but from top to bottom', industry being, for all practical purposes, non-existent.[13] One year later, many of the disappointed original founders of the movement joined the Liberal Party. Social democracy disappeared from the political scene for a full decade. Re-established in 1910, the Party counted among its leaders many intellectuals of foreign origin. Foremost among them was the founding father of Marxist socialist thought in Romania, Constantin Dobrogeanu-Gherea. Born in the Ukraine and formerly active in the Narodnik movement, Gherea, whose real name was Solomon Katz, settled in Romania in 1878.[14] The extent to which socialist doctrines were foreign in the country at the time is attested by a letter he sent to Kautsky in 1894: 'When I first arrived to Romania as a Russian refugee, not even the word "socialism" was known here.'[15] In 1880, after some time spent in Romania in Gherea's company, P. Axelrod commented that 'not even the greatest optimist would dare entertain hopes that modern socialist ideas could take roots' there.[16]

It is doubtful, therefore, that Marxism would have fared significantly better had it arrived to Romania by ways that did not so easily lend themselves to identification of its exponents with one of Romania's 'historical enemies'. For, though Gherea and the early Romanian Marxists by no means advocated policies encouraging Russian expansionism[17], after the First World War opponents of Soviet irredentism over Bessarabia would seldom distinguish between Marxism and pro-Soviet postures. Such a hostile attitude toward socialist ideas, it must be added, was undoubtedly enhanced by the radicalisation of some prominent socialist leaders after the 1917 October revolution. For example, Trotsky's Bulgarian friend C. Rakovsky, who had been active in Romania before 1917 and had denounced the dangers of *imperial* Russian expansion, became an advocate of Bessarabia's reincorporation into the *Soviet* state.[18]

The RCP's position on the question of Greater Romania's territorial integrity, and the regime's successful exploitation of the issue of ethnic composition in the Party's laws, greatly hindered its capacity to mobilise popular support in the interwar period. The foundation congress of the Party took place between 8 and 13 May 1921, with 380 out of the 540 delegates present voting for affiliation to the Third International. Three years later the Party was outlawed, because of expressed support of Soviet refusal to recognise Bessarabia as part of Romania. Among the recommendations of the Third Congress (Vienna, 1924), one finds support of the national minorities' right to self-determination 'up to complete succession from the existing state'. A similar position was expounded at the Fourth Congress (1928) and at the Fifth (1931), held in Kharkov and Moscow, respectively. Many years later, in the midst of the process of 'de-Sovietisation' and 're-Romanisation' of the RCP, Secretary-general Nicolae Ceauşescu would castigate this position, which, according to him, had been imposed through 'tactical orientations and indications' issued by the Comintern.[19] These orders, according to Ceauşescu, contradicted the Romanian 'economic, social, political and national conditions'. The Third International, moreover, had added insult to injury by 'appointing leadership cadres, including the Secretary-general, who were not familiar with the life and with the preoccupations of the Romanian people'. The Secretary-general appointed at the Fourth and Fifth Congresses, Ceauşescu reminded the audience, had not even properly belonged to the RCP.

Many communist leaders belonged to either the Jewish or the

Hungarian minority,[20] and some were what, in the eyes of the Romanian majority, was probably the worst possible combination – Bessarabian or Hungarian Jews.[21] There were also several leaders whose national origin was Slav.[22] Neither the fact that the bulk of the Jewish minority by no means identified itself with the RCP,[23] nor the purge in the 1930s of many communist activists in the Soviet Union[24] significantly altered the Party's 'foreign image'.

After the Fifth Congress, the Soviet grip on the RCP was virtually absolute – but there was hardly any party to speak about. With the Red Army approaching Romania's borders, the RCP was still minuscule in size, ineffective and beset by deep divisions between its leaders. Two main factions competed for leadership, although neither group was strictly cohesive. The first, formed by the so-called 'home communists', consisted of the remnants of activists who had spent the war years in Romania. To this belonged such imprisoned leaders as Gheorghe Gheorghiu-Dej, Chivu Stoica and Gheorghe Apostol. Its background was mostly proletarian, its nationality Romanian. The members of the rival 'Muscovite' faction, who had spent most of the war years in the USSR, were, on the other hand, better educated and the great majority of them belonged to the national minorities. The more prominent leaders of this group were Ana Pauker, Vasile Luca, Iosif Chişinevschi and Leonte Răutu. A somewhat lonely figure was Lucreţiu Pătrăşcanu, an intellectual who had been particularly successful in establishing contacts with circles outside the Party that came to oppose the continuation of the war.

In spring 1944, the Secretary-general of the Party, Ştefan Foriş (of Hungarian origin), came under suspicion of acting in the service of the secret police. At a meeting held in a prison cell on 4 April in the presence of Emil Bodnăraş[25] (especially dispatched from Moscow to help reorganise the Party), Dej and his followers decided to dismiss Foriş. Arrested immediately upon the entrance of the Soviet troops, the former Secretary-general was shot without trial in 1946.[26] The circumstances of his liquidation still remain obscure. According to the official Dejist version, the 'Muscovites', and particularly Pauker, had opposed the move.[27] However, the 1968 Central Committee resolution that rehabilitated Foriş accused *both* Dej and the 'Moscovites' of having ordered Foriş's execution.

The apparently more accurate 1968 version may contribute to the elucidation of the highly relevant issue pertaining to the origins and the development of the Romanian–Soviet dispute. Two main theories about this have dominated the field of Western postwar Romanian studies.

According to the first, the origins of the conflict should be traced to the struggle for power between the 'home communists' and the originally Moscow-supported Pauker faction.[28] The second interpretation, on the other hand, tends to view the 1944–52 events as no more than an episode of internal Party conflicts, with no nationalistic overtones whatsoever, and with *both* factions competing for Soviet support.[29] Only at a much later stage, and in entirely different circumstances, according to this interpretation, did the Romanian-Soviet dispute evolve into an open confrontation. Although marginal to this dispute, the 1968 revelations seem to confirm the latter interpretation, proving that Dej and Pauker could – indeed, occasionally did – act in common, and that, regardless of the competition between the two factions, both fully identified with Soviet-inspired policies.

It was Pătrășcanu and not Dej who at this stage opposed Moscow's grip on the RCP, a 'sin' for which he paid with his freedom – and eventually with his head. Having served as Minister of Justice for four years, he was arrested in 1948 and executed at Dej's personal orders in April 1954, following a show trial at which he was accused of having spied for Antonescu's secret police and for the British and Americans.[30] The execution was carried out hastily, at a time when the Soviet Union encouraged the emergence, in Eastern Europe, of leaders with local appeal. So much for Dej's alleged early nationalist postures.

Aware of its numerical weakness, the RCP, apparently at Pauker's orders[31], launched a huge recruitment campaign almost as soon as it had ceased to be illegal. From fewer than 1000 members in 1944, the number of activists grew to over 200,000 by the end of the following year, and to 714,000 at the end of 1947[32] (see Table 21.1). Many of the new recruits were former members of the fascist Iron Guard movement, co-option being occasionally carried out *en bloc* – i.e. with local organisations being 'transferred' wholesale from the former to the new party.[33] The rewards for such opportunism were obvious, ranging from escape from punishment for former activities to material benefits and jobs, which sometimes simply meant continuation of past employment. The head of Antonescu's secret police, for example, was personally received into the RCP by Bodnăraș and immediately offered a similar position under the new regime.[34]

Using tactics employed all over Eastern Europe, the RCP took over the Social Democratic Party in February 1948. The new united party was named the Romanian Workers' Party (RWP), and new statutes, reflecting complete subservience to Moscow, were adopted. The final resolution adopted at this First RWP (Sixth RCP)[35] Congress, announ-

TABLE 21.1 RCP (RWP) membership, 1944–78

Year	Membership	
1944	less than	1000
1945	over	200,000
1947		714,000
1955		595,398
1960		834,600
1962		1,100,000
1965		1,450,000
1969		1,924,500
1970		1,999,720
1972		2,230,000
1974	approx.	2,480,000
1978 (Mar)		2,747,110

Sources: V. Grigorian, 'Strategiia i taktika leninizma boevoe oruzhie bratskih kompartii', Bolshevik, XVII, no. 7 (1950) 14; P. Lendvai, Eagles in Cobwebs: Nationalism and Communism in the Balkans (London: Macdonald, 1970) p. 287; D. Ghermani, 'Die Rumänische Kommunistische Partei', in K. D. Grothusen (ed.), Rumänien (Göttingen: Vandenhoeck & Ruprecht, 1977) pp. 18–19; Congresul al IX-lea al Partidului Comunist Român (Bucharest: Editura politică, 1966) p. 128; Scînteia, 20 Mar 1970 and 24 Mar 1978; and N. Ceauşescu, România pe drumul construirii societăţii socialiste multilateral dezvoltate, vol. VII (Bucharest: Editura politică, 1973) p. 531, and vol. XI (Bucharest: Editura politică, 1975) p. 84.

ced that a new constitution (adopted on 13 April and valid till September 1952) was about to be drafted, reflecting the new socio-economic structure of the State, providing for a new administrative organisation, and outlining the economic measures intended to put Romania on the path of economic development. Articles 5–15 of this document attested to the new regime's determination to obliterate capitalism and reorganise the economy on the basis of central planning. The nationalisation of industry, in June 1948, was the most significant step taken in this direction. This measure marked also the beginning of a new stage in the Party's rule.

TRANSFORMATION AND CONSOLIDATION UNDER DEJ

In a pioneering methodological study of postwar developments in Romania, K. Jowitt employs the concept of 'breaking through' to analyse RWP motivations and strategies in the post-1948 period.[36] The final aim of the process of 'breaking through' as described by Jowitt is none other but the complete *transformation* of societal structures and values.[37] More specifically, according to Jowitt the process is perceived by the Party as conditioned by achievement of an absolute monopoly of political power; by industrialisation; and by the collectivisation of agriculture. A fourth element, pertaining to a 'cultural breakthrough', should, however, be added to this list.[38] As is easy to see, 'breaking through' amounts to full emulation of the Soviet model.

Transformation, consolidation and *modernisation*, according to Jowitt, constitute the 'core tasks' of Marxist-Leninist regimes. 'Modernisation' will be dealt with later in this chapter. As for 'consolidation', Jowitt defines it as 'the attempt to create the nucleus of a new political community in a setting that ideally prevents existing social forces from exercising any uncontrolled and undesired influence over the development and the definition of the new community'. This definition implicitly views the Party as a monolithic organisation in course of establishing its monopoly over other forces; unwarrantedly, however, it neglects the highly relevant issue of factional struggles within the Party. 'Consolidation' as employed here, therefore, will refer to both the endeavour to ensure the Party's monolithic position in society and to the tactics employed by a leader or a faction (in our case, the Dej group) to concentrate and conserve absolute power in its hands, at the expense of any rivals.

The offensive launched against actual or potential rivals outside the Party began even before 1948; annihilation of the leaders of the opposition, however, started in earnest with the arrest of the National Peasant Party leaders I. Maniu and I. Mihalache in July 1947. They were brought to trial at the end of October and sentenced to life imprisonment. Maniu died in prison and so did his former political Liberal rival D. Brătianu. Many other former politicians met with a similar fate.[39] In August 1947 the two 'historical parties' were outlawed. A new system of justice, emulating the Soviet one and doing away with separation of powers, was instituted in 1949.[40] The former penal code was replaced by laws providing for punishment of acts 'considered as dangerous to society', even if the infringements were not 'specifically provided for in the law as crimes'.[41] Many of those sentenced under the new laws perished in the huge labour camp of the Danube–Black Sea Canal project, which was initiated in 1949 and abandoned in 1953. After a short lull brought about by the 'New Course', a new wave of terror was instituted with Decree no. 318 of July 1958.[42]

Such high incidence of 'irrational violence', Jowitt rightly points out, is not to be explained simply 'in terms of Soviet demands for detailed emulation' but also in terms of the Romanian leadership's uncertainty, owing to its lack of independent experience, as to how else to achieve 'an ideologically and politically correct breakthrough'.[43] As A. G. Meyer remarks, the task of radical transformation of societal structures and values was particularly difficult in such countries as Hungary or Romania, where the new ruling elites were associated with national defeat and their legitimacy was 'lowered even more by the predominance in their leadership of people alien to the dominant [political] culture'.[44] For both ideological and circumstantial reasons, therefore, the new regime's legitimacy at this 'transformative' stage had to be built on what has been termed 'primitive accumulation of legitimacy',[45] by which is meant precisely the attempt to destroy the patterns upon which the hegemony of adversary counter-elites had been based. At this stage, legitimacy may be said to have been largely extra-systemic, exogenous and derivative, i.e. emanating from Moscow, and supra-systemic or supra-national, i.e. emanating from a doctrine which claimed to be universally applicable. So uncertain was Dej of any local roots that, even in those few cases where he could reasonably point to 'continued legitimacy', he preferred to emulate the Soviet line. Thus he stigmatised Gherea, the founder of Romanian Marxist thought, as 'essentially a Menshevik'.[46]

Total identification with, and subservience to, the Soviet Union, were expressed in the 1952 constitution.[47] Both in the Preamble and in article 86, the Party was specifically designated the leading force of the society. Entire paragraphs from the Soviet Constitution were simply incorporated into this document. Moreover, the Soviet Union was specifically mentioned no fewer than three times in the Preamble and once in article 2, which stipulated that the Romanian People's Republic had come into being 'as a result of the historic victory of the Soviet Union over German fascism and of Romania's liberation by the glorious Soviet army'.

By the early 1950s the political power of the opposition had been efficiently wiped out. Annihilation of Party rivals, as Dej was to find out, proved by far more prolonged a process. The first, and undoubtedly the most important, victory registered by the 'home communist' faction was the elimination of the Pauker-Luca group in 1952. Throughout 1951 and 1952, both groups had been making efforts to enlist Moscow's support. It is not entirely clear what finally determined Stalin to decide in Dej's favour, but Pauker's Jewish origin, at a time when the bloc was being swept by a new antisemitic campaign, may have played a more important part than any other argument. In May 1952 Luca was dismissed from the Central Committee and his position as Finance Minister and expelled from the Party, together with the other principal ally of Pauker, Interior Minister Teohari Georgescu. Ana Pauker herself lost all her positions a few weeks later.[48] Dej's victory, however, was not complete, for after the Pauker purge the Political Bureau still included some of her allies, such as Chişinevschi, Miron Constantinescu and the staunchly independent C. Pîrvulescu. It was only in 1957, in circumstances still disputed among Western specialists,[49] that Dej managed to get rid of Chişinevschi and Constantinescu. The two had apparently formed an 'unholy alliance' seeking to exploit the de-Stalinisation campaign in the USSR in order to topple Dej. Having finally eliminated Pîrvulescu in 1961, Dej became the unchallenged leader of Romania.

To achieve this position, he had had to make full use of his political skills, behaving ruthlessly towards foes, relinquishing and taking over key positions as circumstances required, and promoting his own protégés in the Party hierarchy. Paying lip service to de-Stalinisation and 'collective leadership', he gave up the position of First Secretary of the Party from April to October 1955, entrusting it to the hands of his old comrade Apostol while he continued to act as Prime Minister, a position he had held since June 1952. In October 1955 he resumed the first-secretaryship, a far more powerful position, and resigned the premiership, which was taken over by his closest ally, Chivu Stoica. In March 1961 Stoica was succeeded by Ion Gheorghe Maurer, whose association with Dej dated from the early 1940s.[50] Dej himself took over the chairmanship of the newly created Council of State in 1961, thereby combining the highest Party and State positions. Last but not least, among the Dej protégés promoted in the hierarchy were Ceauşescu[51] and Alexandru Drăghci.[52] The former was entrusted with control over the Party apparatus, the latter with the security forces.

The Party's cadre policy up to the 1960s reflected the leadership's unconcealed preference for 'trustworthy elements' belonging to the 'worker elite'. A purge conducted between 1948 and 1950 'cleansed' the RWP of some 192,000 'unhealthy elements', many of them recruited a few years earlier.[53] At the Second RWP (Seventh RCP) Congress in 1955, the statutes were amended, and a 'screening' period of candidacy was introduced. At the end of 1955 total membership stood at 595,398, of which 56,583 were candidate members of the Party. The proportion of workers was 42·61 per cent. Five years later, at the Third (Eighth) Congress, total membership was 834,600, of whom 148,000 held 'candidate' status. The proportion of workers had by then increased to

51 per cent; 34 per cent were peasants, and the remainder 'intellectuals and functionaries' (see Tables 21.1 and 21.2).

TABLE 21.2 Social composition of the RWP/RCP, 1955–78

	Workers No.	%	Peasants No.	%	Intellectuals, etc. No.	%
1955		42·61				
1960		51·00		34·0	70,000	
1965	630,000	44·00	500,000	34·0	145,000	
1969		43·00		28·0		23·0
1972	1,060,000	46·50	526,589	23·1	430,000	18·8
1974		50·00		20·0		22·0
1975	approx. 50·00		approx. 20·0		approx. 22·0	
1978	'Over 73·26 per cent of members are engaged in material production'					

Sources: G. Ionescu, *Communism in Rumania 1944–1962* (London: Oxford University Press, 1964) pp. 243, 319; *Congresul al IX-lea al Partidului Comunist Român*, p. 71; *Congresul al X-lea al Partidului Comunist Român* (Bucharest: Editura Politică, 1969) pp. 127–8; *Scînteia*, 22 June 1973, 25 July 1975, 24 Apr 1976 and 24 Mar 1978.

Industrialisation and collectivisation were also entirely based on the Soviet model. Two five-year plans and a six-year plan, covering the period 1951–65, reflected the leadership's determination to put Romania on the forced-development path. The prime target was industrialisation, with little attention paid to human costs. Investments were consequently oriented towards 'Group A' (heavy industry), with the ratio of investments to consumption one of the highest in the world.[54] By the end of the 1950s, the Romanian leaders could boast of success, having practically reached the stage of 'take-off'. The Six-year Plan, adopted at the Third RWP Congress, continued to provide for a high rate of industrial growth. Its most outstanding symbol was the new Galaţi steel plant, an ambitious project envisaging a production capacity of some 4 million tons in 1970.

The collectivisation process was completed by 1962. Although Dej attempted to blame Pauker and Luca for the harsh treatment of recalcitrant peasants,[55] his own identification with the Stalinist model, as Jowitt indicates, implied a perception of 'social, cultural, political and economic threat . . . as residing in the countryside'. The transformation of agriculture, consequently, was regarded by the Romanian leadership as 'a necessary condition for industrialization', while the latter process, involving mass emigration from the countryside to the city and destruction of traditional village patterns, 'was thought to be essential in redefining and breaking through the existing character of peasant life'.[56]

Finally, the 'cultural breakthrough' envisaged an end to illiteracy, as a *sine qua non* condition of modernisation, and sought a radical transformation of political culture via the agents of socialisation. As regards the latter aspect, the offensive – at its first stage – was directed mainly at the creative intelligentsia, whom the new regime, owing to historical circumstances, perceived as a potential threat. The process was aimed at 'desocialising' and subsequently 'resocialising' into the official political culture those whose role was perceived primarily as one of carrying the Party's word to the masses. Since the Romanian intellectuals had been the most eloquent spokesmen of anti-Russian nationalism, one of the most painful corollaries of the 'cultural breakthrough' was 'de-Romanisation'.[57] 'România' became 'Romînia', Romanian history was distorted so as to stress the alleged 'historical friendship' with Russia, and 'socialist realism' was adopted as the one and only valid model for the arts. In contrast to the RWP's successes in industrialisation, all evidence indicates that the regime failed in its endeavours to transform political culture in general, and intellectual political sub-culture in particular. This failure was to have unexpected consequences in later years.

FROM DEJ TO CEAUŞESCU: NATIONALISM, MODERNISATION, CONTAINMENT

In the early 1960s Romania gradually entered the phase of 'modernisation'. As employed here, the concept does not refer to the processes outlined by K. W. Deutsch in his well known article on social mobilisation and political development.[58] Those approximate to what has been analysed here under the categories of 'transformation' and 'consolidation'. 'Modernisation' is here understood as referring to the 'post-mobilisation' period and, as emphasised by C. Johnson and by S. B. Huntington,[59] as dealing with the dilemmas of institutionalisation and participation in societies whose political elites are faced with the danger of becoming 'victims of their own success'. In other words, having consolidated power and at least partially transformed, i.e. industrialised, society, communist political elites in the 'modernisation' period are faced with the task of finding a suitable political formula which, without compelling them to 'go beyond Leninism',[60] i.e.

renounce the Party's leading role, none the less offers the new socio-economic groups opportunities for political expression. In such circumstances, however, participation seldom amounts to more than 'manipulated participation'. Its chief function is that of pre-empting systemic inputs potentially questioning the validity of the Party's right to an absolute monopoly of power.[61] The corollary of 'modernisation', therefore, is 'containment'.

One of the most important aspects of 'modernisation' is 'political innovation'. At central, intermediary and peripheral levels, new institutions are created or the character of existing institutions is altered, in order to enhance the sense of participation. It is particularly this aspect of the 'modernisation' process that lends itself to analysis in so far as manipulation is concerned. This section will concentrate on political innovation in the Party itself, as a major instrument of manipulation for personal means. Other sections will examine political innovation as an instrument of continued Party supremacy.

On precisely what formula 'modernisation' will principally be based depends on numerous factors, ranging from the particularities of the 'dominant' political culture to alterations in the political environment as a result of either circumstantial or more permanent change. In the particular case of Romania, as we shall see, the new political formula was primarily based on a combination of revived and officially sponsored nationalism and on national pride in the country's industrial achievements.

The most striking development in the last years of Dejist rule was the outbreak and development of the conflict with the Soviet Union. The dispute originated with what Khrushchev saw as the appropriate division of labour within Comecon: this would have turned Romania into mainly a supplier of agricultural products to the industrially advanced members of the community. Dej was faced with the dilemma of having to choose between the Soviet Union and the Soviet model. Paradoxically enough, it was to a large extent his staunch identification with the Leninist-Stalinist values of industrialisation that turned him into a 'national communist'.

By the end of the 1950s there were already signs of an unmistakable reorientation in Romania's foreign trade, with the total Soviet share reduced from 51·5 per cent in 1958 to 47·3 per cent in 1959 and 40·1 per cent in 1960. This trend — which remained constant up to 1974[62] — was largely the result of Soviet unwillingness to support the further expansion of Romanian industrialisation. As a result of these developments, Romania turned to the West for credits — and eventually for

TABLE 21.3 Romanian foreign trade, 1960–76 (million lei)*

	1960	%	1965	%	1970	%	1975	%	1976	%
Total exports	4,302·2	100·0	6,609·2	100·0	11,104·9	100·0	26,546·9	100·0	30,504·5	100·0
Total imports	3,887·1	100·0	6,462·7	100·0	11,760·8	100·0	26,548·5	100·0	30,293·9	100·0
USSR										
Exports	1,688·6	39·2	2,630·6	39·8	3,172·9	28·5	5,278·9	19·8	5,558·6	18·2
Imports	1,595·6	41·0	2,436·9	37·7	3,004·8	25·5	4,578·6	17·2	5,305·1	17·5
Other European communist states										
Exports	1,190·7	27·6	1,674·7	25·3	2,633·3	23·7	5,585·4	21·0	6,937·9	22·7
Imports	1,072·5	27·5	1,351·5	20·9	2,842·3	24·1	5,760·5	21·6	7,304·8	24·1
China										
Exports	200·0	4·6	159·8	2·4	431·2	3·8	1,094·0	4·1	1,236·8	4·0
Imports	141·6	3·6	131·2	2·0	372·1	3·1	1,070·4	4·0	1,003·6	3·3
Other Asian communist states										
Exports	60·0	1·3	55·7	0·8	126·5	1·1	170·6	0·6	172·9	0·5
Imports	32·0	0·8	38·0	0·5	46·0	0·3	106·1	0·3	79·1	0·2
FRG										
Exports	323·4	7·5	430·4	6·5	634·8	5·7	1,339·6	5·0	2,079·5	6·8
Imports	311·1	8·0	375·0	5·8	690·5	5·8	1,569·4	5·9	2,174·2	7·1
USA										
Exports	3·8	a	15·8	0·2	80·5	0·7	485·5	1·8	944·1	3·0
Imports	37·8	0·9	54·8	0·8	358·6	3·0	688·6	2·5	1,375·4	4·5

France										
Exports	116·9	2·7	131·2	1·9	364·0	3·2	747·9	2·8	890·9	2·9
Imports	149·0	3·8	295·3	4·5	673·6	5·7	941·3	3·5	1,266·0	4·1
EEC[b]										
Exports	565·3	13·1	974·1	14·7	2,247·8	20·2	5,627·4	21·1	6,426·3	21·0
Imports	562·3	14·4	1,357·6	21·0	2,582·1	21·9	6,608·7	24·8	6,087·8	20·0

* US $1 = approx. 4.97 lei.
a Less than 1 per cent.
b From 1973 including also the UK, Ireland and Denmark.

Source: Anuarul statistic al Republicii Socialiste România (Direcţia centrală de statistică, 1977) pp. 422ff.

political support (see Table 21.3). As the conflict with the Russians became a matter of public knowledge, the leadership turned to the rank-and-file in search of domestic support.

In order to be effective, however, this campaign could not be limited to Party members only. Gradually it evolved into a search for a new political formula. As long as the Party had identified itself with the Soviet external referent, it had had no choice but to pursue the course of 'primitive accumulation of legitimacy'. The core of the *new* political formula, on the other hand, consisted in the political elite's efforts to rid itself of its previous, derivative image and base its claim to power on historic intra-systemic continuity. From now on the Party was determined to become not only the embodiment of industrial development, but also that of national aspirations for independence. Instead of becoming a 'victim of its own success' in industrialisation, the regime managed to turn into the beneficiary of its own failure to alter the basically nationalist political culture. Discontent and political dissent, instead of being channelled into the system as inputs, were successfully deflected by the regime to external (Soviet) targets as outputs, in a manner reminiscent of the tactics employed by *antebellum* governments.

A carefully concerted campaign of 'de-Sovietisation' and 're-Romanisation', initiated under Dej and reaching often ridiculous peaks under Ceauşescu, was the first step undertaken by the regime in its search for the new political formula. Beginning with the restoration of original Romanian names to streets and places previously Russified, developing into the mass rehabilitation of historical and cultural figures associated with the struggle for political and economic independence and restoring 'Romanianism' to the Romanians, the campaign culminated in the obvious endeavour to build a new image for the Party. The communists were now presented as the direct descendants, followers and continuators of nationalist ancestors, from the Dacian king Burebista onwards. Within the same framework, a new version of the events of August 1944 began to be promoted. First made public in a book review printed in the Party's historical periodical at the end of 1962,[63] the new version rejected the Soviet (and until recently also Romanian) version of the August 1944 events, according to which the country owed its liberation primarily to the Red Army. Instead, the RCP was now credited with organising and carrying out the anti-Antonescu putsch, and only minimal lip service was paid to the Soviet contribution to the defeat of the Nazis. A new and further stage in the campaign for national legitimisation of the Party was reached in 1964, with the publication of Marx's 'Notes on the Romanians'.[64]

Communist ideology now proved perfectly compatible with anti-Russian nationalism, since the founder of scientific socialism himself, as it turned out from Marx's hitherto unknown notes, had denounced Russia's encroachments on Romanian independence in general, and the annexation of Bessarabia in particular.

While appealing to national sentiments, the Party also sought to increase its popularity by an amnesty for former 'class enemies' and 'chauvinist elements' and, above all, by opening its ranks to sections of the population formerly perceived as ideologically harmful. The first step towards turning the RCP from an essentially worker elitist group into a nationally representative organisation was taken in April 1962, when the candidacy or probation period was considerably shortened and in some cases totally abolished. The new Party statutes, adopted at the Ninth RCP Congress in 1965, did away with the candidacy period altogether. As a result of these measures, a significant number of intellectuals joined the Party,[65] symbolically contributing to its further legitimation and to the validation of claims concerning participatory patterns (see table 21.2). By the end of 1962, the Pary had over a million members. For the rest of Dej's leadership and then under Ceauşescu, mass recruitment constituted one of the main instruments of changing the Party's image.

With the RPW's adoption, in April 1964, of its famous 'Statement' concerning the problems of the international communist movement,[66] the neo-nationalist and independent line pursued by Bucharest reached the state of canonisation. Not only did this document restate the Romanian position concerning such issues as Comecon or the role played in the past by the Comintern, but it also bluntly espoused the 'many ways to socialism' school, rejecting any possible Soviet claim to ideological primacy:

> Bearing in mind the diversity of the conditions of socialist construction, there are not, nor can there be, any unique patterns and recipes; no one can decide what is and what is not correct for other countries or parties. It is up to every Marxist-Leninist party, it is a sovereign right of each socialist state, to elaborate, choose or change the forms and methods of socialist construction. . . .
>
> There does not and cannot exist a 'parent' party and a 'son' party, or 'superior' parties and 'subordinate' parties. . . . No party has or can have a privileged place, or can impose its line and opinions on other parties.

Ceaușescu's advent to power in March 1965, following Dej's death, both ensured continuity and brought radical political innovations. The obviously popular line introduced by the previous leadership continued, but gradually Ceaușescu himself came to replace the Party as the personification of the much-heralded 'Romanian national spirit'. Pageants and extravagant displays stressing historical associations with the national struggle for independence were staged in an effort to identify the new leader with the symbols of national pride. 'Ceaușescu-România' – in precisely that order – became the slogan of mass rallies. With the possible exception of Albania, there is no comparable personality cult in any other East European country.

Two important decisions reflecting the course Ceaușescu intended to pursue were made in July and August 1965. At the Fourth RWP Congress, the first chaired by the new leader, it was decided to readopt the name 'Romanian Communist Party', thereby emphasising local, independent roots and further disassociating the Party from the old, derivative RWP image. The July congress consequently became (counting the RPW congresses with the RCP ones) the Ninth Congress of the RCP. Even more expressive was the decision to change the State's denomination from 'People's Republic' to 'Socialist Republic', putting Romania on an equal footing with the Soviet Union. Unlike the 1952 constitution, the new constitution, adopted on 21 August, made no mention of Romania's liberation by the Red Army or of everlasting friendship with Moscow. Instead,[67] 'respect of sovereignty and national independence, equality of rights and mutual advantage, non-interference in internal affairs' – echoing the 1964 'Declaration of Independence' – were the new major themes. The Party's leading role, on the other hand, remained inscribed in the Constitution as the 'leading political force of the whole society'. The new Party statutes, adopted in July, reflected similar trends: on the one hand, provision was made for a continual growth in the Party's role in the society, and, on the other, there was no longer any mention of solidarity with the CPSU.

Since the Party occupies the central role in the Romanian system, it was only natural that political innovation should occur there first. Scrutinising the nature of the innovations, however, one is struck by their highly manipulative and personal nature. Their most blatant feature was their purpose of ensuring that Ceaușescu and his protégés had exclusive control over decision-making.

'Democratisation' of Party life

At the outset of his leadership Ceauşescu was faced with powerful political adversaries – above all, the members of the Dejist 'old guard', who could legitimately claim both seniority and closer association with the deceased leader. The main, though not sole, contender for power was the chief of the security forces, Drăghici. At the Ninth Congress it was decided to set up a commission to investigate and 'clarify the political situation of a number of Party activists who were arrested or sentenced many years ago'.[68] Although for the time being the decision was kept secret, the results of the investigation were a foregone conclusion. Published in April 1968 and resulting in, among other things, Pătrăşcanu's rehabilitation, the investigation led to Drăghici's downfall. At the same time, it neutralised all Dej's other associates who had acquiesced in the former leader's 'illegalities'. Last but not least, Dej himself was made responsible for the brutal repression of political adversaries, and this brought to its culmination the campaign against Dejism that had been tacitly instituted soon after his death. Having rid himself of his predecessor's giant shadow, Ceauşescu could claim sole credit for the nationalist line and add to it the aura of democratiser of a regenerated Party.

The new statutes kept 'democratic centralism' as a leading principle, stipulating, however, that 'collective leadership' was one of the guiding axioms of the Party and that consequently no person should hold office in both Party and State capacities. With the benefit of hindsight, it may now be established that the purpose of this stipulation was to weaken the power base of Ceauşescu's potential adversaries. Drăghici, for instance, was forced to give up his position as Minister of Interior, and this proved to be the first step on his path to political disgrace. Once the rule had served its turn, the statutes were duly changed, making it possible for Ceauşescu to hold a number of positions in State and Party.

Another expression of 'democratisation' introduced by the Ninth Congress was the enlargement of the Central Committee from seventy-nine to 121 full members and from thirty-one to seventy-five candidate members. The measure was supposed to reflect the growth marked in Party membership, and similar measures were passed by the Tenth and Eleventh Congresses, in 1969 and 1974 respectively. At present, the Central Committee has 205 full and 156 candidate members. Many of those promoted in 1965 and 1969, however, were staunch Ceauşescu supporters, and those who lost their positions were political adversaries.

Improving 'efficiency'

The amendment of the Party statutes in December 1967 was carried out in the name of avoiding unnecessary parallelisms. As a result of this amendment, Ceauşescu was elected President of the Council of State, replacing Chivu Stoica, who had inherited Dej's presidential mantle. Stoica practically disappeared from the political scene. An amendment to the Constitution adopted in March 1974 made Ceauşescu President of the Republic, officially doing away with the last vestiges of 'collective leadership'. Another consequence of the 1967 amendment, as will become clear, was the strengthening of Party control over the State apparatus at all levels of the pyramidal power structure.

It was also in the name of improving efficency that the 'rotation principle' was instituted in 1969. According to this principle, high Party dignitaries are required periodically to exchange positions in the central Party apparatus for jobs at lower levels. No precise set of rules for the 'rotation principle' was ever set up, but the only living leader not affected by it at one time or another is the Secretary-general, Ceauşescu. The 'principle' has allowed a constant check on possible power contenders.

A perfect illustration of how 'efficency' may be exploited for radically different purposes is offered by the institutional innovation introduced in March and November–December 1974. At a Central Committee plenum held on 25–26 March it was decided to abolish the Committee's Standing Presidium, whose members were the most influential individuals in the Party, and to replace it with a Permanent Bureau. The Standing Presidium had been created in 1965, replacing the former Political Bureau and heading the Central Committee's Executive Committee, a new intermediary body between the Central Committee and the top Party leadership. The object of the 1965 innovation had been to provide a mechanism for the advancement of Ceauşescu protégés who could not yet make it to the topmost echelons. By March 1974, some of these protégés were well up the hierarchical ladder, and, as Standing Presidium members, were rather powerful. According to the March 1974 decision, the Permanent Bureau was to function on the principle of *ex-officio* membership, i.e. to include the Secretary-general (Ceauşescu), the President of the Republic (also Ceauşescu), plus all Central Committee secretaries, the Prime Minister and several other State and mass-organisation leaders. At the Eleventh Congress, however, new Party statutes were adopted,[69] providing for changes in the structure and composition of the Permanent Bureau. According to the new provisions, the Bureau was to be appointed by the Political Executive

Committee (a new name for the former Executive Committee) from among its own members. Instead of keeping to the originally envisaged composition, the Political Executive Committee nominated only five persons to the Permanent Bureau.[70] At first sight, the change may appear to be rational from the point of view of administrative efficiency, since a smaller forum may reach decisions more rapidly. With the benefit of hindsight, however, it may be established that the 'reform' was not dictated by considerations of 'efficency'. The promotion of four new members to the Bureau in January 1977 increased the number of its members to nine. It therefore appears that the evolution of the new body from March 1974 to January 1977 was a three-step process aimed at the elimination of the former Standing Presidium, whose members might have become too influential and independent. The March reform, having provided for *ex officio* membership, removed most of the members of the former Presidium from the new leading Party forum; as a second step, in November the Political Executive Committee was given power to appoint the Bureau, but the size of the Bureau was much reduced – seemingly creating a more efficient forum. Finally, in January 1977, Ceauşescu's closest collaborators were promoted to the Bureau, thereby ensuring his renewed domination of the decision-making process.

It was certainly not accidental that three of those promoted in January 1977 were relatives of Ceauşescu – his wife Elena, his brother-in-law Ilie Verdeţ and his nephew Cornel Burticǎ. Another brother-in-law, Manea Mǎnescu, had been a member of the Bureau since its establishment, and was Prime Minister between March 1974 and March 1979, when he resigned apparently for health reasons. He was replaced by Ilie Verdeţ. Promotion to high Party and State echelons has indeed often proved simply a function of family connections. Mrs Ceauşescu is nowadays practically the second highest Romanian official. In addition to her Party position (she became an Executive Committee member in June 1973), she is a member of the Grand National Assembly and, as a trained chemist, Director-general of the Central Institute of Chemical Research, Chairman of the Section for Chemical Industry of the Supreme Council for Economic Development, a member of the Technical-sciences section of the Romanian Academy, and Chairman of the National Council of Science and Technology. The latter position, which she has held since June 1979, makes her an *ex officio* member of the government as well. Nicu Ceauşescu, one of the President's sons, is a member of the Secretariat of the Union of Communist Youth; Ilie Ceauşescu (brother) is a deputy secretary in the Higher Political Council of the Romanian Army, with the rank of Major-general; Ion Ceauşescu (brother) is Secretary of State in the Agriculture Ministry; yet another member of the Ceauşescu family, Constantin, is head of the Directorate of Post, Radio and Television, while Florea Ceauşescu, reportedly[71] also a brother of the President, is editor-in-chief of an agricultural publication. The list is far from complete, for it does not include relatives on Mrs Ceauşescu's side of the family. It should also include among others, nephew Ion Ioniţă, Chief-of-staff of the Romanian Army, brother-in-law Gheorghe Petrescu, Minister of Metallurgical Industries; and other, lesser officials.

ORGANISATIONAL PRINCIPLES OF THE RCP

Party organisation in Romania is based on the general model of ruling East European communist parties. The statutes adopted in 1974 insist on strictest Party discipline and respect of 'democratic centralism'. In the name of the need to promote ever better-trained cadres, the statutes provide for an uninterrupted turn-over in the Party hierarchy, from the basic cell up to Central Committee level.

The primary Party level is the basic cell, the general assembly of which elects a bureau. In institutions, factories or agricultural co-operatives where more than one cell function, the general assembly elects a Party committee. On 31 December 1977 the RCP had 59,037 cells.

The RCP is organised according to territorial subdivisions, i.e. villages, cities, municipalities and counties. The territorial organisation's general assembly elects a Party committee. According to the statutes, the highest Party organ is the Congress, which meets every five years. Extraordinary congresses may be convened at the initiative of the Central Committee or at the request of a third of Party members. The Congress elects the Central Committee and the Secretary-general, as well as the Central Revision Commission. The Central Committee nominally directs all Party activity between congresses. It holds plenary sessions at least every four months. When, between congresses, it considers it necessary to debate important matters of policy, it may convene a National Party Conference. As already indicated, the 1974 statutes provide for the election of the Political Executive Committee by the Central Committee. The latter also elects the Secretariat and organises the Central Party College. The Political Executive Committee designates from among its members the Permanent Bureau, headed by the Secretary-general.

GOVERNMENT

The constitution

The 1969 constitution defines Romania as a socialist republic and as a 'sovereign, independent and unitary state of workers from town and village'. According to the first article, Romania's territory is 'inalienable and indivisible'. The second article stipulates that 'the whole power' belongs 'to the people, free and master of its own fate', and is based on the alliance of all classes, regardless of nationality. The leading political force of the entire society is the Communist Party. Article 5 describes Romania's national economy as 'socialist, based on socialist ownership of the means of production'.

The Grand National Assembly

Article 4 of the Constitution stipulates that the people exercises its sovereign right to power through the Grand National Assembly (GNA – Marea Adunare Naţionalǎ) and through the people's councils. The GNA is defined as the 'supreme organ of State power'.

Until 1974, elections to the Assembly, as provided in the Constitution, were based on the Soviet model, i.e. one candidate for each seat (For election results, see Table 21.4.) The candidate was nominated by the Socialist Unity Front (SUF) and elected on a single list by a large majority. Within the framework of stressing participatory patterns during the 'modernisation' period, the electoral system was reformed in 1974, providing for multi-candidate elections similar to those held in Yugoslavia and Hungary. The first multi-candidate elections were held in March 1975, with 488 candidates running for the Assembly's 349 seats. It should be stressed, however, that, in those electoral districts where two candidates opposed each other, *both* endorsed, and were endorsed by, the SUF. Moreover, officials who held important Party and State positions were almost always unopposed, and only in the case of about 40 per cent of the seats was the term 'multi-candidate' actually warranted.[72]

The GNA is elected for a term of five years. It meets in session twice a year and in extraordinary session whenever necessary. Between sessions its work is carried out by the Council of State and by the GNA commissions. There are at present ten standing commissions in the Romanian parliament. Their functions and responsibilities have been substantially increased during the Ceauşescu period.

TABLE 21.4 Romanian election results, 1952–75[a]

Year	Registered voters No.	Votes cast No.	%	Positive No.	%	Against No.	%	Null No.	%
1952	10,574,475	10,353,489	97·9	10,187,833	98·4	165,656[b]	1·6[b]		
1957	11,652,289	11,553,690	98·2	11,424,521	98·2	115,880	1·0	13,289	0·1
1961	12,444,977	12,417,800	99·78	12,388,787	99·7	23,461	0·19	5,552	0·04
1965	12,858,835	12,853,590	99·96	12,834,862	99·85	16,449	0·13	2,279	0·02
1969	13,582,249	13,577,143	99·96	13,543,499	99·75	30,748	0·23	2,896	0·02
1975	14,900,032	14,894,185	99·96	14,715,539	98·80	178,053	1·20	593	0·003

[a] 1952–65 for the Popular Democratic Front; 1969–75 for the SUF.
[b] Includes null votes.

Source: D. Sternberger and B. Vogel, *Die Wahl der Parlamente und anderer Staatsorgane*, vol. I, pt II (Berlin: W. de Gruyter, 1969) pp. 1068–9.

According to article 70 of the GNA regulations,[73] the prerogative of initiating legislation belongs to the Party's Central Committee. The National Council of the SUF, the Council of State and the Council of Ministers – in that order – precede the Assembly in the right to initiate new laws. Moreover, the Party's domination of the GNA is also ensured by the massive presence of Central Committee members in the Assembly. At the 1975 elections, no fewer than 167 full or candidate Central Committee members (47.85 per cent of all deputies) were elected to the GNA.[74]

The Council of State

While in other East European countries it is customary for parliamentary functions to be delegated, between sessions, to a presidium elected from among the deputies, in Romania since 1961 this role belongs to the Council of State. The Council's prerogatives, however, were substantially reduced with the creation, in 1974, of the office of President of the Republic. Officially the Council of State is subordinate to the GNA, to which it is accountable for its activities, and which elects it for the entire length of the parliamentary term. The Council is composed of a President (always the President of the Republic), three vice-presidents and an undefined number of members.

The President of the Republic

With the possible exception of Yugoslavia, in no other East European country is so much power concentrated in the hands of one person.[75] Even though Ceaușescu practically acted as State President ever since his election to the presidency of the Council of State in 1967, the creation of the office of President of the Socialist Republic of Romania was the institutional epitome of the personality cult. The official portraits issued on that occasion, showing Ceaușescu wrapped in the ribbons of office and with a sceptre in his hands, speak for themselves.

The President is elected at the recommendation of the Central Committee of the RCP and at that of the SUF by a two-thirds majority of GNA deputies, for the entire legislative period of the Assembly. He is responsible to the GNA and may be recalled at any time by a three-quarters majority of members.

The head of State is also *ex officio* President of the Council of State, supreme commander of the armed forces and President of the Defence

Council. His prerogatives are considerable, for the Constitution does not require him to submit his decisions for the approval of any organ of State authority.

The Council of Ministers

The Council of Ministers (the Government) is elected by the GNA for the whole parliamentary term and is collectively responsible to it. Its composition is recommended by the Central Committee and by the National Council of the SUF. In exceptional cases, when the Assembly is unable to meet in session, the government may be nominated or revoked by the Council of State.

From the structural point of view, it is possible to distinguish between three categories of membership of the Romanian government.[76] The first, including members nominated by the GNA, is composed of the Prime Minister, his first deputy or deputies, deputy prime ministers, ministers, and secretaries of State. The second category is made up by leaders of public administrative organisations whom special legislation designates as members of the government. Finally, a third category comprises the presidents of a number of mass organisations who belong to the forum *ex officio*.

Local government

The central government's local agents at county, municipality, town or commune level are the people's councils. They are elected for a term of five years, except in communes (villages), where their mandate is for only half that period. The councils and their elected organs function according to democratic centralist principles as well as according to the 'principle of double responsibility': i.e. responsibility both to central government and to higher levels of local government. Nominally at least, they are also responsible to the electors. In practice, each council is above all responsible to the appropriate local Party organisation. Since February 1968 the latter responsibility has been practically institutionalised, with each council being headed by the appropriate Party first secretary.

The functions of local government are manifold, including, among others, the planning and supervision of local economic performance. Although this is officially presented as an expression of ever-increasing local autonomy, the 'principle of double responsibility' hardly allows for any real administrative decentralisation in practice; rather, as one observer has put it, one is faced here with an attempt at administrative deconcentration.[77]

Party – State relations

The programme adopted by the RCP in December 1974, envisages an ever-increasing role for the Party. According to this document, the Party will continue to exist and lead as long as the process of socialist edification and construction continues, and will only gradually wither away 'through its integration in the society's life, through an ever more organic participation of Party members in the entire social life'.[78] In other words, the withering-away process envisaged amounts to a 'take-over from within' of societal structures at all levels. Party leadership, according to the programme, 'must be exercised not from outside, but from inside social, State, and economic organs'.[79]

As has already been seen, ever since 1967 the tendency in Romania has been to merge Party and State activities in the name of avoiding parallelism. In practice, this tendency has given birth to several forms of Party domination over State activities.

First, multiple holding of positions in both the Party and the State apparatus has become the standard practice from top to bottom. At the leadership level, as illustrated in Table 21.5, all members of the Permanent Bureau hold positions in either State or joint Party-State organisations. Of the forty members of the Romanian government in September 1978, only three were not members of the Central Committee; of the remaining thirty-seven, all but one were full members of that forum.

Secondly, while the 'principle of rotation' ensures that no Party leader accumulates enough power and influence to endanger Ceauşescu's position, it also provides an ideal mechanism for Party supervision at all levels. Finally, an institutional innovation of later years provides for the creation of joint Party–State organisations.[80] The juridical status of these bodies is still somewhat obscure,[81] for the Constitution does not provide for organs of such mixed nature. There can be no doubt, however, that in the long run these organisations are aimed at blending Party and State activities and possibly at producing a blueprint for 'take-over from within'.

TABLE 21.5 State or joint State–Party positions held by members of the
Romanian Permanent Bureau, 1978

Nicolae Ceauşescu	President of the Republic
	President, Council of State
	Chairman, National Defence Council
	Chairman, Supreme Council for
	  Economic Development
	Chairman, Commission for Economic and
	  Social Forecasting

Elena Ceauşescu	Chairman, Section for Chemical Industry, Supreme Council for Economic Development
Manea Mănescu	Prime Minister

Gheorghe Oprea	First Deputy Prime Minister
	Chairman, Section for Metallurgical Industry
	  and Machine Building, Supreme Council for
	  Economic Development

Ilie Verdeţ	First Deputy Prime Minister Chairman, State Planning Committee
Cornel Burtică	Deputy Prime Minister Minister of Foreign Trade and International Economic Co-operation
Paul Niculescu	Deputy Prime Minister Minister of Finance Chairman, Council for Co-ordination of Consumer Goods Production
Ion Păţan	Deputy Prime Minister Minister of Technical-Material Supply and Control of Fixed Assets
Gheorghe Rădulescu	Deputy Prime Minister
Ştefan Andrei	Minister of Foreign Affairs
Iosif Banc	Chairman, Central Council of Workers' Control of Economic and Social Activities

MASS ORGANISATIONS

The 'containment' function is fulfilled particularly through the mass
organisations. The biggest and most important mass organisation is the
Socialist Unity Front. The SUF was created in 1968, replacing the
former Popular Democratic Front, and is defined as a 'permanent
political organ of large representation', including 'the Romanian

Communist Party as the leading political force of our society, and the main mass, public and professional organisations'.[82] Its President since its foundation is Ceauşescu.

The 'containment' function of the SUF is perhaps best illustrated by the case of one of its components, the Council of Workers of Hungarian Nationality.[83] The councils of workers of national minorities were established in the year the SUF was founded, and joined it at once. There are at present twenty-nine local minority councils – fifteen Hungarian, ten German, two Serbian and two Ukrainian. Their creation, particularly in the Hungarian case, was intended to help alleviate national grievances in the wake of a territorial reorganisation which abolished the Hungarian Autonomous Region. At that particular period, the Romanian leadership was also troubled by the possibility that the Soviet Union might attempt to exploit dissatisfaction among the national minorities as a pretext for intervention in Romania. After the establishment of the Hungarian Council, the regime made a few minor concessions, particularly in the cultural field, but withdrew most of them as soon as the situation had calmed down somewhat. The Hungarian Council's present activity is limited to occasional plenary sessions. Károly Király, a former Central Committee member, protested in 1977, in letters addressed to prominent Party officials, against the existing situation, pointing out the typically pre-emptive nature of the Council's activities.[84] A similar description, accompanied by proposals for reforms, was provided by former Nationalities Minister and Central Committee member Lajos Takács.[85] Király is reported to be under harassment, though not (yet?) deprived of liberty.

Among other members of the SUF are the General Union of Syndicates (the trade unions), the Union of Communist Youth, the National Council of Women and the National Union of Agricultural Production Co-operatives. The trade unions, allegedly a forum for 'large manifestation of workers' democracy, of syndicate autonomy', are entrusted with the 'growth of economic efficency in all economic sectors', as well as with 'the implementation of the communist principles of order, discipline and work responsibility'.[86] A National Council of the Working People, constituted in October 1977[87] and reorganised in April 1978, is supposed to ensure the workers' participation in the management of society. In so far as can be judged from available material, the organisation is much less an instrument for worker self-management than a mechanism for increased Party supervision of production. Ceauşescu, who was elected Chairman of the Council, stressed in his first speech to it that it must supervise the implementation of economic plans and of Party and State policy in the economic field. The Union of Communist Youth, is the Party's youth branch, organised on the same principles and functioning with a similar structure.

INTERNAL AFFAIRS

Education

As presently conceived, the Romanian educational system provides for pre-school education (ages three to five), followed by ten years' compulsory education and facultative subsequent training. The compulsory stage is divided between the 'schools of general culture', providing elementary (ages six to nine) and secondary (ages ten to thirteen) education, and the 'first stage of the lyceum', providing either theoretical or combined theoretical-vocational training. After successfully completing the ten years of compulsory education, the student may continue, on the basis of a selective entrance examination, to the 'second stage of the lyceum' and eventually to higher studies. Those found ineligible for such studies either start work or may continue to study in vocational schools and courses, lasting from six to eighteen months. The regime attaches particular importance to these schools, which aim at shortening the gap between the knowledge of specialists and that of skilled workers.

There are at present seven universities and various other institutes of higher learning in Romania. The universities are in Bucharest (eleven faculties), Cluj-Napoca (nine faculties), Timişoara (four faculties), Braşov (five faculties), Craiova (seven faculties), Galaţi (three faculties) and Iaşi (nine faculties). The institutes are of several categories: technical, industrial, agricultural, medical, arts and teacher-training with also an academy for economics and an institute of physical education and sports.

Religion

According to Western estimates,[88] some 80 per cent of Romanian citizens are religiously affiliated. The bulk of the population (66 per cent) belongs to the Romanian Orthodox Church; 5 per cent are Roman Catholic; 1·7 per cent are Protestants; 0·4 per cent are Jews; and an even smaller fraction are Moslems.

In 1948 all sects were placed under State supervision[89] and their estates confiscated. The regime attempted to gain control of ecclesiastical affairs through Justinian Marina, a relatively unknown figure who, as a village priest, had hidden Dej in his house in August 1944. Justinian was elected Patriarch and pronounced himself in favour of an accommodation with the regime. According to his supporters, his leadership saved the Church from possibly greater persecution. Although Orthodox priests fell victim to the Party's determination to obliterate any potential form of opposition, the Orthodox Church fared far better than did other sects. A tacit agreement with the communist authorities brought about the forced unification of the Romanian Uniate Church with the Orthodox Church, in December 1948. Uniate priests who refused to convert were arrested and all Uniate churches were turned over to the Orthodox Church. In July 1948 Romania unilaterally abrogated the concordat with the Vatican. A decree issued in August required all religions to accept the Romanian State's authority as supreme. For the Catholics, this amounted to a demand to renounce their ties with the Vatican, which they could not possibly accept. In the circumstances, the Roman Catholic authorities were unable to submit their statutes for approval, as required by law, and in retaliation the regime reduced the number of Catholic sees from five to two. To this date, therefore, the situation of the Catholic Church remains somewhat ambivalent.

At present, religious life in Romania is organised by the Department of (Religious) Cults. The Department was reorganised in August 1970, through a decree[90] providing for a considerable increase in State – in fact, Party – control over religious affairs. In 1974 all religions were ordered to join, collectively, the SUF.[91]

None the less, the situation of religious denominations in general, and of the Orthodox Church in particular has considerably improved since the mid1960s. Within the framework of the nationalist campaign, the leadership acknowledged and heralded the traditional role played by the Church in the process of 'nation-building'. In 1966 Ceaușescu visited the Putna monastery, which was then celebrating 500 years of existence, and in 1967 the entire press carried detailed descriptions of similar festivities at the Curtea de Argeș monastery.

The situation of the Jews has considerably improved since 1967. The Federation of Jewish Communities runs kosher canteens and even organises Hebrew-language classes. Chief Rabbi Rosen, who once played in the Jewish community a role similar to that played by Patriarch Marina in the Orthodox Church, now frequently travels to Israel and to international Jewish gatherings. A mini personality cult of the Rabbi dominates the official life of the community. The Federation has been allowed to extend financial help to needy Jews. On the other hand, emigration to Israel, though not forbidden, is officially discouraged and encounters considerable difficulties. The Federation and Rabbi Rosen personally stress the Romanian Jews' loyalty to the State and their identification with its past, present and future. The 1978–9 calendar published by the Federation lists such significant landmarks in the history of the community as the 1877 Independence War and 26 January 1918 – Ceauşescu's birthday.

Serious problems are encountered by the Protestant churches, albeit for different reasons. The Lutheran Church, the majority of whose believers are village dwellers of German origin, has been affected both by the urbanisation process and by emigration to Germany.[92] Neo-Protestant sects have been particularly successful in proselytism and have consequently encountered the wrath of the regime. Pastors and members of the Baptist, Adventist and other creeds have been persecuted, arrested and beaten for having demanded religious freedom and non-interference in church-affairs.[93]

The economy

Romania was the last East European State to adopt a programme of economic reform, doing so in 1967. The Central Committee directives on 'Perfecting the Management and Planning of the National Economy',[94] approved at the RCP National Conference of December, by no means went as far as the Yugoslav or Hungarian models, but resembled a blend of GDR and Czechoslovak practices, leaning more towards the former. Even so, they were only partially implemented, and it was only in the course of 1978 that new measures, envisaging a fuller implementation of the original model, were adopted.

The core of the 1967 programme[95] consisted in establishing a new, intermediary level between economic ministries and enterprises. The 'democratic centralist' principle in economic organisation was not abolished, for the 'centrals', as the new bodies were called, were still subject to the directives of central planning and one of their main functions was plan fulfilment. The central was envisaged as 'an autonomous economic unit, co-ordinated and controlled by the relevant ministry' and 'set up by the grouping of several enterprises'. It was to be provided 'with material and money resources, operating on the principle of own economic administration'. The draft proposals adopted on this occasion also envisaged modifications in the price system, castigating 'the erroneous idea according to which the prices of the means of production must not wholly reflect the social production expenditure', the consequence of which was that 'a number of enterprises and products . . . have become unprofitable'. For the elimination of such shortcomings it was envisaged that in all economic branches prices must be based on 'social production expenditures', i.e. on real production costs. A more flexible mechanism for establishing prices, it was recommended, should give the centrals some rights in establishing and modifying prices, though no market-supply mechanism was envisaged.

Implementation of the directives, however, proved far more difficult a task than issuing them, partially because the Party seemed to have second thoughts on the consequences of releasing its grip on the economy. Thus, whereas the National Party Conference of December decided to dissolve the economic sections of the Central Committee and transfer Party supervision to the local level, the decision was revised in 1969, when similar Party commissions were established also at district, city and town level. Similarly, a March 1973 Central Committee plenum, while attempting to revive the reform by introducing new organisational measures,[96] established also additional joint Party-State bodies (the Council for Economic and Social Organisation, and the Supreme Council for Socio-economic Development), whose task was to increase Party jurisdiction over economic affairs.

Since March 1978 there are, however, signs that there are thoughts of returning to, and even going beyond, the original 1967 directives. A document approved at the 1978 plenum reflects considerable determination to introduce further decentralisation and improve efficency by allowing for a greater measure of autonomy. It consists of a four-part programme providing for the following.

1. Devolution of responsibility to centrals and enterprises, on the one hand, and enhancement of the authority of central organisations, on the other. It is envisaged that enterprises will be granted greater responsibility in drafting their own plans and for drawing up their budgets. Expansion of banking-credit activities (first introduced in 1967), accompanied by increased bank controls, is also provided for. Central authorities are to be responsible for the harmonisation of economic activities and for ensuring the flow of resources to the centrals and the enterprises.
2. Self-management at all levels of production.
3. Adoption of a profit-sharing scheme (provided for in the 1967

directives, but not implemented) for the purpose of encouraging greater efficency in production.

4. Modification of economic indicators on the lines established in 1967. The main indicator, replacing 'gross output value', will be 'net production', arrived at by subtracting raw-material expenditure from total output.

To what extent were these reforms triggered by the 1977 miners' strikes in the Jiul valley and by other displays of dissatisfaction by workers is difficult to establish. The scheme is to be implemented in stages, which may indicate a cautious approach to the more sensitive aspects of Party control over the economy. A reduction of Party interference in economic affairs is not, in any case, envisaged. In spite of the much-heralded self-management, it should be pointed out that the working people's councils, to which enterprise directors are responsible, are headed by the incumbent Party secretary. Moreover, a missing link in the 1978 scheme as compared with the 1967 directives is the problem of price determination. It is not yet clear whether enterprises and centrals are to be allowed to play any part in their establishment – without which, of course, the system of self-management and profit-sharing is meaningless. Finally, as long as policies continue to favour high investments at the national level, it is questionable whether central controls may really be reduced, and consequently autonomy at central and enterprise levels remains problematic.

FOREIGN AFFAIRS

The basic aims of Romanian foreign policy were established in the 1960s and have hardly changed since. Whether at the United Nations or at international communist gatherings, whether in behind-the-scene diplomatic contacts or in the pomp of State visits, the primary objective of this policy has been, and remains, that of augmenting Romanian independence and room for manoeuvre, with the purpose of checking any possible Soviet designs of forcing Bucharest 'back into the fold'.

The nature of Romania's manifold contacts or semi-alliances, established for this strategic purpose, differs in scope and intensity. It is, however, possible to classify them into a three-dimensional scheme: the international communist movement; the Western world; and the Third World.

The foremost partners in the first dimension have been China and

Yugoslavia, although in recent years the Eurocommunist parties have also come to play a certain role. It is, of course, not accidental that all these movements are 'divergent'. Advocacy of 'unity in diversity', i.e. of an end to polemics and of common action based on shared values, has perfectly served the purpose of perpetuating Moscow's difficulties in its efforts to impose policies on the international movement.

The Sino-Soviet split, which first burst into the open at the Romanian Party Congress in 1960, has been a *sine qua non* condition for the success of Romania's challenge of Soviet policies.[97] Here it is impossible to review the Bucharest-Peking-Moscow triangle in full, but it should be remembered that Dej would hardly had dared to oppose Khrushchev had not the Soviet leader's hands been tied at the time by his endeavours to neutralise Mao; that Romania adopted in the 1960s the 'honest broker' position which allowed her later to oppose Soviet attempts to have the Chinese Communist Party 'excommunicated', and that Chairman Hua's first visit abroad was to Belgrade and Bucharest.

In the wake of the 1968 invasion of Czechoslovakia and the 'Brezhnev doctrine', Chinese support for Romania (which denounced both) was vociferous – but little more than that. Whether or not, as recently alleged in Tirana, Peking sought to forge a military Albanian-Yugoslav-Romanian alliance in 1968[98] is difficult to establish. Regardless of Chinese intentions, it is unlikely that Ceaușescu would have courted disaster in such a manner. Military collaboration between Romania and China, in spite of exchanges of high-ranking delegations and in spite of Chinese verbosity, has up to now amounted to the delivery of a few gunboats to Bucharest.[99] The value of the Chinese deterrent, in so far as the Romanians are concerned, consists more in its combination with other semi-alliances, none of which officially replaces the Warsaw Pact. It is meaningful to remember that Bucharest was active in the Sino-American rapprochement,[100] and that, while such manoeuvres arouse Soviet wrath, they always stop short of offering Moscow an excuse for military intervention.

Similar considerations have determined the development of Yugoslav-Romanian relations. Belgrade's long experience of successful confrontation with Moscow, as well as Yugoslav prestige in the Third World, made Tito Romania's natural ally once the rift with the Moscow had reached the point of 'no return'. Following Ceaușescu's advent to power, the relationship intensified considerably. In April 1966 Tito came to Romania in what subsequently proved to be the first in a series of regular encounters designed to co-ordinate policies and to develop economic and technical co-operation between the two neighbours.

Thirteen such meetings have so far been held. In two instances, in 1968 and in 1978, Tito and Ceauşescu took particular care to establish grounds for common action.

In 1968 the Russians seemed to be particularly wary of the possibility of a revival of the 'Little Entente', socialist style. The invasion of Czechoslovakia ended the Romanian-Yugoslav-Czechoslovak collaboration, but also resulted in further intensification of contacts between Belgrade and Bucharest. Following the Yugoslav example, the Romanians even set up the 'Patriotic Guards' – yet another symbolic gesture designed to emphasise Ceauşescu's determination to resist Soviet pressures. In 1978, Chairman Hua's visit to the two capitals was closely concerted in contacts at the highest level. Whatever may result from the visit, in itself it constituted proof of the importance attached by the RCP to the 'communist diversionist' dimension of its foreign policy.

Securing support in the communist movement was a necessary but insufficient condition for the Romanian 'national deviation' to succeed. No less essential, both economically and politically, were the developing ties with the west. The foremost place among Western creditors is nowadays occupied by the FRG, with which economic relations dramatically improved after 1967, when Romania became the first East European communist country to establish diplomatic relations with Bonn. By 1971, the debt to the FRG was estimated at some 1500 million marks.[101] Generally, Romania's main problem in her trade with developed countries in the West has been her inability to balance substantial imports by corresponding exports. This may partially explain why lately Bucharest has proved less hostile in participating in joint Comecon schemes, although rejection of supranational bodies governed by majority decision has remained as eloquent as ever. Trade with the United States has also improved considerably, and in 1975 Bucharest acquired most-favoured-nation status, conditional on annual revisions under the 'Jackson amendment'. Although, as a Comecon member, Romania does not officially recognise the EEC, its overall trade volume with the EEC in 1977 totalled $2522·4 million.[102] As early as 1971, Bucharest was demanding preferential status from the Community, a request that met with partial success in 1974.

Politics, to be sure, played just as important a part in the relationship. There can be no doubt that the advantageous economic ties pursued with the West enable Romania to maintain her independent policy and that Romania's partners know exactly what they pay for. How valuable Western political support is was perhaps best demonstrated in 1968, when the United States warned the Russians against possible intervention in Romania. Ceauşescu has visited practically all the main Western capitals, has played host to Presidents Nixon and Ford, and has undertaken three extensive trips to America. Apart from the role played in the Sino—American rapprochement, there are also indications that Bucharest was active behind the scenes in mediation between Washington and Hanoi.

Since 1968, a policy of intensive contacts with the Third World is actively being pursued by Bucharest. As a general feature, such contacts are aimed at enlarging world sympathy and support for Romania, even if its effectiveness as an anti-Soviet deterrent is somewhat doubtful. The most substantial victory Bucharest scored in this area was Romania's admission into the 'Group of 77' in February 1976. Economically, apart from such advantages as could come *from the West* as a result of Romania's status as a developing country, there are potential longer-run advantages to be considered. Above all, the Third World countries may be more open to imports of industrial goods of a quality below Western standards.

Occasionally a contradiction may arise between the search for such markets and the quest for Western investments and technology. This was the case with the 'special relationship' developed with Israel in 1966–7, which was part of the reason why Romania refused to break diplomatic relations with Jerusalem following the Six Day War. The intensification of trade and other contacts with Israel generated a temporary crisis in relations with the Arab world.[103] Eventually not only was the crisis overcome, but Ceauşescu played a prominent part in the 1977 Middle East 'breakthrough'.

Romania's attitude on the Middle East question was not, to be sure, the outcome of economic interests alone. Every bit as important was the fact that the development of the Arab-Israeli conflict potentially endangered Romania's own position. At a relatively early stage in the 1967 confrontation, Bucharest apparently realised that the outbreak of hostilities every now and then – whatever their results – was bound to bring about the raising of global tension and carried with it the danger of confrontation between the blocs. Such a confrontation would enhance the chances of a Soviet attempt at forcing Romania back into active Pact membership. For, after all, it is the Pact as the main instrument of Soviet domination that the Romanian leadership fears most. For this reason, Ceauşescu has remained stubborn in his refusal to allow troop manoeuvres on Romanian soil, and, whatever symbolic collaboration with the Pact's High Command Bucharest is forced to maintain, it is certain that its future strengthening is not envisaged.

Nicolae Ceauşescu, Secretary-general of the RCP, was born in 1918 and probably owes his present position, to some extent at least, to the fact that he was imprisoned with Gheorghiu-Dej at the Tîrgu Jiu internment camp in the 1940s. In 1945 he became a candidate Central Committee member and in 1948 he was nominated Deputy Minister of Agriculture. In this capacity Ceauşescu was deeply involved in the collectivisation campaign. In 1950 he became Deputy Minister of the Armed Forces and Chief of the Supreme Political Staff, with the rank of Lieutenant-general. Promoted to full membership of the Central Committee in 1952, he went on to become a secretary of the Committee and a candidate member of the Political Bureau in 1954. His position as secretary in charge of control of the Party apparatus played an important part in securing his election as Dej's follower in 1965. Thereafter he became President of the Council of State (1967), Chairman of the SUF (1968), Honorary President of the Academy for Social and Political Sciences (1970), Chairman of the Commission for Economic and Social Forecasting (1971), Chairman of the Supreme Council for Economic Development (1973) and President of the Romanian Socialist Republic (1974).

Manea Mănescu, born in 1916 and related to Ceauşescu by marriage became a candidate member of the Executive Committee of the RCP in 1966, a full member in 1968, Vice-chairman of the Council of State in 1972, Vice-chairman, of the Council of Ministers in March 1974, and in the same year Prime Minister. Resigned in 1979 for health reasons.

Ilie Verdeţ, born in 1925 and related to Ceauşescu by marriage, became a Central Committee Secretary, a candidate member of the Executive Committee and Vice-chairman of the Council of Ministers in 1965, after Ceauşescu took over the Party leadership. In 1966 he was promoted to full membership of the Executive Committee and of its Permanent Presidium. In 1967 he became First Vice-chairman of the Council of Ministers. From March 1974 to March 1975 Verdeţ was Chairman of the Central Council of Workers' Control of Economic and Social Activities. A member of the Permanent Bureau of the Political Executive Committee since 1977, Verdeţ replaced Mănescu as Prime Minister in March 1979.

BASIC FACTS ABOUT ROMANIA[104]

Oficial name: Socialist Republic of Romania (Republica Socialistă România)

Area: 237,500 sq. km. (91,670 sq. miles).

Population (1977 preliminary figures): 21,599,416.

Population density: 91 per sq km.

Membership of the RCP (Partidul Communist Român) in March 1978: 2,747,110.

Population distribution: 47·5 per cent urban, 52·5 per cent rural.

Administrative division: 39 counties (*judeţe*), 236 towns (incl. 47 municipalities) and 2706 communes.

Ethnic nationalities: [105] Romanians, 88·1 per cent; Hungarians,[106] 7·9 per cent; Germans, 1·6 per cent; Gypsies, 1·0 per cent; others, 1·4 per cent.

Population of major towns (1977 preliminary figures): Bucharest (Bucureşti, the capital) 1,807,044; Timişoara 268,685; Iaşi 264,947; Cluj-Napoca 262,421; Braşov 257,150; Constanţa 256,875; Galaţi 239,306; Craiova 222,399.

National income by sector (1975): industry, 56·2 per cent; agriculture and forestry, 16·5 per cent; construction, 7·6 per cent; transportation and communications, 5·8 per cent; others, 13·9 per cent.

Main natural resources: oil, coal, copper, gold, uranium, timber, bauxite, salt and hydroelectric power.

Foreign trade (1976): exports, 30,504·5 million lei ($6,137·7 million); imports, 30,293·9 million lei ($6,095·4 million); total, 60,798·4 million lei ($12,233·1 million).

Main trading partners (1976): USSR, FRG, GDR, Poland, Czechoslovakia, Iran, USA, China, France.

Rail network: 11,080 km.

Road network: 77,768 km.

Universities: Bucharest, Cluj-Napoca, Iaşi, Timişoara, Braşov, Craiova, Galaţi; number of students in 1976–7 (including those at other institutes of higher education) 177,888.

Foreign relations: diplomatic and consular relations with 130 states; member of the UN since 1955.

NOTES

1. An objective analysis of the circumstances of the birth of the Romanian national movement will be found in S. Fischer-Galaţi, 'Romanian Nationalism', in P. F. Sugar and I. J. Lederer (eds), *Nationalism in Eastern Europe*, 2nd imp. (Seattle: Washington University Press, 1971) pp. 373–95.

2. Institute of Political Sciences and of Studying the National Question, *The Hungarian Nationality in Romania* (Bucharest: Meridiane, 1976) p. 5.
3. The most detailed account of the Sovietisation of Romanian history is to be found in D. Ghermani, *Die kommunistische Umdeutung der rumänischen Geschichte unter besonderer Berücksichtigung des Mittelalters* (Munich: Oldenbourg, 1967). See also M. Rura, *Reinterpretation of History as a Method of Furthering Communism in Rumania: A Study in Comparative Historiography* (Washington, DC: Georgetown University Press, 1961), G. Schöpflin, 'Rumanian Nationalism', *Survey*, XX, nos 2–3 (1974) 84–92.
4. The letters 'â' and 'î' are pronounced similarly in the Romanian language, but, while the former may be traced back to Latin origins, the latter evolved on the basis of the Cyrillic character. A governmental decree issued in September 1953 and enforced in April 1954 obliterated the letter 'â' from Romanian spelling. This 'orthographic reform' was partially altered in 1965, when the neo-nationalist line of the regime generated a 'reform of the reform'. See the texts of the two decrees in Academia Republicii Populare Romîne, Institutul de Linguistică, *Î ndreptar ortografic şi de punctuaţie* (Bucharest: Editura Academiei Republicii Populare Romîne, 1960) pp. 3–4 and Academia Republicii Socialiste România, Institutul de Linguistica din Bucureşti, *Î ndreptar ortografic, ortoepic şi de punctuaţie* (Bucharest: Editura Academiei Republicii Socialiste România, 1965) p. 3
5. These ancient Romanian lands had been annexed by Russia in 1812, when Turkey ceded them to Czar Alexander I.
6. See P. Lendvai, *Eagles in Cobwebs: Nationalism and Communism in the Balkans* (London: MacDonald, 1970) p. 271, and D. Turnock, *An Economic Geography of Romania* (London: G. Bell, 1974) p. 11.
7. See A. G. Lee, *Crown Against Sickle: The Story of King Michael of Rumania*, 2nd ed. (London: Hutchinson, 1955); G. Ionescu, *Communism in Rumania 1944–1962* (London: Oxford University Press, 1964) pp. 83–6; S. Fischer-Galaţi, *The New Rumania: From People's Democracy to Socialist Republic* (Cambridge, Mass.: MIT, 1967) pp. 22–3; and B. Vago, 'Romania', in M. McCauley (ed.), *Communist Power·in Europe 1944–9* (London: Macmillan, 1977) p. 111. For a contemporary Romanian attempt to discredit this largely consensual version, see I. Chiper, 'Istoriografia străină despre insurecţia armată din august 1944 din România', *Studii*, XXII, no. 4 (1969) 733–59.
8. Such resolutions were adopted at the December 1955 Second RWP (Seventh RCP) Party Congress, at the July 1965 Ninth Congress, and, again, at the July 1970 Central Committee plenum. According to the latter decision, publication of the history was envisaged for May 1971, for the fiftieth anniversary of the RCP. At the November 1971 Central Committee plenum, however, one of the participants admitted that the task of drafting the Party history had proved difficult and complex. See G. Gheorghiu-Dej, *Raportul de activitate al Comitetului Central al Partidului Muncitoresc Romîn la Congresul al II-lea al Partidului* (Bucharest: Editura de stat pentru literatură politică, 1956) pp. 155–6; *Congresul al IX-lea al Partidului Comunist Român* (Bucharest: Editura politică 1966) p. 845; 'Hotărîre cu privire la aniversarea semicentenarului Partidului Comunist Român', *Anale de istorie*, XVI (1970) 3–11; and Radio Free Europe, *Situation Report: Rumania*, no. 27 (28 Sep 1974).

9. For histories of the RCP produced in the West, consult Ionescu, *Communism in Rumania* and D. Ghermani, 'Die Rumänische Kommunistische Partei', in K. D. Grothusen (ed.), *Rumänien* (Göttingen: Vandenhoeck & Ruprecht, 1977) pp. 11–41.

10. See S. Fischer-Galaţi, *Twentieth Century Rumania* (New York: Columbia University Press, 1970) p. 75; Vago, in McCauley, *Communist Power*, p. 113; and K. Jowitt, *Revolutionary Breakthroughs and National Development: The Case of Rumania 1944–1965* (Berkeley, Calif.: University of California Press, 1971) p. 79.

11. See V. Grigorian, 'Strategiia i taktika leninizma boevoe oruzhie bratskih kompartii', *Bolshevik*, XVII, no. 7 (1950) 14.

12. On the history of Romanian social democracy, consult T. Petrescu, *Socialismul în România* (Bucharest: Biblioteca socialistă, n.d.). Useful documents may be found in Institutul de Studii Istorice şi Social-politice de pe Lingă CC al PCR, *Presa muncitorească şi socialistă din România*, 4 vols (Bucharest: Editura politică, 1964–71) *Documente din istoria mişcării muncitoreşti din România 1916–1921* (Bucharest: Editura politică, 1966), and *Documente din istoria mişcării muncitoreşti din România 1893–1900* (Bucharest, 1969); and Institutul de Istorie a Partidului de pe Lingă CC al PCR, *Mişcarea muncitorească din România 1893–1900* (Bucharest: Editura politică, 1965).

13. 'What is the result of our socialist movement? The creation of a socialist headquarters of some seventy to eighty people', G. Diamandi disappointedly stated at the Sixth Congress. 'We cannot make propaganda', complained the socialist deputy V. G. Morţun, 'because our pamphlets are not understood.' Institutul de Studii Istorice, *Documente 1893–1900*, pp. 684, 689.

14. On Gherea see Petrescu, *Socialismul in România*, pp. 340–8; H. L. Roberts, *Rumania: Political Problems of an Agrarian State*, 2nd ed. (London: Archon Books, 1969) pp. 243–4; G. Haupt, 'Naissance du Socialisme par la Critique: La Roumanie', *Le Mouvement Social*, no. 59 (1967) 30–48; and S. Voicu, 'Constantin Dobrogeanu-Gherea', *Anale de istorie*, XVI, no. 3 (1970) 3–18.

15. Institutul de Studii Istorice, *Documente 1893–1900*, p. 274.

16. P. Axelrod, 'Bericht über den Fortgang der sozialistische Bewegung: Rumänien', *Jahrbuch für Sozialwissenschaft*, II (1881) 320–6, as quoted by Haupt, in *Le Mouvement Social*, no. 59, p. 31.

17. Fear of provoking the reactionary Russian Empire into intervention determined socialist advocacy of restraint in the implementation of social reforms. Among those who adopted such postures was Gherea himself. See Roberts, *Rumania: Political Problems*, pp. 18–19.

18. See G. Ionescu, *Communism in Rumania*, p. 7.

19. N. Ceauşescu, *România pe drumul desavîrşirii construcţiei socialiste*, vol. I (Bucharest: Editura politică, 1968) pp. 360–1.

20. For instance, the Third Congress had elected as Secretary-general the Hungarian Elek Köblös (Bădulescu), an unlikely popular nomination at a time when Budapest's irredentism was feared in Romania. Among the Party's prominent leaders during the period when it was banned were C. Dobrogeanu-Gherea's son Alexandru, Marcel and Ana Pauker, L. Bechenau, M. Kahana, B. Brainer, R. Kofler, M. Roller, I. Chişinevschi, L.

Răutu and S. Toma (all Jews), and Köblös, K. Berger, A. Kereszi-Krisan, I. Rangheţ, V. Luca and Ş. Foriş (all Hungarians).

21. This was the case of, for example, Chişinevschi and Răutu (Bessarabians) and K. Berger (Hungarian).

22. Among them, the more prominent were B. Ştefanov, P. Tkacenko, P. Borilă, B. Doncev, D. Coliu, D. Kronşev and later E. Bodnăraş.

23. See B. Vago's illuminating article 'The Jewish Vote in Romania between the Two World Wars', *Jewish Journal of Sociology*, XIV, no. 2 (1972) 229–44. It is interesting to remark that the RCP itself did not hesitate to attempt to exploit anti-semitism in its own favour. The Third Congress, for instance, called for struggle against 'the Jewish capital'. See B. Vago, 'The Attitude towards Jews as a Criterion of the Left-Right Concept', in B. Vago and G. Mosse (eds), *Jews and Non-Jews in Eastern Europe* (New York: Wiley, 1974) p. 47.

24. Among these were A. Dobrogeanu-Gherea, M. Pauker, E. Köblös, Aldar Imre, E. Filipovici, Alter Zalic, D. Finkelstein-Fabian, L. Lichtblau, Jaques Konitz, Moscovici Ghelber, L. Marcel, P. Zissu and others. They were rehabilitated *post mortem* in 1968. See *Plenara Comitetului Central al Partidului Comunist Român din 22–25 aprilie 1968* (Bucharest: Editura politică, 1968) p. 75.

25. E. Bodnăraş (1904–76) is undoubtedly one of the most controversial figures in the RCP history. Born in Bukovina, of German-Ukrainian origin, he served as officer in the Royal Romanian army between 1928 and 1932. The following year he defected to Soviet Russia, returning in secrecy in 1944. Bodnăraş took part in contacts with the 'historical parties' and with royal circles in 1944, served as Defence Minister between 1947 and 1956 and held prominent Party and State positions. For many years considered Russia's trustworthy agent in Romania, he none the less supported Dej's change of policies towards Moscow in the 1960s and later became one of the staunch supporters of Ceauşescu's independent policies. See Ghermani, in Grothusen, *Rumänien*, pp. 15–16.

26. See *Plenara aprilie 1968*, pp. 73–4.

27. See, for instance, Ceauşescu's speech at the November–December 1961 Central Committee plenum – *Scînteia*, 13 Dec 1961.

28. The outstanding scholar representing this interpretation is Fischer-Galaţi.

29. See particularly K. Jowitt, *Revolutionary Breakthroughs*, pp. 124–30.

30. See the decision on his rehabilitation in *Plenara aprilie 1968*, pp. 65–71.

31. See the speeches of Dej and Ceauşescu at the November–December 1961 plenum – *Scînteia*, 7 and 13 Dec 1961.

32. Lendvai, *Eagles in Cobwebs*, p. 287.

33. See A. Drăghici's speech at the November–December 1961 plenum – *Scînteia*, 15 Dec 1961, and Ionescu, *Communism in Rumania*, p. 98.

34. See I. Raţiu, *Contemporary Romania* (Richmond: Foreign Affairs Publishing, 1975) p. 9.

35. At the July 1965 Congress it was decided to rename the Party 'Communist' and to count the congresses from 1921. See below.

36. 'Breaking through', as defined by Jowitt, refers to 'the decisive alteration or destruction of structures and behaviours which are perceived by a revolutionary political elite as comprising or contributing to the actual or potential existence of alternative centres of political power' –

Revolutionary Breakthroughs, p. 7. We are told that, along with the task of political integration, 'breaking through' is part of a strategy aimed at the completion of 'nation-building' (ibid.) It is, however, highly questionable whether the concept of 'nation-building' can be applied in a situation in which 'the nation' has, for all practical purposes, already been 'built'. Perhaps 'nation-*re*building' (which implies the necessity of destroying existing national values which contradict the Party's central belief system) would be a more suitable term.

37. Indeed, in another study Jowitt defines 'transformation' exactly in the terms employed in his definition of 'breakthroughs'. See his 'An Organizational Approach to the Study of Political Culture in Marxist-Leninist Systems', *American Political Science Review*, LXVIII, no. 3 (1974) 1174.

38. According to Jowitt, Leninist political elites tend to neglect, during the first phase of their rule, the problem of transforming political culture, adopting instead a strategy of 'commanding heights' (ibid. p. 1184). Alfred G. Meyer, on the other hand, has argued that 'revolutions can be defined as conflicts between modes of consciousness (cultures), with a revolutionary elite seeking to break down the existing culture and replacing it with a new one' – 'Communist Revolutions and Cultural Change', *Studies in Comparative Communism*, v, no. 4 (1972) 360. Such efforts, I believe with Meyer, are not postponed till a later phase of development, but are part of the initial effort to change the face of societies in which communist elites rule. For further elaboration, see M. Shafir, 'Political Culture, Intellectual Dissent and Intellectual Consent: The Case of Rumania', Soviet and East European Research Centre, Research Paper no. 30, (mimeo. – Hebrew University of Jerusalem, 1978) pp. 1–9.

39. See Ionescu, *Communism in Rumania*, pp. 131–6, and V. Ierunca, 'Postface: Le Phénomène Concentrationnaire en Roumanie', in P. Goma, *Gherla* (Paris: Gallimard, 1976) p. 198.

40. See Ionescu, *Communism in Rumania*, p. 172.

41. Free Europe Committee, *Penal Laws and Justice in the Communist Regime of Rumania* (New York, 1952), as quoted in Ionescu, *Communism in Rumania*, p. 172.

42. Ionescu, *Communism in Rumania*, pp. 290–1; Ierunca, in Goma, *Gherla*, pp. 196–7.

43. Jowitt, *Revolutionary Breakthroughs*, p. 102.

44. A. G. Meyer, 'Legitimacy and Power in East Central Europe' in S. Sinanian, I. Deak and P. C. Ludz (eds), *Eastern Europe in the 1970's* (New York: Praeger, 1972) p. 56.

45. See A. G. Meyer, 'The Comparative Study of Communist Political Systems' in F. J. Fleron Jr (ed.), *Communist Studies and the Social Sciences: Essays on Methodology and Empirical Theory* (Chicago: Rand McNally, 1969) p. 192.

46. See G. Gheorghiu-Dej, *Articole și cuvîntări 1959–1961* (Bucharest: Editura politică, 1961) p. 427.

47. See text in J. F. Triska (ed.), *Constitutions of the Communist Party States* (Stanford, Calif.: The Hoover Institute, 1968) pp. 362ff. Short analyses of this document will be found in Ionescu, *Communism in Rumania*, pp. 215–18, and F. Mayer, G. H. Tontsch and I. Iovănas, 'Staat-Verfassung-Recht-

Verwaltung' in Grothusen, *Rumänien*, pp. 54–5.

48. Till her death in 1960, Pauker worked in a Bucharest publishing house. Georgescu disappeared from public life for more than two decades, and was partially rehabilitated shortly before his death. Luca, however, was sentenced to death in 1952, but the conviction was commuted to life imprisonment. He died in prison in 1960. The sentence was reversed *post mortem* in 1968.

49. For two, opposed versions of Constantinescu's purge, see S. Fischer-Galaţi, *Twentieth Century Rumania*, pp. 145–53, and K. Jowitt, *Revolutionary Breakthroughs*, pp. 172–3.

50. A lawyer by training, Maurer had acted as defence counsel in several trial of communists in the 1930s. He helped Dej escape from prison in August 1944 and became a full Central Committee member at the First RWP Congress, in 1948. Soon afterwards, however, he disappeared from political life, apparently a victim of the Pauker-Luca group. Re-emerging at the Second Congress in 1955 as a candidate Central Committee member, he was appointed Minister of Foreign Affairs in June 1957. In January 1958, following Petru Groza's death, he became Chairman of the Presidium of the GNA, i.e. titular head of State. In June 1958 Maurer was promoted to full membership of the Central Committee and two years later to the Political Bureau. As Prime Minister between 1961 and 1974, he is considered one of the main architects of the Romanian independent line.

51. See biographical note towards the end of this chapter.

52. Drăghici became a member of the Central Committee in 1948. In 1951 he became Deputy Minister of the Interior and in 1952 Minister of the Interior, a position he held till 1965. In this capacity he acted as Dej's trusted arm in the liquidation of political adversaries, the foremost of whom was Pătrăşcanu. Like Ceauşescu, he became a full member of the Political Bureau in 1955, and it is possible that their rivalry and competition for Dej's ear dated from that period.

53. For Dej's account of the campaign, see his article 'Für die Reinheit der Partei', *Für dauerhaften Frieden, für Volkdemokratie*, 23 June 1950.

54. The most detailed study of the Romanian industrialisation drive remains M. Montias, *Economic Development in Communist Rumania* (Cambridge, Mass.: MIT, 1967). See also T. Gilberg, *Modernization in Romania since World War II* (New York: Praeger, 1975) pp. 142–52; W. Gumpel, 'Die Wirtschaftssystem', in Grothusen, *Rumänien*, pp. 259–70; and R. Schönfeld, 'Industrie und gewerbliche Wirtschaft', ibid., pp. 295–322.

55. See his speech at the November–December plenum – *Scînteia*, 7 Dec 1961.

56. Jowitt, *Revolutionary Breakthroughs*, pp. 121–2.

57. See above, note 36.

58. See K. W. Deutsch, 'Social Mobilization and Political Development', *American Political Science Review*, LV (1961) 73–99.

59. See C. Johnson, 'Comparing Communist Nations', in C. Johnson (ed.), *Change in Communist Systems* (Stanford, Calif.: Stanford University Press, 1970) p. 14; and S. B. Huntington, 'Social and Institutional Dynamics of One-Party Systems', in S. B. Huntington and C. H. Moore (eds), *Politics in Modern Society: The Dynamics of One-Party Systems* (New York: Basic Books, 1970) p. 32.

60. See Z. Gitelman, 'Beyond Leninism: Political Development in Eastern

Europe', *Newsletter on Comparative Studies of Communism*, V, no. 3 (1972) 18–43.

61. Jowitt's definition of modernisation indeed stresses that the new phase requires 'a rather significant redefinition of the relationship between regime and society, from mutual hostility to the regime's selective recognition and managed acceptance of society'. Selective recognition, according to Jowitt, refers to 'the regime's willingness to expand power by allowing greater functional autonomy in various organizational settings', while managed acceptance 'refers to the regime's organizational pre-emption of social strata with recognition aspiration or demands'. In *American Political Science Review*, LXVIII, no. 3, 1174.

62. See G. E. Schmutzler, 'Die Entwicklung und Struktur der Aussen-handelsbeziehungen Rumäniens', in Grothusen, *Rumänien*, p. 369.

63. See A. Niri's critical review of V. B. Ushakov's book *The Foreign Policy of Nazi Germany*, in *Analele institutului de studii istorice al partidului*, VIII, no. 5 (1962) 179–84.

64. K. Marx, *Însemnări despre români. Manuscrise inedite*, ed. A. Oțetea and B. Schwann (Bucharest: Editura Academiei Republicii Populare Romîne, 1964).

65. See the data provided in the Party's theoretical monthly: 'Munca organizatorică la nivelul sarcinilor actuale', *Lupta de clasă*, XLIII, no. 7 (1963) 5.

66. *Scînteia*, 23 Apr 1964.

67. See *Constituția Republicii Socialiste România* (Bucharest: Editura politică, 1965). The document has been modified several times since its adoption. See Mayer, *et al.*, in Grothusen, *Rumänien*, pp. 55–7.

68. *Plenara aprilie 1968*, p. 64.

69. *Scînteia*, 19 Dec 1974.

70. These were Ceaușescu, Manea Mănescu, Deputy Prime Minister Gheorghe Oprea, Deputy Prime Minister and Minister of Foreign Trade Ion Pățan, and Central Committee secretary Ștefan Andrei. Meanwhile the attributions of the original members, as well as the composition of the Bureau, have been modified. In January 1977 the Political Executive Committee promoted to the Permanent Bureau Mrs. Ceaușescu, C. Burtică, Ilie Verdeț and Gheorghe Rădulescu. In early 1978 Paul Niculescu and Iosif Banc were also co-opted to the leading Party forum.

71. See *Free Romanian Press* (London), XII, no. 36 (1977).

72. See M. E. Fischer, 'Participatory Reforms and Political Development in Romania', in J. F. Triska and P. M. Cocks (eds), *Political Development in Eastern Europe* (New York: Praeger, 1977) pp. 217–37.

73. Mayer *et al.*, in Grothusen, *Rumänien*, p. 74.

74. Fischer, in Triska and Cocks, *Political Development*, p. 230.

75. On this aspect see M. Cismărescu, 'Die verfassungsrechtliche Entwicklung der Sozialistischen Republik Rumänien', *Jahrbuch des öffentlichen Rechts der Gegenwart*, XXIV (1975) 249ff.

76. See Mayer *et al.*, in Grothusen, *Rumänien*, pp. 160–1.

77. Ibid., p. 83.

78. *Programul Partidului Comunist Român de făurire a societății socialiste multilateral dezvoltate și înaintare a României spre comunism* (Bucharest: Editura politică, 1975) p. 111.

79. Ibid., p. 116.
80. Among such organisations are the Supreme Council for Economic Development, the Central Council of Workers' Control of Economic and Social Activity, the National Council of Romanian Radio and Television, the National Council for Science and Technology, the Council for Socialist Culture and Education, the Defence Council, and the Committee for Problems of People's Councils.
81. See M. Cismărescu, 'An Original Legal Experiment in Rumania: The Party and State Bodies', *Review of Socialist Law*, II (1976) 5–13.
82. Academia 'Ştefan Gheorghiu', *Dicţionar politic* (Bucharest: Editura politică, 1975) p. 260.
83. For a Romanian attempt to present the councils as truly representative organisations, see J. Demeter, E. Eisenburger and V. Lipatti, *Sur la Question Nationale en Roumanie: Faits et Chiffres* (Bucharest: Meridiane, 1972) pp. 58–63; and Institute of Political Sciences and of the Studying of the National Question, *The Hungarian Nationality in Romania*, pp. 10–11. See also Schöpflin, *The Hungarians of Rumania*, Minority Rights Group, Report no. 37 (London, 1978), pp. 10–15.
84. The text of Király's letters was published by the Committee for Human Rights in Romania on 30 January 1978.
85. See Schöpflin, *The Hungarians of Rumania*, pp. 12–13.
86. Academia 'Ştefan Gheorghiu', *Dicţionar politic*, p. 609.
87. Working people's councils (*consiliile oamenilor muncii*) were first created in 1968 as a form of management at enterprise and central levels. They are composed of the local Party organisation's secretary, the productive unit's director, his deputies or section directors, specialists, the chief of the local trade-union organisation, the secretary of the local cell of the Union of Communist Youth, and elected representatives of the workers.
88. See W. F. Robinson, 'Selected Demographic and Economic Data on Eastern Europe', in Radio Free Europe, *Background Report*, no. 90 (Eastern Europe) (27 Apr 1977).
89. See E. C. Suttner, 'Kirchen und Staat', in Grothusen, *Rumänien*, pp. 458–83; and Ionescu, *Communism in Rumania* pp. 180–1.
90. Decree no. 334, in *Buletinul oficial*, 15 Aug 1970.
91. Suttner, in Grothusen, *Rumänien*, p. 481.
92. Ibid., p. 476.
93. See ibid., pp. 476–8 for other persecutions and the communiqué published by the Communauté de Secours aux Eglises Martyres, Geneva, 13 Apr 1977.
94. See 'Draft Directions of the Central Committee of the Romanian Communist Party on the Perfectioning of Management and Planning of the National Economy in Keeping with the Conditions of the New Stage of Romania's Socialist Development' (Agerpres, n.d.)
95. See I. Spigler, *Economic Reform in Rumanian Industry* (London: Oxford University Press, 1973); and Gumpel, in Grothusen, *Rumänien*, pp. 270–90.
96. Spigler, *Economic Reform*, p. 34.
97. On the role and importance of the Sino-Soviet conflict for Romania, see S. Fischer-Galaţi, 'Rumania and the Sino-Soviet Conflict', in K. London, (ed.), *Eastern Europe in Transition* (Baltimore: Johns Hopkins, 1966) pp. 261–75, and 'Foreign Policy', in Grothusen, *Rumänien*, pp. 207ff.; and R.

B. King, 'Rumania and the Sino-Soviet Conflict', *Studies in Comparative Communism*, v, no. 4 (1972) 373–93.
98. See L. Zanga, 'The Albanian Letter – A Retaliatory Document', Radio Free Europe, *Background Report*, no. 178 (Albania) (11 Aug 1978).
99. See J. E. Moore (ed.), *Jane's Fighting Ships 1976–1977* (London: Jane's Yearbooks, 1976) pp. 388–9.
100. Romania welcomed the rapprochement: Secretary of State Rogers visited Bucharest in July 1972 to inform on Nixon's February trip to China.
101. See S. Fischer-Galaţi, in Grothusen, *Rumänien*, p. 227.
102. *Romanian Foreign Trade*, 1 (1978).
103. See M. Shafir, 'Rumanian Policy in the Middle East 1967–1972', Soviet and East European Research Centre, Research Paper no. 7 (mimeo. – Hebrew University of Jerusalem, 1974).
104. Unless otherwise specified, all statistics are taken from *Anuarul Statistic al Republicii Socialiste România* (Bucharest: Direcţia Centrală de Statistică, 1977).
105. Preliminary data 5–12 January 1977 census – *Scînteia*, 4 June 1977.
106. This figure does not include 1604 Szeklers, who, for the first time at the 1977 census, were offered the opportunity of returning a nationality different from Hungarian. The overwhelming majority of Szeklers a body of some 600,000–700,000 Unitarian or Calvinist Magyars – failed to do so. This new device may well indicate a new stage in the Romanian authorities' 'salami tactics' of Romanisation of the Hungarian minority. See G. Schöpflin, *The Hungarians of Rumania*, p. 6.

BIBLIOGRAPHY

Academia Republicii Populare Romîne, *Istoria Romîniei*, 4 vols (Bucharest: Editura Académiei Republicii Populare Romîne, 1960–4).
Academia 'Ştcfan Gheorghiu', *Dicţionar politic* (Bucharest: Editura politică, 1975).
Burks, R., V., 'The Rumanian National Deviation: An Accounting', in K. London, *Eastern Europe in Transition* (Baltimore: Johns Hopkins, 1966).
Ceauşescu, N., *România pe drumul desăvîrşirii construcţiei socialiste*, vols I–III (Bucharest, 1968–9).
——, *România pe drumul desăvîrşirii construirii societăţii socialiste multilateral dezvoltate*, vols IV–XV (Bucharest: Editura politică, 1970–7).
Congresul al III-lea al Partidului Muncitoresc Romîn (Bucharest: Editura de stat pentru literatură politică, 1960).
Constantinescu, M. *et al.*, *Études d'Histoire Contemporaine de la Roumanie* (Bucharest: Editions de l'Academie de la Republique Socialiste Roumaine, 2 vols, 1970–1).
Constantinescu, M., Daicoviciu, C. and Pascu, S., *Istoria României*, 2nd ed. (Bucharest: Editura didactică şi pedagogică, 1971).
Cretzianu, A., *The Lost Opportunity* (London: J. Cape, 1957).
—— (ed.), *Captive Rumania: A Decade of Soviet Rule* (London: Atlantic Press, 1956).
Demeter, J., Eisenburger, E. and Lipatti, V., *Sur la Question Nationale en Roumanie: Faits et Chiffres* (Bucharest: Editions Meridiane, 1972).
Dobrogeanu-Gherea, C., *Opere complete* (Bucharest: Editura politică, 1977).

638　　　*Marxist Governments*

Fischer, G., 'Rumania', in A. Bromke and T. Rakowska-Harmstone (eds), *The Communist States in Disarray 1965–1971* (Minneapolis: University of Minnesota Press, 1972).

Fischer, M. E., 'Participatory Reforms and Political Development in Romania', in J. F. Triska and P. M. Cocks (eds), *Political Development in Eastern Europe* (New York: Praeger, 1977).

Fischer-Galaţi, S. (ed.), *Romania* (New York: Praeger, 1957).

——, 'Rumania and the Sino-Soviet Conflict', in K. London (ed.), *Eastern Europe in Transition* (Baltimore: Johns Hopkins, 1966).

——, *The New Rumania: From People's Democracy to Socialist Republic* (Cambridge, Mass.: MIT, 1967).

——, *The Socialist Republic of Rumania* (Baltimore: Johns Hopkins, 1969).

——, *Twentieth Century Rumania* (New York: Columbia University Press, 1970).

——, 'Romanian Nationalism', in P. F. Sugar and I. J. Lederer (eds), *Nationalism in Eastern Europe*, 2nd impression (Seattle: Washington University Press, 1971).

——, 'Moldavia', in Z. Katz (ed.), *Handbook of Major Soviet Nationalities* (New York: Free Press, 1975).

——, 'The Moldavian Soviet Republic in Soviet Domestic and Foreign Policy', in R. Szporluk (ed.), *The Influence of East Europe and the Soviet West on the USSR* (New York: Praeger, 1975).

Floyd, D., *Rumania: Russia's Dissident Ally* (New York: Praeger, 1965).

Gheorghiu-Dej, G., *Articole şi cuvîntări* (Bucharest: Editura pentru literatură politică, 1952).

——, *Raportul de activitate al Comitetului Central al Partidului Muncitoresc Romîn la Congresul al II-lea al Partidului* (Bucharest: Editura de stat pentru literatură politică, 1956).

——, *Articole şi cuvîntări 1959–1961* (Bucharest: Editura politică, 1961).

Ghermani, D., *Die kommunistische Umdeutung der rumänischen Geschischte unter besonderer Berücksichtigung des Mittelalters* (Munich: Oldenbourg, 1967).

Gilberg, T., *Modernization in Romania Since World War II* (New York: Praeger, 1975).

Giurescu, C. C., *The Making of the Romanian Unitary State* (Bucharest: Meridiane Publishing House, 1975).

Giurescu, C. C. and Giurescu, D. C., *Istoria Românilor* (Bucharest: Editura Albatros, 1971).

Grothusen, K. D. (ed.), *Rumänien* (Göttingen: Vandenhoeck & Ruprecht, 1977).

Institute of Political Sciences and of Studying the National Question, *The Hungarian Nationality in Romania* (Bucharest: Meridiane Publishing House, 1976).

Institutul de Istorie a Partidului de pe Lîngă CC al PCR, *Mişcarea muncitorească din România 1893–1900* (Bucharest: Editura politică, 1965).

Institutul de Studii Istorice şi Social-politice de pe Lîngă CC al PCR, *Presa muncitorească si şi socialistă din România*, 4 vols (Bucharest: Editura politică, 1964–71).

——, *Documente din istoria mişcării muncitoreşti din Romănia 1893–1900* (Bucharest: Editura politică, 1969).

Ionescu, G., *Communism in Rumania 1944–1962* (London: Oxford University Press, 1964).

Jowitt, K., *Revolutionary Breakthroughs and National Development: The Case of Rumania 1944–1965* (Berkeley, Calif.: University of California Press, 1971).

King, R. B., *Minorities under Communism: Nationalities as a Source of Tension among Balkan Communist States* (Cambridge, Mass.: Harvard University Press, 1973).

Lee, A. G., *Crown against Sickle: The Story of King Michael of Rumania*, 2nd ed. (London, 1955).

Lendvai, P., *Eagles in Cobwebs: Nationalism and Communism in the Balkans* (London: MacDonald, 1970).

Montias, M., *Economic Development in Communist Rumania* (Cambridge, Mass.: MIT, 1967).

Muşat, M. and Ardeleanu, I., *Viaţa Politică în România 1918–1921*, 2nd ed. (Bucharest: Editura politică, 1976).

Oţetea, A. (ed.), *Istoria Poporului român* (Bucharest: Editura ştiintifică, 1970).

Pătrăşcanu, L., *Un veac de frămîntări sociale 1821–1907* (Bucharest: Editura politică, 1969).

——, *Sub trei dictaturi* (Bucharest: Editura politică, 1970).

——, *Curente şi tendinţe în filozofia românească* (Bucharest: Editura politică, 1971).

Petrescu, T., *Socialismul in România* (Bucharest: Biblioteca Socialistă, n.d.).

Plenara Comitetului Central al Partidului Comunist Român din 22–25 aprilie 1968 (Bucharest: Editura politică, 1968).

Programul Partidului Comunist Român de făurire a societăţii socialiste multilateral dezvoltate şi înaintare a României spre comunism (Bucharest: Editura politică, 1975).

Remington, R. A., *The Warsaw Pact: Case Studies in Communist Conflict Resolution* (Cambridge, Mass.: MIT, 1971).

Roberts, H. L., *Rumania: Political Problems of an Agrarian State*, 2nd ed. Archon Books, 1969).

Rura, M., *Reinterpretation of History as a Method of Furthering Communism in Rumania: A Study in Comparative Historiography* (Washington, DC: Georgetown University Press, 1961).

Schöpflin, G., 'Rumanian Nationalism', *Survey*, xx, nos 2–3 (1974) 77–104.

——, *The Hungarians of Rumania*, Minority Rights Group Report no. 37 (London, 1978).

Shafir, M. 'Die Bukarester Nahostpolitik', *Wissenschaftlicher Dienst Südosteuropa*, xxii, nos 11–12 (1973) 173–9.

——, 'Rumanian Policy in the Middle East 1967–1972', Soviet and East European Research Centre, Research Paper no. 7 (mimeo. – Hebrew University of Jerusalem, 1974).

——, 'Who is Paul Goma?', *Index on Censorship*, vii, no. 1 (1978) 29–39.

——, 'Political Culture, Intellectual Dissent and Intellectual Consent: The Case of Rumania', Soviet and East European Research Centre, Research Paper no. 30 (mimeo. – Hebrew University of Jerusalem, 1978).

Spigler, I., *Economic Reform in Rumanian Industry* (London: Oxford University Press, 1973).

Turnock, D., *An Economic Geography of Romania* (London: G. Bell, 1974).

Vago, B., 'Romania', in M. McCauley (ed.), *Communist Power in Europe 1944–1949* (London: Macmillan, 1977).

22 Somali Democratic Republic

IOAN LEWIS

Lying in the extreme north-eastern corner of the Horn of Africa, the Somali Democratic Republic was formed in 1960 by the union – on their attainment of independence from colonial rule – of the former British Somaliland Protectorate and Italian-administered United Nations trust territory of Somalia. The resulting Somali Republic (as it was known until the military coup of 1969) was based on the principle of national self-determination applied to these two divisions of the Somali people, leaving three neighbouring parts of the nation still under alien rule in French Somaliland (later called the Territory of the Afars and Isas), in eastern Ethiopia (the Ogaden and adjacent areas, regarded by Somalis as 'western Somalia') and in north-eastern Kenya. In this incomplete nation state, created prior to Kenya's independence, there was a strong presumption that as colonial rule receded in response to the independence struggle, the remaining three Somali communities would gain autonomy and join the Republic, with the resulting expanded state embracing the whole nation. This aim was enshrined in the Somali Republic's constitution and symbolised in the five-pointed star on the national flag. A bitter guerrilla campaign in north-eastern Kenya (1962–7) and full-scale war in the Ogaden (1977–8) failed to achieve this aim, while the former French Somaliland became independent under the name of Jibuti in June 1977 without joining the Republic.

Today an estimated 3·5 million Somalis live in the Somali Democratic Republic, while the remaining 1·5 million ethnic Somalis are distributed in eastern Ethiopia (750,000 to 1 million), the north-eastern region of Kenya (250,000) and Jibuti (approximately 100,000), which they share with the Afars, who like the Somalis are Cushitic-speaking Moslems living mainly as pastoral nomads. While the Somalis are sharply distinguished from the Christian and Semitic-speaking Amharas, who

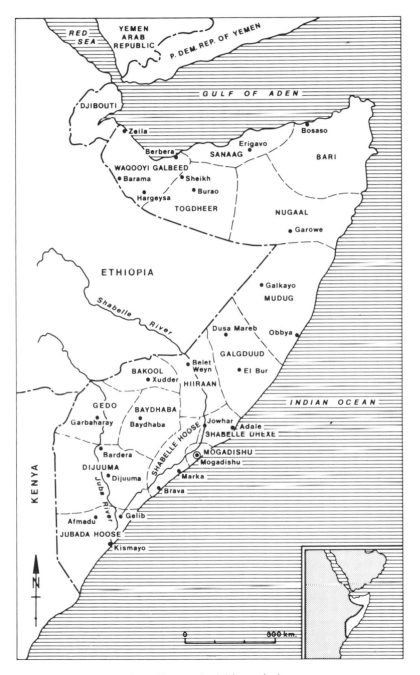

Somalia: provincial boundaries

have held a monopoly of power in Ethiopia for generations, they are quite closely related to the Cushitic-speaking Oromo (formerly known by the derogative title 'Galla') and particularly the Moslem Arussi branch of the nation in Bali province, neighbouring the Ogaden. This affinity is reflected in the close alliance between the Arussi Somali Abo Liberation Front,[1] fighting against the Ethiopian central government in Bali, and the Western Somali Liberation Front in the Ogaden. The Oromo, with a population estimated at 12 million, are at least twice as numerous as the Amhara and form the largest ethnic group in the multinational Ethiopian conquest state. Ethiopia achieved its maximum extent under the forceful rule of Emperor Menelik, whose armies began to impose Amhara rule in the Ogaden and Somali areas surrounding the ancient Islamic citadel of Harar (seized in 1886) at the end of the nineteenth century, at the height of the European scramble for influence in the Horn of Africa. At this time the principal rivals were France and Britain, competing for control of the Nile. In this contest Britain used Italy as a convenient ally, while France made similar use of Russia, whose ambitions towards Ethiopia were advanced under the banner of the Orthodox Church.[2] After the Ethiopian defeat of the Italians at the battle of Adowa in 1896, the remaining European powers with interests in the area saw the necessity of coming to terms with Ethiopia. Menelik considered it prudent to concede the coast to the French, British and Italians (Russia had dropped out of the game) while gaining European recognition for his recent conquests amongst the Cushitic-speaking peoples and other tribesmen. It was this that led to the fivefold division of the Somali people, who formed a culturally distinct congeries of clans and tribes rather than a unified state. It was against this multiple Christian colonisation by Ethiopia, France, Britain and Italy that the fiery Somali sheikh Mohamed Abdille Hassan proclaimed his 'holy war' to liberate his compatriots from 'infidel' domination. The ensuing guerrilla campaign, which lasted from 1900 to 1920, ironically ended with the foreign rulers more firmly and deeply entrenched in Somali territory than they had been at the outset.

Modern Somali nationalism developed strongly during the Second World War, when, following the Italian defeat in East Africa, the whole region came under British military administration. When the issue of the future status of the former Italian colonies (Libya, Eritrea and Somalia) was debated first by the Big Four powers and later by the United Nations, Britain unsuccessfully proposed the formation of a 'Greater Somalia' to include British, Italian and Ethiopian Somali territories. Instead Somalia was transformed into a United Nations trust territory and Italy returned to administer it with a ten-year mandate to independence. The formation of the Somali Republic in 1960 by the union of ex-Italian Somalia and the British Somaliland Protectorate followed naturally from these earlier events. It left, as has been emphasised, an incomplete state containing only part of the nation on which it was based. The unsolved problem posed by Somali 'irredentism' was further aggravated by the opposed expansionist dynamic enshrined in the neighbouring conquest state of Ethiopia. The fact that one side was Moslem and the other Christian and that both had traditions of centuries of conflict[3] added to the intractable nature of the issue. This brief historical background is indispensable for an understanding of recent developments under the banner of socialism in an area where nationalism remains the most powerful ideology.

THE PRE-REVOLUTIONARY STATE

From its creation in 1960 to the military coup staged in 1969, the Somali Republic had a succession of civilian governments elected by universal suffrage. The dominant party was the Somali Youth League, a progressive nationalist organisation, which had originated as a youth club in 1943. In common with its smaller rivals, this party was inevitably in practice a consortium of competing clan and clan segment interests. The majority of the population were pastoral nomads with a deeply entrenched attachment to their clan divisions, which constituted their traditional political structure and guaranteed the security of life and prosperity of individual members.[4] Crucial and closely related institutions here were the blood feud and blood compensation, valued in camels and paid not on an individual but on a group basis. The development of a strong nationalist movement and of an extremely lively parliamentary democracy did little to change these traditional allegiances, which remained the fundamental basis of co-operation in politics and of all aspects of government and administration. Clan nepotism became, inevitably, a deeply entrenched phenomenon, tending both to weaken governments and to lead to appointments and preferments in the civil service, where family ties counted for more than education and ability. Governments were formed on a tacit principle of clan balance, all the major lineage blocs, or clan confederations, being allocated at least one minister (see Table 22.1). Some indication of the growing tension between transcendent nationalist aims and local clan realities can be gained from a revealing practice which developed during

TABLE 22.1 Composition of Somali governments[a] by major lineage blocs, 1960—75

	1960[b]	1966[c]	1967[d]	1969[e]	1975[f]
Darod	6	6	6	6	10
Hawiye	4	3	4	5	4
Digil and Rahanweyn	2	3	3	2	0
Dir	0	1	1	0	2
Isaq	2	3	4	5	4
Total	14	16	18	18	20

[a] Only Cabinet ministers, and, after 1969, members of the Supreme Revolutionary Council, are included here. The Somali nation as a whole comprises the five major lineage blocs [or 'clan families', as I have called them in previous publications: see I. M. Lewis, *A Pastoral Democracy* (1961)], whose representation in successive Somali governments is shown in the table.

[b] The first administration of Somalia formed after independence in 1960, headed by Premier 'Abd ar-Rashid 'Ali Shirmarke (Darod). The President and non-executive head of State was Adan 'Abdulle Isman (Hawiye).

[c] Government formed under the leadership of 'Abd ar-Razaq Haji Husseyn (Darod), Adan 'Abdulle Isman remaining President of the Republic.

[d] Government formed by Muhammad Haji Ibrahim Igal (Isaq) from the northern (ex-British) regions of the Republic. Dr 'Abd ar-Rashid 'Ali Shirmarke (Darod) had now become President.

[e] Second government formed by Muhammad Haji Ibrahim Igal following March 1969 elections, Dr 'Abd ar-Rashid 'Ali Shirmarke remaining President.

[f] Supreme Revolutionary Council as of 1975, following various changes in composition since the military coup of October 1969. The Council was officially dissolved in July 1976 with the formation of the Somali Socialist Revolutionary Party. This had a Central Committee of seventy-three members and a political Bureau of five (see Table 22.2), presided over by the head of State and Party Chairman, General Mohamed Siyad Barre.

the early years of the parliamentary democratic period. This involved the adoption into standard Somali speech of the Latin prefix 'ex' to denote clans and their divisions. Instead of speaking in the embarrassingly direct terms of clan divisions and loyalties, it became fashionable among the Westernised elite to speak of 'ex-clans'. It was thus possible to talk about the political realities of the present as though they existed only in the past. Thus the troubling 'problem of tribalism' was solved, ostensibly at least, by an ingenious trick of language.

Apart from thus distributing resources amongst the competing clans, whose parliamentary representatives were expected to be active in promoting clan interests, the main internal problem in the first years of independence was that of amalgamating the separate and often conflicting Italian and English colonial traditions. By 1964 the mechanics of integrating the civil service, the judiciary and education had largely been achieved, with more success than might have been expected. Internal cohesion was fostered by an increasingly aggressive pursuit of the pan-Somali issue. When Britain announced in the spring of 1963 that, contrary to the findings of the commission of inquiry that it had established, the Somali populations of northern Kenya would not be allowed independence separately from the rest of Kenya, the Somali Republic broke off relations with the United Kingdom. Clandestine support was consequently given to the ensuing Somali nationalist guerrilla movement in northern Kenya. At the same time, the long train of border incidents with Ethiopia had by 1964 escalated into a brief outbreak of open war between the two states. It was in this context that a generally pro-Western, if officially neutralist, Somali government rejected an offer of Western military assistance in favour of a large Soviet package. This was largely a matter of expediency and had no ideological significance. The Somali government of the time, led by a man with a reputation for conservative religious views, simply reasoned that, since its major opponents, Ethiopia and Kenya, were dependent on Western military support, it would be unwise to rely on the same source.

A change of President (by the constitutional method of election in the National Assembly) and a change of government in 1967 led to a shift of policy on the pan-Somali issue. The new Prime Minister, a northerner from the ex-British Protectorate, embarked on an active policy of detente with Kenya and Ethiopia. The north-eastern Kenya Somalia guerrilla war fizzled out, diplomatic relations with Britain were restored, and Somalia assumed a less isolated position on the OAU stage, where the sensitivity of member states on the inviolability of frontiers had generated a hostile reaction to the pan-Somali case. However realistic this new accommodation might have been, it gave the Prime Minister's enemies ammunition for criticism at home. However, in Somalia's last general election, held in March 1969, the government party was returned to power with substantially increased support. Some sixty-two parties, mainly thinly disguised clan organisations, fielded over 1000 candidates for the 124 seats in the Assembly. This anarchic situation, which indicated the continuing strength of parochial kinship loyalties, was followed by an increasingly despotic style of government and an alarming increase in nepotism and corruption. There was no longer any effective parliamentary opposition – except inside the government party. Matters were brought to a head by the assassination of the

President on 15 October 1969. The Prime Minister, who was out of the country at the time, returned precipitately to Somalia to secure the election of a new president who would reappoint him as Premier. When it became clear that this outcome was imminent, the Army, in the early hours of 21 October, just before the formal election of the new president, seized power in a smoothly executed and bloodless coup. Ministers and other leading figures (including the influential former police chief) were placed in detention or under house arrest, the Constitution was suspended, the Supreme Court abolished, the National Assembly closed, and political parties were banned. The country was thenceforth to be ruled by a Supreme Revolutionary Council (SRC) composed of military and police officers and chaired by the existing Army commander, General Mohamed Siyad Barre.

THE SOMALI REVOLUTION

Unlike its later Ethiopian counterpart, the twenty-five-man SRC, presided over by General Siyad, consisted solely of officers from the rank of captain to that of general, and with a noticeable thinning at the level of colonel, where, significantly, much of the impetus for the *coup d'état* had originated. The inclusion of senior police officers signalled their acquiescence rather than active participation in the coup, and imported a minor element of tension. This reflected a certain rivalry between the two forces, sharpened by the dependence of the police on Western equipment and the Army's growing reliance on the Soviet Union. Execution of the policies decided by the SRC was entrusted to a fourteen-member Committee of Secretaries, whose members possessed quasi-ministerial functions and were all, save one, civilians. With considerable initial public support, the new regime got down to business, seeking to apply military discipline and efficiency to the country's basic problems: poverty, disease and underdevelopment. Civilian district and provincial governors were replaced throughout the country by military personnel, who were installed as chairmen of local revolutionary councils modelled on the SRC.

In the same way as previous civilian governments had been non-aligned but in effect pro-West, the new leaders, following the direction of their arms supply, inclined to the Eastern bloc. The official commitment of the State to scientific (in Somali literally 'wealth-sharing based on wisdom') socialism was announced on the first anniversary of the coup, in October 1970. Under this banner, with the aid of a small radical intelligentsia, national campaigns and 'crash programmes' were inaugurated against corruption and tribalism, and effigies representing these archaic evil forces were burnt at official ceremonies early in 1971. In the same spirit, official clan chiefs and elders were renamed 'peace seekers'. The rallying cries of 'self-help',[5] 'self-reliance' and 'unity' were invoked to galvanise public energies in a concerted effort to achieve real progress. The term *jaalle*, meaning 'comrade' or 'friend', was thrust into circulation to replace the traditional greeting 'cousin' or 'uncle', which, because of its divisive clan connotation, was no longer acceptable. Locally based people's vigilants (the Victory Pioneers) were recruited from amongst the un- and under-employed to organise community development projects. Destitute children and orphan street boys were herded into revolutionary youth centres, where they were clothed, fed, and educated in the new revolutionary ideals. The same values were inculcated, along with military discipline, at the National Orientation Centre and former military academy (renamed 'Halane', after a Somali lieutenant who had died in the 1964 Somali–Ethiopian fighting) in Mogadishu.

Under the vigilant direction of the Ministry of Information and National Guidance, a national cult, blending Chinese, North Korean and Nasserite as well as Soviet influence, was created round the head of State as benevolent 'Father' of a nation whose 'Mother' was the 'Glorious Revolution'. This cult of the President was elaborated by the publication of pithy extracts from his speeches and sayings, printed in the propagandist official paper, *October Star*, and by radio programmes, which carefully syncretised these and Marxist themes with Moslem motifs. The political office of the Presidency was expanded into a national organisation of apparatchiks to staff local orientation centres, set up in all major settlements.

In large towns these new developments were depicted on crude posters, and the walls of orientation centres were adorned with the new trinity: Jaalle *Markis* (Marx), Jaale Lenin and Jaalle Siyad. The maintenance of these revolutionary ideals was reinforced by two powerful ancillary organisations: the National Security Service – with arbitrary powers of arrest and detention – and the National Security courts, which, dispensing with legal safeguards on individual liberty, dealt out a somewhat rough justice.

Official rhetoric stressed the two-way system of communication that the 'Victorious Leader', President Siyad, sought to establish with his subjects through this elaborate apparatus connecting the rural population to the central authorities. If, however, it was clear that it seemed better to disseminate instructions downwards from the top, rather than suggestions upwards from the bottom, the nomadic population still remained a recalcitrant and far from easily controlled force. Clan and kinship ties – 'tribalism' in its special Somali form – moreover, obstinately refused to wither away. In a further effort to grapple with this problem, rooted in the nomadic way of life, the State's eight provinces were reconstituted in 1974 as fifteen regions (see map accompanying this chapter), renamed, where necessary, to eliminate clan associations. Renewed emphasis was placed on the settlement as the basic unit of association; and, in a further endeavour to stamp out lingering lineage loyalties, people were requested to abandon their traditional tribal weddings in favour of ceremonies conducted at orientation centres. Despite these concerted attempts to transform the traditional social structure of a predominantly nomadic people, outside the few urban centres the pastoralists remained little affected by developments that in fact touched them only spasmodically and fleetingly. Much of the structure described remained a cosmetic surface phenomenon, and it is thus not surprising that a Marxist Polish critic should have described Somali socialism as 'an industry for power'.[6]

SOCIALISM AND THE ECONOMY

Further evidence for this view might be cited from the regime's policy in economic matters. The main export product continued to be livestock and livestock produce from the pastoral economy. Livestock on the hoof and other animal products were bought and sold directly by private entrepreneurs and shipped to the Arabian Gulf. Some meat, it is true, found its way to the Russian-built State-owned meat-processing factory at Kismayu. Hides and skins from the same source were mainly marketed and exported through a government agency. The banana crop, the other main export product, was grown on a variety of plantations – mostly privately owned – and sold through an official board. Farmers, mainly in the relatively fertile land between the Shebelle and Juba rivers in southern Somalia, were obliged to sell the bulk of their grain crop to the Agricultural Development Agency, which stored it and later distributed it to retailers or purchasers via orientation centres. Imported goods were likewise handled primarily by a State agency. The main government enterprises in this essentially agricultural country were meat and fish canneries and a sugar-processing plant. The existence of these State-run organisations, as well as State farms, drawing their work force partly from prisons, left ample scope for private enterprises, even if these often found it convenient to disguise themselves as co-operatives.

Alongside this in practice mixed economy, SRC's revolutionary ideals were pursued through a succession of national 'crash programmes' launched by the President with full military honours. The most impressive of these were the urban and rural mass literacy campaigns of 1973 and 1974. No previous government had been sufficiently confident of its position to resolve the delicate issue of choosing between the rival scripts proposed for Somali. Arabic, although technically less suitable than the Roman script, enjoyed wide religious support, while other Somalis favoured Somali-invented script. President Siyad's regime took the bold and sensible decision of adopting the Latin script, which, whatever its secular implications, was the most convenient written medium for the national language. In the 1973 urban campaign, officials were given courses which they were obliged to pass if they were to retain their posts. Adult literacy classes proved popular, and in the summer of 1974 the more ambitious rural mass literacy campaign, aimed at the nomads, was launched. Literacy here was part of a wide development package, containing hygiene, civic and veterinary components, designed to share the fruits of the revolution with the neglected nomads. This grandiose campaign involving 30,000 secondary-school student 'volunteers' and teachers happened, unfortunately, to coincide with one of the worst droughts in Somali history. What began as the 'Rural Prosperity Programme' was thus transformed into a desperate relief operation in which the urgent needs of a quarter of a million destitute nomads had to be met. Advantage was taken of the situation to settle these famine-stricken pastoralists in three huge settlement schemes (effectively State farms) and in a larger number of smaller fishing co-operatives along the coast. It was in such practical measures as these that scientific socialism might be seen in operation in Somalia.

The Party

Especially after the signature of the Somali–Soviet treaty of friendship signed in July 1974, the Somali regime seems to have been under powerful pressure to adopt a civilian party structure, based on the Soviet model. In the same year Somalia had joined the Arab League, partly to gain leverage in her increasingly binding relationship with Russia, and had acted as host to the OAU under President Siyad's chairmanship. It was not, however, until June 1976 that the Party was launched, in the wake of the successful response to the 1975 drought. The Somali Socialist Revolutionary Party, as it was called, was equipped with a widely representative seventy-three-man Supreme Council (replacing the former military SRC). The Central Committee, presided over by the State President, Party Secretary and Chairman of the Council of Ministers, Jaalle Mohamed Siyad Barre, included all the members of the former SRC plus nineteen others, not exclusively military personnel. Each member of the Central Committee held responsibility for a particular government department. Separate government ministers (all, with one exception, members of the Central Party Committee) were appointed to exercise authority in co-ordination with the Party bureaux. An interesting development here was the abolition of the Ministry of the Interior and its replacement by a Ministry of Local Government and Rural Development. The central offices of the Party comprised fifteen departments. The key Political Bureau (see Table 22.2) had five members: the President, the three Vice-presidents, and the head of the National Security Service; all were military officers (see Figure 22.1 for a diagram of central Party structure.)

TABLE 22.2 Political Bureau of the Somali Socialist Revolutionary Party

President of the Republic and Party Chairman	Major-General Mohamed Siyad Barre
Vice-President and Minister of Defence	Lieutenant-general Mohamed Ali Samatar
Vice-President and Assistant to the President for Presidential Affairs	Major-general Hussein Kulmiye Afrah
Vice-President and Assistant to the Chairman for Party Affairs	Brigadier-general Ismail Ali Abokar
Member and Head of the National Security Service	Brigadier-general Ahmed Suleman Abdulle

As formerly the central SRC structure had been replicated at regional and district level by corresponding councils, so now these administrative units came under the authority of corresponding local Party committees. The posts of regional governor (or district governor) and regional party secretary (or district secretary) merged, this key official being aided by a first assistant for Party affairs and a second assistant for administrative affairs. In residential areas or in centres with work forces, Party 'cells' and 'units' were formed. A cell consists of one or two Party

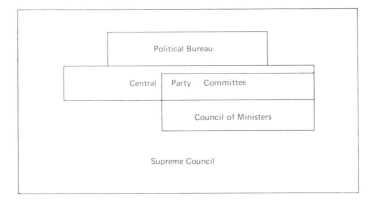

FIGURE 22.1 Central structure of the Somali Socialist Revolutionary Party

members; a unit is formed by three or more members; when it has fifty-one or more members, it elects a member committee, with a secretary and assistant and with three branches dealing with organisational, ideological and secretariat matters, respectively. Centrally organised seminars are regularly held for district and regional Party officials and branch secretaries.

There are three 'mass' social organisations: the General Confederation of Somali Trade Unions (GCSTU); the Somali Revolutionary Youth Union; and the Somali Democratic Women's Organisation. These predate the Party, and GCSTU and Women's Organisation have action programmes as well as constitutions. Each organisation has a central committee, secretariat and central inspectorate. All are most active in urban centres and least active in rural areas, where there are often no local representatives or members. Membership of the GCSTU is, at least in theory, compulsory for all workers. In 1977, out of a total work force officially recorded at 260,000, the GCSTU had 147,000 members – mostly State employees.[7] The three mass organisations hold local and national conferences and training programmes, the effectiveness of which is limited by the shortage of trained cadres and inaccessibility of the mobile nomadic population.

In this vastly expended complex structure there were certainly more civilians in senior positions, but power still lay ultimately in the hands of the small military oligarchy which had ruled Somalia since 1969: the President and his vice-presidential amanuenses. The formation of the

Party simply provided a wider framework for the existing power structure. Despite all the rhetoric that had been directed against tribalism and the policies designed to eliminate it, Siyad's regime was in fact based on a stout framework of traditional clan allegiances. The key group was his own clan, the Marrehan, members of which were entrusted with various delicate positions. Power was shared with two other clans: that of the President's mother – the powerful Ogaden, from whom the disputed area in eastern Ethiopia (western Somalia) takes its name; and that of the President's son-in-law and commander of the National Security Service. This clan, the Dulbahante, was also especially significant in that, straddling the old boundary separating the former British and Italian Somali territories, it formed a natural bridge linking these two parts of the state. Although it would have been risking imprisonment to refer openly to this triple power base in the Siyad regime, it was, of course, public knowledge and widely debated and criticised in private. This gave rise to a new series of political circumlocutions, by which, in an atmosphere where tribalism was officially dead, the President's clan was referred to indirectly as '21 October', his mother's as '22 October' and his son-in-law's as '23 October'. Later developments associated with the 1977–8 Ogaden conflict led, as we shall see, to a further entrenchment of the President's clan ties. They, far more than any organ of the Party, held the key to Siyad's power in Somalia. The Party, with its labyrinthine committees, remained a surface phenomenon, providing prestigious positions for some of the younger, more ideologically oriented members of the Somali intelligentsia who had not already sought refuge outside Somalia – in Kenya, the Arab states or elsewhere.[8] By 1978 the Party officially claimed 20,000 members in a population of some 3.5 millions. The Central Committee was less a genuine parliament than a sounding board for the President's plans. Ironically, its most momentous decision to date was that taken on 13 November 1977, when, provoked by Russia's massive military assistance to Ethiopia (a direct violation of the Somali–Soviet friendship treaty), Somalia expelled the 6000 Russians in the country and withdrew all their military facilities.[9] Thus, the organisation which the Russians had pressed on their Somali clients formally annulled the Somali–Soviet entente; and the Russians who had, in effect, come in with the Ogaden issue, went out with it.

ISLAM AND FOREIGN POLICY

The Russian rupture demonstrated the pervasive force of Somali nationalism, which had been significantly enhanced by written Somali. Despite considerable Russian and Cuban diplomacy directed at finding a solution to the Ogaden problem through a federal arrangement between neighbouring socialist states, neither the Somali nor Ethiopian leaders showed any enthusiasm for this. As so often elsewhere, socialism had ultimately to bow to the prior claims of nationalism, and a similar tension and order of priorities existed with Islam.

Commitment to socialism did not supersede allegiance to the Moslem faith, which, in its ideal form at least, was essentially socialist in spirit. As President Siyad declared shortly after seizing power,

> Our Islamic faith teaches us that its inherent values are perennial and continually evolving as people progress. These basic tenets of our religion must be interpreted not in a static sense, but rather as a dynamic source of inspiration for continuous advancement. . . . To help our brethren and our fellows, we must go beyond the concept of charity and reach the higher and more altruistic concept of co-operation on a national scale. We must strive with enthusiasm and patriotism to attain the highest possible state of general welfare for all.

And, as General Siyad pointed out in a speech directed at young secular radicals, 'The founders of scientific socialism were not against religion in particular but they exposed and disproved the reactionary elements of religion that dominate [the] sound reasoning of mankind and hence hinder [the] progress of society.' This, as the President was repeatedly to insist, did not entail abandoning belief in the divinity of God, since, unlike Islam, socialism was not 'a heavenly message' but merely a way of regulating the relations between men and productive resources. Scientific socialism was thus simply a means to an end, and not an end in itself. As a young Somali intellectual put it in a heated conversation with a well-known French Marxist anthropologist, 'We don't need Marx: Marx needs us!'

This endeavour to root the new socialist path in the Islamic tradition reflected internal and external developments and tensions. Conservative Islamic opinion inside Somalia and outside it in the Arab League had grave reservations about this marriage between Marx and the Prophet Mohamed. These doubts often crystallised in concrete issues – as for instance, in the reaction to the Somali government's liberalisation of family law, giving women the same inheritance rights as men. The implementation of these new measures as the Somali contribution to Women's Year in 1975 provoked a traditionalist gut reaction led by a small group of sheikhs who accused the government of heresy. The public execution of these reactionary religious figures startled public opinion and provoked hostile reactions in the conservative Arab states on which Somalia was becoming more and more dependent for financial aid. These increased their pressure on the Somalis to sever or reduce their links with Russia. It was, however, as we have seen, not Arab pressure, nor even an internal conservative Islamic backlash, that produced this result, but the force of pan-Somali nationalism in the context of the western Somali struggle for independence from Ethiopian rule.

Up till 1974, Siyad's regime concentrated primarily on internal problems – consolidating its position within Somalia and ostentatiously promoting development. Siyad's chairmanship of the OAU in 1974 presented an opportunity for a more thrusting foreign policy. Here, partly inspired by and at the expense of the Sudan, the line taken was that Somalia was the 'natural' bridge between Arab North Africa and Black sub-Sahara Africa. With this general orientation, conveniently accommodating entry to the Arab League, Somalia loudly espoused the cause of the liberation movements struggling to gain independence in the few remaining territories still under colonial rule. Here the OAU context, which recognised white but not black imperialism (as in Ethiopia), made the continuing French presence in Jibuti the most obvious target. Elections in the French Territory of the Afars and Issas (as it was then called) in November 1974 demonstrated the strength of official, French-supported Afar dominance at the expense of the rival Somali community. This led to a powerful Somali backlash, which with diplomatic support from the Somali Republic gradually redressed the balance. Without going into details,[10] after much local political upheaval, to which events in Ethiopia contributed, the territory finally became independent in June 1977 under a Somali President and Afar Prime Minister.

A few days before this, the vital railway connection between Jibuti and Addis Ababa had been blown up by Somali guerrilla forces (with, perhaps, some Afar support) as the Western Somali Liberation Front (WSLF)[11] swung into action in the Ogaden and surrounding Somali regions. Existing under this name since 1975, but with roots going back to the first days of Ethiopian colonisation in 1900, the Front's pressure on the Siyad regime for support had become irrepressible as disorder and chaos spread through Ethiopia in the wake of Emperor Haile Selassie's overthrow in September 1974. When, in the spring of 1977, it became clear that Russia was moving into the power vacuum left in Ethiopia by the American withdrawal, the Somalis judged that they had to act at once if they were not to miss a golden opportunity. The ensuing campaign, with dramatic if bitterly short-lived success, gained much from the parallel insurgent movement amongst the ethnically related and Moslem Arussi division of the Oromo (Galla) people – a movement that from 1976 went under the banner of the 'Somali Abo Liberation Front', a name emphasising the close religious and ethnic links between the two peoples. Without going into details here,[12] by November WSLF forces (unofficially supported by units of the Somali Republic's army) had successfully liberated the Ogaden and were strongly attacking the Ethiopian defences in the ancient Islamic city of Harar. The speed with which the Somali forces were able to evict the occupying Ethiopians reflected the unanimous support of the local population in this ethnically totally Somali area (named Ogaden after a local Somali clan) and the low morale of the Ethiopians, who could scarcely be blamed if they did not share the enthusiasm that their new military dictator, Mengistu, displayed for the region.

The Somali victory and Ethiopian humiliation were, however, short-lived, and here super-power strategy proved decisive. Having become involved in Ethiopia, the Soviet Union and her satellites (including Cuba, the GDR and so on) proceeded to shore up Mengistu's disintegrating polity. The situation evoked an unusual pattern of alliances, in which, in addition to the military support of the Eastern bloc, crucial contributions came from Libya, South Yemen and Ethiopia's old ally, Israel. Since, as colonial creations, most African states shared Ethiopia's character as a loose assemblage of ethnic groups defined most unambiguously by her boundaries, the Ethiopian view of the Somalis as aggressors was widely accepted. The Russians and Cubans, indeed, claimed to be defending the Ethiopian revolution and the integrity of an African state threatened by external attack. In these circumstances, Western states were extremely reluctant to respond to the Somali clamour for urgent military aid, and limited their contribution to exhortations to Russia and Cuba not to exploit African internal problems, warning that Western countries could not remain indifferent to the growing Russo-Cuban presence in Africa. More specifically, in March 1978, once the massive Cuban- and Yemeni-stiffened Ethiopian counter-attack had got under way, the United States provided a face-saving formula which enabled Somalia, which had now officially entered the war, to withdraw her troops from the Ogaden in return for an assurance that the Ethiopian reconquest would stop at the Republic's frontier.

THE AFTERMATH OF THE OGADEN WAR

The expulsion of the Russians when nationalist feelings and fortunes were in the ascendant was immensely popular. In the wake of the Ethiopian victory in the Ogaden, this super-power vacuum added to Somalia's internal problems. These were multiple: there was bitter recrimination on all sides on the conduct of the war, and a great upsurge of divisive tribal loyalties, which had been suppressed during the Ogaden struggle. Paradoxically, the great influx of foreign aid for civilian projects, mainly now from Western and Arab sources and in some cases a direct substitute for the military aid still so ardently requested, added to the country's internal dissensions. It was thus not surprising that units of the armed forces attempted in April to overthrow President Siyad. However, although there was widespread criticism of the President's regime, the attempted coup was poorly organised and was too closely identified with one particular clan to capture this potential national support. Fighting was in fact limited mainly to skirmishes on the outskirts of the capital, Mogadishu, and the dissident forces were quickly overcome by troops loyal to the President. The President's reaction was predictable: the ringleaders and other suspects were arrested, and a number of changes were made in key posts. These changes had the effect of further entrenching the hegemony of the President's own clan, both directly and, through the appointment of people from neutral or weak groups in the traditional clan structure, indirectly. In thus taking advantage of the new upsurge of clan rivalry to consolidate his own, unenviably vulnerable position, President Siyad was aided by the extraordinarily injudicious overtures made by some of the April coup leaders to the Ethiopian regime.

These expedients, of course, did not solve the more basic problem of recovering some of the public support which he had lost. Here the President continued his desperate search for Western military support, visiting Scandinavia, Italy and Belgium in September 1978, while developing new measures at home. It was difficult to know whether putting all the director-generals of ministries and government agencies on a five-month course at Halane was to be interpreted as a defensive measure after the abortive April coup, as a means of preparing for a major policy shift, or as a device for providing an ostensibly objective aptitude test for further promotion of the country's most senior civil servants. There was certainly no sign of any sudden rejection of the socialist path, although this was now less invariably qualified by the adjective 'scientific'. Relations with China continued to be strong and friendly, as the visit of the Chinese Vice-premier in August 1978 indicated.

The abortive April coup and the ensuing counter-measures, involving quite widespread arrests within the army, did little to silence the widely based public criticism, which continued to be expressed, more openly than ever before, throughout the summer. In August the captured coup leaders were brought to trial and seventeen were sentenced to death. Others were released or given prison sentences. There were rumours that the clan to which most of the defendants belonged had taken hostages from the President's clan and some commentators prophesied an outbreak of tribal war. The President gave some indication of how he intended to respond to this situation when, on 21 October 1978, to mark the ninth anniversary of the revolution he announced the release of nearly 3000 prisoners, the creation of a new constitution and the formation of a parliament. These conciliatory gestures, designed to win back much-needed public support, were quickly followed by the public execution of the convicted leaders of the coup. It would obviously take some time to assess the significance of these new developments, which can be seen as logical developments of the formation of the Party in 1976. Certainly there was little to suggest that the President proposed to encourage a return to the excesses of the old multi-party civilian democracy. The parliament, when it was formed, would have to behave 'responsibly', within well-defined guidelines. Nor was there any indication that these new changes would modify the head of State's dedication to socialism, a system which his cynical Somali critics considered particularly appropriate for the perpetuation of his form of personal rule.

FROM MARXISM TO 'SOMALI SOCIALISM'?

There was, however, an interesting and significant shift in the inspiration and direction of Somali Socialism signalled by a decreasing emphasis on the qualifying adjective 'scientific'. Following October 1978, this sensitive word became less prominent in official statements and publications. Somalia appeared to be in a state of transition from qualified Marxism ('scientific socialism') to unqualified socialism. This gradual movement towards a less committed socialism and a more positive non-alignment in the international field reflected the delicate interplay of internal and external forces in Somali politics. The same interdependence between external and domestic interests was evident in the novel emphasis in Somali foreign policy on human rights, an issue which in the Somali view applied just as acutely in Ethiopia as in South Africa. These developments notwithstanding, the trajectory of Somali policy was not as inconsistent as some critics claimed. General Siyad had always stoutly maintained that socialism had to be pragmatically adapted to local Somali circumstances. Nationalism remained the key Somali priority.

BIOGRAPHY

General Mohamed Siyad, President of the Republic, was born 1919 in Lugh (Kansa Dere) district on the Juba River in southern Somalia. He grew up in the nomadic interior, intermittently attending Quranic school (religious studies) from the age of ten after has father's death. During the British military administration of Somalia (1942–1950), he joined the police force, receiving an education to secondary-school standard. He reached the rank of chief inspector and was in charge of the Upper Juba region and involved in Somali Youth League politics leading to independence. In 1950, during the Italian trusteeship administration, he was awarded a scholarship to study at a military academy in Italy. After completing his military training, he studied political science and administration, and in 1954 he returned to Somalia as an officer in the security forces. In 1965 he became a regimental commander and in 1966 he became General and Commander of the Army.

Source: Jama Umar 'Ise, *Thawra 21st Uktwbir* (Mogadishu, 1972).

BASIC FACTS ABOUT SOMALIA

Official name: Somali Democratic Republic (Jamhuriadda Dimoqradiga Somaliya)
Area: 637,657 sq. km. (246,201 sq. miles).
Population (1976 unofficial census): 3,500,000.
Population density: 5·5 per sq. km.
Population distribution: 15 per cent urban, 75 per cent rural (mainly nomadic pastoralists).
Membership of the Somali Socialist Revolutionary Party (1977): 12,330 (over half 'workers'; 'peasants' numbered 735). (Source: *Halgan*, July 1977.)

Administrative division: 15 regions, comprising 78 districts.

Ethnic nationality: Somali.

Religion: Moslem (Sunni; mainly Shafi Law School).

Population of major towns: Mogadishu (the capital), 350,000 (1973 est.); Hargeisa, 80,000 (1978 est.); Burao, 50,000 (1966 est.); Kismayu, 60,000 (1966 est.).

Industry: Somalia is primarily an agrarian country; there are currently no large-scale industries.

Main natural resources: pasture, gypsum, minerals.

Foreign trade (1975, Somali shillings) [US $1 = approx. 6.233 Somali shillings]: exports (mainly livestock and livestock products and bananas) 557·6 million (US $89.5 million); imports 1021·2 million (US $163.8 million); total 1578·8 million (US $253.3 million).

Main trading partners (1974): main sources of imports – Italy and the USSR, followed by China, Kenya and Thailand; main destination of exports – Saudi Arabia, Italy, Iran and the USSR.

Budget (Somali shillings): current budget (1973), 396·1 million (largest item general administration and defence); development budget (1974–8 proposed expenditure), 3617 million (largest items agriculture, transport and communications).

Rail network: none.

Road network: approx. 2400 km. all-weather metalled roads.

Universities: 1 – National University, Mogadishu, with approx. 3000 students in 1978.

Foreign relations: diplomatic relations with 31 countries; member of the OAU and UN since 1960 and of the Arab League since 1974.

NOTES

1. This organisation takes its name from the expression 'Somali Abo' coined in 1976 to assimilate Moslem pro-Somali Oromo (mainly Arussi) to the Somali nation. In Oromo the exclamation *abo* is used to attract someone's attention, in much the same way as the word *wariya* is used in Somali. Hence the terms 'Somali Abo' and 'Somali Wariya' are used to imply that the Arussi (and other Moslem Oromo) are a distant branch of the Somali nation. The alliance is, of course, primarily one of common hostility to the Semitic-speaking, Christian Amhara.
2. See C. Jesman, *The Russians in Ethiopia: An Essay in Futility* (1958).
3. See J. S. Trimingham, *Islam in Ethiopia* (1952).
4. For a detailed analysis of this social system see I. M. Lewis, *A Pastoral Democracy* (1961).
5. These terms antedate the revolution. Self-help schemes were introduced in the British Somaliland Protectorate in the early 1950s. The Somali term for

'socialism' was invented by broadcasters on the BBC Somali programme at about the same period.

6. See A. Wolczyk, 'Il "Socialismo" Somalo: Un Industria per il Potere', *Concretezza*, Jan 1972, pp. 23–6.
7. For further information on the Party and these organisations, see Omer Salad Elmi *et al.*, 'Party Life', in *Halgan*, July 1977, pp. 9–33.
8. Although hard to quantify, it seems safe to say that thousands of Somali nationals have left the Republic since 1969. Nor is the exodus restricted to intellectuals and members of the professions. A large number of emigrants are unskilled or semi-skilled workers (drivers and others) who have found lucrative employment in the Gulf States and Saudi Arabia. This reflects the very low level of salaries in the Republic. Remittances from migrant wage-earners now play an important role in the Somali economy.
9. These included the port complex and missile-storage and handling base at Berbera in the north.
10. On developments in the territory, see articles by I. M. Lewis in the annual survey *Africa South of the Sahara.* See also I. M. Lewis, *A Modern History of Somalia: Nation and State in the Horn of Africa*, (1979) ch 9 and 10.
11. On the WSLF, see I. M. Lewis, 'The Western Somali Liberation Front and Sheikh Hussein of Bali', in *Congress of Ethiopian Studies: Nice 1976* (1979).
12. For fuller details, see Lewis, *A Modern History of Somalia*, ch. 10.

BIBLIOGRAPHY

Davidson, Basil, 'Somalia: towards Socialism', *Race and Class*, XVII (1975) 19–38.
Halgan, official journal of the Somali Revolutionary Socialist Party, People's Hall, Mogadishu (PO Box 1204), published monthly in Somali, Arabic and English.
Jesman, C., *The Russians in Ethiopia: An Exercise in Futility* (London, 1958).
Lewis, I. M., *A Pastoral Democracy* (London: Oxford University Press, 1961).
——, in *Africa South of the Sahara* (London: Europa, 1970–1 [annual]).
——, *A Modern History of Somalia: Nation and State in the Horn of Africa* (London: Longman, 1979).
——, 'The Western Somali Liberation Front and Sheikh Hussein of Bali', *Congress of Ethiopian Studies: Nice 1976* (Paris, 1979).
Pestalozza, L., *Somalia: Cronaca della rivoluzione* (Bari, 1973).
Trimingham, J. S., *Islam in Ethiopia* (London: Oxford University Press, 1952).
Wolczyk, A., 'Il "Socialismo" Somalo: Un Industria per il Potere', *Concretezza*, Jan 1972.

23 Union of Soviet Socialist Republics

RONALD J. HILL

GEOGRAPHICAL AND SOCIAL BACKGROUND

With a territory covering one-sixth of the land surface of the globe, the Soviet Union, inheritor of the pre-1917 Tsarist Russian Empire, is by far the largest territorial state in the world today. It stretches 5000 km. from north to south, and 10,000 km. from east to west: from the frozen wastes of the Arctic to the scorching deserts and rugged mountains of Central Asia; from Poland to the International Date Line, within fifty miles of Alaska – itself formerly a Russian colony and now part of the United States. When Muscovites are rising in the morning, the people in the Far East are already home after a day's work; some Soviet citizens live to the east of China and Japan. The USSR, in other words, spans both Europe and Asia. From Norway and Finland in the north-west, round via Poland, Czechoslovakia and Hungary, on past Romania, Turkey, Iran and Afghanistan, to China, Mongolia and finally Korea, the Soviet Union has land borders with twelve foreign states; Japan is separated from it only by the Sea of Japan; North America is within easy reach by jet or missile over the North Pole.

These basic features alone create certain problems which have to be faced by the society and government of the country. The vast distances (the train journey across Siberia from Moscow to Vladivostok takes the best part of a week; that from Moscow to Tashkent, in Central Asia, two days or more) and the lack of adequate road systems, particularly in rural areas, present real problems of *communication* between the political centre and the provinces, and this may have a marked impact on the degree of control that the centre can exercise. This poses the problem of *centralisation and decentralisation*, which can best be put by asking a number of questions. How can the country be held together and

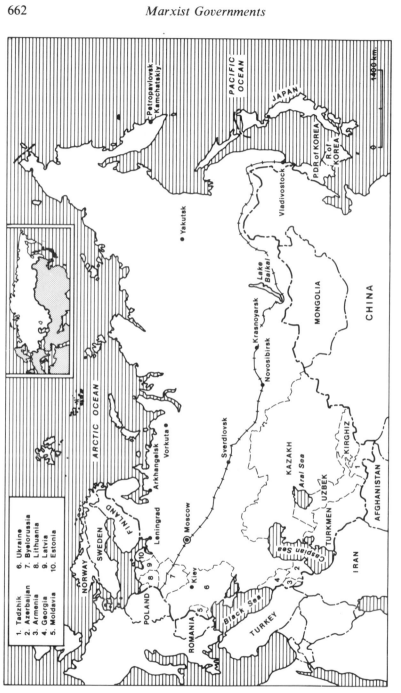

Union of Soviet Socialist Republics

ruled from a single capital city? Can it at all? How can disintegration be prevented? It also poses the problem of *defence*: the Soviet territory is vulnerable from all sides, with potential enemies able to attack from any direction, in particular along the 6000 km. frontier with China, or overland from Europe, from where Russia has been seriously threatened three times in the past two centuries. There is also the *economic* dimension: is it possible to develop a single, co-ordinated economy in such a vast country? Particularly when there are other problems, which will become clear in a moment. And the *social* aspect: can a unified, harmonious society – a 'nation' – be built, when its members are dispersed in such a vast land?

Those are some of the problems associated with the sheer size of the country. There is one obvious benefit: in conventional warfare, withdrawal to the interior can be used, as it has been in the past, against Napoleon and Hitler; moreover, the vast distances between China and the most developed areas of the present-day USSR may be of defensive value. Yet the geographical situation of Russia and the Soviet Union means, in our day, that the country is almost bound to engage in *global* diplomacy.

There are other underlying factors that affect how the country deals with its problems. The broad *climatic variations*, with vast tracts of frozen tundra in the north and east, and the uninhabitable deserts in the south, with summer temperatures reaching 80° C, obviously mitigate the effects of size, but also create further problems and, at the same time, opportunities. There is little need for a communications network in areas where practically no one lives: the communications substructure can be concentrated in the west–central region (essentially that area to the west and south of the Ural mountains), where the majority of the population lives. Moreover; the variety of climatic conditions also gives the country a potential for growing a wide range of its own requirements in food and agricultural produce, including both temperate crops (wheat and other grains, roots, apples and soft fruits), and also sub-tropical varieties (citrus fruits, tea, cotton). Yet the climate can be fickle, leading to disastrous harvests, such as occurred in 1972, when severe January frost destroyed winter wheat and barley, to be followed by spring drought in the western grain-growing areas, and early snow at harvest time in Kazakhstan. Such unreliability can obviously place great strains on a society and economy; and yet the USSR's potential as an agrarian country is considerable.

The Soviet Union's potential as an industrial power is even more impressive. The full extent of the country's wealth of economically valuable resources is not known. Prospecting proceeds apace, and the number of specialists has expanded rapidly: the number of third-level students of geology and related disciplines rose from 16,200 in 1950 to 38,000 in 1976, while those in disciplines connected with working mineral deposits expanded from 20,900 to 55,900 over the same period.[1] What is known is that the resources of energy and valuable minerals are vast: sufficient coal to last thousands of years at present extraction rates, abundant natural gas and oil, two-thirds of the world's peat deposits, millions of cubic metres of timber, and a tremendous potential for hydroelectricity. Thus, despite imports of 34·3 million tonnes of fuel resources in 1976,[2] and speculation about an energy shortage[3] (in part associated with exports of 273·4 million tonnes[4]), known stocks place the 'energy crisis' in perspective and offer excellent prospects for medium- and long-term supply.[5] The same applies to other valuable resources, including iron ore, manganese, potassium, lead, silver, uranium, gold and platinum.

The implication of all this is obviously that the Soviet Union has a tremendous potential for creating an industrial economy. This has been the motif of twentieth-century development, with transformation from a backward peasant society into the world's second industrial power; moreover, this has been achieved largely by relying on native resources. Such is the mineral and other natural wealth of the territory that industrial self-sufficiency is possibly a realistic policy: naturally, that has implications for the economic independence and political power of the USSR in the international arena. At the very least, these resources present a 'prodigious potential' for *sustained* economic growth.[6]

Yet once again we find that the geographical factor affects the realisation of that potential. Much of these resources lies in the inhospitable parts of the country, remote from where the majority of the people live. The cost of exploiting these riches is raised by the need to transport extracted minerals over great distances, or to attract workers and bring in supplies to cater for their needs – again at great cost in terms of inducements and the extra expenditures needed in order to overcome the rigours of isolation and climate. One result has been the virtual impossibility, since the abandonment in the post-Stalin era of directing labour eastwards, of building up a stable work force in the eastern areas,[7] and foreign companies, particularly from Japan and the United States, have been invited in to help with economic development in those regions.[8]

So much for the economic resources available in developing the Soviet Union. What of the *social* resources? The population in 1977 stood at almost 260 millions, the third largest after China and India, and continuing to expand, although at a slower rate than hitherto. This slowing-down in the rate of expansion has been associated with industrialisation,[9] an interpretation that is borne out by the pattern of regional variations: the birth rate in the more industrialised regions stands at roughly fifteen per thousand population, while in the rural areas of Central Asia – Tadzhikistan, Turkmenia and Uzbekistan – there is a population explosion, with a birth rate of over thirty per thousand.[10] There have been many indications in recent years that the authorities are worried both by the slowdown in the rate of growth and by the regional imbalances. As to the first, there is no doubt that the economic and territorial resources are sufficient to sustain a substantially larger population,[11] while the serious regional imbalances threaten to alter the national make-up of the population, with potential political implications. It is symptomatic of the offical concern that Leonid Brezhnev called at the Twenty-fifth Congress of the CPSU, in February 1976, for an effective population policy to be worked out.[12] Reports of the establishment of computer-dating and holidays for single persons are a further indication of how the problem is being tackled.

Other aspects of the demographic dimension of Soviet society have caused concern, in particular the gross imbalance between the sexes, which has been especially pronounced since the Second World War, and which amounted in 1970 to a surplus of 18·1 million females (itself a reduction from well over 20 million in the early postwar years).[13] This has naturally had its impact on the employment of women, leading to further exacerbation of the birth-rate problem.[14] It may also be a contributory factor to the very high divorce rates prevalent in Soviet society in recent years.

A further important element in the social structure, at the outset of the Soviet regime, was its backwardness. Despite attempts in the last decades of the Tsarist era to establish an industrial society, attempts which led to the growth of an industrial work force of some 3 million and an urban population of 26 million by 1914, the country remained essentially agrarian. In 1914 over four-fifths of the population were peasants, with all the connotations of illiteracy, ignorance, and lack of the skills (including political skills) needed to run a modern society. It was not until 1961 that the country became predominantly urban.[15]

Another factor in the composition of Soviet society, which will be more fully discussed below, is its national, cultural and linguistic variety. With over one hundred nationalities, speaking scores of languages and using five alphabets, the problems facing any government are formidable indeed. The issue of communication – in *which* language or languages? – is a central dilemma, compounded by the very different sizes of the national groups and their varying levels of cultural development. The Russian and Soviet experience in coping with the problem raises fundamental questions about 'development' in a diverse society: how can these sub-groups be united under a coherent policy and developed to form a single nation? More basically: is it *possible*, without destroying at least some of those cultures? And is it in any case *desirable* to try to do so?

We have now identified the basic geographical and social realities that have characterised the Soviet Union: the size of the country, its geography, its varied climate, its economic wealth, its underdevelopment, and its diverse social composition. *Any* government, whether it adhered to the principles of Marxism-Leninism or not, would have been faced with these factors, which both pose problems and offer solutions. In its role in organising society, any government of that territory would have as its basic goals to *create institutions* and *devise policies* that will (1) 'solve' – i.e. eliminate, neutralise, or reduce the impact of – the problems; and (2) in the twentieth century, permit the development of the potential. As for the specifically *Soviet* government, the Marxist-Leninist ideology strongly indicates the way in which those goals shall be achieved: by building an industrially based, socialist society, giving way eventually to a communist society in which the 'new Soviet man' will live in harmony with his fellows, collaborating to produce wealth for the common good of all, and with the members of society ruling themselves in 'communist self-administration'. In a real sense, the ideology prescribes a further goal: to transform the *culture* of the society, by replacing the traditional outlook and mores by a new, 'communist' culture.[16] The means of achieving this cultural transformation is a process of *mobilisation*, seen as 'an induced attempt to raise the level of acculturation',[17] and involving education, training, communications and information control, and what one might term 'encouraged participation'.

In order to move towards this goal, the regime has set up a range of institutions and established conventions by which to control the course of the society's development. Over the past sixty-odd years, the society has been upturned, and the Soviet Union today ranks economically and militarily with the United States of America as a 'superpower'. In subsequent sections of this chapter, I shall survey the political structures, the economy and the society; I shall examine the problem of the nationalities, and see how far it has been 'solved'; and I shall conclude with a brief analysis of Soviet foreign relations.

POLITICAL INSTITUTIONS

The central institution in the Soviet political system is the Communist Party of the Soviet Union (CPSU). The 1977 Constitution, article 6, explicitly asserts the position of the Party as the 'leading and guiding force of Soviet society and the nucleus of its political system'. Since the early 1920s, the CPSU has been the *only* political party in the country, a fact that, above all others, has led hostile critics to brand the system as fundamentally undemocratic. The Soviet system has been defined as a 'partocracy'; the single party was one of the characteristics of the totalitarian model; and two Soviet scholars have noted, not without foundation, that 'the apostles of anti-communism pounce with particular fury on the position of the Party in the republic of soviets, making it object number one for their slanderous fabrications, their verbal subversions of the foundations of socialist society'.[18]

Quite clearly, a single party ('a contradiction in itself', in the well known judgement of Sigmund Neumann[19]) is in a fundamentally different position from parties in competitive systems, and somewhat different from the communist party in socialist systems in which non-communist parties exist and work within the framework of communist leadership. The CPSU is a permanently ruling party, with no rivals for power or even influence. It bases its position on the fact that it alone is capable of correctly understanding the 'scientific laws of social development' enshrined in the ideology, and hence it can provide the necessary guidance and leadership required by any society that is aiming to build communism. 'Without the leading role of the party of communists', according to one recent writer,

the state and public organisations would inevitably function in disunity, risking going astray from the correct path. Only a party of the Leninist type, armed with knowledge of the objective laws of social development, and expressing the interests of the foremost and most revolutionary class in society, the working class, can by right exercise leadership over the activities of these mass organisations, imparting to them a planned and purposeful character.[20]

Such an interpretation naturally begs the questions of whether the ideology *is* 'correct', and whether the party *does* understand it and express the interests of the working class (it begs several other questions as well). Nor is it clear precisely how the ideology is used in the policy-making process: on the face of it, the writings of Marx, Engels and Lenin would have little to say about whether or not to produce platform-soled shoes or colour television sets, or which side to support in the Horn of Africa. Moreover, there is plenty of evidence that, despite its supposed appreciation of scientific laws, the Party in the past has chosen disastrous and contradictory policies, and been obliged to make sharp reversals and cover its tracks as best it could.[21] Nevertheless, with no legitimate opposition to challenge this interpretation, the CPSU can use the ideology as a powerful legitimising tool, and perform its self-appointed role of leader, organiser, co-ordinator, catalyst – concepts and metaphors that have been used by Soviet writers to depict the Party's role in the system.[22]

As the 'leading and guiding force', the CPSU consists of over 16 million dedicated men and women drawn from all sectors of the adult population, and hence able to present itself as 'the party of the whole people'. Although its composition does not accurately reflect the social composition of the population[23] (workers and peasants are severely under-represented; so are women; so too are many of the minority nationalities), the Party can nevertheless claim with justification that it is broadly representative; it has also, in the past few years, been making strenuous efforts to even out the imbalances in its own membership, whilst weighing this against other factors, including its position as a vanguard, and its traditional association with certain managerial and government occupations.[24] Recruitment is highly selective and aims to admit only 'the best'. Over two-thirds of new members rise from the ranks of the Komsomol (Young Communist League),[25] in a complex selection procedure that involves formal application, supporting references, several assessments, and a year's probation before full membership is granted.

Once a member, the individual is obliged to be active and to submit to Party discipline. The Party rules require all members to be exponents of Marxism-Leninism, to serve as examples of the communist attitude towards work, to improve their skills, to explain Party policy to the masses, and in general to take an active part in the country's political life; in return, they gain the right to participate in the internal life of the Party and thereby, if only remotely, in policy-making.[26] Passivity is not merely frowned upon: it is a serious form of indiscipline, punished in the last resort by expulsion. Indeed, there are only two ways of leaving the

Party: expulsion and death. It is, of course, possible to engineer one's own dismissal (a form of resignation) by ceasing to be actively involved, but the stigma that attaches to such expulsion is equivalent to discharge with ignominy, and it severely restricts the individual's further prospects. Nevertheless, in the review of membership and exchange of Party documents that took place between 1971 and 1975, about 347,000 were declined a renewal of their membership cards.[27]

Soviet writers are emphatic that the CPSU does not form an elite, pointing out that 'Lenin was implacably opposed to all attempts to use Party membership in order to gain any advantages or benefits, or to act in contravention of Soviet laws'.[28] Nevertheless, it is clear that the rights of membership do place the Party member in a politically advantaged position, in that he can have some indirect say in policy-making and in the selection of leaders; he gains prestige in official eyes; his chances of advancement to positions of responsibility and high salary are vastly improved; and – despite the provisions of Party rule 12 that members who infringe the law shall be expelled and prosecuted in the courts – in practice Party membership can offer immunity from prosecution.[29] Moreover, the very fact that admissions are carefully controlled and restricted tends towards creating an exclusive, 'elitist' organisation.

The Party's most powerful, permanent body is the Political Bureau, consisting of about two dozen men (there has only ever been one woman), 'leaders of higher Party and State organs, the most prominent and experienced politicians'.[30] These include at present the Secretary-general of the Party (Brezhnev), the Prime Minister (Kosygin), the Ministers of Defence (Ustinov) and Foreign Affairs (Gromyko), the head of the KGB security police (Andropov), and the Party heads from the Ukraine (Shcherbitskii), Belorussia (Masherov), Leningrad (Romanov) and elsewhere. The average age of this body, well over sixty-five, with several members over seventy, has been the subject of comment by Western writers for a number of years,[31] and the trend, reported by Brezhnev to the CPSU's Twenty-fourth Congress in 1971, of replacing veteran cadres with 'young, promising functionaries' has so far had little impact on the top leadership itself.[32] At the same congress, Brezhnev reported that this august body meets weekly to review 'the most important and urgent questions of the Party's internal and foreign policy',[33] and there can be little doubt that the Political Bureau ultimately determines policy, although in consultation with a wide variety of other organs and institutions, including the central Party Secretariat, the Council of Ministers, and republican and provincial

Party and State bodies. As policy-maker, the Political Bureau is the 'government' of the USSR.

Policy, once formulated, is endorsed by the Central Committee, a 400-strong body of influential figures from all spheres and all parts of the country, elected for a five-year term of office by the Party Congress, to which it formally reports, through the Secretary-general. It is perhaps not inappropriate to see the Central Committee as the Soviet 'establishment', containing as it does political leaders from the higher ranks of Party and State, the editors of major newspapers and journals, famous writers, ambassadors, the President of the Academy of Sciences, the former astronaut Valentina Nikolaeva-Tereshkova, a host of other luminaries, and a sprinkling of lesser notables – representatives of the 'ordinary' Party members.[34] The full Central Committee meets in formal session (plenum) twice a year, or as necessary, and issues authoritative statements on any aspect of Soviet policy, as well as giving approval to measures introduced by the Political Bureau. It is at such plenums that changes in personnel are formally made, such as the dropping of Shelepin from the Political Bureau in April 1975 or of Podgorny in May 1977.[35] In certain circumstances the Central Committee may play a key role, by serving as a court of appeal from a deadlocked Political Bureau: precisely such a role was performed in 1957, when Khrushchev's leadership was challenged (unsuccessfully), and in 1964, when he was removed from office.[36]

Beneath the CPSU Central Committee there are republican central committees, provincial, territorial, urban and district committees, each formally elected by a Party conference at the appropriate level, and headed by first secretary, who is without doubt the most powerful individual at that level of administration.[37] The secretaries have ultimate responsibility for all that goes on within their territory, political and economic.

At the grass-roots level, every communist belongs to a primary Party organisation, formed in institutions where a minimum of three Party members work. There were 414,000 such organisations in 1977, some subdivided into Party groups and over 80 per cent of them containing under fifty members, but with an average of ninety-five members in industrial units and a tendency for the size of organisations to increase.[38] These basic institutions are the bodies through which Party policies are ultimately implemented, through a system of Party *assignments*. These are specific tasks allocated to the members, on a short- or long-term basis, and may include single obligations – writing an article for the factory's newspaper, or giving a lecture – or more onerous duties, such as running a Komsomol branch or a trade-union group. It is by this 'allocation of cadres' (placing its members where they can be of greatest use) that the Party performs its leading role throughout society; moreover, in an extension of this principle, Party members must obtain party permission to change jobs.[39] The principle of 'democratic centralism', which makes the decisions of higher bodies binding on all lower bodies and their members, acts as a unifying feature to the structure as a whole, and ensures compliance and discipline on the part of ordinary members, on pain of reprimand or, ultimately, expulsion.

The basic ideological statement for Party members is the Party Programme. The third one, adopted in 1961, is still current, although a number of its wilder predictions about the impending advent of communism have been quietly dropped. That document, which mapped out in general terms and in detail the road to communism, forms the basis on which party policy is supposedly founded. Moreover, although it is technically binding only on Party members, it is regarded as having become the 'ideological constitution of the country'.[40] The plain fact is, however, that the rest of the country has not been consulted on the matter.

Soviet writers continually stress that the Party *rules*, but does not govern or administer. That role is performed by the Soviet State, whose structure is divided into two basic types of institution: the representative institutions ('organs of State power' – the soviets of people's deputies) and the administrative organs, or executive committees, with their departments, committees and, at State level, ministries, each responsible for a specific area of administration.

The soviets are elected by the adult population, under the careful supervision of the Party, for a thirty-month term of office. Their deputies, of whom 2,229,641 were elected in June 1977, are broadly representative of the population, and carefully chosen as 'the best sons and daughters' of the people.[41] The local soviets meet six times a year, the Supreme Soviet twice yearly, with deputies maintaining their regular employment, thereby retaining contact with their constituents, and not becoming preoccupied with their position as 'parliamentarians'. Such, at any rate, is the theory: however, since the early 1960s there have been many calls and some serious attempts to 'professionalise' the role of deputy, so that greater emphasis is now placed on the effective representation of constituents' interests, in a campaign that began after the Twentieth Party Congress (1956) to revitalise the governmental system.[42] Thus, although the formal decision-making role of the soviets amounts in practice to little more than an act of rubber-stamping Party policy, there is now a significant role for the deputies to play outside the two-monthly sessions, particularly as members of the 'permanent commissions' that check up on the efficiency of administration.[43] Moreover, even the rubber-stamping is not regarded as a mere formality: rather, it is seen as the important stage in the political process without which Party-approved policy does not have any legal force. Even though the Party's members form a majority of deputies at any level of importance (rising to about 75 per cent in the Supreme Soviet); and even though the voting (by show of hands, rather than by either secret or recorded ballot) is always unanimous, this stage is accorded significance in Soviet accounts of the political system.

After all, it was the Congress of Soviets (precursor of the Supreme Soviet) that endorsed the revolution in October 1917: in the celebrated words of eyewitness John Read, the Bolsheviks 'seized the state power of Russia and placed it in the hands of the Soviets'.[44] It was the fact that the soviets were spontaneously created by the workers themselves in the revolutions of 1905 and 1917 that caused Lenin and the Bolsheviks to attach such importance to them that they were made the basis of the post-revolutionary State, and gave their name to that state. Thus, even though they now bear very little resemblance to the strike committees formed in the revolutionary period, the soviets are a highly symbolic feature of the Soviet political structure. Moreover, new legislation is being introduced, beginning in the late 1960s, to redefine the functions and duties of these institutions, strengthen their financial basis, and raise the social and political stature of the deputies, so that they can, as resolved by the Twenty-fourth Party Congress (1971) 'still more fully carry out their functions, exert effective influence on the development of the economy and culture and raising the people's welfare, more persistently deal with questions of everyday services to the population and the maintenance of public order'.[45]

That is one area of development in the Soviet political system over the past decade or so: extending the powers of *representative* institutions, raising the demands placed on the deputies, and giving training so that they can play this enhanced role more effectively. A further area of reform is in the staffing of the *administrative* apparatus, in particular by means of more careful selection of personnel, to replace those of the previous generation. Those were chosen for their political reliability and suitably proletarian social origins, rather than for their training or competence as administrators, and sent, after training lasting perhaps a few months, to run whole provinces. It can be argued that their crude methods worked when the country had one or two main goals: building up heavy industry as quickly as possible, or winning a war. But, as Soviet scholars have argued with increasing frequency and urgency in recent years, such crudity is totally inadequate to run a complex, differentiated and educated society, in which the range of legitimate interests (over and above the common interest in building a communist society) is vast. As two writers at the beginning of the present decade put it,

> In the process of communist construction there takes place the development of both social and private interests of the workers. The study and reflection of these interests in the activity of the state . . . is an important condition for the satisfaction of the requirements of the popular masses and the needs of society.[46]

Hence there is a need for leaders themselves to be sophisticated, educated, responsive, and even – a basic requirement, one would have thought – to know the law that they are supposed to be applying.[47]

Such developments, if they are successfully introduced, will lead to a very different type of political system from the crude, bullying model that has been Stalin's legacy. In 1978, however, one is obliged to stress the conditional quality of this proposition. There can be little doubt that there is taking place what one Soviet scholar in conversation called a 'change of generations'; nevertheless the severity with which leading exponents of dissident opinion continue to be dealt with by Soviet courts (which are, of course, subject to strong political influence) is ample evidence that even the 'new' leaders are not sufficiently sophisticated to be able to cope with fundamental criticism without resorting to harshly repressive measures. One might argue that much of the infringement of civilised standards of administrative and political behaviour stems from the incapacity of the centre to control the localities, while yet placing extremely high demands on local leadership. After all, the members of the Political Bureau have few opportunities to discriminate against Jews or religious believers: that is done by the manager of a town's housing list, who keeps such families permanently at the bottom, or by schoolteachers who make fun of children from such families. In the country much may happen of which the Kremlin politicians are unaware. Yet it is no doubt true that a stronger lead from the centre would help enormously; and the severe waves of suppression by the KGB cannot but be sanctioned by the top leadership.

A further point that needs to be borne in mind when assessing the Soviet political system, however, is whether it is even appropriate to speak of 'the leadership'. The principle of 'collective leadership', which is stressed even in a period of clear dominance by one leader, means that it is difficult to be certain about disagreements and divergences of opinion among the ruling group. Yet not only have the 'Kremlinologists' such as Tatu and Conquest succeeded in producing highly plausible and entertaining accounts of Soviet politics based on an assumption of conflict; not only have scholars such as Pethybridge and Ploss likewise pieced together evidence of divergent opinions among leaders over specific topics; but, furthermore, the dissident Soviet historian Roy Medvedev, himself generally in favour of the aims of the system, has convincingly outlined several major strands of political opinion among Soviet leaders.[48] Indeed, a political process can hardly be envisaged without such disagreements. What it implies, however, is that it is inappropriate to assume that there is a single, unified leadership which has complete control over all that takes place in the country, and that the highly centralised model of the system, introduced by the theorists of totalitarianism, that dominated Western thinking about the Soviet Union for two decades or more is at best an aspiration by some of the leaders. It also implies that those among the leadership who may wish to reform or develop the system may be faced with severe political obstacles.[49] What is clear, in the mind of this writer, is that the general overall trend is towards greater rationality, sophistication and re-sponsiveness on the part of the political system, while continuing to deal severely with those who reject the system, regarding them as, at best, unpatriotic and, at worst, downright subversive.

It is easy for liberals to see repressive actions as merely attempts by a group of 'frightened' men to maintain themselves in office and the system through which they exercise power (and from which they obviously gain) in existence. Obviously, all politicians, in any system, have a strong sense of political (and physical) self-preservation, and any system will strive above all to maintain itself, by whatever means are necessary, in the face of external attack or internal subversion: events in the summer of 1978 in Iran, Nicaragua and Rhodesia are cases in point. In the Soviet case, tough measures are made so much more acceptable by the political culture, which includes 'the fear of chaos' and 'propensity to regard as "normal" such phenomena . . . as strictly hierarchical poli-tical organisation, political police surveillance, administrative exile, literary censorship, and internal passports'.[50] Further, a vital element in the official culture is the insistence that the communist society will not come about of its own accord: it has to be planned, organised; society has to be led in the appropriate direction, and, as we saw, that leadership function is exercised by the CPSU. In the next section, we shall look more closely at the 'Soviet model' of the economy and society that is deemed to be appropriate.

ECONOMIC AND SOCIAL DEVELOPMENT

As we saw earlier, Russian society at the time of the revolution was overwhelmingly rural and agrarian. Its peasants (commonly referred to as *chernye lyudi*, 'black people') and their way of life were characterised by illiteracy, poverty, ignorance, lack of facilities, superstition – characteristics that had already led Marx, referring to the French peasantry, to speak of 'the class that represents barbarism within civilisation'.[51] The ideology of Marxism–Leninism, however, which came to dominate in Russia after the successful defence of the revolution in the Civil War (1918–21), posited the goal of a communist society based on an advanced industrial economy and a high material standard of living, with industrial workers forming the vast bulk of society. There was clearly a great gulf between that hypothetical society and the social material on which the Bolsheviks had to work. On the other hand, as we have seen, the material resources were available in abundance for industrial development. What was required was the means of allocating resources in order to change the nature of the economy and society in the desired direction: economic *plans* fitted the bill. Beginning with the First Five-year Plan, introduced in 1928, and now working through the Tenth, covering 1976 80, the Soviet Union has radically restructured its entire economy, by giving primacy to the development of heavy industry and defence-related industries, and only in recent years beginning to allow for the satisfaction of consumer demands.

The point about the Soviet planning system, unlike that in some other socialist countries, is that it presupposes that the political authorities know what should be produced. On the basis of that knowledge, the planners draw up complex sets of directives and issue instructions to individual enterprises, informing them 'what to produce and what to deliver, and to whom, at what prices, and from whom to obtain needed inputs'.[52] This system is known as 'directive planning' and is administered by the political authorities in precisely the same fashion as other forms of policy: the Political Bureau decides overall priorities, which are then formulated as guidelines or 'directives'; these are endorsed by the Central Committee and Party Congress (one reason for holding Party congresses at five-yearly intervals is that this fits in well with the planning system[53]), and subsequently framed as 'control figures' by the State Planning Commission (Gosplan) and the various ministries, and made law by the Supreme Soviet; in applying the Plan, local legislative bodies endorse similar plans for their territories. In addition, current or operational plans exist for each individual production unit, indicating that enterprise's required contribution for the current quarter or year to the overall national Plan.

The State owns most of the country's productive capacity, and, since the plans have the force of law, it is a serious matter if a plan is not fulfilled. Inevitably, however, bottlenecks occur, accidents interrupt supply, resources have to be diverted, and a thousand and one other factors intervene to inhibit the perfectly smooth-running implementation of directives. In consequence, management – State-employed, and enjoying relatively little freedom of manoeuvre, even following the modest decentralising reforms of the past decade – has had to devise a range of legal and semi-legal (and sometimes plainly illegal) devices in order to reduce wastage of labour or materials and manage to fulfil quotas. Bribery, black-marketeering, fixing up dubious deals with unauthorised suppliers: these and other features have long been established elements in the Soviet economy.[54]

One can easily fault Soviet economic performance and challenge the very principle of planning, which rejects the market as a mechanism for determining what should be produced, in what quantities, and at what prices. The Soviet press is full of tales of woe about shoddy, poorly designed, unwanted (and ultimately wasted) produce lying in warehouses or shops. Any visitor to a Soviet town quickly appreciates the shortages of many basic goods that are taken for granted even in some of the less wealthy parts of the world: toilet paper, soap, fruit and vegetables, footwear and clothing. Yet the fact remains that, in global terms, this system has achieved a complete transformation in the nature of the Soviet economy and society. It may well be that a similar result could have been achieved by free-market methods, and without all the coercion that characterised the early years of industrialisation: I do not propose to be drawn into that debate.[55] The point is that, by using its own methods, the Soviet Union has virtually destroyed the traditional peasant way of life and replaced it by a modern, urban, industrial society, all within the space of half a lifetime. Moreover, the process of development is not simply one of lifting the peasants up and setting them to work in factories. The process has a whole series of facets, each of which has implications for the nature of contemporary Soviet society.

Obviously, the change in the social structure from peasant- to worker-dominated, with a rapid rise too in the 'intelligentsia', is one important element in this development. The traditional peasantry, farming by primitive methods, with the household as the basic productive unit, has all but disappeared.[56] It has been replaced by a *collectivised peasantry*, co-operatively using modern equipment and farming techniques, and now guaranteed a minimum monthly wage. Although there are significant forms of social differentiation within the peasantry (according to type of occupation, income, status, involvement in social affairs, use of cultural amenities, and so on) and regional variations (depending on such features as soil, proximity of a town, and religious and other cultural factors that affect family size),[57] Soviet analysis categorises collective farmers together as a distinct class, since they collectively own buildings, equipment, seeds and produce, which they sell under contract to the State. In 1970 the peasantry (including dependants) constituted 20·5 per cent of the population; this had dwindled to 15·7 per cent by 1977,[58] and is likely to be yet further reduced as agriculture becomes more efficient, following significant investment in recent years, and as the manpower shortage in industry continues to be filled mainly by drawing in from the countryside. A further element is the expansion of *State farms*: there were 19,617 of these in 1976, employing almost 11 million workers, and increasing (as against 27,700 collective farms, with 14·8 million workers, and decreasing).[59] State farms tend to be larger than collective farms, and specialised; and, since they are wholly State-owned, and their workers directly employed by the State on a par with industrial workers, they are regarded as part of the working class (rather than the peasantry), and their expansion forms a somewhat artificial element in the growth of the working class.

Yet the growth of the *industrial proletariat* continues apace: there were just over 11 million industrial workers in 1940, on the eve of Soviet involvement in World War II; their numbers had swelled to over 23 million by 1965, and 29 million by 1976; workers in transport numbered 8·2 million in 1976, with a slightly smaller number in construction.[60] Alongside the expansion of the number of industrially employed workers, there has also been a rapid growth in the number of managerial, supervisory and administrative personnel, who in Soviet parlance are regarded as part of the *intelligentsia,* together with 'intellectuals' in the Western sense of the word. In an essay published in the early 1970s, L. G. Churchward, defining the intelligentsia in terms of employment in positions that require third-level education, and including tertiary students and unemployed graduates, arrived at an estimate of 10,676,000 for 1967. Given that tertiary institutions have released over half a million graduates annually since then (rising to 734,600 in 1976), that figure could probably be increased by 5–6 million by the late 1970s.[61]

Thus, the changing social structure has been one important constituent element in the process of development. Urbanisation has been another. The Soviet definition of 'urban' (based on either population or function) classifies as 'urban-type settlements' many small communities that are really little more than villages, so that the category includes a wide variety of settlements with vastly different facilities and other characteristics. Nevertheless, the urban way of life is now the dominant pattern. There are now fifteen cities with over 1 million inhabitants, and a further twenty-seven with over half a million; 1151 new urban settlements have been established since 1917; and the urban population stood at 159,593,000 in 1977, or 62 per cent of the total;[62] of these, almost 60 per cent (94,561,000) lived in large cities of over 100,000 inhabitants.[63] The Soviet Union has thus, within a relatively short period, become a nation of urban dwellers.

This has in large measure been achieved through migration of peasants, and in particular of the younger, able-bodied and ambitious among them. This has naturally affected the quality of the agricultural work force, which has tended to age and not to require and retain in the countryside the mechanical and similar skills needed for running a modern agricultural sector: thus, Soviet agriculture has long been over-staffed while suffering severe shortages of skilled labour (and this has doubtless contributed to the inefficient use of what equipment has been made available);[64] migration also helps to keep village cultural standards at a low level, by creaming off to the towns the brighter, better educated and more demanding youngsters, who would perhaps stimulate social and political life in the countryside if they stayed.

Migration has also had its impact on the towns. As a recent Soviet writer pointed out, while rural migration has been regarded simply as the means of getting manpower for the industrial cities, 'migration of the rural population presents significant interest not only for the economist, but also for the sociologist and social psychologist, for the demographer and ethnographer, for the social hygiene specialist and the architect and planner'.[65] The same writer favours migration into the new cities (which, in the process of expansion by this means, remain essentially cities of young people, with a high demand for educational and other facilities for the migrants' children), since it fulfils the purpose of expanding industry, and the migrants are sufficiently flexible in attitude to create for themselves a social existence and sense of community. The problem is less satisfactory in the long-established European cities, to which the majority of migrants move. There, this supply of unskilled labour has tended to depress technological levels in industry, which in turn has encouraged further migration of relatively low-skilled workers: hence, there exists a *hidden surplus of labour* in certain branches of industry.[66]

Moreover, there are also effects not directly connected with industry, since 'the contemporary town is a complex social system, and therefore one must not approach it simply as a means for attaining economic goals. . . . One must not regard its growth as a mechanical process.'[67] Not only does the provision of services – education, health provision, sewage disposal, transportation – take on a completely new dimension as a city expands, but in addition the social balance, built up perhaps over generations, can be upset by a sudden influx of migrants, sometimes of diverse nationalities, bringing peasant standards and attitudes and maintaining peasant rates of reproduction. One can thus see that urban expansion is as much a cultural as an economic phenomenon, and requires adjustments in attitudes that can be acquired only through education and experience. Where (as sometimes happens) whole villages migrate *en bloc*, the problem of integration can be quite significant.[68] The psychological impact on relatively unsophisticated, unmarried young peasants, suddenly transported to live in a hostel in an alien city, may be a contributory factor to the problem of delinquency and alcoholism, which has been particularly virulent in recent years.[69] These are problems of which Soviet scholars and, through them, planners and politicians are becoming increasingly aware.

From the inception of industrialisation and urbanisation on a massive scale in the late 1920s and the 1930s, the emphasis has been mainly on the production of goods in quantity. With the Ninth Five-year Plan (1971–5) came somewhat greater emphasis on the production of consumption goods and services for the population, while the current plan, dubbed the 'Plan of Quality', aims to continue the upward swing:

The main task of the Tenth Five-year Plan consists in the continued implementation of the Communist Party's course for raising the material and cultural living standard of the people on the basis of the dynamic and proportional development of social production, and raising its efficiency, an acceleration in scientific and technical progress, growth in labour productivity, and an improvement by all means in the quality of work in all sectors of the national economy.[70]

In particular the Plan envisages greater efficiency in the utilisation of manpower; investment in housing and amenity construction in the east in order to encourage manpower migration; greater efficiency and rationality in resource utilisation; more effective application of science and technology; better managerial methods and techniques; and greater attention to the protection of the environment.[71]

The last point is an indicator of the growing sophistication of Soviet society. It also – and this is what gives it its special significance in the Soviet context – challenges the growth ethic that has dominated Soviet developmental thinking since its inception, inspired by what one Western commentator has referred to as the 'produce-or-perish mentality', coupled with a great sense of the vastness of the territory and its 'seemingly inexhaustible resources', waiting to be exploited.[72] It must have required considerable courage, for author, editor and censor alike, to publish a recommendation that Soviet economic growth be slowed down by 7–10 per cent 'for several years to divert funds to rescuing the balance of nature'.[73] The reviewer who cited this was pessimistic about the impact of scholarly and other concerned public opinion on the Soviet governmental planners; yet progress has been observed in this area, in the form of anti-pollution legislation filling a 'sizable' volume,[74] the introduction of which at least one Soviet scholar attributed to the impact of public opinion.[75]

The fact that the environmental question is now incorporated by Party Congress in its resolutions on the five-year plans is further evidence that this issue is now considered to be an important one. It also tells us much, in my opinion, about the changing nature of Soviet society and its political system. The totalitarian model of Soviet politics left no room for public opinion to challenge and influence official thinking in this way: according to that model, government decided, and its policy was implemented without question. On the face of it, indeed, there was no need for the permanently ruling Party, backed up by powerful security agencies, to respond to pressures from below. Now, it appears, this is no longer the case, and in the next section I shall attempt to find explanations for this development.

DEVELOPED SOCIALIST SOCIETY

Immediately following the October revolution of 1917, the Bolsheviks introduced a system of government referred to as the 'dictatorship of the proletariat', whose task it was to bring about the fundamental realignment of political and social forces in the country. By 1936 it was declared that the basic socialist transformation of society had been achieved, and article 1 of the Stalin constitution, introduced in that year, declared the USSR to be 'a socialist state of workers and peasants'. Khrushchev, anxious to demonstrate the further progress under his leadership, declared that the stage of the 'unfolding' or 'rapid building of communism' had been attained – a cumbersome phrase in both English and Russian – and he established a commission in 1961 to draft a fresh constitution reflecting this change. His successors dropped the 'unfolding building of communism', discovered 'developed' or 'mature socialism' (a much slicker, more positive slogan), and finally brought in the awaited constitution in 1977.[76] This declares in its Preamble that 'in the USSR a developed socialist society has been built', and that such a society is 'a natural, logical stage on the road to communism'.

One of the characteristics of this society (again, according to the Constitution) is the high level of culture and science that has been created, and indeed, the tremendous rise in the general educational level of the population is a further important part of the process of 'development' discussed above. Not only was education regarded as a good thing in itself, but in addition it was a *sine qua non* in creating a skilled work force capable of planning, designing and operating new industrial and urban complexes without relying heavily on imported expertise and technology. Some foreign technology was made use of, including whole factories transferred as reparations from the Soviet Zone of the defeated Germany after the Second World War; but for the most part the Soviet Union developed by her own efforts, brutally enforced by Stalin under his policy of building 'socialism in one country'. Part of that policy, over the years, has been to raise the level of skills in the population, by establishing a State-run, comprehensive education system.

Soviet statistics showing the expansion of education are extremely impressive: the number of individuals of all ages involved in the system has risen from 47,547,000 in 1940–1 to 79,634,000 in 1970–1 and 93,708,000 in 1976–7; of the 1976–7 total, 4,950,000 year were in higher institutions, 4,623,000 in special secondary schools and 3,552,000 in trade schools; during the years 1918–76, 67·8 million citizens acquired secondary education. The total number of higher educational institutions rose from 105 in 1914–15 to 817 in 1940–1 and 859 in 1976–7, with a rise in the number of special secondary schools over the same period (1914–77) from 450 to 4303. In the same years, the numbers of students and pupils in higher institutions rose from forty-one per 10,000 population to 192, with a similar rise from fifty to 179 in special secondary schools.[77] Such impressive statistics could go on. They tell us nothing about quality, of course, and the problems of rural schools, in particular, are given frequent airing in the press.[78] Yet the net result has been to create a population, technically educated and literate, at least on a par with most other modern societies.

Moreover, as the 'scientific and technological revolution' has an ever greater impact in the 1970s, further training among the working class (encouraged by a payment system that rewards formal qualifications) is said to be leading to a blurring in role distinctions between technically trained workers, technicians and the lower margins of the technical intelligentsia.[79] In other words, education has had a dual impact on the developing Soviet Union: it has raised the general level of skill, and extended the range of special skills available to the society in solving the problems posed by an industrial economy; and it has raised the general training of individual citizens. Moreover, the explicit attempts from an early age to instil certain communal values into the population, reinforced by political education throughout life (in part formally and semi-formally, through the adult education and lecture courses, and in part informally, through the State-sponsored mass media), attempt to involve the whole population in the country's political life, at least as interested and committed observers.[80] The outcome of these various educational processes may well have been, as the 1977 constitution states, to create a new historical entity, 'the Soviet people'. Yet it is a people consisting of ever better educated and increasingly diverse individuals, more aware of their own position and their own identity and that of the various social groups to which they belong. This is a development the significance of which has been noted by Soviet scholars in the past fifteen years or so and is now having an impact on politicians.

As Lane and others have noted, Soviet society is a complex organism, with many forms of differentiation and stratification, based on sex, occupation, earnings, prestige, religion, nationality and other factors.[81] Although the existence of any such differentiation in a 'socialist' society may be used by left-wing idealists and right-wing opponents in order to discredit the Soviet system, and although 'official' Soviet interpretations of the system tend to ignore or minimise such inequalities,[82] the scholarly literature of Soviet philosophers, sociologists and other social scientists has, nevertheless, in recent years paid considerable attention to the question, and examined its implications in the political sphere. Over two decades ago, the philosopher G. M. Gak argued that 'alongside the development of production and the growth of material culture, ever new personal interests arise', including, for example, the interests of the individual as a consumer. G. Y. Glezerman later stated his view that in any more or less developed society there is a mass of multifarious interests – personal, group, class, public, and so on – reflecting needs arising from the social conditions. Moreover, it cannot be assumed that people's *specific* interests will be compatible with one another: on the contrary, there may be contradictions among them, leading to possible collision.[83]

Such a view has obvious relevance for the political system, bearing as it does the implication that such potential conflicts need to be resolved through a political mechanism. As Georgi Shakhnazarov has well expressed it,

> the absence of antagonisms does not signify an identity of the needs of the different social groups. Along with the complete and permanent coincidence of the fundamental interests of all classes and social groups, there may arise, and does arise, a lack of coincidence of specific interests. This is a contradiction of a kind which, while not being antagonistic, can become aggravated unless it is resolved in good time.

He later states that 'no political organisation can function effectively without being constantly informed about the aspirations and requirements of all the classes and sections of society and without reacting to them in some form or another'.[84] In other words, unlike the highly authoritarian political system of a generation ago, the Soviet Union today needs a system of government that takes individual and group interests into account in formulating policies. One writer holds up the disastrous administrative rearrangements of Khrushchev, introduced with no consultation of local or professional opinion, as an example of how not to run the modern Soviet State.[85] Other writers, notably R. A. Safarov, have developed this theme, stressing the importance of taking public opinion into account if policies are to be effective.[86]

Politicians too have taken up the argument. At the Twenty-fifth Party Congress (1976), Brezhnev spoke of the need to study public opinion as a means of developing the State, and specifically referred to letters addressed by members of the public to the Party organs as 'an important link between the Party and its Central Committee, and the masses'.[87]

The implication of all this – and one should stress that so far the arguments have not found firm reflection in the system's institutional policy-making arrangements – is that the Party no longer believes it always knows what is best for people in all circumstances and at all times. It still claims that through its understanding of the ideology it can identify the *basic* needs of the population; but in a complex society the range of legitimate 'secondary' interests is so vast that they need to be communicated to the decision-makers in Party and State.

A further point, and one that has direct relevance to the improved educational level of society as a whole, is that, for such opinion to be valuable and effective, it must be competent. That involves not only a high level of information, but also the possession of certain political skills. In this connection, B. N. Topornin has pointed out that today's public is better educated and also much more experienced in the skills of participation in political life than its predecessors, while N. P. Farberov, in a contribution to the same book, argues that 'the higher the political consciousness of the masses, and their culture, the more successfully does democracy develop'.[88] Shakhnazarov has openly argued for much more openness in government: in particular he wants to see the regular publication of a whole range of information on social and economic matters, in order that the public may 'know the facts'. Indeed, he sees this as 'the precondition for active participation by citizens in political life' – one of the stated aims of the regime.[89]

The politicians are clearly not ready for such a radical opening-up of the system at this stage. It may be, as some argue, that the system is incapable of reforming itself in this way.[90] Time alone will tell. Yet the Soviet Union has changed, is changing, and in my view the pace and direction of change must not be measured solely by reports of economic shortfall or by the treatment of dissidents. What is clear, as Moshe Lewin has also shown,[91] is that Soviet society is proving itself capable of generating critical analyses and reformist ideas: it is thus not the stagnant pool that many critics take it to be.

Problems are certainly present. Indeed, political leaders occasionally admit this,[92] although some of the problems are such that they cannot be mentioned in public. One of these is the nationality question, which is of such potential significance that it deserves a brief discussion.

THE NATIONALITIES

Soviet leaders have long been firm in their assertion that the national question in the USSR has been 'solved', and that all national groups live harmoniously side by side in what one writer referred to as a 'fraternal family of nations'.[93] The Prologue to the new constitution refers to the 'juridical and factual equality of all [the country's] nations and nationalities and their fraternal co-operation'. Not all observers share this view. At the other extreme, the dissident historian Andrei Amalrik (now living in exile) envisages that the USSR might in certain circumstances disintegrate into 'anarchy, violence and intense national hatred' while the experienced Western commentator Zbigniew Brzezinski foresaw a decade ago that this problem might become more important politically than the racial issue has been in the United States.[94] My own view is that national relations within the Soviet Union are neither as good as the official statements would have us believe, nor necessarily as bad as the pessimistic critics maintain. Yet the question is obviously one of great complexity, and it is hard to say what constitutes 'solving' the problem: indeed, it may be ultimately insoluble.

There are many dimensions to the question. One is the number and range of nationalities. There are over 100 recognised groups, ranging from 129 million-odd Russians and 41 million Ukrainians to 1089 Orochi and 441 Aleutians at the time of the 1970 census. There were approaching 2 million Germans, over 1 million Poles, and significant numbers of other nationalities with a state outside the USSR, adding a foreign-policy dimension. Some, such as the Russians, Ukrainians, Georgians, Armenians and others, possess an ancient cultural heritage and a long historic identity as distinct nations, while others (particularly in Central Asia) were largely illiterate and traditional bearers of a common Moslem culture. Certain groups, such as the Roman Catholic Lithuanians and the Buddhist Kalmyks, are identified with particular religions, adding a religious aspect to policy-making in this area. Several of these factors unite in the very special case of the Jews – combining with long-standing anti-semitism in some parts of the western USSR, and with the principles of Zionism, which are seen as racialist by the Soviet regime – to create a problem which has risen to a central position in East-West relations in recent years.

The problem of resolving the potential tensions associated with the existence of such a wide diversity of national units is formidable. Clearly, the application of concepts of equality and national self-determination becomes highly problematical in these circumstances. In recent years, a cause of grave concern has been the recurrent manifestations of nationalist sentiment, particularly in the Ukraine and Lithuania, and among sections of the Russians.[95]

It can be seen that the nationality question is multi-faceted, and policy-making here involves policy in many other areas. A further angle is the impact of industrialisation. One result of the association between birth-rate and industrial development, which has caused rates of reproduction to differ widely between national groups, is that the urbanised European areas of the Soviet Union are facing a severe labour shortage, while the less developed areas, particularly of Central Asia, possess a surplus. Western Europe solved its labour shortage in the 1950s and 1960s by bringing in immigrants or 'guest workers' from outside Europe. That may be a solution for the Soviet economy. Yet it would impose a strain on the older cities, with the greatest labour shortages, and the migrants might end up in the less skilled positions (as in Western Europe). Their inadequate cultural training to cope with Russian city life, coupled with lack of proper facilities for maintaining their own traditions, might lead to precisely the same type of tensions that have become established in some British cities. The other solution (which, in essence, represents the Soviet response to the problem) is to take economic growth and development to the poorer areas. In this field, the Soviet Government can claim considerable success: the cities of the outlying republics can boast a record in job creation and can display a range of cultural and other facilities that few non-metropolitan cities in other parts of the world can match. And yet the danger remains that this may be greeted with resentment, since it is the Russians, above all, who are bringing in their skills and upsetting the traditional way of life of non-European peoples, organising them, imposing an alien set of values, showing the way, and thereby perforce dominating.

This is, of course, the dilemma of a developing country, where an urban elite has to impose its values on an unsophisticated populace: in the Soviet Union, the national question adds a further problem to be overcome. In this connection it is interesting to note that Soviet writers in recent years have been emphasising the importance of recruiting and training local leaders in the national areas;[96] and yet that very policy might encourage the nationalism that might threaten the unity of the system. By the same token, by encouraging local ethnic cultural activities, establishing administrative units based on the national principle, and inserting national identification in citizens' internal passports, the Government risks fostering an awareness of national distinctions that could be exploited for subversive purposes or help to maintain prejudices; on the other hand, not to do so might lay it open to charges of Russian chauvinism, since, in view of their numerical preponderance and their high cultural and economic level, the Russians are bound to retain the leading position in the State as a whole; alternatively, it could be accused of neglecting to recognise the national minorities' legitimate interests and aspirations for advancement.

The nationalities question is thus extremely intricate, and it is inextricably bound up with problems and policies in other areas, any one of which might seem overwhelmingly important at any time. Given this interdependence of problems and issues, and the many pressures that face the political leadership at any time; given too the apprehensions that they doubtless experience about what might happen to the country if they were to permit the free play of political and other forces; and given the daily examples around the world of terrorism for nationalist purposes – by South Moluccans in the Netherlands, by the IRA in Northern Ireland, by Croatian exiles in Sweden, the FRG and elsewhere: given all this, the safest course, when viewed from the Kremlin, may well be to pursue present policies, in the expectation that economic development, combined with a relatively high level of internal migration and consequent intermixing, will ultimately lead to a diminishing in the importance of national distinctions.

FOREIGN RELATIONS

In the previous sections of this chapter, I have been concerned almost exclusively with internal developments in the Soviet Union; I conclude with an excursion into foreign relations.

In the opening section, we saw the strategic position of the territory of the USSR: vulnerable, in these days of intercontinental missiles, from all quarters. Not only are NATO countries within striking distance of Soviet cities over the Pole, in Western Europe, and on the south-western flank, in Greece and Turkey, but in addition the Chinese present a constant challenge over the long border across Asia, with Mongolia forming a territorial buffer for part of the distance, but also needing permanent Soviet buttressing. As was noted, the USSR willy-nilly is engaged in world-wide diplomacy, for basic strategic and defensive reasons. As Hammer has noted, 'an overriding, possibily pathological concern about national security' has always inspired Soviet foreign policy.[97] Whether such concern is justified, it is hard to say. But memories of ham-fisted foreign intervention shortly after the revolution, and especially memories of the tragic losses in the Second World War, still inspire mistrust of foreigners that is not entirely the product of official propaganda.

These memories, fears and suspicions, sometimes encouraged by impressive if sentimental films, also inspire a genuine popular horror of war among the Soviet masses. In view of this, there can be little doubt that the Soviet Union's international rise in stature – whether measured by Brezhnev's overseas travels or the visits of Western leaders to Moscow, or by the military hardware displayed on anniversary parades in the Soviet capital and other cities – is a reassurance to Soviet citizens and leads them to support a regime that protects them in this way. Soviet citizens see it as perfectly natural for their country to be involved in world affairs to the same degree as the United States, and employing similar means of displaying that involvment. If the United States can 'legitimately' intervene in the Dominican Republic, involve itself in Chile or the Middle East, and have warships cruising around the globe, then the Soviet Union has the same rights. Such an attitude is reflected in a view which I heard more than once during the period of the 'Prague Spring' of 1968, to the effect that the people of Czechoslovakia – and Romania, Poland and other countries of Eastern Europe – should remember who saved them from fascism (namely, the Soviet Union), with the implication that they should eternally express their gratitude by adhering to the Moscow line. Popular attitudes, therefore, form an internal dimension to Soviet foreign relations. They probably do not act as a serious constraint, restricting the Government's policies, provided these do not lead to the ultimate of armed conflict with the West; on the contrary, as I have argued, the fact that the regime shows itself capable of ensuring the country's capacity to defend itself helps to win popular support. The related programme of space research fulfils a similar purpose.

In addition to defensive concerns, the Soviet Union's growing population and developing economic strength have placed her in a position of might comparable with the great powers, thereby achieving under Stalin and his successors what Russia ultimately failed to attain under the Tsars: acceptance as an equal by the great powers of the day. Under Khrushchev, the Soviet Union became a *global power*, and policy in the past decade, in particular, has been to place at the country's disposal the military capacity which it feels is required, and in such deployment as to play such a role effectively. That included in 1976–7 a defence expenditure estimated at 50,000–75,000 million rubles ($115,000–125,000 million), an armed force of 3,650,000, disposed in an army of 1,825,000, a navy of 450,000 and an air force of the same number, plus 350,000 border and security troops. The bulk of the army – 106 divisions – was in Europe (including those in Warsaw Pact countries), with forty-three divisions on the Sino-Soviet border; the navy included forty nuclear attack and forty-four nuclear cruise-missile submarines, one aircraft-carrier, and a naval air force of about 645 combat aircraft.[98] A significant development in the past decade has been the deployment of an Indian Ocean fleet and of a significant force in the Mediterranean: these have modified the world's strategic balance and been an object of great concern among the Soviet Union's adversaries. As David Holloway has observed, it is hard to estimate whether this fresh deployment of the Soviet navy represents an attempt to counter Western naval power around the globe, or a move in preparation for an aggressive foreign policy,[99] pursued essentially by proxy, in Africa, southern Asia and the Middle East. It hardly needs pointing out that such deployment places the Soviet Union in a position to interfere with Western oil supplies should this be desired. But, whatever might be said about the specific contents of such developments, there can be no doubt that the overall trend signifies further enhancement of the USSR's international position, finds general support domestically, and taxes the patience and political skills of the Soviet Union's opponents.

In order to assess the significance of these changes in the Soviet Union's international behaviour, it is necessary to consider the *ideological dimension* of Soviet policy-making. Indeed, this may be seen as the crucial issue in trying to understand Soviet intentions. The question that arises is, how far does the USSR behave as a great-power state, and how far as the bearer of the creed of communism? Obviously, it performs both roles, and it might be argued that it is of little real consequence which factor dominates: an aggressive foreign policy is likely to bear roughly the same content whether from a great power or from an ideologically motivated one; only the rhetoric is likely to differ.

What is clear, however, is that, from the very inception of the Soviet regime, leaders have tended to identify the interests of communism with those of the Soviet Union. Experienced students of Soviet foreign policy point out that ideology has steadily waned as a factor that *inspires* Soviet actions, implying that, given the way the Soviet mood has developed, the chances of a Soviet-led communist crusade are now negligible. As Hammer points out, the ideology is not a blueprint: it is more a 'way of looking at the world', and over time the interests of the Soviet State have come to take precedence over the interests of revolutionary communism.[100] Another writer, Vernon Aspaturian, refers to the 'progressive de-ideologization of Soviet foreign policy goals',[101] so that, far from contemplating a risky campaign to bring revolutionary communism to the whole world, the Soviet Union tends to be conservative, cautious and deliberate, carefully calculating the risks before engaging in action.[102] The fact that it may miscalculate (as happened in Cuba in

1962) is a separate issue, and such miscalculations may reflect the level of efficiency of the Soviet intelligence agencies.

Yet if the communist ideology does not inspire Soviet foreign policy, it nevertheless plays an important part in Soviet foreign relations, if only to provide a suitable rhetoric for justifying policies and actions adopted or engaged in for essentially different reasons. Obviously, the Soviet profession of Marxism-Leninism dictates the posture adopted by Western governments, particularly the United States. The fear of 'communism' is at least as great as the fear of the USSR as a great power. Similarly, the way China perceives Moscow's 'distortions' of the ideology has influenced the development of Sino-Soviet relations as much as the territorial disputes and other bones of contention between China and the USSR as states.

The official Soviet view of the world is one in which the capitalist states are in deepening crisis; in which the socialist states, led by the USSR, are continuously growing in economic power and political prestige; and in which the Third World states are engaged in the struggle against the exploitation of the capitalist states, and are assisted by the Soviet Union and her allies. China, according to the Soviet view, pursues policies aimed against the majority of the socialist states and close to the position of 'the most extreme reaction in the whole world', including 'the racists of South Africa and the fascist rulers of Chile'.[103] This is obviously a view of the world through the prism of Marxism-Leninism, or Moscow's interpretation of the ideology, which serves to indicate who are the Soviet Union's friends and potential friends, and who her enemies, and to justify foreign-policy initiatives.

As far as relations with her allies are concerned, there are a number of principles that govern Soviet policies and actions. The first is that the Soviet Union, as the first state to achieve the socialist revolution, has always claimed to be the 'leader' in building communism. More than that, under Stalin it was declared that the Soviet way was the only correct way, which the countries of Eastern Europe were obliged to imitate, regardless of economic, social and political divergences among them. Since the mid 1950s this insistence of copying the Soviet model has been discarded in favour of 'polycentrism': the notion that each communist party within its respective country is in the best position to determine the appropriate road to communism for that country. (This principle, which Moscow even now sometimes seems to accept with reluctance, is of particular relevance in the Soviet Union's relations with West European communist parties.) Since the events in Czechoslovakia in the spring and summer of 1968, that doctrine has been further refined and modified, and the Soviet Union insists that certain characteristics are essential in a state that purports to be building communism. Above all stands the insistence on the the 'leading and guiding' role of the communist party, under whatever name, with everything that this implies for the independence and competence of all other organisations and institutions.[104] The case of Czechoslovakia proves that a loyal foreign policy is not sufficient for an ally of the Soviet Union: indeed, Romania has succeeded in steering a relatively independent foreign policy. When, however, it appears (when viewed from the Kremlin) that the communist party is beginning to lose its grip, then the socialist countries, led by the USSR, have the right and duty to intervene and rescue that state. Such, in essence, is the so-called 'Brezhnev doctrine', enunciated by the Soviet leader in the months following August 1968. That interpretation of the Soviet Union and her allies' 'internationalist duty' to each other has remained a central part of Soviet foreign perspectives.

Further elements also influence Soviet relations with other socialist countries, in particular membership of the Warsaw Treaty Organisation and Comecon. The Warsaw Treaty of 1949 established a military alliance as a counter to NATO, and is to be regarded for strategic purposes as an extension of Soviet military might; policy objectives are co-ordinated through the Pact's Political Consultative Committee. Comecon, which also dates from 1949, is the main instrument for intra-bloc trade and economic development, and attempts to co-ordinate the plans of the various member countries. The construction of oil and gas pipelines, the establishment of a power grid, and now the beginnings of a motorway network, all tend to cement the various countries together in firm economic substructure links.

At the same time, the development of Comecon and the hostility towards capitalism do not preclude extending economic ties with the advanced countries of the non-communist world, despite Western attempts – which provoke indignation and dismay in Moscow – to link the sale of grain or advanced technology with the emigration of Soviet Jews or with the treatment of dissidents. There may be several reasons why the Soviet Union regards improved relations with the West as of particular significance, as witness the insistent calls for a relaxation of tension (detente) in recent years: indeed, it is no exaggeration to say that Brezhnev has staked his reputation on such an achievement.

One view is that detente is intended to lull the West into a sense of security, of which the Soviet Union may be able to take advantage later. A second possible reason for detente is that it permits the country to concentrate her energies in that region where she feels ultimately most vulnerable: involvement in a conventional war with China probably appears a greater real threat than does a nuclear war with the West. And, in weighing the military and strategic balance, the Soviet leaders have to consider not only external strength, but also the reliability of their own national minorities, and that of their Warsaw Pact allies in any confrontation in Europe: loyalty to socialism may not necessarily prove strong enough to overcome traditional dislike of the Russians.

A further set of important reasons links detente with the needs of the Soviet economy. As we noted above, after years of deprivation the Soviet people are now beginning to enjoy the fruits of their effort and are rapidly becoming intent on enriching themselves with consumer goods and services. The likely impact of this growing wealth on the population's potential willingness to fight is a complex question that I shall leave aside. What is clear, though, is that a reduction in military expenditure would release substantial funds for investment in the provision of more consumer goods, as a means of winning popular support and gaining legitimacy. However, the level of wealth in Soviet society is already such that the demand can be met only by producing, efficiently and in volume, high-quality, sophisticated products to match those originally developed in the more advanced economies of the West.

In the past generation we have witnessed the rise of the Soviet consumer.[105] In the 1950s, with a devastated country still recovering from the ravages of war, and practically isolated from the outside world, the population could be fobbed off with few goods of poor design and quality. That is no longer possible, or desirable. Basic provision is already made, and a richer society becomes more discriminating. Soviet taste is becoming educated, largely through contact with the outside world, through tourism in both directions, informal contacts, exchanges of students, scholars and others, and through radio and television. Soviet citizens are often remarkably well informed about life abroad, including living standards and the range and quality of goods available in the advanced countries. Moreover, the Polish riots of December 1970, which brought down Gomułka's government precisely over the issue of consumer goods, cannot but have had some impact on the Soviet leaders, and served as a warning of the possible results of too long ignoring the interests of the consumer. The importation of Western consumer-goods technology, the best-known example of which is the Fiat automobile works at Togliatti, on the Volga, has thus become a significant element in Soviet foreign relations, although its impact on overall Soviet economic performance has apparently been slight.[106]

The involvement of Japanese and American technology in the exploitation of Siberia's frozen wealth is of potentially greater longer-term significance. A rapprochement with China, particularly if coupled with Japanese advanced technology, leading to joint exploitation of Siberia's wealth to supply the Chinese and Asian market, would be a development of gigantic dimensions, portending a shift in the centre of gravity of world economic activity.[107]

For the foreseeable future, such a development is out of the question. Economists, regrettably but perhaps wisely, rarely make predictions about the probable form of human economic activity in, say, 200 or 500 years' time. But, if there is to be any future for industrialism, this kind of development seems almost bound to come about sooner or later. For the moment, in Siberia the Soviet Union possesses 'one of the last and greatest undeveloped areas',[108] the exploitation of which offers a challenge and an opportunity for the future of the USSR and for her relations with the world outside.

CONCLUSION

In this chapter I have been concerned to portray the Soviet Union not simply in ideological or great power or similar terms, stressing one dominant element that is of particular concern. Such an exercise, while it has its uses for policy-making, cannot, in my view, permit one to take an overall perspective. I am reminded of this whenever I visit the USSR: fed on a Western newspaper diet of economic problems and depressing reports of official treatment of dissidents, it is a salutary reminder to arrive in Moscow and see, amid these persistently grimmer aspects, that people do nevertheless smile on the streets, couples embrace in the parks, save up for things, go out for restaurant meals, and generally go about their business.

For anyone raised in the Western tradition of political freedom, life in the Soviet Union remains restricted. Shortages prevail; facilities are lacking; standards are low; quality is inferior. Yet to say this does not adequately cover Soviet reality. Soviet society, as any other, is a complex whole, and the features discussed in this essay form some of the more significant elements. Change is constantly occurring, and, while the political leaders attempt to control the pace and direction of change, fresh developments inside and outside the country add further stimulus. Despite the grim truth of the regime's treatment of dissidents, very many citizens in all walks of life – perhaps the majority – share a sense of optimism, of satisfaction that things are getting better, life is getting fuller and freer, in spite of everything. A further encouraging sign is that the present leaders themselves acknowledge that problems exist that need to be tackled; and, as I have shown, quite apart from the dissidents, there is a body of scholars and intellectuals who are developing and circulating sophisticated ideas and opinions, coming to grips with the problems posed by advanced technology, and working out their implications for the future of society. Given the absence of major catastrophes, and given longer experience of involvement in an educated and sophisticated society, the Soviet Union in a generation or two from today is likely to look significantly different from the image it has enjoyed in the past. Whether it will be any closer to the traditionally held view of 'communism' is perhaps a separate question.

BIOGRAPHIES

Leonid Il'ich Brezhnev, leader of the CPSU since 1964 and President of the USSR since 1977, has led an essentially Party-oriented career. Born in 1906 into a working-class family, he graduated from the Dneprodzerzhinsk metallurgical institute in the Ukraine. He joined the Party in 1931, and six years later began his political career, as deputy chairman of the Dneprodzerzhinsk city soviet. In subsequent years he held successive provincial party positions in the Ukraine, leading up to his first major appointment, as trouble-shooting first secretary of the party in Moldavia, the tiny republic reincorporated into the USSR during the war.

After two years in Moldavia, he was called to the central Party Secretariat in Moscow and subsequently assigned as a political adviser to the army and navy. At the Nineteenth Party Congress (1952) he was elected to the CPSU Central Committee and elevated to candidate membership of the Political Bureau.

In 1954 he was sent to Kazakhstan to supervise the campaign to bring vast tracts of virgin lands under the plough, and two years later he returned to Moscow for a spell in the Secretariat, until his transfer in 1960 to the presidency, a move that was interpreted in the West as demotion.

However, in 1963 he again took on a Party central secretaryship, working under Khrushchev as First Secretary, while retaining his State position. With the palace revolution of October 1964, in which

Khrushchev was ousted from his posts as First Secretary and as Prime Minister, Brezhnev was one of the triumvirate (together with Kosygin as Prime Minister, and Anastas Mikoyan as President, soon to be replaced by Nikolai Podgorny) who took over the leadership of the country. Brezhnev was Party First Secretary, a title altered in 1966 to Secretary-general of the CPSU Central Committee, a post which he has retained, and to which in June 1977, following Podgorny's removal, he again added the presidency. In the 1970s Brezhnev has come to dominate the Soviet political scene.

Aleksei Nikolaevich Kosygin, born in Leningrad in 1904, and a graduate of that city's textile institute, has been Chairman of the USSR Council of Ministers (Prime Minister) since October 1964.

After a brief early career involving consumers' co-operatives in Siberia and textile-factory management in Leningrad, his first political appointment was as Mayor of Leningrad, in 1938. In the following year, at the age of thirty-five, he was promoted to be Minister for the Textile Industry, in Moscow, and a year later he became a Deputy Prime Minister.

A Party member since 1927, he was elected to the Central Committee in 1939 and raised to candidate membership of the Political Bureau in 1946 (two years later he became a full member). During the war he was responsible for co-ordinating the food and light industries, and during 1942 he had special responsibility for supplies in blockaded Leningrad. To his other responsibilities he added the post of Prime Minister of the RSFSR in 1943.

Further ministerial appointments followed the war: finance, light industry, consumer-goods industries, again Deputy Prime Minister of the USSR, and First Deputy Chairman of Gosplan, of which he became chairman in 1959.

His Party career suffered a setback in 1952, when he was demoted to candidate membership of the Political Bureau. The following year he was removed from it entirely. This demotion was associated with a severe purge of the Leningrad apparatus and those connected with it, embarked upon in 1948. In 1957, however, Kosygin returned to the Political Bureau as a candidate member, and in 1960 he recovered full membership; that same year, he also became First Deputy Prime Minister, directly under Khrushchev as Premier – a position which he took over when Khrushchev's posts were split.

In that position, for several years, Kosygin worked to reform and reorient the economy, and also undertook foreign tours. In the 1970s his position in the 'collective leadership' has increasingly become subordinated to that of the Party Secretary-general.

BASIC FACTS ABOUT THE USSR

Official name: Union of Soviet Socialist Republics (Soyuz Sovetskikh Sotsialisticheskikh Respublik).

Area: 22,402,200 sq. km. (8,620,000 sq. miles).

Population (mid 1977): 258,900,000.

Population density: 11·6 per sq. km.

Population distribution: 62 per cent urban, 38 per cent rural.

Membership of the CPSU (Kommunisticheskaya partiya Sovetskogo Soyuza) *at 1 July 1977*: 16,203,446.

Administrative division: 15 union republics; 20 autonomous republics; 8 autonomous provinces; 126 provinces; 10 national areas. (See Table 23.1.)

Major ethnic groups (1970): Russians, 53·4 per cent; Ukrainians, 16·9 per cent; Uzbeks, 3·8 per cent; Belorussians, 3·7 per cent.

Population of major cities (1977): Moscow (Moskva, the capital), 7,819,000; Leningrad, 4,425,000; Kiev, 2,079,000; Baku, 1,435,000; Kharkov, 1,405,000.

National income by sector (1978): industry, 64·6 per cent; agriculture, 14·0 per cent; construction, 10·5 per cent; transport and communications, 4·3 per cent; trade, catering and others, 6·6 per cent.

Major natural resources: timber, oil, natural gas, coal, platinum, iron, gold, uranium, diamonds, lead, zinc, nickel, tin.

Foreign trade (1976): exports, 28,022 million rubles; imports, 28,731 million rubles; total, 56,753 million rubles. (1 ruble = $1·32.)

Structure of foreign trade (1976): with socialist countries, 55 per cent; with capitalist countries, 33 per cent; with developing countries, 12 per cent.

Rail network: 138,500 km. (39,700 km. electrified).

Road network: 1,405,600 km. (689,700 km. surfaced).

Oil pipelines: 58,600 km.

Gas pipelines: 103,500 km.

Higher educational institutions (1976–77): 859, with 4,950,200 students (734,600 graduates in 1976).

Publications (1978): newspapers – 7844 titles, 38,458 million copies; books – 84,156 titles, 1737·2 million copies; periodicals – 4859 titles, 3068·8 million copies.

TABLE 23.1 USSR: administrative divisions, 1 January 1977

Administrative units

Union republics (15)[a]	Population (million)	Autonomous republics	Autonomous oblasts[b]	National areas	Krais and oblasts[b]	Rural districts	Urban districts	Cities and towns	Urban-type settlements	Village soviets
RSFSR	135·6	16	5	10	55	1,783	344	995	2,015	22,710
Ukraine	49·3	–	–	–	25	477	115	398	896	8,542
Byelorussia	9·4	–	–	–	6	117	16	96	109	1,512
Uzbekistan	14·5	1	–	–	11	134	12	82	84	977
Kazakhstan	14·5	–	–	–	19	210	29	82	189	2,174
Georgia	5·0	2	1	–	2	65	8	51	62	923
Azerbaijan	5·8	1	1	–	–	61	10	60	125	1,051
Lithuania	3·3	–	–	–	–	44	7	92	20	594
Moldavia	3·9	–	–	–	–	34	3	21	37	712
Latvia	2·5			–	–	26	6	56	36	507
Kirgizia	3·4	–	–	–	3	34	4	17	32	362
Tadzhikistan	3·6	–	1	–	2	41	4	18	47	293
Armenia	2·9	–	–	–	–	36	7	24	33	469
Turkmenia	2·7	–	–	–	5	40	3	15	73	229
Estonia	1·4	–	–	–	–	15	4	33	26	194
USSR, total	257·8	20	8	10	126	3,117	572	2,040	3,784	41,249

Source: Yezhegodnik Bol'shoi Sovetskoi Entsiklopedii, 1977 (Moscow: Sovetskaya Entsiklopediya, 1977) p. 15; population figures for 1 Jan 1977 from Narodnoe khozyaistvo SSSR za 60 let (Moscow: Statistika, 1977) p. 42.

[a] The listing of Union republics follows the Soviet rank-ordering, which is according to population in 1947.

[b] Krai = territory; oblast = province.

Foreign relations (beginning of 1977): diplomatic relations with 128 countries; member of UN, Comecon, WTO, etc.

NOTES

1. Narodnoe khozyaistvo SSSR za 60 let (Moscow: Statistika, 1977) p. 585. (Hereafter referred to as Narkhoz 1977.)
2. Ibid., p. 83.
3. For example, Iain F. Elliot, The Soviet Energy Balance (New York: Praeger, 1974) pp. 252–9; Herbert L. Sawyer, 'The Soviet Energy Sector:

Problems and Prospects', in *The USSR in the 1980s* (Brussels: NATO, Directorate of Economic Affairs, 1978) pp. 33–51.

4. *Narkhoz 1977*, p. 83.
5. Elliot, *The Soviet Energy Balance*, p. 263.
6. E. Stuart Kirby, *The Soviet Far East* (London: Macmillan, 1971) p. xiii.
7. Ibid., pp. 17–26.
8. Robin Edmonds, *Soviet Foreign Policy, 1962–1973* (London: Oxford University Press, 1975) pp. 159–61.
9. J. A. Newth, 'Demographic Developments', in Archie Brown and Michael Kaser (eds), *The Soviet Union since the Fall of Khrushchev*, 2nd ed. (London: Macmillan, 1978) p. 75.
10. *Narkhoz 1977*, pp. 72–3. For an interpretation in terms of urbanisation and industrialisation, see Rein Taagepera, 'National Differences Within Soviet Demographic Trends', *Soviet Studies*, XX (1969) 478–89.
11. Mervyn Matthews, *Class and Society in Soviet Russia* (London: Allen Lane, 1972) p. 17.
12. *XXV s"ezd Kommunisticheskoi partii Sovetskogo Soyuza: Stenograficheskii otchet* (Moscow: Politizdat, 1976) vol. I, p. 98.
13. *Narkhoz 1977*, p. 40.
14. Lotta Lennon, 'Women in the USSR', *Problems of Communism*, XX, no. 4 (July–Aug 1971) esp. pp. 54–5.
15. Pierre Sorlin, *The Soviet People and Their Society* (New York: Praeger, 1969) pp. 21–2, 29; *Narkhoz 1977*, p. 7.
16. For an argument along these lines, see Robert C. Tucker, 'Culture, Political Culture, and Communist Society', *Political Science Quarterly*, LXXXVIII (1973) 173–90.
17. J. P. Nettl, *Political Mobilization: A Sociological Analysis of Methods and Concepts* (London: Faber, 1967) p. 70.
18. G. V. Barabashev and K. F. Sheremet, 'KPSS i Sovety', *Sovetskoe gosudarstvo i pravo*, 1967, no. 11, p. 31. On the USSR as a 'partocracy' see Abdurakhman Avtorkhanov, *The Communist Party Apparatus* (Chicago: Henry Regnery, 1966). On the single party as a characteristic of totalitarianism, see Carl J. Friedrich and Zbigniew K. Brezezinski, *Totalitarian Dictatorship and Autocracy*, 2nd ed. (New York: Praeger, 1966) p. 21 and ch. 4.
19. Sigmund Neumann, 'Toward a Comparative Study of Political Parties', repr. in Jean Blondel (ed.), *Comparative Government: A Reader* (London: Macmillan, 1969) p. 69.
20. *Voprosy vnutripartiinoi zhizni i rukovodyashchei deyatel'nosti KPSS na sovremennom etape* (Moscow: Mysl', 1974) p. 247.
21. See, for example, Sidney I. Ploss, *Conflict and Decision-making in Soviet Russia: A Case Study of Agricultural Policy, 1953–1963* (Princeton, NJ: Princeton University Press, 1965); Joel J. Schwartz and William R. Keech, 'Group Influence and the Policy Process in the Soviet Union', *American Political Science Review*, LXII, 2 (1968) 840–51. Khrushchev's blanket denunciation of Stalin after 1956 is the most massive single example of such rejection of previous policy.
22. See, for example, Barabashev and Sheremet, in *Sovetskoe gosudarstvo i pravo*, 1967, no. 11, p. 34; *Politicheskaya organizatsiya razvitogo sotsialist-*

icheskogo obshchestva (pravovye problemy) (Kiev: Naukova dumka, 1976)
p. 421 and *KPSS — rukovodyaschee yadro politicheskoi sistemy Sovetskogo obshchestva* (Moscow: Mysl', 1977) pp. 4–5.

23. For a thorough analysis of this question, see in particular the work of T. H. Rigby: *Communist Party Membership in the Soviet Union, 1917–1967* (Princeton, NJ: Princeton University Press, 1968); and 'Soviet Communist Party Membership under Brezhnev', *Soviet Studies*, XXVIII (1976) 317–37.

24. Ibid. For an excellent analysis of the problem of regulating the composition of the Party, see Peter Frank's contribution to Brown and Kaser, *The Soviet Union since the Fall of Khrushchev*, pp. 96–120; also Darrell P. Hammer, 'The Dilemma of Party Growth', *Problems of Communism*, XX, no. 4 (July–Aug 1971) 16–21.

25. *XXV s"ezd*, vol. I, p. 89.

26. See rules 2 and 3; English version reprinted in David Lane, *Politics and Society in the USSR*, 2nd ed. (London: Martin Robertson, 1978) pp. 514–31.

27. *XXV s"ezd*, vol. I, p. 89

28. *Demokratiya razvitogo sotsialisticheskogo obshchestva* (Moscow: Nauka, 1975) p. 100.

29. See Brown and Kaser, *The Soviet Union since the Fall of Khrushchev*, p. 273, note 79.

30. *Partiinoe stroitel'stvo: uchebnoe posobie*, 3rd ed. (Moscow: Politizdat, 1972) p. 162.

31. See, for example, Michel Tatu, *Power in the Kremlin* (London: Collins, 1969) pp. 538–9; Brown and Kaser *The Soviet Union since the Fall of Khrushchev*, pp. 111–12, 306–7; and esp. Rein Taagepera and Robert Dale Chapman, 'A Note on the Ageing of the Politburo', *Soviet Studies*, XXIX (1977) 296–305.

32. Brown and Kaser, *The Soviet Union since the Fall of Khrushchev*, pp. 112–13. Brown connects the Brezhnev 'personality cult' with this problem in an extremely interesting speculation: see ibid., pp. 312–13.

33. *Partiinoe stroitel'stvo*, p. 162.

34. For an analysis of the Central Committee and the principles governing its composition, see Michael P. Gehlen and Michael McBride, 'The Soviet Central Committee: An Elite Analysis', *American Political Science Review*, LXII (1968) 1232–41.

35. Reported in *Pravda*, 17 Apr 1975, and 25 May 1977.

36. John A. Armstrong, *Ideology, Politics and Government in the Soviet Union: An Introduction*, 3rd ed. (London: Nelson, 1973) p. 90.

37. Derek J. R. Scott, *Russian Political Institutions*, 4th ed. (London: Allen and Unwin, 1969) p. 140.

38. *Partiinaya zhizn'*, 1977, no. 21, pp. 36–8; that issue contained comprehensive statistics on the Party.

39. *Organizatsionno-ustavnye voprosy KPSS* (Moscow: Politizdat, 1973), pp. 179–80.

40. G. K. Shakhnazarov, *Sotsialisticheskaya demokratiya: nekotorye voprosy teorii* (Moscow: Politizdat, 1972) p. 86. For the text of the 1961 programme and analysis of it, see Leonard Schapiro (ed.), *The USSR and the Future* (New York: Praeger, 1963).

41. On the composition of the deputies, see Everett M. Jacobs, 'The Composition of Local Soviets, 1959–1969', *Government and Opposition*, VII (1972) 503–19; and Ronald J. Hill, 'Patterns of Deputy Selection to Local Soviets', *Soviet Studies*, XXV (1973) 196–212.
42. A fuller discussion of the points raised in this paragraph appears in Ronald J. Hill, *Soviet Politics, Political Science and Reform* (forthcoming); see also Ronald J. Hill, *Soviet Political Elites: The Case of Tiraspol* (London: Martin Robertson, 1977) *passim*.
43. Ibid., pp. 19, 101–3.
44. John Read, *Ten Days that Shook the World* (Harmondsworth: Penguin, 1966) p. 9.
45. *XXIV s"ezd. . . . Stenograficheskii otchet* (Moscow: Politizdat, 1971) vol. II, p. 233. On the developments in the early 1970s, see Ronald J. Hill, 'Recent Developments in Soviet Local Government', *Community Development Journal*, VII, no. 3 (1972) 169–75.
46. V. A. Kim and G. V. Nechitailo, *Otrazhenie interesov naseleniya v deyatel'nosti mestnykh Sovetov deputatov trudyashchikhsya* (Alma-Ata: Nauka, 1970) p. 3. On Soviet views of interests, see Hill, *Soviet Politics, Political Science and Reform*, ch. 5.
47. *Organizatsiya i deyatel'nost' Sovetov i organov gosudarstvennogo upravleniya Armyanskoi SSR* (Erevan: Izdatel'stvo Akademii Nauk Armyanskoi SSR, 1970) p. 165; on the old-style leader and his training, see *Internatsional'nyi printsip v stroitel'stve i deyatel'nosti KPSS* (Moscow: Politizdat, 1975) pp. 160–1; and on the demands made of the 'modern' leader, see ibid., p. 165.
48. Tatu, *Power in the Kremlin*; Robert Conquest, *Power and Policy in the USSR* (London: Macmillan, 1961); Roger Pethybridge, *A Key to Soviet Politics* (London: Allen and Unwin, 1962); and Ploss, *Conflict and Decision-Making*; Roy A. Medvedev, *On Socialist Democracy* (Nottingham: Spokesman Books, 1975) ch. 48.
49. This point is argued more fully in my *Soviet Politics, Political Science and Reform*, ch. 9.
50. Brown and Kaser, *The Soviet Union since the Fall of Khrushchev* ; p. 267.
51. Karl Marx, 'The Class Struggles in France, 1848–1850'; excerpt in Theodore Shanin (ed.), *Peasants and Peasant Society* (Harmondsworth: Penguin, 1971) p. 229.
52. Alec Nove, *The Soviet Economic System* (London: Allen and Unwin, 1977) p. 18.
53. *XXIV s"ezd*, vol. I, p. 123.
54. Nove, *The Soviet Economic System*, pp. 99–108.
55. For a discussion of this point, see Alec Nove, *Was Stalin Really Necessary?* (London: Allen and Unwin, 1964) pp. 17–39.
56. Ian H. Hill, 'The End of the Russian Peasantry?', *Soviet Studies*, XXVII (1975) 109–127.
57. On social differentiation within the peasantry, see Matthews, *Class and Society*, ch. 6.
58. *Narkhoz 1977*, p. 8.
59. Figures ibid., pp. 350 (collective farms), 370 (State farms).
60. Ibid., p. 466 (including junior service personnel and security staff).

61. Figures ibid., p. 593; Churchward's estimate in L. G. Churchward, *The Soviet Intelligentsia* (London: Routledge and Kegan Paul, 1973) p. 7. David Lane, using a different definition, arrives at a figure of 24 million in December 1976, including 10 million employed third-level graduates, but excluding students and unemployed graduates, such as pensioners and housewives: see Lane, *Politics and Society*, p. 390. See also Matthews, *Class and Society*, pp. 141–8.
62. *Narkhoz 1977*, pp. 68, 49.
63. Calculated from ibid., pp. 59–68.
64. See Nove, *The Soviet Economic System*, ch. 5, for an interesting discussion of this and other problems in Soviet agriculture.
65. V. I. Staroverov, *Gorod ili derevnya* (Moscow: Politizdat, 1972) p. 60.
66. Ibid., p. 61; see also Nove, *The Soviet Economic System*, pp. 220–1.
67. Staroverov, *Gorod ili derevnya*, p. 62; cf. E. Zagorodnaya, 'Budushchee malykh gorodov', *Sovetskaya Moldaviya*, 23 Jan 1976, p. 2.
68. Staroverov, *Gorod ili derevnya*, pp. 64–5.
69. Ibid., p. 64; Walter D. Connor, *Deviance in Soviet Society* (New York: Columbia University Press, 1972) pp. 173–5.
70. *XXV s"ezd*, vol. II, p. 233.
71. Ibid., pp. 233–42.
72. Jack Perry, 'The USSR and the Environment', *Problems of Communism*, XXII, no. 3 (May–June 1973) 53; see also Keith Bush, 'Environmental Problems in the USSR', ibid., XXI, no. 4 (July–Aug 1972) 21–31.
73. P. Oldak, in *Literaturnaya gazeta*, 3 June 1970; cited by Perry in *Problems of Communism*, XXII, no. 3, p. 54.
74. Bush, ibid., XXI, no. 4, p. 28.
75. R. A. Safarov, *Obshchestvennoe mnenie i gosudarstvennoe upravlenie* (Moscow: Yuridicheskaya literatura, 1975) p. 169.
76. English text in Lane, *Politics and Society*, pp. 553–84.
77. Statistics from *Narkhoz 1977*, pp. 575–98.
78. See, for example, *Sovetskaya Moldaviya*, 26 Apr 1973.
79. L. Blyakhman and O. Shkaratan take a positive view of this trend in *Man at Work* (Moscow: Progress Publishers, 1977), ch. 4. See also Matthews, *Class and Society*, pp. 109–10, for a different view of the likely impact.
80. On childhood socialisation, see Urie Bronfenbrenner, *Two Worlds of Childhood* (Harmondsworth: Penguin, 1974) chs 1–3; on adult political education, see Stephen White, 'Political Socialization in the USSR: A Study in Failure?', *Studies in Comparative Communism*, X (1977) 328–42.
81. See in particular David Lane, *The End of Inequality? Stratification under State Socialism* (Harmondsworth: Penguin, 1971), and *Politics and Society*, chs 12 and 13. See also Matthews, *Class and Society*, chs 4 and 6; and Frank Parkin, *Class Inequality and Political Order* (London: Paladin, 1972), ch. 5.
82. Lane, *Politics and Society*, p. 419.
83. G. M. Gak, 'Obshchestvennye i lichnye interesy i ikh sochetanie pri sotsializme', *Voprosy filosofii*, 1955, no. 4, pp. 17–28; G. Y. Glezerman, 'Interes kak sotsiologicheskaya kategoriya', ibid., 1966, no. 10, pp. 14–26; Yu. V. Shabanov, *Problemy Sovetskoi sotsialisticheskoi demokratii v period stroitel'stva kommunizma* (Minsk: Nauka i tekhnika, 1969) p. 261; B. M.

Lazarev, 'Sotsial'nye interesy i kompetentsiya organov upravleniya', *Sovetskoe gosudarstvo i pravo*, 1971, no. 10, pp. 86, 89–91.
84. Georgi Shakhnazarov, *The Role of the Communist Party in Socialist Society* (Moscow: Novosti, 1974) pp. 29, 42.
85. V. A. Nemtsev, 'Ob ispol'zovanii konkretno-sotsiologicheskogo metoda dlya izucheniya problem administrativno-territorial'nogo deleniya', in *Nekotorye voprosy sotsiologii i prava* (Irkutsk, 1967) p. 231.
86. Note, in particular, his monograph on the question, *Obshchestvennoe mnenie i gosudarstvennoe upravlenie* (Moscow: Yuridicheskaya literatura, 1975).
87. *XXV s"ezd*, vol. I, pp. 92, 98.
88. *Demokratiya razvitogo sotsialisticheskogo obshchestva*, pp. 86, 38.
89. Shakhnazarov, *Sotsialisticheskaya demokratiya*, p. 137.
90. See for example, Eugene Lyons, in *Problems of Communism*, July–Aug 1966; repr. in Zbigniew Brzezinski (ed.), *Dilemmas of Change in Soviet Politics* (New York: Columbia University Press, 1969), p. 51.
91. See Moshe Lewin, *Political Undercurrents in Soviet Economic Debates* (London: Pluto Press, 1975).
92. For example, the Ukrainian Party leader, V. V. Shcherbitskii, wrote in a recent book, 'At the Twenty-fifth CPSU Congress it was underlined that not all problems are yet resolved, that better than all our critics we know our deficiencies, we see the difficulties, and we are successfully overcoming them' – quoted in G. Glezerman and M. Iovchuk, 'Sovetskii obraz zhizni i formirovanie cheloveka', *Kommunist*, 1978, no. 4, p. 124.
93. I. Groshev, *A Fraternal Family of Nations* (Moscow: Progress Publishers, 1967).
94. Andrei Amalrik, *Will the Soviet Union Survive until 1984?* (London: Allen Lane, 1970) p. 61; Zbigniew Brzezinski, Foreword to Vyacheslav Chornovil, *The Chornovil Papers* (New York: McGraw-Hill, 1968) p. vii.
95. For a succinct survey of the development of nationalism in different parts of the Soviet Union, see Peter Reddaway's contribution to Brown and Kaser, *The Soviet Union since the Fall of Khrushchev*, pp. 121–56, esp. pp. 135–46.
96. See, for example, *Voprosy vnutripartiinoi zhizni* . . . , p. 192; B. N. Topornin, *Sovetskaya politicheskaya sistema* (Moscow: Politizdat, 1975) p. 61.
97. Darrell P. Hammer, *USSR: The Politics of Oligarchy* (Hinsdale, Ill.: Dryden Press, 1974) p. 387.
98. Figures on Soviet military strength from *The Military Balance, 1976–1977* (London: International Institute for Strategic Studies, 1976) pp. 8–10, and 109–10.
99. David Holloway, 'Foreign and Defence Policy', in Brown and Kaser, *The Soviet Union since the Fall of Khrushchev*, p. 55.
100. Hammer, *USSR*, pp. 384–6.
101. Vernon V. Aspaturian, 'Foreign Policy Perspectives in the Sixties', in Alexander Dallin and Thomas B. Larson (eds), *Soviet Politics since Khrushchev* (Englewood Cliffs, NJ: Prentice-Hall, 1968) p. 132.
102. Jan F. Triska and David D. Finley, *Soviet Foreign Policy* (New York: Macmillan, 1968) esp. ch. 9 (cited in Hammer, *USSR*, p. 387).
103. Brezhnev, in *XXV s"ezd*, vol. I, p. 33.

104. See, for example, the comments of V. V. Platkovskii in 'Partiya –
     rukovodyashchaya sila sotsialisticheskogo gosudarstva', *Sovetskoe gosud-
     arstvo i pravo*, 1970, no. 8, p. 8.
105. See Margaret Miller, *The Rise of the Russian Consumer* (London: Institute
     of Economic Affairs, 1965).
106. See the assessment by Philip Hanson, 'The Import of Western
     Technology', in Brown and Kaser, *The Soviet Union since the Fall of
     Khrushchev*, pp. 16–48.
107. Kirby, *The Soviet Far East*, p. 2.
108. Ibid., p. 254.

BIBLIOGRAPHY

There is an enormous literature on the Soviet Union, in English and other
languages, and the titles which follow are necessarily selective. For further
reading, see David Lewis Jones, *Books in English on the Soviet Union, 1917–1973*
(New York and London: Garland Publishing, 1975); for specialised reading,
including articles, note the bibliographies following each chapter of David Lane,
Politics and Society in the USSR, 2nd ed. (London: Martin Robertson, 1978).
Significant documents originating in the USSR are to be found in Bogdan
Szajkowski (ed.), *Documents in Communist Affairs – 1977* and *1979* (Cardiff:
University College Cardiff Press); and *Documents in Communist Affairs – 80*
(London: Macmillan, annual).

General

Amalrik, Andrei, *Will the Soviet Union Survive until 1984?* (London: Allen Lane,
     1970).
Berner, Wolfgang *et al.* (eds), *The Soviet Union: Domestic Policy, Economics,
     Foreign Policy* (London: C. Hurst, annual [since 1975]).
Brown, Archie and Kaser, Michael (eds), *The Soviet Union since the Fall of
     Khrushchev*, 2nd ed. (London: Macmillan, 1978).
Cliff, Tony, *Russia: A Marxist Analysis* (London: Socialist Review Publications,
     1964).
Davies, R. W. (ed), *The Soviet Union* (London: Allen and Unwin, 1978).
Kaiser, Robert G., *Russia: The People and the Power* (London: Secker and
     Warburg, 1976).
Morton, Henry W. and Tökés, Rudolf L. (eds), *Soviet Politics and Society in the
     1970s* (New York: The Free Press, 1974).
Nogee, Joseph L. (ed.), *Man, State, and Society in the Soviet Union* (London:
     Pall Mall, 1972).
Rositzke, Harry, *The USSR Today* (London: Abelard-Schuman, 1973).
Salisbury, Harrison E. (ed.), *Anatomy of the Soviet Union* (London: Nelson,
     1967).
Shakhnazarov, G. K., *Sotsialisticheskaya demokratiya: nekotorye voprosy teorii*
     (Moscow: Politizdat, 1972).
Smith, Hedrick, *The Russians* (London: Times Books, 1976).
Vladimirov, Leonid, *The Russians* (London: Pall Mall, 1968).

Werth, Alexander, *Russia: Hopes and Fears* (Harmondsworth: Penguin, 1969).

Historical background

Carr, E. H., *A History of Soviet Russia*, 11 vols (London: Macmillan, 1950–78).
Conquest, Robert, *The Great Terror* (London: Macmillan, 1968).
Deutscher, Isaac, *The Unfinished Revolution* (London: Oxford University Press, 1967).
———, *Russia after Stalin* (London: Jonathan Cape, 1969).
Ginzburg, Evgenia S., *Into the Whirlwind* (London: Collins, 1967).
Keep, John, *The Russian Revolution* (London: Weidenfeld and Nicolson, 1976).
Mandelstam, Nadezhda, *Hope against Hope* (Harmondsworth: Penguin, 1975).
———, *Hope Abandoned* (Harmondsworth: Penguin, 1976).
McCauley, Martin (ed.), *The Russian Revolution and the Soviet State, 1917– 1921: Documents* (London: Macmillan, 1975).
McNeal, Robert H., *The Bolshevik Tradition* (Englewood Cliffs, N.J.: Prentice-Hall, 1975).
Medvedev, Roy, *Let History Judge* (London: Macmillan, 1972).
Nettl, J. P., *The Soviet Achievement* (London: Thames and Hudson, 1967).
Nove, Alec, *Stalinism and After* (London: Allen and Unwin, 1975).
Pethybridge, Roger, *The Social Prelude to Stalinism* (London: Macmillan, 1974).
Read, John, *Ten Days that Shook the World* (Harmondsworth: Penguin, 1977).
Treadgold, Donald W. (ed.), *The Development of the USSR* (Seattle: University of Washington Press, 1964).
Trotsky, Leon, *The Revolution Betrayed* (London: New Park Publications, 1967).
Tucker, Robert C., *The Soviet Political Mind* (London: Allen and Unwin, 1972).
Von Laue, T. H., *Why Lenin? Why Stalin?* (London: Weidenfeld and Nicolson, 1966).

Geography, resources, environment

Cole, J. P., *Geography of the USSR* (Harmondsworth: Penguin, 1967).
Conolly, Violet, *Siberia Today and Tomorrow* (London: Collins, 1975).
Elliot, Iain F., *The Soviet Energy Balance* (New York: Praeger, 1974).
Goldman, Marshall I., *The Spoils of Progress* (Cambridge, Mass.: MIT Press, 1972).
Harris, Chauncy D., *Cities of the Soviet Union* (Chicago: Rand McNally, 1970).
Kirby, E. Stuart, *The Soviet Far East* (London: Macmillan, 1971).
Lydolph, Paul, *Geography of the USSR*, 3rd ed. (New York: Wiley, 1977).
Mathieson, R. S., *The Soviet Union: An Economic Geography* (London: Heinemann, 1975).
Mints, A. *et al.*, *Geography of the USSR* (London: Collet's, 1975).
Morey, George, *The Soviet Union: The Land and its People* (London: Macdonald Educational, 1975).
Pryde, Philip R., *Conservation in the Soviet Union* (London: Cambridge University Press, 1972).

Singleton, Fred (ed.), *Environmental Misuse in the Soviet Union* (New York: Praeger, 1976).
St George, George, *Siberia: the New Frontier* (London: Hodder and Stoughton, 1969).
Symons, Leslie and White, Colin, *Russian Transport* (London: G. Bell, 1975).

Politics

Armstrong, John A., *Ideology, Politics and Government in the Soviet Union*, 3rd ed. (London: Nelson, 1973).
Barghoorn, Frederick C., *Politics in the USSR*, 2nd ed. (Boston and Toronto: Little, Brown, 1972).
Barry, Donald D. *Contemporary Soviet Politics* (Englewood Cliffs, N.J.: Prentice-Hall, 1978).
Brown, A. H.,*Soviet Politics and Political Science* (London: Macmillan, 1974).
Brzezinski, Zbigniew K. (ed.), *Dilemmas of Change in Soviet Politics* (New York: Columbia University Press, 1969).
Churchward, L. G., *Contemporary Soviet Government*, 2nd ed. (London: Routledge and Kegan Paul, 1975).
Cocks, Paul with Daniels, Robert V. and Heer, Nancy W., *The Dynamics of Soviet Politics* (Cambridge, Mass.: Harvard University Press, 1976).
Cornell, Richard, *The Soviet Political System: A Book of Readings* (Englewood Cliffs, N.J.: Prentice-Hall, 1970).
Dallin, Alexander and Larson, Thomas B. (eds), *Soviet Politics since Khrushchev* (Englewood Cliffs, N.J.: Prentice-Hall, 1968).
Dallin, Alexander and Westin, Alan F. (eds), *Politics in the Soviet Union: 7 Cases* (New York: Harcourt, Brace and World, 1966).
Fainsod, Merle, *Smolensk Under Soviet Rule* (London: Macmillan, 1958).
Fainsod, Merle and Hough, Jerry, *How the Soviet Union is Governed* (Cambridge, Mass.: Harvard University Press, 1978).
Gilison, Jerome M., *The Soviet Image of Utopia* (Baltimore: Johns Hopkins University Press, 1975).
Hammer, Darrell P., *USSR: The Politics of Oligarchy* (Hinsdale, Ill.: Dryden Press, 1974).
Hill, Ronald J., *Soviet Political Elites: The Case of Tiraspol* (London: Martin Robertson, 1977).
Hough, Jerry, *The Soviet Union and Social Science Theory* (Cambridge, Mass.: Harvard University Press, 1978).
Juviler, Peter H. and Morton, Henry W., *Soviet Policy-making* (London: Pall Mall, 1967).
Laird, Roy D., *The Soviet Paradigm* (New York: The Free Press, 1970).
Lane, David, *Politics and Society in the USSR*, 2nd ed. (London: Martin Robertson, 1978).
Latov, Vitali, *The Soviet Electoral System* (Moscow: Novosti, 1974).
Lewin, Moshe, *Political Undercurrents in Soviet Economic Debates* (London: Pluto Press, 1975).
Marcuse, Herbert, *Soviet Marxism* (London: Routledge and Kegan Paul, 1958).
McAuley, Mary, *Politics and the Soviet Union* (Harmondsworth: Penguin, 1977).

Medvedev, Roy A., *On Socialist Democracy* (London: Macmillan, 1975).
Meyer, Alfred G., *Leninism* (Cambridge, Mass.: Harvard University Press, 1957).
——, *The Soviet Political System: An Interpretation* (New York: Random House, 1965).
Moore, Barrington, Jr, *Soviet Politics – the Dilemma of Power* (New York: International Arts and Sciences Press, 1976).
Osborn, Robert J., *The Evolution of Soviet Politics* (Homewood, Ill.: Dorsey, 1974).
Schapiro, Leonard (ed.), *The USSR and the Future* (New York: Praeger, 1963).
——, *The Government and Politics of the Soviet Union*, 6th ed. (London: Hutchinson, 1977).
Scott, D. J. R., *Russian Political Institutions*, 4th ed. (London: Allen and Unwin, 1969).
Tatu, Michel, *Power in the Kremlin* (London: Collins, 1969).
Taubman, William, *Governing Soviet Cities* (New York: Praeger, 1973).
Topornin, B. N., *Sovetskaya politicheskaya sistema* (Moscow: Politizdat, 1975).

The Party

Armstrong, John A., *The Politics of Totalitarianism* (New York: Random House, 1961).
——, *The Soviet Bureaucratic Elite* (London: Atlantic Books, 1959).
Djilas, Milovan, *The New Class* (London: Allen and Unwin, 1966).
Gehlen, Michael P., *The Communist Party of the Soviet Union: A Functional Analysis* (Bloomington: Indiana University Press, 1969).
Hough, Jerry F., *The Soviet Prefects* (Cambridge, Mass.: Harvard University Press, 1969).
Kommunisticheskaya partiya v politicheskoi sisteme sotsialisticheskogo obshchestva (Moscow: Mysl', 1974).
Moses, Joel C., *Regional Party Leadership and Policy-making in the USSR* (New York: Praeger, 1974).
Partiinoe stroitel'stvo: uchebnoe posobie, 3rd ed. (Moscow: Politizdat, 1972).
Rigby, T. H., *Communist Party Membership in the USSR, 1917–1967* (Princeton: Princeton University Press, 1968).
Schapiro, Leonard, *The Communist Party of the Soviet Union*, 2nd ed. (London: Methuen, 1970).
Shakhnazarov, Georgi, *The Role of the Communist Party in Socialist Society* (Moscow: Novosti, 1974).
Stewart, Philip D., *Political Power in the Soviet Union* (Indianapolis and New York: Bobbs-Merrill, 1968).

The State

Barabashev, G. V. and Sheremet, K. F., *Sovetskoe stroitel'stvo*, 2nd ed. (Moscow: Yuridicheskaya Literatura, 1974).
Bezuglov, A. A., *Soviet Deputy (Legal Status)* (Moscow: Progress Publishers, 1973).

Carson, George Barr, Jr, *Electoral Practices in the USSR* (London: Atlantic Press, 1956).
Cattell, David T., *Leningrad: Case Study of Soviet Urban Government* (New York: Praeger, 1968).
Mote, Max E., *Soviet Local and Republic Elections* (Stanford, Calif.: Hoover Institution, 1965).
Narkiewicz, Olga, *The Making of the Soviet State Apparatus* (Manchester: Manchester University Press, 1970).
Saifulin, R. A. (ed.), *The Soviet Form of Popular Government* (Moscow: Progress Publishers, 1972).
Vanneman, Peter, *The Supreme Soviet* (Durham, NC: Duke University Press, 1977).

Interest groups

Remnek, Richard B. (ed.), *Social Scientists and Policy Making in the USSR* (New York: Praeger, 1977).
Safarov, R. A., *Obshchestvennoe mnenie i gosudarstvennoe upravlenie* (Moscow: Yuridicheskaya literatura, 1975).
Skilling, H. Gordon and Griffiths, Franklyn (eds), *Interest Groups in Soviet Politics* (Princeton, N.J.: Princeton University Press, 1971).

Society

Brokhin, Yuri, *Hustling on Gorky Street* (London: W. H. Allen, 1976).
Chinn, J. H., *Manipulating Soviet Population Resources* (London: Macmillan, 1977).
Churchward, L. G., *The Soviet Intelligentsia* (London: Routledge and Kegan Paul, 1973).
Connor, Walter D., *Deviance in Soviet Society* (New York: Columbia University Press, 1972).
Fischer, George, *The Soviet System and Modern Society* (New York: Atherton Press, 1968).
Hollander, Paul (ed.), *American and Soviet Society: A Reader* (Englewood Cliffs, N.J.: Prentice-Hall, 1969).
——, *Soviet and American Society* (New York: Oxford University Press, 1973).
Inkeles, Alex and Bauer, Raymond A., *The Soviet Citizen* (New York: Atheneum, 1968).
Kassof, Allen (ed.), *Prospects for Soviet Society* (London: Pall Mall, 1968).
Klassy, sotsial'nye sloi i gruppy v SSSR (Moscow: Nauka, 1968).
Lane, David, *The End of Inequality?* (Harmondsworth: Penguin, 1971).
——, *The Socialist Industrial State* (London: Allen and Unwin, 1976).
Matthews, Mervyn, *Class and Society in Soviet Russia* (London: Allen Lane, 1972).
——, *Privilege in the Soviet Union* (London: Allen and Unwin, 1978).
Osipov, G. V. (ed.), *Town, Country and People* (London: Tavistock, 1969).
Parkin, Frank, *Class Inequality and Political Order* (London: Paladin, 1972).
Reshetov, P. and Skurlatov, V., *Soviet Youth* (Moscow: Progress Publishers, 1977).

Sorlin, Pierre, *The Soviet People and Their Society* (New York: Praeger, 1969).
Yanowitch, Murray, *Social and Economic Inequality in the Soviet Union* (London: Martin Robertson, 1977).

The nationalities

Allworth, Edward (ed.), *The Nationality Question in Soviet Central Asia* (New York: Praeger, 1973).
Clem, Ralph S., *The Soviet West* (New York: Praeger, 1975).
Conquest, Robert (ed.), *Soviet Nationalities Policy in Practice* (London: Bodley Head, 1967).
——, *The Nation-killers* (London: Macmillan, 1970).
Dzyuba, Ivan, *Internationalism or Russification?* (London: Weidenfeld and Nicolson, 1970).
Groshev, I., *A Fraternal Family of Nations* (Moscow: Progress Publishers, 1967).
Katz, Zev (ed.), *Handbook of Major Soviet Nationalities* (New York: The Free Press, 1975).
Kochan, Lionel (ed.), *The Jews in Soviet Russia Since 1917*, 3rd ed. (London: Oxford University Press, 1978).
'Nationalities and Nationalism in the USSR', special issue of *Problems of Communism*, XVI, no. 5 (Sep–Oct 1967).
Rakowska-Harmstone, T., *Russia and Nationalism in Central Asia* (Baltimore: Johns Hopkins University Press, 1970).
Schlesinger, Rudolf, *The Nationalities Problem and Soviet Administration* (London: Routledge and Kegan Paul, 1956).
Simmonds, George W. (ed.), *Nationalism in the USSR and Eastern Europe* (Detroit: University of Detroit Press, 1977).

Religion

Bociurkiw, B. R. and Strong, J. W. (eds), *Religion and Atheism in the USSR and Eastern Europe* (London: Macmillan, 1975).
Bourdeaux, Michael, *Opium of the People* (London: Faber, 1965).
——, *Faith on Trial in Russia* (London: Hodder and Stoughton, 1971).
—— (ed.), *Religious Minorities in the Soviet Union, 1960–1970* (London: Minority Rights Group, 1973).
——, *Patriarchs and Prophets* (London: Mowbrays, 1975).
Kolarz, W., *Religion in the Soviet Union* (London: Macmillan, 1962).
Lane, Christel, *Christian Religion in the Soviet Union* (London: Allen and Unwin, 1978).
Lawrence, John, *Russians Observed* (London: Hodder and Stoughton, 1969).
Powell, David E., *Antireligious Propaganda in the Soviet Union* (Cambridge, Mass.: MIT Press, 1975).
Zernov, Nicolas, *The Russians and their Church*, 3rd ed. (London: SPCK, 1978).

Education

Bereday, G. Z. F. *et al.* (eds), *The Changing Soviet School* (London: Constable, 1961).

Bronfenbrenner, Urie, *Two Worlds of Childhood* (London: Allen and Unwin, 1971).

Grant, Nigel, *Soviet Education* (Harmondsworth: Penguin, 1968).

Jacoby, Susan, *Inside Soviet Schools* (New York: Schocken Books, 1975).

Lane, David and O'Dell, Felicity, *Soviet Industrial Workers: Social Class, Education and Control* (London: Martin Robertson, 1978).

Price, Ronald F., *Marx and Education in Russia and China* (London: Croom Helm, 1977).

Dissent

Barghoorn, Frederick C., *Detente and the Democratic Movement in the USSR* (New York: The Free Press, 1976).

Barker, Francis, *Solzhenitsyn: Politics and Form* (London: Macmillan, 1977).

Bloch, Sidney and Reddaway, Peter, *Russia's Political Hospitals* (London: Gollancz, 1977).

Carter, Stephen, *The Politics of Solzhenitsyn* (London: Macmillan, 1977)

Chornovil, Vyacheslav, *The Chornovil Papers* (New York: McGraw-Hill, 1968).

Feldbrugge, F. J. M. (ed.), *Samizdat and Political Dissent in the Soviet Union* (Leyden: A. W. Sijthoff, 1975).

Lader, Malcolm, *Psychiatry on Trial* (Harmondsworth: Penguin, 1977).

Marchenko, Anatoly, *My Testimony* (London: Pall Mall, 1969).

Medvedev, Zhores and Roy, *A Question of Madness* (London: Macmillan, 1971).

Reddaway, Peter (ed.), *Uncensored Russia* (London: Jonathan Cape, 1972).

Sakharov, Andrei D., *Sakharov Speaks* (London: Collins/Harvill Press, 1974).

Solzhenitsyn, Alexander, *Letter to Soviet Leaders* (London: Collins/Harvill Press, 1974).

Tőkés, Rudolf L. (ed.), *Dissent in the USSR* (Baltimore: Johns Hopkins University Press, 1975).

The economy

Bernard, Philippe J., *Planning in the Soviet Union* (London: Pergamon, 1966).

Clarke, Roger, *Soviet Economic Facts, 1917–70* (London: Macmillan, 1972).

Dyker, David, *The Soviet Economy* (London: Granada, 1976).

Ellman, Michael, *Planning Problems in the USSR* (London: Cambridge University Press, 1973).

Hanson, Philip, *The Consumer in the Soviet Economy* (London: Macmillan, 1968).

Kaşer, Michael, *Soviet Economics* (London: Weidenfeld and Nicolson, 1970).

Miller, Margaret, *The Rise of the Russian Consumer* (London: Institute for Economic Affairs, 1965).

Nove, Alec, *An Economic History of the USSR* (Harmondsworth: Penguin, 1969).

——, *The Soviet Economic System* (London: Allen and Unwin, 1977).

Industry, working class

Amann, R. *et al.* (eds), *The Technological Level of Soviet Industry* (New Haven: Yale University Press, 1977).
Andrle, Vladimir, *Managerial Power in the Soviet Union* (Farnborough, Hants: Saxon House, 1976).
Berliner, J. S., *Factory and Manager in the USSR* (Cambridge, Mass: Harvard University Press, 1957).
Blyakhman, L. and Shkaratan, O., *Man at Work* (Moscow: Progress Publishers, 1977).
Brown, Emily C., *Soviet Trade Unions and Labor Relations* (Cambridge, Mass.: Harvard University Press, 1966).
Iovchuk, M. T. and Kogan, L. N. (eds), *The Cultural Life of the Soviet Worker* (Moscow: Progress Publishers, 1975).
McAuley, Mary, *Labour Disputes in Soviet Russia, 1957–1965* (Oxford: Clarendon Press, 1969).
Osipov, G. V. (ed.), *Industry and Labour in the USSR* (London: Tavistock, 1966).
Zdravomyslov, A. G. *et al.* (eds), *Man and His Work* (New York: International Arts and Sciences Press, 1972).

Agriculture, peasantry

Laird, Roy D. and Laird, Betty A., *Soviet Communism and Agrarian Revolution* (Harmondsworth: Penguin, 1970).
Lewin, Moshe, *Russian Peasants and Soviet Power* (London: Allen and Unwin, 1968).
Millar, James R., *The Soviet Rural Community* (Urbana: University of Illinois Press, 1971).
McCauley, Martin, *Khrushchev and the Development of Soviet Agriculture* (London: Macmillan, 1976).
Ploss, Sidney I., *Conflict and Decision-Making in Soviet Russia* (Princeton, N.J.: Princeton University Press, 1965).
Shaffer, Harry G., *Soviet Agriculture* (New York: Praeger, 1977).
Simush, P. I., *Sotsial'nyi portret Sovetskogo krest'yanstva* (Moscow: Politizdat, 1976).
Strauss, E., *Soviet Agriculture in Perspective* (London: Allen and Unwin, 1969).
Wädekin, K.-E., *The Private Sector in Soviet Agriculture* (Berkeley, Calif.: University of California Press, 1973).

Foreign relations

Aspaturian, Vernon V., *Process and Power in Soviet Foreign Policy* (Boston, Mass., and Toronto: Little, Brown, 1971).
Edmonds, Robin, *Soviet Foreign Policy, 1962–73* (London: Oxford University Press, 1975).
Fischer, L., *The Soviets in World Affairs*, 2 vols (London: Jonathan Cape, 1930).
Hoffman, E. P. and Fleron, F. J. (eds), *The Conduct of Soviet Foreign Policy* (London: Butterworth, 1971).

The Military Balance (London: International Institute for Strategic Studies, annual).

Moseley, Philip E., *The Kremlin and World Politics* (New York: Vintage Books, 1960).

Rubinstein, A., *The Foreign Policy of the Soviet Union* (New York: Random House, 1966).

Rush, Myron (ed.), *The International Situation and Soviet Foreign Policy* (Columbus, Ohio: Charles E. Merrill, 1970).

Szporluk, Roman (ed.), *The Influence of East Europe and the Soviet West on the USSR* (New York: Praeger, 1976).

Ulam, Adam B., *Expansion and Coexistence* (London: Secker and Warburg, 1968).

Lenin

Cliff, Tony, *Lenin*, 3 vols (London: Pluto Press, 1975–6).

Deutscher, Tamara (ed.), *Not By Politics Alone* (London: Allen and Unwin, 1973).

Harding, Neil, *Lenin's Political Thought* (London: Macmillan, 1977).

Lewin, Moshe, *Lenin's Last Struggle* (London: Pluto Press, 1975).

Payne, Robert, *The Life and Death of Lenin* (London: W. H. Allen, 1964).

Schapiro, Leonard and Reddaway, Peter (eds), *Lenin* (London: Pall Mall, 1967).

Shub, David, *Lenin: A Biography* (Harmondsworth: Penguin, 1976).

Shukman, Harold, *Lenin and the Russian Revolution* (London: Longman, 1977).

Trotsky, Leon, *The Young Lenin* (Harmondsworth: Penguin, 1974).

Ulam, Adam B., *Lenin and the Bolsheviks* (London: Fontana, 1969).

Stalin

Alliluyeva, Svetlana, *Twenty Letters to a Friend* (London: Hutchinson, 1967).

Deutscher, Isaac, *Stalin: A Political Biography* (Harmondsworth: Penguin, 1966).

Killingray, David, *Stalin* (London: Harrap, 1976).

Rigby, T. H. (ed.), *Stalin* (Englewood Cliffs, N.J.: Prentice-Hall, 1966).

Tucker, Robert C., *Stalin as Revolutionary, 1879–1929* (London: Chatto and Windus, 1974).

Ulam, Adam B., *Stalin: The Man and his Era* (London: Allen Lane, 1974).

Trotsky

Carmichael, Joel, *Trotsky: An Appreciation of his Life* (London: Hodder and Stoughton, 1975).

Deutscher, Isaac, *Trotsky*, 3 vols (London: Oxford University Press, 1960–3).

Knei-Paz, Baruch, *The Social and Political Thought of Leon Trotsky* (Oxford: Clarendon Press, 1978).

Smith, Irving H., *Trotsky* (Englewood Cliffs, N.J.: Prentice-Hall, 1973).

Leon Trotsky Speaks (New York: Pathfinder Press, 1972).

Trotsky, Leon, *My Life* (Harmondsworth: Penguin, 1975).

Khrushchev

Crankshaw, Edward, *Khrushchev* (London: Collins, 1966).
Frankland, Mark, *Khrushchev* (Harmondsworth: Penguin, 1966).
Khrushchev, Nikita, *Khrushchev Remembers*, 2 vols (Harmondsworth: Penguin, 1977).
Linden, Carl A., *Khrushchev and the Soviet Leadership* (Baltimore: Johns Hopkins University Press, 1966).
Medvedev, Roy A. and Zhores A., *Khrushchev: The Years in Power* (London: Oxford University Press, 1977).
Page, Martin and Burg, David, *Unpersoned: The Fall of Nikita Sergeyevitch Khrushchev* (London: Chapman and Hall, 1966).

Brezhnev

Dornberg, John, *Brezhnev: The Masks of Power* (London: Andre Deutsch, 1974).
Institute of Marxism–Leninism, CPSU Central Committee, *Leonid Ilyich Brezhnev: A Short Biography* (Oxford: Pergamon Press, 1977).

Statistics

Itogi Vsesoyuznoi perepisi naseleniya 1970 goda (1970 USSR Census) 7 vols (Moscow: Statistika, 1972–4).
Mickiewicz, Ellen, *Handbook of Soviet Social Science Data* (London: Collier-Macmillan, 1973).
Narodnoe khozyaistvo SSSR (Moscow: Statistika, annual).
Scherer, John L., *USSR Facts and Figures Annual*, vol. I (1977) (Gulf Breeze, Fla.: Academic International Press, 1977).
The USSR in Figures (Moscow: Statistika, annual).

Specialist journals

Canadian Slavonic Papers.
Current Digest of the Soviet Press.
Coexistence: An International Journal.
Critique.
Problems of Communism.
Revue d'Études Comparatives Est–Ouest.
Soviet Analyst.
Soviet Jewish Affairs.
The Soviet Review.
Soviet Law and Government.
Soviet Studies.
Studies in Comparative Communism.

24 Socialist Republic of Vietnam

DAVID ELLIOTT

Despite its image as a small country (it is the sixteenth largest country in the world), the Socialist Republic of Vietnam (SRV) is the world's third most populous communist state. Vietnam's geography has been a major factor in its historical development, particularly with regard to its northern neighbour, China. A thousand years of Chinese occupation between 111 BC and 939 AD left a lasting imprint on Vietnamese culture and institutions. It also left a strong desire for national independence, which subsequently manifested itself in bitter struggles against the Mongols in the thirteenth century, the Ming dynasty in the fifteenth century, and France and the United States in the twentieth century. Although Vietnam has long been viewed in the West as the 'smaller dragon' – a miniature replica of China – modern scholarship has uncovered important cultural and linguistic differences between the two countries, and these in many ways show Vietnam to be more closely linked to its South-east Asian neighbours than to China.

Geography is a factor that assisted Vietnam in preserving its autonomy from China. Their common border lies mainly in mountainous terrain, inhabited primarily by ethnic minorities. Vietnam's two major agricultural areas in the northern and southern deltas are connected by a narrow strip of land between the rugged Annamite mountain chain in the West and the Pacific Ocean. Vietnam reached its present southern boundaries after a process of expansion that nearly doubled its territory between the fifteenth and eighteenth centuries. This process of southward expansion left marked regional differences between the north, central and southern parts of the country, but these local characteristics were placed within a framework of linguistic and cultural unity which proved to have a powerful integrative force, despite long periods of debilitating civil strife. This unity did not always include

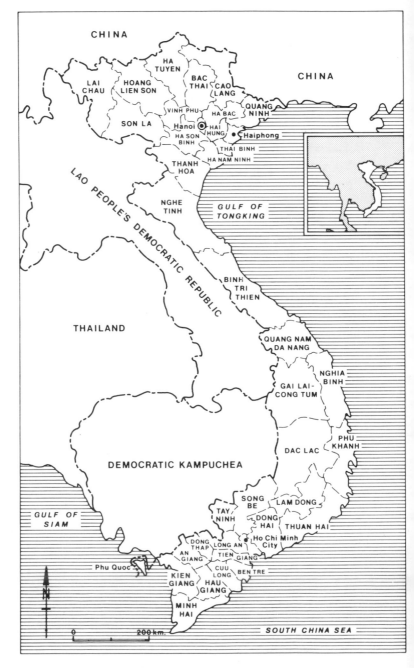

Vietnam: provincial boundaries

the minority groups, however. The ethnic Vietnamese (*nguoi Kinh*) have had a mixed record in their relationships with other ethnic groups. The Kinh comprise 87 per cent of the population. Although minority groups total only about 13 per cent of the SRV's population, they occupy about 75 per cent of the total land area, including many of Vietnam's most sensitive border regions.[1]

Vietnam's communist party was an outgrowth of the upsurge of nationalist anti-colonial movements after the First World War. The major figure in Vietnamese communism, Ho Chi Minh, was a founding member of the French Communist Party in 1920, received a brief period of training in Moscow, and engaged in Comintern activities in Canton in the mid 1920s. In Vietnam itself in 1926, a rising generation of student activities demonstrated against the colonial regime in protest against the ban on organising funeral observances for a leading figure of the early nationalist movement, Phan Chu Trinh. This student protest was an important element in creating the climate in which the precursors of Vietnam's communist party were organised. Some of those who had fled to escape colonial reprisals in Vietnam joined Ho Chi Minh's Thanh Nien (Youth) Party in Hong Kong, while others joined proto-communist groups in Vietnam. The clandestine circumstances in which these groups operated made it difficult to achieve a broad co-ordination of revolutionary activities, and by 1930 three separate communist parties had been formed.

The unification of these parties was carried out under the leadership of Ho Chi Minh in Hong Kong on 3 February 1930.[2] At this time Ho, under the alias of Nguyen Ai Quoc (Nguyen the Patriot), was well known among Vietnamese nationalists for his anti-colonial activities in France and elsewhere. His authority over the movement was further enhanced by his status as a Comintern representative. Initially the Party was called the Vietnamese Communist Party, in order clearly to set it apart from the splinter groups which had preceded it. This name was changed to the Indochinese Communist Party (ICP) in October 1930, because the Comintern felt that since Vietnam, Laos and Cambodia were linked together by the colonial administration they should be guided by a single party. Repression following a premature anti-colonial uprising in 1930 resulted in the virtual extinction of the Viet-Nam Quoc-Dan Dang (VNQDD), a non-communist nationalist party and the major political alternative to the ICP. The ICP itself was devastated by repression following peasant revolts in the revolutionary strongholds of Nghe An and Ha Tinh provinces in central Vietnam. Ho was not in Vietnam at the time, but was arrested in Hong Kong and briefly imprisoned by the British authorities. After his release, Ho went to Moscow in 1933 and stayed there until late 1938.[3]

While Ho was abroad, important changes took place within Vietnam as a result of the formation of the Popular Front government in France. This led to the release of political prisoners, including many who became leading figures in the Vietnamese Party. Some political freedoms were allowed; communist candidates ran for local office in parts of Vietnam and were able to publish their own newspapers. Figures such as Pham Van Dong, Truong Chinh and Vo Nguyen Giap became prominent in Hanoi during this period. Looking forward to a possible change in French policy, the ICP kept a clandestine branch of the Party near Saigon, in southern Vietnam; the current Party Secretary-general, Le Duan, played a key role in this branch. When the Popular Front collapsed, the Party reverted to secrecy and established bases in the rural areas.

The Japanese occupation was a major turning point in the development of Vietnamese communism. It dealt the colonial system a blow from which the French never recovered, despite the Japanese decision to allow the Vichy authorities to exercise nominal control over the administration of Indochina. As a means of diverting the Vietnamese from an alliance with the Japanese based on the idea of an Asian order from which Europeans could be excluded, the Vichy regime encouraged the formation of Vietnamese youth groups under close French scrutiny, and took the calculated risk of encouraging, within limits, expressions of Vietnamese nationalism, which had up to then been strictly forbidden. As the war drew to a close, the Japanese authorities suspected that the colonial regime was preparing to switch its allegiance to de Gaulle and on 9 March 1945 conducted a coup which led to the formation of an 'independent' Vietnamese government under the sponsorship and control of the Japanese. This government was unable to respond to the pressing tasks before it, including massive famine in northern Vietnam, where 2 million people – nearly a fifth of the region's total population – died of starvation.[4] The solution to this catastrophe was clear: to seize the rice stockpiles which the Japanese had set aside in case of an Allied invasion. Most of the anti-communist groups were collaborating with the Japanese and were thus unable to move against their patrons, while the small remnant of the VNQDD was waiting in China, dependent on Nationalist assistance. Only the Viet Minh, led by the ICP, was in a position to move. Many Viet Minh cadres had infiltrated the youth groups and newly organised Japanese militia and it was this force which aided peasants in storming the rice depots to end the famine.[5] This alliance of veteran cadres and rural youths constituted the core of the Party in the subsequent struggle against the French.[6] To this was added the urban bourgeoisie, which supported the Viet Minh during the seizure of power in Hanoi, Hue and Saigon during the period following the Japanese surrender. Ho Chi Minh, who had been directing the anti-Japanese struggle from his mountain base near the Chinese border, entered Hanoi and proclaimed an independent and unified Democratic Republic of Vietnam (DRV) on 2 September 1945. The thirty-year conflict that ensued stemmed from the efforts of external forces to reverse this verdict.

The government of the newly established DRV was a coalition of political forces, dominated by the communists. National elections were held in early 1946, resulting in a large Viet Minh majority. This soon became academic, as the French started their reoccupation of Indochina and the Viet Minh were once again forced to flee to the mountainous base areas. At the time of the August revolution, the ICP numbered around 5000 members, of whom 20 per cent were in prison.[7] By 1946 Party membership had risen to 20,000.[8] In an attempt to rally wide support in their anti-colonial struggle, the ICP announced that it would be dissolved and its members regrouped into Marxist studies associations. This tactical manoeuvre did not prevent a dramatic growth in Party membership, which reached 700,000 by 1950.[9] In effect, the ICP had broadened the united front *within* its own ranks. Instead of becoming a highly disciplined 'steel framework' within the anti-colonial movement, the ICP relaxed its admission criteria to include anyone who was effective in organising the struggle against the French, regardless of class background.

As the resistance to the French dragged on, the Viet Minh leadership began to question this approach. Many of the urban bourgeoisie tired of the struggle and returned to the cities, and it became more difficult to mobilise support in the countryside. The first response to this was the re-emergence of the Communist Party, renamed the Vietnam Workers' Party (VWP) at the Second Party Congress in 1951, into a position of visible and direct leadership. Recognising the different situations of Vietnam, Laos and Cambodia (Kampuchea), the latter two countries were left to form their own anti-colonial organisations and the concept of a single Indochinese party was abandoned. A freeze on Party recruitment was instituted and efforts were made to tighten discipline within its ranks.[10] A second response was to give greater emphasis to the social content of the revolution. In an attempt to appeal for continued sacrifices for the poor peasant majority, which now played the key role in the struggle, the VWP instituted a land reform in 1953. It was not until 1955–6, however, that the main phase of the land reform was launched.

After the French defeat, the Geneva agreements signed on 20 July 1954 provisionally divided Vietnam into two separate zones. Some 80,000 Viet Minh troops regrouped to North Vietnam, to await the expected reunification elections.[11] In the South, around 15,000 Party members stayed behind under orders to push for the implementation of the Geneva agreements.[12] The government of Ngo Dinh Diem in South Vietnam refused to participate in a unification election and instead opted to consolidate power by eliminating the political opposition of Viet Minh resistants. Prohibited from legally engaging in the political process and hunted down by the police, the Viet Minh (now designated 'Viet Cong' – Vietnamese communists – by the Diemists, in order to underscore their communist leadership) responded by taking up arms. Sporadic guerrilla resistance began in 1957 and accelerated during 1958. The DRV leadership, under pressure from the Soviet Union, pursued a policy of non-military struggle. By early 1959, however, Party ranks in the South had been reduced to 5000 members, and it was clear that Hanoi would have to ratify the unauthorised decision by individual southerners to defend themselves by guerrilla warfare, or else risk losing the nucleus of their revolutionary movement in the South.[13] This was done at the Fifteenth Plenum, in January 1959.[14]

As the conflict with the Saigon government escalated, a new generation was recruited into the Party. The southern branch of the Party was controlled by the Central Office for South Vietnam which had been established at the Third Party Congress of September 1950.[15] In December 1960 the National Front for the Liberation of South Vietnam was set up to mobilise broad opposition to the Diem government. The core of the revolutionary movement was provided by the southern branch of the Party, which in early 1962 renamed itself the People's Revolutionary Party and defined itself as 'the Party of all patriots in South Vietnam . . . struggling to overthrow the rule of the imperialists and the feudalists . . . and liberate Vietnam'.[16] Tactically this was intended to underline the southern orientation of this branch of the Party, and organisationally it was designed to separate the tasks of the two branches of the Party: national liberation in the South and socialist construction in the North. By 1962, according to some estimates, membership of the People's Revolutionary Party was 35,000.[17] At its height the southern branch of the Party had about 400,000 members, but this was reduced to about 200,000 by the end of the war in 1975.[18] Party membership in the North rose from 500,000 in 1960 to over 1 million by 1970.[19]

After 1954 the Party leadership had to formulate policies with an eye to both the North and the South. The first major policy implemented in the North was an accelerated land-reform campaign. Although this achieved its objective of breaking the hold of landlords over rural society, it created great turmoil in the North and an adverse reaction in the South. In part this was because of the violence of the campaign. No accurate figures exist for the number of people killed or unjustly accused during the campaign, but the chaos caused by the actions of the land-reform teams forced the DRV to bring the campaign to a halt and to institute a Rectification of Errors Campaign.[20] Party Secretary-general Truong Chinh was held responsible for the excesses of the land reform and removed from his post. His successor, Le Duan, was formally named First Secretary of the Party in September 1960 but had been acting in that capacity prior to this official appointment[21] even though Ho himself had nominally assumed the title of Secretary-general after the removal of Chinh.

At about the same time as the decision to allow armed struggle in the South was made, the DRV also determined to proceed with socialist construction without waiting for the unification of Vietnam, which, it was now recognised, was a long way off.[22] Collectivisation of agriculture was the main decision of the Fourteenth Plenum in November 1958, and the second DRV constitution, which had been in preparation since 1956, was not issued until the end of 1959, suggesting that Hanoi had been reluctant to formalise its separate path of development until it was absolutely certain that national unification would not be forthcoming. The first stage of co-operativisation was completed by mid 1960 and the first stage of socialist transformation was considered basically complete by 1961. Higher-level co-operatives were set up gradually. By 1967 only three-quarters of co-operatives had moved to the advanced stage; the remainder attained the higher-level stage of organisation in the late 1960s and early 1970s.[23]

Relations with the Soviet Union and China fluctuated during the 1954–75 period. Both the USSR and the People's Republic were instrumental in pressing the Viet Minh in 1954 to accept less at the bargaining table than it had won on the battlefield.[24] Moscow even proposed in 1957 that both North and South Vietnam should be accepted into the United Nations.[25] Although the early phase of Sino-Soviet polemics centred around the issue of supporting national liberation movements, China itself did not actively support the move to armed struggle in South Vietnam until challenged by the establishment of the US Military Assistance Command in early 1962.[26] Following the Nuclear Test-ban Treaty, however, the DRV apparently concurred with China's negative assessment of Soviet policy and, during the period from Liu Shao-ch'i's visit to Hanoi in May 1963 until the overthrow of Khrushchev, leaned toward the Chinese position on international communist affairs.[27] Even during this period, however, the DRV attempted to play a mediating role, and in February 1964 the Party's official newspaper, *Nhan dan*, published a major document attempting to heal the rift between the communist powers.[28] When the United States directly entered the conflict, the DRV began to rely more heavily on Soviet political support and military aid and, during the latter phases of the war, was alienated from China's criticism of its strategy for ending the war.[29]

The escalation of the war greatly affected the developmental policies of the DRV, as it was increasingly compelled to devote its resources to military requirements. The First Five-year Plan (1961–5) was not followed with a formal plan until after the unification of Vietnam, when the Second Five-year Plan (1976–80) was implemented. North Vietnam, with a gross national product of about $1700 million suffered, by late 1967, bombing damage estimated to be in excess of $370 million.[30] By the end of the air war, a Japanese firm estimated that restoring North Vietnam's economic infrastructure to its prewar state would require expenditures of between $11,000 million and $15,000 million. Another wartime impact was the decentralisation of industry as the DRV leaders tried to reduce their vulnerability and achieve greater flexibility in responding to war-related tasks.[31] This policy was reassessed at the Nineteenth Plenum, in 1971, and, following the signing of the Paris accords in January 1973, a major process of recentralisation took place.[32]

Nearly one year after the military victory of 1975, elections for a unified National Assembly were held. Despite profound differences in the social and economic patterns of the two regions of Vietnam, the two-track policy of leadership was implicitly abandoned. Unified Vietnam was renamed the Socialist Republic of Vietnam (SRV) and the VWP became the Vietnam Communist Party. These changes were intended to emphasise that, having accomplished the unification of the country, all energies would be devoted toward 'building socialism'.[33] Institutional adjustments were made to cope with the special problems of the old South, but overall policy guidance now was given by the enlarged State Council and the new Political Bureau and Central Committee elected at the Fourth Party Congress in December 1976.[34]

Unable to attract the economic assistance required for major industrial development, and beset by agricultural production problems, in the Second Five-year Plan the SRV reoriented its priorities from industry to agriculture.[35] Relations with China deteriorated, as China suspected that Vietnam was a political rival for influence in South-east Asia and an outpost of Soviet expansion in Asia.[36] In 1978, China finally cut off all economic assistance and withdrew its technicians from Vietnam, replicating the Soviet actions against China in 1960 that had marked the irreparable break in the Sino-Soviet dispute.[37] Without Chinese assistance and in the face of American disinterest in achieving a closer relationship with the SRV, the Vietnamese had only the Soviet Union to turn to for support in their dispute with China. Vietnam's 1978 decision to join Comecon may have been intended as a message for the Chinese.[38] It seems unlikely, especially in the face of reported East European dissatisfaction with the SRV's entry, that any substantial degree of economic integration will occur.[39]

The postwar period for Vietnam may be characterised as transition in a time of crisis. In the face of desperate internal economic problems and external pressures from the major power in the region, Vietnam has not yet been able to develop stable long-range domestic or external policies. Immediately after the end of the war, Vietnam appeared to view itself as a Third World country with a principal interest in developmental issues.[40] It has now become embroiled once again in the Sino-Soviet controversy, and its support of the Soviet position on a broad range of foreign-affairs issues has contributed to the rupture with China. Domestically, its policies have been largely improvisatory, responding to the continuing challenges of economic stagnation.

As it faces the future, the SRV will be confronted with a formidable array of challenges. The central problem will be to achieve a decent standard of living for its people. Not only did Vietnam suffer great economic damage during the war years, it also lost a decade of development. Without improvement in the economic situation, the process of reintegrating the groups that opposed the revolution will be difficult indeed. Many of the political problems in the southern part of Vietnam appear to be largely owing to the bleak economic situation there, and will probably not improve until living standards are significantly raised.

Although Vietnam's problems are formidable, its assets are considerable. Foremost among these is a political leadership with an experience and tradition of unity that is unique among ruling communist parties. It has frequently been observed that the greatest test of a communist political system is the political succession from one leader to another. Vietnam's first succession came in late 1969, following the death of Ho Chi Minh. Despite a brief intensification of policy disputes during this period, the leadership closed ranks around Party First Secretary (now Secretary-general) Le Duan. At the same time, the frequent postwar shifts of policy indicate that the decision-making system is quite flexible, and that decision-making is a collective process. The more complex questions are (1) whether a leadership formed in conditions of continuous struggle is knowledgeable and flexible enough to manage the transition to a peacetime economy, and, if so, (2) what happens when the next generation of leadership takes over? It may be premature to pass judgement on the first question, since the expected peace has once more given way to conflict. None the less, the pragmatic policies of the SRV leadership, their use of incentives, their willingness to experiment, do not indicate a leadership whose only response to the complexity of peacetime management is guerrilla discipline. As for the next generation, it is too early to tell if there are pronounced generational differences in outlook and leadership methods. It does seem to be the case that the SRV is committed to a developmental process that will place heavy reliance on technological expertise. If the past is any guide to the future, one may expect a further development of an elaborate set of bureaucratic institutions providing the State framework within which a pragmatic Party leadership will pursue developmental policies based on maximum utilisation of skilled manpower and external resources. But the past also suggests a vulnerability to external challenges, which continue to make it difficult for the SRV to follow its preferred direction.

THE VIETNAM COMMUNIST PARTY

The present statute of the Party, adopted at the Fourth Party Congress in December 1976, defines the position of the Vietnam Communist Party as the 'leadership nucleus of the dictatorship of the proletariat in our country', having the responsibility of exercising 'unified leadership over all activities of the State and society, focusing the efforts of the entire people, successfully building socialism in the entire country, and safeguarding the permanent independence and unification of the Fatherland'.

Organisation

As with all ruling communist parties, the guiding organisational principle is democratic centralism, which is intended to serve two functions: ensure the 'initiative and creativity of every Party organisation and member' in carrying our Party policies while also ensuring unity of thought and action within the Party. These goals are summarised in the VCP slogan 'collective leadership with individual accountability'. The institutional framework in which democratic centralism is embodied is an electoral process which selects Party executive committees from the local level to the Central Committee. Party policies are ratified by resolutions passed by the majority vote at the periodic Party conferences, from the lowest level to the Central Committee. Despite the formal democratic aspects of the Party institutions, effective authority lies with the twenty-three man Political Bureau (fourteen voting members and nine alternates) and the 133-member Central Committee (101 full members and thirty-two alternates).[41]

According to the Party statutes the Central Committee is the highest leadership organ of the Party between Party congresses, which are supposed to be held every five years.[42] (The clandestine revolutionary struggle and the subsequent division of Vietnam and the wartime situation resulted in an irregular schedule of Party congresses: the first was held in 1935, the second in 1951, the third in 1960 and the fourth in 1976). Between the semi-annual plenums of the Central Committee, the Political Bureau 'takes the place of the Central Committee in exercising leadership over Party tasks' in accordance with the resolutions of the last plenum. In practice, therefore, the Political Bureau is the highest leadership body in the SRV political system. Although it is not known precisely how decisions are made within the Bureau, it appears that decisions often reflect a compromise between its senior members. On occasion important decisions have been altered during the implementation phase. Le Duan, the Secretary-general of the Party, presides over another body elected by the Central Committee – the Party Secretariat – which 'directs the tasks of Party organisation and the coordination among the various organisations in the system of the dictatorship of the proletariat (e.g. both Party and State bureaucracies) in carrying out the resolutions of the Central Committee and the Politburo, and supervising the implementation of Party resolutions at each level and in each branch of activity'. Whereas the Political Bureau is the forum for collective leadership and decision-making, the Secretariat is the instrument of the Party Secretary-general, who derives much of his power and influence from his role in policy implementation.[43] This is particularly true in a highly bureaucratised, pragmatic, problem-oriented political system such as the SRV's.

Membership

Any citizen of Vietnam over the age of eighteen who 'has engaged in labour and not been an exploiter' may become a Communist Party member. Membership of the VCP at the Fourth Party Congress was 1,553,500, or 3·13 per cent of the total population, of which about 273,000 are in southern Vietnam, representing about 1·3 per cent of the population of that region (see Table 24.1).[44] To a great extent the number of Party members has influenced its composition. In 1953 it was noted that 'of 1,365 students (in Party training courses) occupying leading positions, only 139 are workers and 351 working peasants'.[45] In 1960 it was reported that, of the approximately 55,000 Party members who held full-time positions in the State and Party bureaucracy, the

TABLE 24.1 Development of the Vietnamese Party: membership 1945–78

Year	Total	North Vietnam	South Vietnam
1945	5,000		
1946	20,000		
1947	50,000		
1948	168,000[a]	102,000	23,000
1950	700,000		
1955			15,000
1959			5,000
1960		500,000	
1962			35,000
1966			100,000
1968		800,000	
1970		1,100,000	
1975			200,000
1976	1,553,500		
1978			273,000

[a] This total includes 43,000 in central Vietnam, which encompasses part of both post-1954 Zones of Vietnam.

number of full-time cadres from petty-bourgeois backgrounds exceeded those from the 'basic classes' (workers and poor peasants), who represented only 32·7 per cent of the total.[46] By 1962, workers comprised only 5 per cent of the total Party membership.[47] Most of the top-ranking Political Bureau members (including Ho Chi Minh) came from an academic–official background, and many of the early adherents of the Party were students.

To solve the ideological problems raised by this sociological fact, in the late 1920s and early 1930s a programme of 'proletarianisation' was instituted: Party members were sent to the factories, mines and plantations, both to recruit and to become proletarians through immersion in the workers' milieu. As the centre of gravity of Party tasks shifted to the peasants in the countryside, and then to leading all social classes in a resistance against foreign intervention, the concern with the class composition of the Party diminished.

Despite (or perhaps because of) the weak representation from the 'basic classes', the Party has opposed discrimination on the grounds of class origins, and, while class background is a major factor in the selection of Party recruits, their potential leadership and technical skills are often given at least equal weight.[48] Beyond this, there is the post-reunification problem of determining a policy on the admission into the Party of persons from families who had opposed the revolution. The SRV has calculated that 30 to 50 per cent of youths in the South had no major connection with the United States or the former Saigon regime, and thus would be eligible for Party membership.[49] Even those with such connections will apparently be considered for Party membership on a case-by-case basis.[50] Because of the lack of emphasis on class background, no systematic compilation of statistics on the class composition of the Party is available.

Since 1954 the Party has been concerned with the problem of producing a new generation of leadership, but it has met with difficulties in the endeavour – first, because of the reluctance of older Party members from the resistance period fully to accept youths who had not shared the trials and hardships of that experience, and, secondly, because of the weakening of the Party organisation in South Vietnam. As late as 1962, nearly 70 per cent of the VWP's membership (around 500,000 at the time) had joined the Party prior to 1954, and less than 10 per cent of Party members were under twenty-six years of age.[51] During the First Five-year Plan, a concentrated effort was made to recruit young people into the Party, and nearly 80 per cent of the 300,000 increase in Party membership between 1960 and 1965 were under thirty years of age.[52] Total mobilisation during the post-1965 period brought even more young people into the Party, including a significant representation of young women, who were called on to perform production and administrative leadership jobs in North Vietnam. Future Party members are normally recruited from the Ho Chi Minh Communist Youth League, whose membership consists of around 30 per cent of all fifteen to thirty year olds in northern Vietnam, but only 10 per cent in the old South, where membership in the Youth League was only about 200,000 in 1977.[53] This geographic variation in potential Party recruits indicates the probability of future problems in Party building in southern Vietnam.

Middle-level leadership within the Party underwent considerable transformation: nearly one half of district Party committee members in the north were replaced in the leadership elections at this level during the period 1971 to 1976.[54] At the Central Committee level there has also been considerable change. Nearly half of the 1976 full members of the Central Committee were newly elected to that body.[55] (All of the alternates were, of course, first-term Central Committee members.) The Political Bureau has remained largely the same, adding four more full members and three new alternate members. (One member of the Third Congress Political Bureau was dropped for political reasons.) It has been calculated that the average age of Central Committee members is around sixty, while the average Political Bureau member is in the mid sixties.[56] A dearth of reliable biographical information makes it difficult to be exact, but it is clear that the VCP's top leadership is aging. The problem of political succession – the transfer of authority from a ruler or government to a successor – has been characterised as the most serious endemic problem of communist ruling regimes. In Vietnam the first phase of this succession took place in 1969, following the death of Ho Chi Minh, and passed without major difficulties. At that time the Party was strongly united under a unified and tested leadership of great prestige during a time of war. The Party's ability to provide continuity of leadership and produce a new generation of leaders in a time of staggering external and internal challenges will be put to the test in the years to come.

GOVERNMENT

The constitution

The Socialist Republic of Vietnam is a successor regime to the Democratic Republic of Vietnam, founded in 1945. Three constitutions have been promulgated since that time, one in 1946, one in 1960 and the new SRV constitution which was released in 1979.[57] The new constitution takes into account the completion of the process of reunification and the current task of building socialism in the entire country. Previous constitutions had stressed the multi-ethnic character of Vietnam, but the autonomous minority zones which the 1960 Constitution said 'may be established' were abolished in 1976. None the less, the special position of minorities, which in 1960 were granted 'the right to preserve or reform their own customs and habits, to use their spoken and written languages, and to develop their own national culture' will probably be reaffirmed, though the conflict between the SRV and elements of the Chinese minority, the reported dissidence of some groups in the Central Highlands of southern Vietnam, and the increasingly sensitive position of the border areas populated by ethnic minorities and to which members of ethnic Vietnamese are being transferred under a programme of resettlement, may bring about changes in the political relationship of minority groups with the central government.

Most basic civil rights are guaranteed by the Constitution, but these are also carefully circumscribed by the wide latitude which Party and State enjoy in interpreting these rights, and the stipulation that 'the State forbids any person to use democratic freedoms to the detriment of the interests of the State and the people'.[58] In addition to these rights, however, the State guarantees a comprehensive range of 'social rights', including the rights to have a job, to receive education and to receive 'material assistance in old age in the case of illness or disability'. Despite the tenuous nature of the constitutional guarantee of civil rights in the SRV, the State has tried to fulfil its obligations in the social-rights sector, recently eliminating hospitalisation fees and attempting to improve access to education, despite a seriously troubled economy.

Structure

The National Assembly is the highest organ of State authority in the

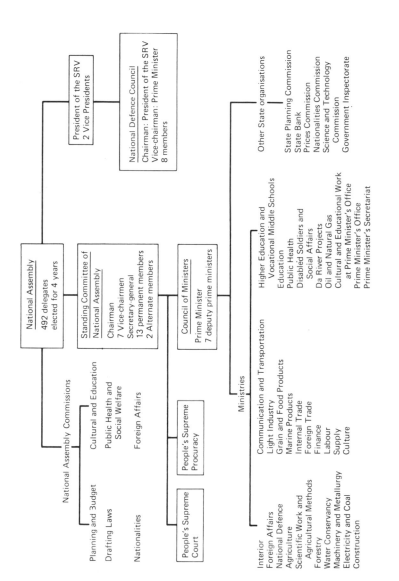

FIGURE 24.1 Governmental structure of the SRV (Compiled by Bogdan Szajkowski)

SRV. (See Figure 24.1, which shows the governmental structure diagrammatically.) The 1960 Constitution specified that elections are held every four years and that the Assembly should meet twice a year. Its constitutional responsibilities are to elect the Chairman and Vice-chairman of the Republic, to appoint the Prime Minister of the government on the recommendation of the Chairman and Vice-chairman, and members of the State Council (Cabinet) on the recommendation of the Prime Minister.

A new National Assembly was elected in April 1976 in conjunction with national reunification and it proclaimed the establishment of the SRV on 2 July 1976. A total of 492 delegates were elected to the Assembly (see Table 24.2).[59] The first (333-member) National Assembly, elected in 1946, was unable to carry out its constitutional functions, owing to the dispersion of the government during the resistance.[60] The National Assembly functioned sporadically as an advisory body, but had no direct policy rule. After the division of Vietnam, the DRV decided to strengthen the Assembly, and in 1957 it established a more powerful Standing Committee, headed by Ton Duc Thang (later elected head of State), and expanded the committees of the Assembly to give it greater scope in reviewing and overseeing the policies of the government.[61] In 1960 the new constitution again strengthened the National Assembly and increased the powers of its Standing Committee.[62] Truong Chinh has headed the Standing Committee from

TABLE 24.2 Results of the 1976 National Assembly elections in Vietnam

Total elected: 492

Composition by occupation:

- 80 workers
- 100 peasants
- 6 manual workers
- 54 military personnel
- 141 political cadres
- 98 representatives of intellectuals and democratic personages
- 13 religious representatives

Composition by individual characteristics:

- 132 female representatives
- 127 youth representatives
- 67 ethnic-minority representatives
- 31 labour heroes and heroes of the armed forces

(*Source: Nhan dan*, 24 June 1976.)

TABLE 24.3 Posts held by members of the Political Bureau of the VCP, 1977

Political Bureau	In the Party			Standing Committee of National Assembly	In the Government	
	Secretariat of the VCP	Department(s) of VCP Central Committee headed	Central Military Party Committee		Council of Ministers	National Defence Council
Full members						
Le Duan	First Secretary					Member
Truong Chinh		Legislation; Research on Party History		Chairman		Member
Pham Van Dong					Prime Minister	Vice-chairman
Pham Hung					Deputy Prime Minister	Member
Le Duc Tho	Member	Organisation				
Vo Nguyen Giap			Member Secretary		Deputy Prime Minister; Minister of National Defence	Member
Nguyen Duy Trinh	Member				Deputy Prime Minister; Minister of Foreign Affairs	Member
Le Thanh Nghi		Emulation			Deputy Prime Minister; Chairman of State Planning Commission	Member
					Minister of Interior	Member

Name			
Tran Quoc Hoan			Member
Van Tien Dung		Deputy Secretary	
Le Van Luong	Member		
Nguyen Van Linh			
Vo Chi Cong			Deputy Prime Minister; Minister of Marine Products
Chu Huy Man			
Alternate members			
To Huu	Member	Science and Education: Propaganda and Training	
Vo Van Kiet			
Do Muoi			Deputy Prime Minister; Minister of Construction

Source: W. S. Turley, 'Vietnam since Renunification', *Problems of Communism*, Mar–Apr 1977, p. 39.

1960 until the present, and outranks Premier Pham Van Dong in Party standing, giving additional authority to the operations of the Committee.

The Council of Ministers carries out State policies under the supervision of the Standing Committee of the National Assembly. Co-ordination between Party decisions and government operations is quite close, owing in part to the fact that the seventeen full and alternate members of the Political Bureau include the Prime Minister, six deputy prime ministers and one minister (see Table 24.3). Relations between the Party Secretariat and the State Council are not as clear, and there does not appear to be any strict dividing line between their respective roles in policy implementation. In conjunction with the decision, in 1978, to accelerate socialist transformation, two important joint Party-State bodies were established: the Private Capitalist Industry and Commerce Reform Committee and the Central Agricultural Reform Committee.[63] These joint bodies appear to diminish even further the distinction between Party and State operations. One possible reason for this tendency toward merging the parallel hierarchies of Party and State may be the increasing dissatisfaction of the SRV leadership with the performance of Party cadres. One response to charges of corruption and inefficiency in cadre ranks has been to set up an elaborate inspectorate system, including the Inspectorate Committee, established by order of the State Council in 1977, which appears to duplicate some of the functions of the Party (which along with the mass organisations is already responsible for 'controlling the activities of State organs in all areas') and the State Procuracy which 'controls the observance of the law by all departments of the State Council, all local organs of State, persons working in organs of State, and all citizens'. In addition, elected people's inspectorate committees have been instituted to watch over the activities of local government in such sensitive areas as food-rationing, family registration, transfer to 'new economic zones' and labour conscription.[64]

Local government

Vietnam has traditionally had four levels of territorial administration: central, province, district and village. The most important levels of local administration have been the province and the village, while for most of the period 1954–5 the role of the district was vaguely defined. An effort was made in 1971 to upgrade the responsibilities of the district and make it the focal point of local administration, but this policy did not become a major priority until the Fourth Party Congress.[65] The SRV now views the district as 'no longer just an administrative management level' but as the focal point for economic management in the countryside.[66] The enlargement of the agricultural co-operatives will make the economic management of the district even more important, as economic specialisation and mechanisation places heavier demands of leadership and co-ordination on that level. At the same time, the Vietnamese have retained the village people's committee as an important element of village government, even though many co-operatives now encompass an entire village, and carry out many of the important leadership and administrative tasks at that level, through the management committee elected by the members of the co-operatives.

Mass organisations

The popular associations (*doan the quan chung*) include the Youth, Women's, and Farmers' Federations. They provide mechanisms for disseminating Party policies and a training ground for potential Party recruits. The most important of these is the Women's Federation, since its tasks and constituency are distinct from those of all other organisations in the SRV. The Ho Chi Minh Youth League is largely responsible for the Youth Federation, and the local Party and agricultural co-operative organs assume leadership over the Farmers' Federation. The importance of the Women's Federation reflects the critical role played by women in Vietnam's revolution, but at the same time suggests that there are still sufficient social barriers to equal participation in the political process to warrant the continuing existence of a special role for the Federation.

The Vietnam General Confederation of Labour (Tong Lien Doan Lao Dong) was formally established in August 1946. Its principal task during the 1946–54 period was mobilising workers in war-related industries. After the DRV had reassumed governmental authority in North Vietnam, the task of the more than 6000 primary trade unions in North Vietnam was to organise workers for emulation campaigns to increase production.[67] The DRV adopted the Soviet 'single-manager system' in industry, which gave factory administrators a wide margin of latitude in factory management and placed a correspondingly heavy burden on labour unions to exercise political leadership among the workers. Although the Confederation does not function as a Western-style bargaining unit, it is entrusted with the responsibility of safeguarding worker welfare. Since many northerners considered factory jobs to be better paying, less onerous, and more 'modern' than most other employment opportunities, worker dissatisfaction did not seem to be a major problem in the 1955–75 period. The labour movement in the South during 1961–75 largely focused on political struggle, led by the South Vietnam Federation of Trade Unions (founded in 1961), against the Saigon government-sponsored trade union. In 1976 the southern organisation merged with the northern one.[68]

Vietnam's umbrella organisation for non-Party political groupings is the Fatherland Front (Mat Tran To Quoc). This organisation grew out of the Lien Viet Association of non-communist political groupings opposed to the French during the First Indochina War. After the 1954 Geneva agreements, the Lien Viet was transformed into the Fatherland Front (September 1955) with the mission of mobilising non-communist support for the reunification of Vietnam. In December 1960 the National Liberation Front was formed in South Vietnam to rally all political forces to overthrow the Saigon government and proceed toward reunification. The Fatherland Front, the National Liberation Front and the Alliance of National Democratic and Peace Forces, formed during the Tet Offensive of 1968 to appeal to the 'Third Force', were merged in June 1976.[69]

SOCIAL AND POLITICAL INTEGRATION

Among Vietnam's many postwar problems are the integration of groups that did not fully participate in the revolution or who actively opposed it. These include religious groups, especially the Catholics, ethnic groups such as the Montagnard tribes in the Central Highlands of southern Vietnam, and a variety of Vietnamese opposed to the revolution on political or class grounds. After the signing of the Geneva agreements of 1954, the Church hierarchy organised a Catholic exodus to South Vietnam totalling 600,000 of the more than 800,000 refugees from the North. 700 priests and ten bishops also fled, leaving only 340 priests and two bishops to minister to a Catholic community which by 1971 had grown to nearly 2 million.[70] This allowed the subsequent appointment of eleven new bishops who were apparently acceptable to both the DRV and the Vatican. Many initial problems were encountered with the predominantly rural Catholic community in North Vietnam, particularly during the land-reform campaign, but these were eventually resolved. In South Vietnam the Catholic community also grew to a total of several million, and were among the strongest supporters of the anti-communist policies of the United States and successive Saigon governments. Towards the end of the war, however, the important changes that had taken place in Vatican policy toward communism and social revolution led the Church in southern Vietnam to adopt a more neutral position, and after 30 April 1975 it urged its members to comply with the policies of the new regime.[71] Ironically, the southern Vietnamese Buddhists, many of whom opposed the war policies of the US and Saigon governments, have had a more difficult time adjusting to the new order. There have been unverified reports of discrimination against members of the Buddhist clergy, whose numbers have declined from 30,000 to 10,000.[72]

A potentially serious political problem for the SRV has been the role of the ethnic minorities in the new Vietnamese polity. In the north of the country, it was the Tay and Nung ethnic minorities that provided crucial support to the Vietnamese struggle against the French. Their special contributions were recognised, and the DRV adopted a policy of facilitating a special path of political, cultural and economic development of the tribal groups within the framework of autonomous highland regions. These regions were, however, abolished after 1975, on the grounds that the political and economic differences between the tribal groups and the lowland Vietnamese were no longer great enough to warrant separate treatment.[73] A probable major consideration was the SRV programme of shifting lowland Vietnamese into the mountainous areas to relieve over-population in the delta, to exploit an under-utilised source of land and, as later became apparent, to provide additional security along Vietnam's sensitive border with China. In the Central Highlands of southern Vietnam, many Montagnards had supported the Viet Minh against the French and the National Liberation Front against Saigon and the United States. Some of these Montagnards moved away from the revolutionary side, partly as a result of the war's toll of the politically astute cadres who were familiar with Montagnard ways, and partly as a result of the programme of moving lowland Vietnamese into the area. Unverified reports suggest that relations between Montagnards and the SRV are tense, and that sporadic armed conflict still goes on. The same is said to be true of the strongly anti-communist Hoa Hao sect in the lower Mekong delta, but the extent and gravity of the problem and the degree to which it has been affected by the Kampuchean border fighting is unknown. In the urban areas, the Chinese minority has posed a special problem for the SRV, discussed below in the context of SRV-China relations.

Finally, there are the Vietnamese who opposed the revolution on political or economic grounds. The numbers of these groups have grown substantially since the early period of the revolution, when the overwhelming majority of Vietnamese supported the Viet Minh against the French. The growth of an urban middle class, stimulated by the artificial war economy and US aid policies, increased opposition to the revolution, and the National Liberation Front also lost the support of an increasing number of rural Vietnamese who either profited from rising agricultural prices or fled to the cities as refugees. During the Second Indochina War, the class composition in the countryside was substantially altered, and the percentage of poor peasants was reduced from a prewar level of over 60 per cent to a current level of 30–40 per cent of the peasant population.[74] This will certainly affect the types of policies that can gain widespread political support during the process of co-operativisation. In the cities, it is recognised, support for Party policies is quite weak. The SRV calculates that between 50 and 80 per cent of young urban Vietnamese had personal or family ties with the United States and the former Saigon regime, which poses obvious difficulties for the government in building an acceptable core of future leaders.[75] Many of the problems of political integration, however, are in reality problems of economic development. The lack of adequate resources to meet the demands of the population make it difficult for the SRV to offer inducements to support its policies and erodes support among its marginal adherents. It is likely that the success of political integration in the future will be closely linked to the SRV's ability to solve its primary economic problems.

INTERNAL AFFAIRS

Education and culture

Vietnam's leadership has always given a high priority to education. SRV leaders have emphasised that of the three revolutions – the revolution in production relations, that in culture and ideology, and the technical revolution – the last is considered to be the most important.[76] None the less, cultural matters – in particular, literature and history – are also given great attention in the SRV educational system. The SRV leaders are proud of their literary heritage and view Vietnam's history of opposing foreign aggression as an inspiration to youth. Inquiry in the fields of literature and history is to some extent restricted by consider-ations of ideological orthodoxy, but Vietnamese scholars have conducted quite lively debates on key questions in the cultural field, and the SRV policies on intellectual comformity have relaxed considerably since the crack-down on the Nhan Van 'hundred flowers' group in 1956–8.

The first great educational policy was proclaimed in 1945 by Ho Chi Minh, who then identified the three main enemies of the Vietnamese people as foreign oppression, hunger and illiteracy and instituted a massive literacy campaign. By 1958, illiteracy in North Vietnam was considered to have been eliminated among ethnic Vietnamese under the age of fifty.[77] In South Vietnam, expanded educational opportunities provided by both the Saigon government and the National Liberation Front helped to reduce illiteracy, but the dislocations of the war deprived many Vietnamese children of an education. According to SRV statistics, in 1975 20 per cent of the southern population was illiterate, but by 1978 the abolition of illiteracy was 'basically completed'.[78]

The SRV educational system is divided into three levels: the first consisting of four grades for children seven to eleven years old, the second with three grades for eleven to fourteen year olds, and the third level with three grades for fourteen to seventeen olds. By 1971 every village in North Vietnam had a first-level school (many had second-level schools as well) and all districts had a third-level school. In the 1977–8 school year 11·4 million general-education students were enrolled in these three levels (4·7 of them in southern Vietnam). In addition there were 125,000 vocational school students and 47,700 university students. There are sixty-three universities and colleges and 268 vocational middle schools in the SRV.[79]

The economy

Vietnam's economy reflects its turbulent political history, shaped by colonialism, large infusions of external aid in the post–1954 period to both North and South and, of course, the devastation of thirty years of conflict. After 1954, the DRV embarked on a three-year transitional plan in 1958–60, followed by the First Five-year Plan (1961–5). During the war most heavy industry was either destroyed or dismantled and removed to rural areas. Recentralisation of the economy began in 1971 but was interrupted by the re-escalation of US bombing. By late 1974, after the Paris agreements, recentralisation in the northern region was basically completed.[80] National reunification was accompanied by the promulgation of the Second Five-year Plan (1976–80). However, its targets were predicated on an infusion of investment capital which was not forthcoming (see below, on foreign affairs) and Vietnam had to shift its plan priorities to the agricultural sector.[81] A sequence of weather calamities, including the catastrophic typhoon of 1978, seriously affected agricultural production, making it impossible for this sector of the economy to accumulate internal investment capital. Caught in a severe economic bind, the SRV joined Comecon as a means of gaining increased access to external assistance.[83]

A persistent debate in the SRV has been over the question of the efficacy of political and organisational solutions to economic problems or, in Marxist terms, whether or not changes in the relations of production are more crucial to economic development than increases in the forces of production. Party Secretary Le Duan has taken the position that 'the development of the forces of production remains the most decisive means to consolidate and perfect the new relations of production'.[84] During the Vietnam war, for example, strict implementation of new statutes outlining a move toward increased collective control in agricultural co-operatives was set aside in the interests of assuring maximum production for the war effort.[85] The progressive elimination of alternative development options after 1975, however, led the SRV leadership to propose a rapid acceleration of the socialist transformation of the economy in southern Vietnam, even though the economy was encountering serious problems. In the spring of 1978, major commercial enterprises were nationalised and the southern currency was unified with that of the former DRV.[86] Agricultural co-operativisation was pushed forward, and in early 1978 the goal was set of 'basically familiarising the peasants' with rudimentary forms of co-operative agriculture by the end of the year.[87] Although land redistribution was carried out in some areas, no major land-reform programme was required, owing to the many previous redistributions by the Viet Minh, the National Liberation Front and the Saigon government. The target size of co-operatives in the south is the comparatively large one of 200 hectares – nearly the size of an average southern hamlet and two-thirds the size of northern co-operatives which have been in existence for nearly twenty years. This, the Party official in charge of co-operativisation in the southern region noted, 'compared with the size of the first northern cooperatives in the past, already represents a skipping of stages'.[88] The goal of co-operativisation is political as well as economic, for the SRV hopes to 'use the movement to push the movement' – that is, to initiate the programme even before an adequate leadership cadre is available, in the hope that one will emerge in the process.[89]

SRV hopes for economic development rest on revitalising the

agricultural sector to promote investment funds for industry, attracting foreign aid and investment, and realising revenue from the country's oil deposits. SRV economic planners calculate that each 1 per cent increase in population requires a 2·5 per cent growth in food production to keep pace, and, with a 3 per cent annual growth rate in population, the projected 8 per cent annual increase in agricultural production will not result in any surplus.[90] Moreover, the Vietnamese have been reluctant to squeeze the agricultural sector. During the DRV's initial stage of collectivisation, capital accumulation as a percentage of total accumulation/consumption was around 17–18 per cent, compared with a Chinese figure of 20–22 per cent and a Soviet figure of around 26 per cent at a comparable stage in development.[91] This leaves the Vietnamese heavily reliant on external sources of investment funds and technology for their future development.

EXTERNAL AFFAIRS

As a small country in a world of larger powers, Vietnam has had to attempt to manoeuvre through the currents of international politics without becoming engulfed by them. Ho Chi Minh was attracted to communism because he observed that the Third International was the only major global political force sympathetic to the plight of colonial countries. Ho's internationalism was demonstrated through service as a Comintern representative in south China and South-east Asia. He was convinced that there was a close relationship between the interests of the Soviet Union, world revolution and Vietnam's own interests. This connection was first put to the test in the 1930s, when the Vietnamese Communist Party was induced to put aside its own revolutionary interests in order to support France; then in 1945, when the Soviet Union failed to recognise the newly established DRV; in 1954, when Vietnam was persuaded by Moscow and Peking to sign an agreement which sacrified the Viet Minh's battlefield advantage for the greater interests of the international communist movement; in 1957, when Moscow proposed dual United Nations membership for North and South Vietnam, despite the fact that this would be a serious obstacle to future reunification; and during the 1958–60 period, when Hanoi attempted to control the burgeoning revolutionary movement in the South to support Moscow's peaceful coexistence policy.[92]

Not until 1963 did the DRV become fully convinced that its interests could no longer be reconciled with the Soviet interpretation of proletarian internationalism, leading it openly to support the Chinese position in the Sino-Soviet dispute.[93] The fall of Khrushchev in 1964 and the need for Soviet military and diplomatic aid with which to resist the US escalation of the war led Hanoi toward a reconciliation with Moscow. Despite important material assistance from both China and the Soviet Union, the DRV resisted the attempts of both to influence its war strategy. The US-China rapprochement was described as 'throwing a life raft to a drowning pirate' and Hanoi could hardly have been pleased by Moscow's decision not to let US re-escalation of the bombing in 1972 interfere with its detente policy toward the United States.[94]

Hanoi was disappointed with the meagre response to its pleas for aid from China and the Soviet Union after the end of the war. The precise sequence of events which precipitated the open break between Vietnam and China, culminating in the July 1978 Chinese decision to suspend all aid to the SRV, and in a series of border clashes, is not known. Some observers point to Le Duan's trip to Peking in September 1975, when the Vietnamese refused to accept the Chinese view that the Soviet Union is the main threat to world peace, while the Chinese refused to provide Vietnam with the amount of aid requested.[95] The position of the more than 1 million Chinese residents in Vietnam was also an irritant. Vietnam accused China of using this group to foment opposition to SRV policies, while China accused Vietnam of discriminating against this minority. Many Chinese businessmen were affected by the elimination of large-scale commercial activities in southern Vietnam, but China itself had done this, as a normal stage of the socialist transformation of China's economy. Moreover, much of the problem involved the Chinese minority in northern Vietnam, many of whom occupied key positions in the Vietnamese industry and economy. Whatever the specific events leading to the open break, it seems clear that Peking's concern with denying the Soviet Union any influence in South-east Asia was a major cause.

The serious conflict that broke out along the Vietnam-Kampuchea border in 1977 was the culmination of longstanding tensions that had existed between the revolutionary movements of these countries. In the Kampuchean view, Hanoi was attempting to establish an Indochinese Federation to ensure Vietnamese dominance of Laos and Kampuchea, and Chinese support was a necessary counter-balance to this.[96] The Vietnamese were dissatisfied with the policy, now ascribed to Kampuchean Communist Party leader Pol Pot, of giving top priority to the internal goals of the Kampuchean revolution rather than supporting Sihanouk and the united-front struggle against foreign intervention in

Indochina. Moreover, the Vietnamese were openly critical of the domestic policies of the Kampuchean Party and government, which they viewed as travesties of 'scientific socialism'.[97] A mixture of concerns led the Vietnamese to support Kampuchean dissidents in the hope (now realised) of overthrowing the Phnom Penh regime. First was the Vietnamese insistence on a 'special relationship' as a recognition of past co-operation between the two movements, but which the Kampucheans felt involved a recognition of Vietnamese dominance in the region. In addition there were territorial disputes, some involving prospective oil reserves. Finally, there was the issue of China's role in Kampuchea, which the Vietnamese saw as a threat to the 'special relationship' and their own security. In supporting an anti-Pol-Pot revolt, the Vietnamese needed to take the Chinese reaction into serious consideration, along with the opposition of other South-east Asian countries, who would like to see a buffer between themselves and Vietnam. The SRV has become increasingly conciliatory toward the non-communist grouping of the Association of South-east Asian States (ASEAN) and hopes to win diplomatic support from ASEAN countries in its quarrel with the China.[98]

An important event in the SRV's foreign policy was the signing of a friendship and co-operation treaty with the Soviet Union in November 1978.[99] In view of the tensions with China and the US opposition to normalising relations with Vietnam, this may have appeared necessary to SRV leaders on both security and economic grounds. A Vietnamese official said that the primary purpose of the treaty 'is to obtain economic and technical cooperation from the Soviet Union on a long term basis for Vietnam war recovery work and to contribute to the peace and stability of Southeast Asia'.[100] The military clauses of the treaty call only for 'immediate consultation' in case either country is attacked. Observers have commented that the treaty contains no specific provisions for military action and offers no promise to the Soviet Union of bases in Vietnam, and that the treaty was aimed at 'political effect' rather than military alliance. The other major party in Vietnam's diplomacy is the United States, which rejected the initial SRV position that the United States must fulfil its 1973 pledge of economic assistance as part of the normalisation process. In November 1978 the US State Department acknowledged that Vietnam no longer insisted on a prior commitment of aid and was willing to normalise relations immediately. The manner in which the United States responds to the new Vietnamese position and the future role it will play in Asia will be a major factor in shaping Vietnam's future diplomacy, the options of which have been seriously circumscribed by Chinese hostility, ASEAN suspicions and US indifference.

Le Duan, Secretary-general of the VCP, has the most influence of any Vietnamese leader, but very little is known of his personal background or even the details of his revolutionary career. In part this is because he spent much of his career in clandestine operations, while other revolutionary leaders were in the public view during periods of legal political activity in the 1930s, as members of the Viet Minh government in 1945 and during the resistance years, and as leading figures of the DRV after 1954. Le Duan was born around 1907 in Hau Tien, a village in Trieu Phong district, Quang Tri province, just south of the post-1954 Demilitarised Zone along the 17th parallel. Nothing reliable is known about his parents' social and economic status, although when Le Duan revisited his native village in 1974, after a fifty-year absence, the foundations of his family home were still there, suggesting that he came from a reasonably prosperous family who could afford a sturdy house in this impoverished region. He left the village at the age of seventeen 'to engage in revolutionary activities'. He joined the Thanh Nien Party, the precursor of the ICP in 1928 and became a founding member of the ICP in 1930. Duan was appointed a member of the North Vietnam Region Party Committee in 1931, but was arrested in Haiphong the same year, sentenced by the French authorities to twenty years in prison and sent to Con Son island until 1936, when he was released under a general amnesty during the Popular Front period. At least six of the current members of the Political Bureau (Pham Van Dong, Pham Hung, Le Duc Tho, Nguyen Duy Trinh, Le Thanh Nghi and Le Van Luong), as well as head of State Ton Duc Thang, also were imprisoned in Con Son. During this period Le Duan was also briefly incarcerated at Son La prison in northern Vietnam, along with Truong Chinh. This experience evidently impressed these young revolutionaries with the importance of solidarity. Engaged in political struggles against their VNQDD nationalist political opponents and faced with the brutality of the prison regime, their very physical survival depended on mutual support. Le Duan was later rearrested and spent the period 1940–5 in prison, again on Con Son island. He recalled that during this period the majority of the political prisoners died. Other sources note that he himself narrowly escaped death.

In his first prison term in Con Son, Le Duan had demonstrated sufficient grasp of Marxism-Leninism to be, along with Nguyen Van Cu who was to be Party Secretary-general from 1938 to 1940, the principal instructor in revolutionary theory. Upon his release in 1936, he returned to Quang Tri and then operated a bookshop in Hue as a cover for his revolutionary activities. During this period he became head of the Central Vietnam Regional Committee of the ICP. In August 1939 the Party returned to clandestine activities as the Popular Front tolerance of the ICP came to an end. Shortly thereafter Le Duan and Nguyen Van Cu went to Saigon and convened the Sixth Plenum of the ICP, which replaced the 'Democratic Front' by the 'United Front Anti-Imperialist Front'. In 1940 Duan was arrested again and imprisoned until 1945. Upon his release from prison Duan assumed a key leadership role in southern Vietnam, attending a key meeting of the South Vietnam Regional Committee on 25 October 1945. It is not clear when he assumed overall leadership of the revolution in the south, but it is probable that he was the key Party figure there from 1945 until his departure for the north in 1953. (Some sources say he left the south after 1945 and returned in 1948 to assume leadership there.)

Unlike the other top leaders of the ICP, Le Duan apparently had relatively little personal contact with Ho Chi Minh prior to his return to the Viet Bac base area in 1953. During that year he worked with Ho in the Tan Trao base area near the Chinese border. During 1955 and 1956 (after the Geneva agreements), Duan operated clandestinely in South Vietnam from a base in Ca Mau province. After the removal of Truong Chinh from the post of Party Secretary-general (which Ho nominally assumed until 1960), Le Duan was recalled to North Vietnam and, in effect, replaced Truong Chinh as the chief Party organiser. It may have been that Ho found it less painful to choose a person with whom he had had comparatively little personal contact, rather than persons such as Vo Nguyen Giap or Pham Van Dong, who, like Chinh, had been personally close to him since the early 1940s. Moreover, moving outside Ho's close personal circle and selecting a man on the basis of 'universal' criteria may have been intended to strengthen the legitimacy of the Party leadership in a period of crisis. Finally, it marked a switch in Party policy toward giving increased emphasis on the revolution in South Vietnam, a constant preoccupation of Le Duan until the final victory of the revolution on 30 April 1975. Duan was finally elected Party First Secretary at the Third Party Congress in September 1960, and has served in that capacity ever since.

Despite his deserved reputation as a pragmatist and revolutionary practitioner, Le Duan also has claims to being a theoretician. We have seen that he was entrusted with teaching Marxism-Leninism to other high-ranking Party cadres in Con Son prison. Around 1950 he wrote a major theoretical work on the revolution in Vietnam, and while in Ca Mau in 1956 he wrote the key document of the post-Geneva period, 'The Path of Revolution in the South', advocating a political solution to the difficulties faced by the revolution in South Vietnam. After the shift to armed revolution was made in 1959, Duan personally supervised many of the operations aimed at aiding the South. During the period 1965–75, he constantly argued for a high priority for the needs of the southern battlefield, even if building socialism in North Vietnam was set back or delayed. He engaged in a political debate with Truong Chinh which intensified after the death of Ho Chi Minh in September 1969. By February 1970, however, Le Duan had issued a comprehensive statement of revolutionary objectives which signified the consolidation of his position as 'first among equals' in the Political Bureau. After 1975, however, he evidently shared the views of his Political Bureau colleagues, who advocated faster social, political and economic transformation of the southern region. He was re-elected Secretary-general of the Party at the Fourth Party Congress in December 1976, and remains first among equals in the leadership of the SRV.

Truong Chinh. Dang Xuan Khu, better known by his revolutionary alias, Truong Chinh (Long March), was born in 1908 in the textile-manufacturing town of Nam Dinh in the Red River delta of northern Vietnam. His father was a teacher and his family had been active in revolutionary circles. Chinh himself had been active in student demonstrations in the late 1920s and is reported to have received his baccalaureate from the prestigious Lycée Albert Sarraut in Hanoi. He became a member of the Thanh Nien Party in 1928 and a founding member of the ICP in 1930. He was arrested in 1931 and, like Le Duan, released under the general amnesty of 1936. He went to Hanoi and worked for several French-language newspapers, but quickly moved into full-time political activity, becoming, in autumn 1937, the political director of all Party organs in northern Vietnam. Shortly thereafter he fell ill with tuberculosis. It was probably during his convalescence that he and Vo Nguyen Giap wrote *The Peasant Question*, which focused attention on the revolutionary potential of Vietnam's peasants.

Chinh was elected acting Secretary of the ICP Central Committee at the Party's Seventh Plenum, in November 1940. The following years, at the historic Eighth Plenum, presided over by Ho Chi Minh, who had just returned to Vietnam after an absence of two decades, he became Secretary-general. His main tasks during the period 1940–5 were building up Party strength in the areas around Hanoi and in the Red River delta. During the momentous events of the August revolution, Chinh played a major role, especially during the period just prior to the seizure of power, when Ho was critically ill. Chinh wrote a major book on the August revolution which has been widely reprinted in the West. He served as Ho's principal lieutenant during the First Indochina War, and an official biography said that, 'while President Ho Chi Minh is the soul of the Vietnam revolution and Vietnam's resistance, comrade Truong Chinh is the builder and commander'. After the Geneva accords, Chinh played a prominent role in the land-reform campaign; he was subsequently held accountable for the excesses of this movement, and in 1956 was forced to resign. Despite this, he evidently was never in political disgrace, for he remained a member of the Political Bureau. He was appointed Deputy Prime Minister in 1958 and briefly served as acting Prime Minister in that year.

In 1960 Chinh became head of the Standing Committee of the National Assembly, the highest governmental office, and assumed the third-ranking position in the Party hierarchy after Ho and Le Duan. He also served as head of the Party Historical Commission, a job of considerable sensitivity and political influence, as well as being the head of the Nguyen Ai Quoc Party Training School, further strengthening his reputation as the Party's main ideologist. Subsequently Chinh wrote a number of important theoretical statements, including, in 1968, a lengthy review of the legacy of Karl Marx, which work was hailed as 'a new contribution to the storehouse of theory on the Vietnamese revolution'. Shortly thereafter, Chinh wrote a major critique of the progress in agricultural co-operativisation in North Vietnam, advocating a 'consolidation of the relations of production' at a higher level of socialist ownership and a tightening up of practices that had been tolerated as expedients to sustain production at a time when the rural North was being drained of manpower to fight the war in the South. After Ho's death, several months of debate over the relative priorities of North and South ensued, with Chinh arguing for paying more attention to problems in the North and Le Duan insisting on the primacy of the struggle in the South. The debate was settled by a compromise which basically favoured Le Duan's position. After the revolutionary victory of 1975, however, both leaders publicly endorsed the position of the other, and SRV policies since that time have moved in the direction of tightening up the 'relations of production' in Northern Vietnam and also accelerating socialist transformation in the old South. Truong Chinh remains the second-ranking figure in the SRV, and his impact in matters of both ideology and practice is considerable.

BASIC FACTS ABOUT VIETNAM*

Official name: Socialist Republic of Vietnam (Công Hòa Xã Hôi Chu Nghĩa Viêt Nam)
Area: 335,400 sq. km. (129,000 sq. miles).
Population (1978 est.): 50 million.
Population density: 150 per sq. km.
Population distribution: 16 per cent urban 84 per cent rural.
Membership of the VCP (Dang Cong San Viet-Nam) in 1978 (est.): 1,626,500.
Administrative division: 35 provinces.
Ethnic nationalities: about 84 per cent of the population of Vietnam are Vietnamese (Kinh); there are also over 60 minority groups, of which the largest are as follows (1976 figures) – Tay 742,000, Khmer 651,000, Thai 631,000, Muong 618,000, Nung 472,000, Meo 349,000, and Dao 294,000.
Population of major towns (1976): Hanoi (the capital), 1,443,500; Ho Chi Minh (Saigon), 3,460,500; Haiphong, 1,190,900.
Cultivated land area (1977 est.): 5·5 million hectares.
Rice production (1977 est.):12·7 tons.
Main natural resources: anthracite, lignite, coal, apatite and oil.
Main trading partners: USSR, China, Japan, Singapore, Hong Kong.
Rail network: 1895 km.
Road network: 29,905 km. (5908 asphalted).
Universities: 3 – in Hanoi, Ho Chi Minh City and at Ban Me Thuot (the Central Highlands University); in all, there are 63 institutions of higher education in the SRV).
Foreign relations: diplomatic relations with over 90 countries; 28 diplomatic missions established in Hanoi; member of the UN (since 1977), Comecon (since 1978) and the Conference of Non-aligned Nations.

* Compiled by Bogdan Szajkowski.

NOTES

1. Viet Chung, 'National Minorities and Nationality Policy in the D. R. V.', in Nguyen Khac Vien (ed.), *Mountain Regions and National Minorities in the Democratic Republic of Vietnam*, Vietnamese Studies, no. 15 (1968) p. 4.

2. Ban nghien cuu lich su Dang Trung-uong, *Bon muoi nam hoat dong cua Dang* ('Forty Years of Party Activities') (Hanoi: Su That, 1972) p. 9.

3. Nguyen Khanh Toan, 'Gap Bac o Lien Xo (1933–38)', in *Bac Ho hoi ky* ('Memoir About Uncle Ho') (Hanoi: Van Hoc, 1960) pp. 121–8.

4. Tang Xuan An, 'Nan doi nam At Dau – 1945' ('The Famine of 1945'), *Su dia* (Saigon) nos 17–18 (1970) pp. 167–76.

5. Huynh Kim Khanh, 'The Vietnamese August Revolution Reinterpreted', *Journal of Asian Studies*, Aug 1971, p. 776.

6. D. W. Elliot, 'Revolutionary Reintegration: A Comparison of the Foundation of Post-liberation Political Systems in North Vietnam and China' (unpublished Ph. D dissertation, 1976) pp. 104–5, 540.

7. Ibid., p. 99.

8. B. B. Fall, *The Viet Minh Regime: Government and Administration in the Democratic Republic of Vietnam*, Cornell University, South-east Asia Program, Data Paper no. 14 (1954) p. 35.

9. Din, 'We are Sure of Final Victory', in *For a Lasting Peace, For a People's Democracy* (Bucharest, 21 Aug 1953). Another source gives a figure of 750,000. Cf. *Ba muoi lam nam dau tranh cua Dang* ('Thirty-five Years of the Party's Struggle') (Hanoi: Su That, 1971) p. 96.

10. Ibid.

11. B. B. Fall, *Vietnam Witness (1953–66)* (1970) p. 76.

12. Carlyle A. Thayer, 'Southern Vietnamese Revolutionary Organizations and the Vietnam Workers' Party: Continuity and Change, 1954–1974', in J. J. Zasloff and M. Brown (eds), *Communism in Indochina: New Perspectives* (1975) p. 34.

13. D. G. Porter, *A Peace Denied* (1975) p. 13.

14. Ibid.

15. Cf. article 24 of the VWP 1960 statute in R. F. Turner, *Vietnamese Communism: Its origins and Development* (1975) p. 404.

16. D. Pike, *Viet Cong: The Organizations and Techniques of the National Liberation Front of South Vietnam* (1966) pp. 137–8.

17. Ibid.

18. Alexander Casella, 'Managing the Peace', *Foreign Policy*, Spring 1978, p. 172. By 1978 Party membership in the South was 273,000 (*Los Angeles Times*, 18 Oct 1978).

19. David W. P. Elliott, 'North Vietnam Since Ho', *Problems of Communism*, July–Aug 1975, p. 46.

20. Cf. D. G. Porter, *The Myth of the Bloodbath: North Vietnam's Land Reform Reconsidered*, Cornell University International Relations of East Asia Project (1972); and Edwin W. Moise, 'Land Reform and Land Reform Errors in North Vietnam', *Pacific Affairs*, Spring 1976, pp. 70–92.

21. Le Duan was referred to as 'representing the Secretariat' – i.e. functioning as acting First Secretary of the Party – by *Nhan dan* on 3 Apr 1960, five months before the Third Congress.

22. Elliott, 'Revolutionary Reintegration', p. 147.
23. Full statistics on the progress of co-operativisation of agriculture in the DRV are presented in Tong Cuc Thong Ke (General Statistics Office), *30 nam phat trien kinh te va van hoa cua nuoe Viet Nam Dan Chu Cong Hoa* ('Thirty Years of Economic and Cultural Development in the Democratic Republic of Vietnam') (Hanoi: Su That, 1978) p. 98. A discussion of the co-operativisation period can be found in David W. P. Elliott, 'Political Integration in North Vietnam: The Cooperativization Period', in Zasloff and Brown, *Communism in Indochina: New Perspectives*.
24. G. McT. Kahin and J. W. Lewis, *The United States in Vietnam* (1967) pp. 45–6.
25. *The Pentagon Papers: The Defence Department History of the United States Decisionmaking on Vietnam*, vol. I (1972) p. 247.
26. Porter, *A Peace Denied*, p. 43.
27. John C. Donnell, 'North Vietnam: A Qualified Pro-Chinese Position', in R. A. Scalapino (ed.), *The Communist Revolution in Asia* (1965) pp. 154–62.
28. Ibid., p. 165.
29. Mao himself had urged the Vietnamese to be more flexible and the Chinese were openly critical of Vietnam's 1972 offensive, which ultimately led to the signing of the Paris accords. Cf. Tad Szulc, 'Behind the Vietnam Cease Fire Agreement', *Foreign Policy*, Summer 1975, pp. 44–5.
30. R. Littauer and N. Uphoff (eds), *The Air War in Indochina* (1972) p.147.
31. J. M. Van Dyke, *North Vietnam's Strategy For Survival* (1972).
32. Elliott, in *Problems of Communism*, July–Aug 1975, pp. 45–6.
33. William S. Turley, 'Vietnam since Reunification', ibid., Mar–Apr 1977, pp. 45–58.
34. Ibid., pp. 38–43.
35. *Nhan dan*, 26 Aug 1977.
36. *Far Eastern Economic Review*, 30 June 1978, pp. 8–9.
37. *Los Angeles Times*, 31 May 1978.
38. A Vietnamese statement of 3 July 1978 said that, although the Chinese aid cut-off would create difficulties for Vietnam, these would be overcome by expanding the spirit of self-reliance and especially by 'the support of fraternal socialist countries – Foreign Broadcast Information Service, *Daily Report: Asia and Pacific*, 10 July 1978, p. K2.
39. *Far Eastern Economic Review*, 18 Aug 1978, pp. 9–10.
40. *Nhan dan*, 16 Aug 1976.
41. For an analysis of the composition of the Fourth Congress Central Committee see Turley, in *Problems of Communism*, Mar–Apr 1977, pp. 38–43.
42. The text of the Fourth Congress Party Regulations is published in *Tap chi cong san*, no. 2 (Feb 1977) pp. 8–36.
43. Elliott, in *Problems of Communism*, July–Aug 1975, pp. 43–4.
44. *Los Angeles Times*, 18 Oct 1978.
45. Din, in *For a Lasting Peace*.
46. *Nhan dan*, 8 Sep 1960.
47. *Nhan dan*, 7 Apr 1962.
48. Elliott, in *Problems of Communism*, July –Aug 1975, p. 49.

49. *Thanh nien*, Jan 1978.
50. Ibid.
51. Elliott, 'Revolutionary Reintegration', p. 292.
52. Ibid., p. 306.
53. *Thanh nien*, Jan 1978, and *Thanh nien*, Feb 1978.
54. *Nhan dan*, 28 Nov 1977.
55. Turley, in *Problems of Communism*, Mar–Apr 1977, p. 38.
56. Ibid.
57. Cf. David W. P. Elliott, 'Vietnam: Transition in a Time of Crisis', in *Southeast Asian Affairs*, 1978.
58. A text of the 1960 constitution may be found in B. B. Fall, *The Two Vietnams* (1963). The text of Vietnam's 1979 constitution was unavailable at the time of going to press.
59. *Nhan dan*, 24 June 1976.
60. Elliott, 'Revolutionary Reintegration', p. 246.
61. Ibid., p. 247.
62. Ibid., p. 252.
63. *Nhan dan*, 1 Dec 1977 and 20 Jan 1978.
64. *Nhan dan*, 16 Sep 1977.
65. *Nhan dan*, 26 Dec 1976.
66. *Tap chi cong san*, Mar 1978, p. 34.
67. B. B. Fall, *Le Viet Minh: La République Démocratique du Viet-Nam, 1945–1960* (1960).
68. *Nhan dan*, 9 June 1976.
69. *Nhan dan*, 21 June 1976.
70. Elliott, 'Revolutionary Reintegration', p. 209.
71. *Far Eastern Economic Review*, pp. 10–15.
72. *Vietnam Today* (Australia), Oct–Dec 1978, p. 7. Much of the reduction may be owing to the fact that many young men became monks during the pre-1975 period in order to avoid the draft.
73. *Nhan dan*, 1 Mar 1976.
74. *Nhan dan*, 11 Jan 1978.
75. *Thanh nien*, Jan 1978.
76. Elliott, 'Revolutionary Reintegration', p. 593.
77. Nguyen Khac Vien (ed.), *General Education in the D. R. V. N.*, Vietnamese Studies no. 30 (1971) p. 9.
78. Vietnam News Agency report in Foreign Broadcast Information Service, *Daily Report: Asia and Pacific*, 10 July 1978, p. K14.
79. Ibid.
80. Elliott, *Problems of Communism*, July–Aug 1975, p. 45.
81. *Far Eastern Economic Review*, 4 Feb 1977.
82. *Nhan dan*, 26 Aug 1977.
83. *Far Eastern Economic Review*, 4 Aug 1978, pp. 12–13.
84. For a discussion of this issue, see Elliott, in *Problems of Communism*, Mar–Apr 1977, pp. 40–1.
85. Ibid., p. 41.
86. *Nhan dan*, 25 Mar and 5 Apr 1978.
87. *Nhan dan*, 13 Jan 1978.
88. Foreign Broadcast Information Service, *Daily Report: Asia and Pacific*, 10 July 1978, p. K12.

89. *Nhan dan*, 13 Jan 1978.
90. *Nhan dan*, 3 July 1977.
91. Elliott, 'Revolutionary Reintegration', p. 378.
92. Cf. J. Race, *War Comes to Long An* (1972) p. 80.
93. Donnell, in Scalapino, *The Communist Revolution in Asia*, pp. 154–62.
94. Porter, *A Peace Denied*, pp. 112–13.
95. *Far Eastern Economic Review*, 14 July 1978, p. 8.
96. For a discussion of these views see, 'Two Views on the Vietnam–Kampuchea War', *Southeast Asia Chronicle*, no. 64 (Sep–Oct 1978).
97. *Far Eastern Economic Review*, 13 Jan 1978, pp. 11–15.
98. Ibid., 15 Sep 1978, pp. 19–23.
99. Ibid., 17 Nov 1978, pp. 8–11.
100. Foreign Broadcast Information Service, *Daily Report: Asia and Pacific*, 10 July 1978, p. K2.

BIBLIOGRAPHY

See also articles and Vietnamese-language publications listed in Notes.

An Outline History of the Viet Nam Workers' Party (1930–1970) (Hanoi: Foreign Languages Publishing House, 1970).
Aperçu sur les Institutions de la République Démocratique du Viet-Nam (Hanoi: Éditions en Langues Étrangères, 1972).
Bodard, Lucien, *The Quicksand War: Prelude to Vietnam* (Boston, Mass.: Atlantic Monthly Press, 1967).
Burchett, Wilfred, *North of the 17th Parallel* (Hanoi, 1955).
——, *Vietnam: Inside Story of the Guerrilla War* (New York: International Publishers, 1965).
——, *Vietnam North* (New York: International Publishers, 1966).
Buttinger, Joseph, *A Dragon Embattled*, 2 vols (New York: Praeger, 1967).
Chaliand, Gerard, *The Peasants of North Vietnam* (Harmondsworth: Penguin Books, 1969).
Chesneaux, Jean, *Contributions a l'histoire de la nation vietnamienne* (Paris: Éditions Sociales, 1955).
——, *Tradition et révolution au Vietnam* (Paris: Anthropos, 1971).
Chu Van Tan, *Reminiscences on the Army for National Salvation*, trs. Mai Élliott, Cornell University South-east Asia Program, Data Paper no. 97 (Ithaca; N.Y.: Cornell University, 1974).
Conley, Michael Charles, *The Communist Insurgent Infrastructure in South Vietnam: A Study of Organization and Strategy*, Department of the Army Pamphlet no. 550–106 (Washington, DC: Center for Research in Social Systems, Mar 1967).
Constitution of the Democratic Republic of Viet-Nam (Hanoi: Foreign Languages Publishing House, 1969).
The Democratic Republic of Viet-Nam (Hanoi: Foreign Languages Publishing House, 1960).
The Democratic Republic of Vietnam on the Road of Socialist Industrialization (Hanoi: Foreign Languages Publishing House, 1963).

Devillers, Philippe and Lacouture, Jean, *End of a War: Indochina, 1954* (New York: Praeger, 1969).

——, *Histoire du Viet-Nam de 1940 a 1952* (Paris: Éditions du Seuil, 1952).

Doan Trong Truyen and Phan Thanh Binh, *L'Édification d'une Économie Nationale Independante au Vietnam (1945–1965)* (Hanoi: Éditions en Langues Étrangères, 1966).

Doyen, Jacques, *Les Viet Cong* (Paris: Denoel, 1968).

——, *Les Soldats Blancs de Ho Chi Minh* (Paris: Fayard, 1973).

Duiker, William J., *The Rise of Nationalism in Vietnam 1900–1941* (Ithaca, N.Y.: Cornell University Press, 1976).

Duncanson, Dennis J., *Government and Revolution in Vietnam* (London: Oxford University Press, 1968).

Elliott, David W. P., *N. L. F.–D. R. V. Strategy and the 1972 Spring Offensive*, Interim Report No. 4, Cornell University International Relations of East Asia Project (Ithaca, N.Y., Jan 1974).

——, *'Revolutionary Reintegration: A Comparison of the Foundation of Postliberation Political Systems in North Vietnam and China'* (unpublished Ph.D dissertation, Cornell University, Ithaca, N.Y., 1976).

Fall, Bernard B., *The Viet Minh Regime: Government and Administration in the Democratic Republic of Vietnam*, Cornell University South-east Asia Program, 4 Data Paper no. 14 (Ithaca, N.Y., 1954).

——, *Le Viet-Minh, la République Démocratique du Viet-Nam 1945–1960* (Paris: Librairie Armand Colin, 1960).

——, *The Two Vietnams* (New York: Praeger, 1963).

——, *Vietnam Witness (1953-66)* (New York: Praeger, 1966).

——, *Last Reflections on a War* (New York: Doubleday, 1967).

——, (ed.), *Ho Chi Minh on Revolution* (New York: Signet, 1968).

Fenn, Charles, *Ho Chi Minh: A Biographical Introduction* (New York: Charles Scribner's Sons, 1973).

Gouvernement Général de l'Indochine, Direction des Affaires Politiques de la Sûreté Générale, *Contribution a l'Histoire des Mouvements Politiques de l'Indochine Française*, 5 vols (Hanoi: IDEO, 1930–3).

Halberstam, David, *Ho* (New York: Random House, 1971).

Hammer, Ellen, *The Struggle for Indochina 1940–1955* (Stanford, Calif.: Stanford University Press, 1966).

Hemery, Daniel, *Révolutionnaires Vietnamiens et Pouvoir Colonial en Indochine* (Paris: Maspero, 1975).

History of the August Revolution (Hanoi: Foreign Languages Publishing House, 1972).

Ho Chi Minh et al., *A Heroic People: Memoirs from the Revolution* (Hanoi: Foreign Languages Publishing House, 1965).

Ho Chi Minh, *Selected Works*, 4 vols (Hanoi: Foreign Languages Publishing House, 1960–2).

Ho Chi Minh: Notre Camarade (Paris: Éditions Sociales, 1970).

Hoang Van Chi, *From Colonialism to Communism* (New York: Praeger, 1964).

Honey, P. J., *Communism in North Vietnam* (Cambridge Mass.: MIT Press, 1963).

——, (ed.), *North Vietnam Today* (New York: Praeger, 1962).

Huynh Kim Khanh, *'Vietnamese Communism: The Pre-power Phase (1925–*

1945)' (unpublished Ph.D dissertation, University of California at Berkeley, 1972).

Kahin, George McT. and Lewis, John W., *The United States in Vietnam* (New York: Delta, 1967).

Lacouture, Jean, *Vietnam between Two Truces* (New York: Random House, 1966).

———, *Ho Chi Minh* (New York: Random House, 1968).

Le Chau, *Le Viet Nam Socialiste* (Paris: Maspero, 1966).

Le Duan, *On the Socialist Revolution in Vietnam*, 3 vols (Hanoi: Foreign Languages Publishing House, 1965–7).

———, *The Vietnamese Revolution: Fundamental Problems and Essential Tasks* (New York: International Publishers, 1971).

Le Thanh Khoi, *Socialisme et developpement au Viet Nam* (Paris: Presses Universitaires de France, 1978).

Lewis, John Wilson, *Peasant Rebellion and Communist Revolution in Asia* (Stanford, Calif.: Stanford University Press, 1974).

Littaver, Raphael and Uphoff, Norman (eds), *The Air War in Indochina* (Boston, Mass.: Beacon Press, (1972).

McAlister, John T., *Viet-Nam: The Origins of Revolution* (New York: Knopf, 1969).

McLane, Charles B., *Soviet Strategies in Southeast Asia* (Princeton, N.J.: Princeton University Press, 1966).

Marr, David G., *Vietnamese Anticolonialism* (Berkeley, Calif.: University of California Press, 1971).

Mus, Paul, *Sociologie d'une Guerre* (Paris: Éditions du Seuil, 1952).

Mus, Paul and McAlister, John T., *The Vietnamese and Their Revolution* (New York: Harper, 1970).

Ngo Vinh Long, *Before the Revolution: The Vietnamese Peasants Under the French* (Cambridge, Mass.: MIT Press, 1973).

Nguyen Khac Vien, *Tradition and Revolution in Vietnam* (Berkeley, Calif.: Indochina Resource Center, 1974).

——— (General ed.), Vietnamese Studies: a monograph series on various aspects of Vietnamese political, economic and social life (Hanoi).

Nguyen Khanh Toan, *Twenty Years' Development of Education in the Democratic Republic of Vietnam* (Hanoi: Ministry of Education, 1965).

Nguyen Thi Dinh, *No Other Road to Take*, trs. Mai Elliott, Cornell University South-east Asia Program, Data Paper no. 102 (Ithaca, N.Y., June 1976).

Nguyen Tien Hung, *Economic Development of Socialist Vietnam 1955–80* (New York: Praeger, 1977).

Our President Ho Chi Minh (Hanoi: Foreign Languages Publishing House, 1970).

O'Ballance, Edgar, *The Indochina War (1945–54)* (London: Faber and Faber, 1964).

O'Neil, Robert J., *General Giap: Politician and Strategist* (New York: Praeger, 1969).

Party Documents (1939–1945) (Hanoi: Su That, 1963).

The Pentagon Papers: The Defense Department History of the United States Decisionmaking on Vietnam, 4 vols (Boston: Beacon Press, 1971).

Pike, Douglas, *Viet Cong: The Organizations and Techniques of the National*

Liberation Front of South Vietnam (Cambridge, Mass.: MIT Press, 1966).

Porter, D. Gareth, *North Vietnam's Land Reform*, Cornell University International Relations of East Asia Project, Interim Report no. 2, (Ithaca, N.Y., 1972).

——, *The Myth of the Bloodbath: North Vietnam's Land Reform Reconsidered*, Cornell University International Relations of East Asia Project (Ithaca, N.Y., 1972).

——, *A Peace Denied* (Bloomington: Indiana University Press, 1975).

Race, Jeffrey, *War Comes to Long An: Revolutionary Conflict in a Vietnamese Province* (Berkeley: Calif.: University of California Press, 1972).

Sacks, I. Milton, 'Communism and Revolution in Vietnam, 1918–1946' (unpublished Ph.D dissertation, Yale University, 1960).

Sainteny, Jean, *Ho Chi Minh and His Vietnam* (Chicago: Cowles, 1972).

Scalapino, Robert (ed.), *The Communist Revolution in Asia* (Englewood Cliffs, N.J.: Prentice-Hall, 1965).

Thayer, Carlyle A., 'The Origins of the National Front for the Liberation of South Viet-Nam (unpublished Ph.D dissertation, Australian National University, Canberra, 1977).

Third National Congress of the Vietnam Workers' Party: Documents (Hanoi: Foreign Languages Publishing House, n.d.).

Thirty Years of Struggle of the Party (Hanoi: Foreign Languages Publishing House, 1960).

Tongas, Gérard, *J'ai Vecu dans l'Enfer Communiste au Nord Viet-Nam et J'ai Choisi la Liberté* (Paris: Nouvelles Éditions Debresse, 1960).

Trager, Frank N. (ed.), *Marxism in Southeast Asia* (Stanford, Calif.: Stanford University Press, 1959).

Tran Huy Lieu, *Les Soviets du Nghe Tinh* (Hanoi: Éditions en Langues Étrangères, 1960).

Tran Nhu Trang, 'The Transformation of the Peasantry in North Vietnam' (unpublished Ph.D dissertation, University of Pittsburgh, 1972).

Truong Chinh, *Primer for Revolt: The Communist Takeover in Vietnam* (New York: Praeger, 1963).

Truong Chinh and Vo Nguyen Giap, *The Peasant Question*, trs. Christine White, Cornell University South-east Asia Program, Data Paper no. 94 (Ithaca, N.Y., Jan 1974).

Turley, William S., 'Army, Party and Society in the Democratic Republic of Vietnam: Civil-Military Relations in a Mass Mobilization System' (unpublished Ph.D dissertation, University of Washington, 1972).

Turner, Robert F., *Vietnamese Communism: Its Origins and Development* (Stanford, Calif.: Hoover Institution Press, 1975).

Van Dyke, Jon M., *North Vietnam's Strategy for Survival* (Palo Alto, Calif.: Pacific Books, 1972).

Vo Nguyen Giap, *People's War, People's Army* (New York: Praeger, 1962).

——, *Military Art of People's War* (New York: Monthly Review, 1970).

——, *Unforgettable Months and Years*, trs. Mai Elliott, Cornell University South-east Asia Program, Data Paper no. 99 (Ithaca, N.Y., 1975).

White, Christine, *Land Reform in North Vietnam*, Agency for International Development, Country Paper (Washington D.C.: AID, June 1970).

Woodside, Alexander, *Community and Revolution in Modern Vietnam* (Boston, Mass.: Houghton Miflin, 1976).

Zasloff, Joseph J. and Brown, MacAlister (eds), *Communism in Indochina: New Perspectives* (Lexington, Mass.: D. C. Heath, 1975).

25 People's Democratic Republic of Yemen

TAREQ Y. ISMAEL

GEOGRAPHY

On 30 November 1967 the People's Republic of South Yemen (PROSY), encompassing the former British colony and protectorate of Aden and the offshore islands of Perim, Kamaran and Socotra, which elected to join the new republic, was founded.[1] The new constitution of November 1970 changed the Republic's name to People's Democratic Republic of Yemen (PDRY). The country has ill defined and in places disputed borders with the Yemen Arab Republic (north-west), Saudi Arabia (north) and Oman (north-east).

The Republic includes some of the most rugged, varied and inhospitable terrain in the Arabian peninsula. Composed of ancient African granites covered in many places with younger sedimentary deposits, the plateau has undergone downwarping to the east and uplifting in the west; consequently mountains of 3000 metres thrust above the Red Sea, gradually giving way to tableland merging with the Arabian desert inland. The Wadi Hadhramaut – an immense valley running parallel to the coast 150–200 km. inland – is host to a seasonal torrent which permits the alluvial soils of its upper reaches to be cultivated. Water is too erratic and scanty for it to be possible to farm the mouth of the Hadhramaut.

Rainfall varies, though nowhere is it plentiful. The coastal mountains play a crucial role in the east-west distribution of moisture carried by the westerly winds off the Red Sea: thus, Aden has approximately 125 mm. per annum, all of this falling in winter (December to March); the mountains and foothills above Aden have an annual rainfall of 900 mm. (mainly falling in summer), which figure decreases gradually to approximately 500 mm. in the eastern highlands, and decreases steadily as

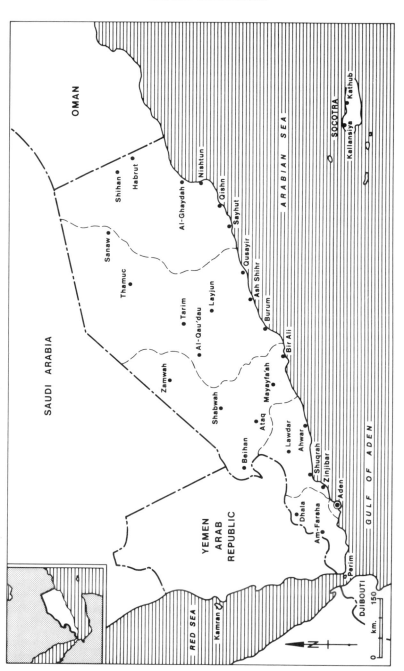

People's Democratic Republic of Yemen: boundaries of governorates

one proceeds inland north to the fringes of the Arabian desert, where ten years may pass without any rain falling.[2] Temperatures are high, particularly on the coastal plain: Aden has a January mean of 24°C and a June mean of 27°C, with the temperature often reaching the 40–50°C range.

Apart from shrubs and dwarf trees in the highlands and irrigated tracts on the coastal plain and in the Hadhramaut, the Republic's terrain is barren. Natural cultivation is confined to terraces on river-beds and the sides and bottom of the Wadi Hadhramaut. Irrigation from wells is practised at Lahej (near Mukalla) on the coastal plain and in the upper Hadhramaut.[3]

HISTORY

Before independence

Long before the age of exploration, Aden was a thriving seaport poised at the gates of the Red and Arabian Seas. When Portuguese navigators entered the Indian Ocean at the turn of the sixteenth century, Aden was a major port of call for ships bound from India to the Red Sea, not to mention local trade with the Arabian Gulf and the trade with East Africa.

Successfully warding off the Portuguese and other European intruders, the Ottoman Turks subdued the Sultan of Aden and took the city in 1538, beginning the first of three centuries of precarious Ottoman rule. The Turks successfully quelled two serious and sustained Yemeni revolts in 1547–51 and 1566–70. The decay of the Empire during the next 150 years reduced Ottoman suzerainty to a façade and restored power to the tribal sheikhs, notably the Sultan of Lahej.

Except for the coffee trade, the commercial importance of Aden languished as a result of the discovery of the Cape route to India and the energetic exploitation of the eastern trade by France, Britain, Portugal and Holland. However, British strategic interest in Aden was kindled by Napoleon's brief Egyptian campaign in 1798, which led directly to the occupation of Perim Island, controlling what was then the only entrance to the Red Sea, and the conclusion of a friendship treaty with the Sultan of Laheh. The introduction of steam navigation, however, greatly increased the strategic importance of Aden to Britain. In an episode of gunboat diplomacy in 1839, Britain took possession of Aden. In a subsequent peace treaty, Aden became part of the British Empire administered by the British Government of India, and the Sultan received a token annual tribute from Britain of $6500 (which tribute continued until World War I). The opening of the Suez Canal in 1869 revitalised Aden, which became a major coaling and fuelling station for the British Navy in the Indian Ocean.

In 1935 Aden was incorporated as a Crown colony. The hinterland of Aden was organised as a West Protectorate and an East Protectorate. These protectorates comprised the territories of the petty rulers who, between 1882 and 1914, had alienated their sovereignty to Britain in exchange for Britain's protection of their internal prerogatives and privileges. The Aden Protectorate, then, comprised three administrative units: (1) the City of Aden, a Crown colony administered by the Colonial Office in London through the appointment of a governor; (2) the Western Protectorate, a conglomeration of seventeen petty principalities whose rulers accepted administration by the British Governor of Aden; and (3) the Eastern Protectorate, comprising three principalities – Hadhramaut, Mahra and the island of Socotra – administered by a British political agent appointed by the Governor of Aden.

The constitutional route to independence envisioned by the Colonial Office went much further awry in southern Yemen than in most British colonies in Africa and Asia. In both 1954 and 1956, the British authorities discussed with interested sheikhs the possible formation of the Federation of Arab Emirates of the South (FAES), an embryonic south Yemeni puppet state bound to Britain by treaty in foreign affairs and protected by the British Army. The nucleus of the Federation – without Aden – was formed in February 1959, from six states of the Western Protectorate.

Analysing Britain's motives in this period, a distinguished student of south Yemeni politics observed:

> The evacuation of British forces from the Suez Canal resulted in the necessity of moving the centre of British forces in the Middle East to Aden. The establishment of a federated state encompassing southern Yemen tied to His Majesty's Government in defence and co-operation was the greatest guarantee of control over a powerful imperial position in a strategic location. . . . The signing of the Yemeni-Egyptian-Saudi Pact of 1956 (indirectly) entered Aden and its protectorate within the sphere of the Arab Mutual Defense Pact. Thus, found itself seriously threatened . . . and the Governor of Aden called upon the Amirs in 1956, with a final draft for

federation. . . . However, this step did not lead to federation, because
of the tripartite aggression on the Suez. . . . . The relations deteriorated between the Arab world and the West to a degree that
neither Britain or the local Arab chiefs would not dare to announce
the creation of the federated state.[4]

In a classic case of too little, too late, the colonial authorities tried to
render the colonial administration of Aden more democratic before
independence. Thus, a legislative council for Aden was granted in 1944
and became operative in 1946. In December 1955 it was expanded to
include a minority elective element. Many popular candidates were
barred from running in the 1959 elections; the newly elected Council was
discredited in the eyes of most of the population, i.e. the Arabs, who
boycotted the polls *en masse*. In fact, only 24 per cent of the electorate
participated in the election. Constitutional talks between the Aden
government and the FAES in London in July 1962 aimed at incorporat-
ing Aden City and other states into the Federation were denounced by
the Aden Trade Union Congress – an umbrella organisation covering
more than thirty trade unions – on the grounds that the Legislative
Council was unrepresentative. The Congress demanded new elections,
in which anti-federation candidates would presumably win. The conference nevertheless recommended incorporation, which took place in
January 1963, unleashing riots, demonstrations, fire-bombings and an
abortive attempt on the life of the Governor, which provoked harsh
repressive measures from the authorities.

In the context of the ferment of nationalism in the Arab world in this
period – Egypt's nationalisation of the Suez Canal (1956), the formation
of the United Arab Republic (1958), the Iraqi revolution (1958) – the
nebulous national liberation currents in southern Yemen began to take
shape. The first and most cohesive was the National Liberation Front
(NLF). When established in 1963, the NLF had two segments: the
liberal-democratic wing under Qahtan al-Shaabi, which included many
prominent émigrés and exiles who took no active part in Yemeni
politics, and the Marxist wing under Abdul Fattah Ismail.[5] Their
differences were submerged in the common interest of party unity.

Most future NLF members underwent a similar political evolution
during the 1950s – all were alienated by a society in which power rested
with a condominium of foreign capitalist and native feudal interests.
Conventional political opposition seemed destined to fail. All were
drawn to Nasserism, so, after the Nasserite revolution in San'a in
September 1962, many went to North Yemen, where they were greeted

warmly by the Egyptian Expeditionary Corps. Nasser armed and trained NLF cadres, who opened the armed struggle with Britain in October 1963. Owing to its efficiency, the NLF rapidly took hold in the countryside.

On the ideological plane, the NLF Left became increasingly disenchanted with what Secretary-general Abdel Fattah Ismail termed in retrospect 'the Arab chauvinism and petty-bourgeois reformism'[6] of Nasserism. The First Congress of the NLF, convened in June 1965, adopted a Marxist platform, which antagonised the Egyptians. The Egyptians set about establishing a rival, Nasserist, pro-Egyptian national liberation group from the People's Socialist Party (led by Abdullah al-Asnaj), the Committee for the Liberation of South Yemen and the South Arabian League, which early in 1965 agreed to form the Organisation for the Liberation of the Occupied South (OLOS). This merged with the radical National Front for the Liberation of the Occupied South to form the Front for the Liberation of South Yemen (FLOSY). However, repelled by the former's terrorism, the South Arabian League soon withdrew from FLOSY. In January 1966, Egypt tried to reconcile FLOSY and the NLF, ending in a permanent rupture between the two groups in July 1966, after which the NLF received no further overt support from abroad. The rump of FLOSY espoused Nasserism and the annexation of Aden by radical North Yemen.[7] The traditional tribal sheikhs were allied with the colonial authorities against these disparate nationalist factions.

A conference on the future of Aden was convened in London in September 1965, and, though all the major parties were represented, it ended in failure: there was no political common ground left in South Yemen. The political façade of the Protectorate began to crumble: the Council of Ministers was disbanded and the Constitution suspended in August 1965 in the face of mounting turmoil. In a White Paper submitted to Parliament in February 1966, the British Government proposed a new Federated Republic of South Arabia, to become independent in February 1968. The political basis for this proposal, had it even existed, was immediately destroyed by a defence paper released the same month which bluntly declared that all British forces would be withdrawn from Aden by independence and that there would be no defence agreement with the new state. This declaration alarmed tribal supporters of the FAES, who soon persuaded Britain to provide a lump sum of £5 million to re-equip and train the Federal Army and an additional £7·1 million per year after independence to meet the Army payroll.[8]

Adapting to a volatile and dynamic situation, in mid 1967 Britain set about establishing an all-party provisional government to hold power until independence and elections under the new constitution, which states in the East Protectorate were still only considering. But the NLF and FLOSY both spurned the offer, rejecting out of hand any scheme for power-sharing with the sheikhs. The denouncement unfolded on the battlefield: the Federation's fledgling army was powerless to stop the NLF from taking over most FAES territories by September 1967 and the undecided East Protectorate states by October. The Federation collapsed. Britain began negotiations with the NLF and FLOSY, who were themselves locked in a fierce struggle for the leadership of the nationalist movement. There were several reasons for the NLF's ultimate victory over FLOSY:

(1) the NLF drew members from all over South Yemen, hence could credibly claim to be an authentically Yemeni movement, untainted by intrigues with Egypt, Saudi Arabia or Britain;
(2) the NLF had greater internal discipline and unity than its rival;
(3) the wavering Federal Army committed itself to the NLF at a decisive stage in the fighting in September 1967;
(4) Egypt's withdrawal from North Yemen following the June 1967 Arab–Israeli war cut off FLOSY's main source of funds and weapons.[9]

Britain sped up her withdrawal timetable and by November 1967 the last British troops were gone. Negotiations between the British government and representatives of the NLF in Geneva in November 1967 culminated in the proclamation, on 30 November, of the People's Republic of South Yemen (PROSY) under President Qahtan al-Shaabi. This ended more than four centuries of exploitation under foreign rule in South Yemen.[10]

After independence

The first years of the PROSY were turbulent, beset by many, interrelated problems. By far the most serious was the chronically depressed economy. Before independence, Britain made a direct grant to Aden to make up the difference between revenues and expenditures; expenditures usually outstripped revenues by two to one – up to £20 million per annum in 1967, a very significant portion of national income – and the precipitate stoppage of this grant caused havoc in Aden. The destruction of the FAES as the vehicle of South Yemeni independence foreclosed the possibility of British civil or military aid after 30 November 1967. The naval installations at Aden were closed on the eve of independence at a direct cost of 25,000 jobs. Convinced that the city had no economic future, 80,000 people – many in the trade and services sector – left Aden. Finally, closure of the Suez Canal in June 1967 reduced the number of ships calling at Aden from 650 to 100 per month, drastically cutting port revenues and repair and servicing charges.[11] With the reopening of the Canal, in mid 1975, the government invested heavily in port expansion and improvement, but the number of vessels calling at Aden increased to only 150 per month by 1976, far below pre-1967 levels, so the loss to the South Yemeni economy appears to be permanent.

To make up the difference, the South Yemen government had to seek foreign aid, largely from the Soviet bloc countries and China, though the extent and nature of foreign aid caused acrimonious political in-fighting in the NLF. In addition, the power of the tribal sheikhs, who still held most of the land in rural Aden, remained intact. Land reform was therefore a crucial and divisive issue. Also, tribal rivalries which the British had successfully exploited reappeared – particularly the traditional animus between the Aulaqis, whom the British had favoured, and the Dathina, which the PROSY Government favoured. This of course set the Aulaqis against the government.

Furthermore, remnants of FLOSY, though weakened by Egypt's withdrawal from North Yemen, remained on the border, a constant threat to the security of the Aden regime. Saudi Arabia continued to back forces of the South Arabian League. There was also the problem of the PROSY's relations with the Oman government, exacerbated by Britain's decision in 1968 to award the Kuria Muria Islands to Oman. In 1965 an insurgent group known as the Popular Front for the Liberation of Oman (PFLO), with ideological aims similar to those of the NLF and dedicated to the overthrow of Sultan Qahbus, occupied the rural lands of eastern Oman adjacent to the sixth governorate of South Yemen, which they used as a sanctuary with the latter's consent. Whether and to what extent to support the PFLO also became a potent political issue in South Yemen.

These pressing political problems put the unity of the National Front (NF)[12] to severe test. Viewed schematically, the moderates and rightists, headed by President Qahtan al-Shaabi and other prominent Yemenis, stressed the importance of restoring the productivity of the national economy to pre-independence levels. They introduced and passed a land-reform law formally redistributing the land from the sheikhs to the peasants, but which was in fact plagued by corruption. The al-Shaabi faction sought to enlist foreign aid from all sources, even the West; a conciliatory attitude toward reactionary Saudi Arabia and the Gulf emirates was thought not too high a price to pay for large sums of aid. Finally, the moderates were wary about risking a clash with Oman by out-and-out support for the PFLO.

The leftists, led by party ideologist Abdul Fattah Ismail and a recent convert from the FLOSY, Salem Rubayi Ali, subordinated all issues to the cause of political and social revolution in South Yemen. The service-oriented economy had to become geared to increased agricultural and industrial production. In the countryside, this required radical steps to break up the large feudal land holdings of the sheikhs, redistribute the land among the poor peasants and establish collectives; in industry, it required State-led planning and investment. In the foreign sphere, radicals associated with Abdul Fattah Ismail favoured close association with the Soviet bloc, while Salem Rubayi Ali preferred the Chinese revolutionary model, or at least Chinese aid to Soviet aid. The radicals strongly supported the struggle of the PFLO. Both Left and Right could agree on the practical need to repress the South Arabian League and FLOSY, the importance of the public sector in the national economy and, on a loftier plane, the desirability of Yemeni unity, solidarity with the Arab revolution and moral support for the Palestinians. The showdown was not long in coming.

At the NF's Third Annual Congress, in March 1968, the Right managed to pass a moderate land-reform law which the Left severely criticised.[13] The Left in turn proposed forming a people's militia with NF political commissars on the Red Army model, as well as popularly elected soviets in each governorate, which would in turn nominate those who would govern the country as a whole. These proposals were rejected by the Right and the army forced several radical ministers to resign their posts. However, the radicals controlled the eastern governorates and went ahead with these proposals, ignoring the protests of legal Aden-appointed governors. After many frustrating months, al-Shaabi was forced to resign by the radicals in what has become known, in the argot of the Yemeni revolution, as the 22 June 'corrective step'.[14]

After the 'corrective step', the revolutionary leadership undertook to change the political and social relations prevailing in all State organisations. The civil service, with its coveted plum jobs, the security forces and the militia, police and Army leaderships were purged, restaffed with

NF appointees and democratised. The Army was particularly affected. According to Ali Antar, Commander of the Army and Deputy Minister of Defence, before the revolution,

> the forces used to be composed of the sons of sheikhs, emirs, and big land-owners, and were formed on tribal lines. In fact, they were formed from a specific tribe, even if other tribes were represented, and their tribe, for example, would be predominant in the command of the army and the armed forces. This structure did not come about by accident; rather, it was designed [by the British] to break down the unity of the country through tribal conflict.
>
> Even after independence, no apparent change was allowed in the structure of this organisation, because the middle-of-the-road forces in the revolution, by virtue of their bourgeois mentality and political dominance, were afraid of radical change.
>
> After the Corrective Step of November 22, 1969, the revolutionary leadership . . . purged the army of elements wishing to preserve their old political and class privileges, and we began to construct our armed forces on new bases which would enable the sons of workers, peasants, nomads, and fishermen to occupy a role in these forces. From among the ranks of these participating classes we prepared technical and administrative leadership cadres so that they could participate in the building, protection and support of the revolution.[15]

This became the main function of the post-revolutionary army. The army established an ideological and technical Military Training College in Aden, staffed by Soviets and Cubans. The army also has established four collective farms, in districts 14, 20, 22 and 30.[16] In addition, new compulsory State-run mass organisations – trade unions and student, women's and youth groups – were established.

On the economic front, there were two salient changes. Foreign–mainly British and French–banks, insurance companies, port firms and commercial and ship supply companies were nationalised.[17] A State monopoly on foreign trade was imposed as the only way to free the country from domination by capitalist markets.[18] Draconian austerity measures were imposed: civil service and army wages were cut by up to 60 per cent to reduce non-productive expenditure and to reduce the ratio between maximum and minimum incomes.

The second important economic step was land reform. As noted above, the first land-reform law was in several respects inadequate.

More thoroughgoing measures were needed. These were embodied in article 19 of the State Constitution of the PDRY, which states,

> The Properties of the Sultans, Amirs, Sheikhs, and rulers of the expired regime and those of all persons stated in the agrarian reform laws shall be sequestrated without compensation. The land shall be utilized by farm workers, poor farmers, the citizens migrating from towns and the deserts. . . . The State shall enforce agrarian reform in the shortest possible time in all parts of the country according to the principles of social justice and with the participation of farm workers and farmers. The State shall encourage the formation of agricultural cooperative societies and shall establish state farms.[19]

The feudal lands had been only partly confiscated and were often inequitably distributed by corrupt civil servants for the benefit of rich peasants. With regard to implementation Salem Rubayi Ali stated,

> The land does not give up itself. It must be taken. The National Front encourages peasant uprisings and other people's revolts because only revolutionary violence is suitable for bringing about a final separation between the big owners and workers and creating an impassable gulf between the exploiters and the exploited. Furthermore, the method has fundamental consequences. The peasants, fishermen and workers have set up militias to defend their social conquests. . . .[20]

Peasant take-overs began in October 1970. Hundreds of peasants armed with pitchforks and scythes arrested landlords and set up a committee apportioning three to five feddans (approx. 1·038 acres divided into 24 kirats) per family. As the take-overs spread throughout the countryside, a golden opportunity was afforded to settle personal and tribal scores under a cloak of revolutionary legality. Faced with a mounting public outcry, in May 1970 the government moved to control excesses. Later take-overs were supervised by NF cadres. The original land law 'encouraged rural capitalism without increasing production', so the authorities set up elective peasant committees to oversee land redistribution and serve as the nuclei of agricultural collectives, which the State was committed to support.[21] By 1972, twenty-one collective and twenty-four State farms had been established, rising to fifty-nine collectives and twenty-six State farms by 1974.[22] It is perhaps still too early to assess the outcome of the reorganisation of Yemeni agriculture; the most recent statistics (see below, under 'Basic facts') suggest that for most commodities output has increased to marginally above pre-independence levels.

THE CONSTITUTION

The State Constitution of the People's Democratic Republic of Yemen is obviously a very important document and merits close attention.[23] Promulgated on 30 November 1970, it is divided into six parts:

Part i: Foundations of the National Democratic Social System and the System of the State (three chapters, articles 1–32).
Part ii: Citizens and their Organisations (two chapters, articles 33–61).
Part iii: Organisation of the State Authority (four chapters, articles 62–115).
Part iv: Democratic Law and Justice (one chapter, articles 116–24).
Part v: National Defence and Security (one chapter, articles 125–30).
Part vi: Interim and Final Orders (one chapter, articles 131–5).

Chapter 1 of Part i lays the political foundation of the State. It contains four important provisions: first, it commits the PDRY to seek a united Yemeni state, since the Yemeni nation is a single entity.[24] Secondly, it claims that the State is based on a class alliance 'between the workers, farmers, intelligentsia and petty bourgeoisie' against reactionary forces at home, in the Arab world and abroad.[25] Thirdly,

> the alliance between the democratic forces of the people expresses itself . . . through the National Front organization. The National Front organization on the basis of scientific socialism leads political activity of the public and public organizations in order to develop the society in a manner which achieves national democratic revolution following a non-capitalist course.[26]

Fourthly, citizens' political participation takes place through free elections to the local people's councils[27] and the People's Supreme Council.[28]

Chapter 2 specifies the economic basis of the State. It contains five important provisions concerning property. While guaranteeing the right to private property[29] and the accumulation of wealth by the private sector,[30] it holds that, 'the State must develop the national economy into a productive economy and shall ensure a fair distribution of the fruits of society between the citizens. Each individual shall be rewarded according to the work or service he gives for the purpose of promoting industrial and social relations'.[31]

Article 15 nationalises foreign commercial enterprises; article 17 holds that the State economy shall not be dictated by impersonal market forces but shall be directed in accordance with a development plan prepared by the State; this plan shall have the force of law and shall override any other law. Article 19, as we have already seen, concerns land law. Finally, article 21 confers a monopoly of foreign trade on the State.

These articles seem to envision a biased mixed-market economy: a market economy in view of the broad right to buy, sell and transmit private property; mixed in the sense that the State plan has a paramount role in government spending; biased in the sense that the bounds of private enterprise are set in principle by consideration of the public good: 'ownership is a social responsibility and its use should not conflict with public welfare'.[32] Chapter 3 commits the State to raising the political, cultural, ideological and physical level of the people.

Part 2 deals with the rights and duties of the citizens and their public organisations. All citizens are formally equal in rights and duties. The list of rights is impressive: right to an education (also a duty); right to personal freedom; right to a court trial; nationality rights; sanctity of home; secrecy of communication; freedom of religious belief;[33] freedom of artistic, literary, scientific and cultural expression; right to assemble 'within the spirit of the constitution';[34] right to medical care; and freedom of movement within the State frontiers. Duties are defence of the domestic order and the Republic's frontiers; public service; and payment of income tax. The government has often invoked article 55 to offer safe haven to Palestinian liberation groups. Chapter 2 defines the purpose and legal status of the trade unions, women's and youth organisations and agricultural co-operative societies.

Part III deals with the formal political organisation of the State. Chapter 1 treats of the People's Supreme Council (PSC), the formal source of sovereign authority in the State. It consists of 101 members, elected triennially through general, equal and direct elections in the governorates. The electorate may request that their members be recalled through petition. The PSC issues legislation covering the whole gamut of State business. The PSC debates and lays down guidelines for the Presidential Council and Council of Ministers in foreign and domestic policy. It must ratify foreign treaties, the national plan, and the annual

State budget. Finally, the PSC elects from its membership all members of the Presidential Council and a majority of the members of the Council of Ministers. The Prime Minister himself must be a member of the PSC, to which he is accountable on a vote of confidence.

Chapter 2 deals with the executive of the PSC, the Presidential Council, consisting of at least three and no more than seven members.[35] It is charged with actually executing State policy and overseeing the work of the government. Unlike,the PSC, its powers are, as a whole, concrete, specific and sweeping. It is empowered

(1) to represent the Republic at home and abroad;
(2) to fix dates for PSC and local people's council elections;
(3) to nominate the Prime Minister and Cabinet;
(4) to appoint members of defence council;
(5) to propose draft legislation (most legislation in fact originates with the PSC);
(6) to issue laws passed by the PSC;
(7) to appoint and discharge leading State officials;
(8) to appoint and discharge leaders of the armed forces;
(9) to appoint and discharge Supreme Court judges;
(10) to award decorations;
(11) to approve treaties not requiring approval of the PSC;
(12) to appoint and discharge the State's diplomatic representatives;
(13) to accredit representatives of foreign governments;
(14) to grant amnesty;
(15) to grant asylum;
(16) to declare emergency powers and mobilise the army; and
(17) to declare a state of national defence.[36]

The Presidential Council is the real focus of power in the PDRY. It is expected, though not required, to present its views on foreign and domestic policy to the PSC, and may periodically ask the Prime Minister for reports on specific programmes. The Council may initiate debates in the PSC and propose legislation on specific matters. When the Chairman of the Council resigns, whether in mid-term or when his term lapses, the Council as a whole resigns.

Chapter 3 establishes the Council of Ministers, consisting of the Prime Minister and his ministers,[37] which is the supreme administrative and executive body of the State. Each minister is separately responsible for his department to the Prime Minister, and the Council as a whole is responsible to the PSC.[38] It is the Council's task.

(1) to propose broad lines of internal and external government policy;
(2) to submit draft legislation to the PSC;
(3) to prepare and execute the State economic plan and national budget;
(4) to appoint members of Supreme Council for national planning;
(5) to audit the final accounts of the State;
(6) to approve the form of treaties and agreements before submission to the PSC and Presidential Council;
(7) to safeguard internal and external security;
(8) to direct, co-ordinate and supervise government departments; and
(9) to appoint, discharge, transfer and punish leading State officials.[39]

Chapter 4 treats of the formation of local people's councils, whose powers and responsibilities are vague and whose relation to the central authorities is obscure. Eventually the people's councils are intended to administer the governorates within the framework of democratic centralisation.

Part IV deals with technical aspects of the legal and judicial system.

Part V deals with national defence. As noted above, the Presidential Council appoints and discharges the leading members of the armed forces including the Supreme Council for National Defence.

Part VI consists of provisional measures to apply in the interim before the new State organisation begins to function.

The first elections to the People's Supreme Council took place early in 1971. Most but not all of those elected were members of the National Front; a handful of Ba'athists and communists were also elected. As envisioned in the Constitution, the People's Supreme Council, though sovereign, is a passive entity which discusses and almost invariably approved measures put forward by the Presidential Council. It is important in so far as it recruits competent people for the Council of Ministers. There is unfortunately a dearth of information on relations between the Council of Ministers and the Presidential Council.

FOREIGN POLICY

'The PDRY has become like a peninsula surrounded by hostile forces.'[40] This statement by Rubayi Ali succinctly expresses Yemen's relations with neighbouring states during much of the early 1970s; only after the rapprochement with Saudi Arabia and Oman beginning in 1976 did the hostile ring begin noticeably to loosen.

Most factions of the NF supported union with North Yemen, and the

1970 constitution regards national unity as a paramount goal of the PDRY's foreign policy, although no concrete steps were taken to promote unity after 1967. The gap between San'a and Aden widened during the early part of the decade. The reasons for this trend were manifold. The Yemen Republic harboured remnants of FLOSY and other defeated groups after the NF had come to power – a perennial irritant to Aden; it also furnished a haven for the many splinters of the NF who grew disaffected with the ruling leaderships of al-Shaabi and Ali. Mercenaries also operated along the common border of the Yemens with the tacit consent of San'a. Commenting in 1971, Rubayi Ali said,

> It is only natural that we cannot separate the political and economic developments in the PDRY from those in North Yemen. Also, it is natural that the difficulties facing the cause of unity among progressive forces do not exclude the effects of the colonial period. British colonialism implanted undesirable customs and traditions and evil procedures in the ruling system in South Yemen. They have reflected a certain mentality in all the peoples. At the same time, we do not forget the backwardness and isolation that we had lived in the Imamate period, which led to division and conflict between the regions and tribes. . . . [To attain unity] San'a is required to provide a proper atmosphere that will allow broader practice of democracy by the masses. We are required to preserve the achievements of the October revolution.[41]

Rubayi Ali doubted that unity at the State level could be attained in the near future, but thought that at the popular level there was and remained a unity of interest. 'The people in the North have expelled the sultans and mercenaries who opposed our regime and the South took the same position against opponents of the revolution of the republican regime in the North.[42] Relations on the State level appeared cordial and co-operative; the Presidents exchanged annual visits, beginning in 1974,[43] and consultations on a ministerial level took place regularly. The objective of political unity between the two states had apparently yielded to practical co-operation on a day-to-day or month-to-month basis.[44] However, the assassination of North Yemen's President, Ahmad Hussain al-Ghashmi (allegedly engineered by Salim Rubayi Ali), and the subsequent attempted coup d'état in the PDRY in June 1978 (discussed below) have renewed tension between San'a and Aden.

Relations with the Gulf states, Oman and Saudi Arabia have been almost unremittingly poor, owing to the PDRY's strong support for the

PFLO in Dhofar province, bordering the PDRY's seventh governorate. The insurgency began in June 1965. During the period 1970–5, Omani troops and aircraft repeatedly crossed into the PDRY in pursuit of guerrillas, destroying PDRY citizens' property and lives in the process. When its position deteriorated in 1973, the Oman government invited Iranian troops and advisers to help contain what it called the Marxist threat, emanating from Aden, to the security of the Gulf. This intervention and the subsequent intensification of the fighting merely strengthened the PDRY's support for the beleaguered insurgents.[45]

A very important breakthrough took place on 10 March 1976, when after protracted negotiations, Saudi Arabia and the PDRY agreed to establish diplomatic relations. Though denied by Aden, it is thought that a number of secret conditions were attached: Aden would receive $400 million from Saudi Arabia, of which $100 million was actually transferred almost before the ink of the agreement was dry.[46] The PDRY was expected to drop its support for the PFLO forthwith, though in compensation Iranian troops would be withdrawn from Oman and the PDRY could expect further aid from Gulf states. The Saudis also exhorted Yemen to lessen its dependence on Soviet foreign aid and advisers. This interpretation was borne out by the fact that in March and July 1976 the PDRY Foreign Minister and a delegation of other ministers paid visits to various Gulf capitals and Riyadh in search of funds. Meanwhile the pace of fighting in Oman slackened noticeably. Since the attempted coup d'état of June 1978, which resulted in the execution of Salim Rubayi Ali, the new leadership in Aden has identified the nascent ties with Saudi Arabia as part of Ali's collusion with imperialist powers in a plot to undermine the Yemeni revolution.

President Numeiry of Sudan brought the PDRY and Oman together for a summit in Taiz, North Yemen, in February 1976, and at the time this was widely and erroneously regarded as marking the final conciliation between the two countries. Aden refused to recognise any agreement with Oman until Iranian troops were withdrawn and Oman agreed to recognise the PFLO. At the United Nations in autumn 1977, the PDRY Foreign Minister delivered a scathing attack on the Oman government's intransigence on this point. Relations with Saudi Arabia swiftly deteriorated; Riyadh recalled the Saudi ambassador from Aden on 14 November 1977.[47] By January 1978, fighting was reported on the common frontier of the two states, and the Yemeni forces were said to have the upper hand.[48]

To cope with its budgetary difficulties, the PDRY government has been constrained to seek large amounts of aid from abroad, without being too discriminating in terms of the political colours of the donor, the quantities involved and the conditions attached. After a few minor deals with other non-aligned nations and the Federal Republic of Germany, in July 1969 it began a major shift toward the Soviet bloc and China. In 1971 both the communist super-powers were contributing about £25 million,[49] with the major difference that Moscow's aid came mainly in the form of loans repayable at 25 per cent interest, while Peking's came in loans repayable without interest over seventeen to twenty-two years.[50] The Chinese – who came first – have concentrated on building up the country's infrastructure, providing financial and technical aid for agriculture, industry, roads and health facilities. The Chinese efforts have elicited praise from the PDRY's leadership: 'The People's Republic of China stood by our people in defence of the Yemen's revolution and in constructing the new society.'[51]

The Soviet Union, its East European allies and Cuba also participate heavily in projects in the PDRY. Soviet aid finances dams, wells, irrigation canals and geological studies, and equips and trains the armed forces.[52] Soviet sources stress the civilian facet of military aid.[53] The GDR supplies light arms and specialists to reorganise the police and security forces, and conducts mineralogical studies. Hungary is financing a number of agricultural aid projects throughout the country.[54]

Rising Soviet influence has had a noticeable impact on the PDRY's attitude to the conflict in the Horn of Africa. The PDRY's natural sympathies lay with Somalia and Eritrea, against Ethiopia. When the Soviet Union switched sides in 1975, the PDRY reluctantly followed suit but still supported the Eritrean Liberation Movement, which maintained an office in Aden. Yielding to Soviet and Ethiopian pressure, the Government ended support for the Eritreans and closed down their Aden office in June 1976. Since then, a Yemeni contingent has fought for Ethiopia on the Ogaden front.

The country has since 1971 attempted to extend its lines of credit in the Arab world and abroad. The oil-rich Arab countries – notably, Iraq, Libya and Kuwait – have extended loans and aid to the PDRY under various forms. In 1975 the PDRY launched a diplomatic offensive to improve relations with the oil-rich Gulf states.

POLITICAL DYNAMICS

Under article 7 of the Yemeni Constitution, the National Front is the leading political organisation in the PDRY. Its ties with the State are very close, although the NF organisation is quite distinct from it. Its fundamental principles are based on scientific socialism. The organisational structure is shown in Figure 25.1. Power emanates from the leadership on typical democratic centralist lines, though there is provision for lower-echelon members to criticise leadership, within certain bounds. The General Congress is the supreme authority of the NF. The Central Committee runs the party between congresses and is therefore its main institution. Like its Soviet counterpart, the NF plays a pivotal part in the central State organisation, implementing congress resolutions, appointing representatives to the highest agents of the State and economy, ratifying the nomination of representatives to the PSC, guiding the work of elected State institutions, and even appointing magazine and newspaper editors. Local organisations take their cue on problems from the Congress and, between congresses, the Central Committee.[55] The NF also operates cells in the army and the youth, trade-union and women's organisations. One estimate places membership at 26,000, with workers and peasants accounting for 12 and 4·8 per cent respectively.[56]

In October 1975 the National Front, the People's Democratic Union (a Marxist party) and the Ba'ath Party (renamed the Party of People's Vanguard in 1974) united to form the Unified Political Organisation – National Front (UPO– NF). This organisation was envisaged to serve as 'a transitional stage towards the establishment of a vanguard party in Democratic Yemen'.[57] According to the National Front programme adopted at the Unification Congress, in the first stage of unification

It [The National Front] is a tool of the national democratic revolution within the general framework of a broad class alliance between all social democratic forces who have a real interest in the national democratic revolution, i.e., the workers, peasants, soldiers, revolutionary intellectuals, and petit bourgeois.[58]

The aim of the UPO–NF, then, was the transformation of the united political organisation into a vanguard Maxist-Leninist party. Initiation of this transformation began with the preparation of an analytical document prepared for the Central Committee's Seventh Session. The aim was the completion of the process of transformation to the new vanguard party by mid 1978. To this end, the document analysed the ideological, class and organisational issues raised by the transformation. On 11 October 1978, the UPO–NF transformed itself into the Yemeni

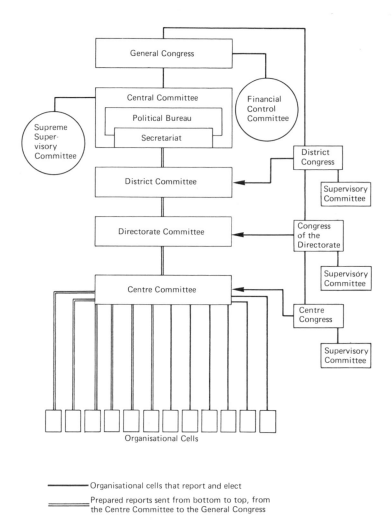

FIGURE 25.1 Organisational structure of the National Front of the PDRY

Source: National Front, *Al-Thawrah al-Wataniyah al-Dimuqratiyah fi al-Yaman* (Beirut: Dar Ibn Khaldun, Nov 1972) p. 130.

Socialist Party (al-Hizb al-Ishtiraki al-Yemeni). The basic organisational structure and leadership of the UPO–NF remained unchanged.
According to the Secretary-general of the Party, Abdul Fattah Ismail,

> The Yemeni Socialist Party is the vanguard of the Yemeni working
> class aligned with the peasants and other working segments of the
> population and revolutionary intellectuals. It is the living expression
> of this class consciousness – a consciousness of its real interests,
> future and historic role. The aim of the Party is to transform the
> society in a revolutionary manner to consolidate the achievements of
> the national democratic revolution and the transition to socialism.
> [This transition] is guided by . . . the theory of scientific socialism
> which takes into account local conditions of growth and the
> development of the national democratic revolution in our country.[59]

THE ATTEMPTED COUP OF 25 JUNE 1978

The present elite has remained in power with few changes since 1969
precisely by accommodating traditional and modern conflicts of interest
between different elements in South Yemen. By the mid 1970s there was
evidence of increasing ideological tension between the two leading elite
figures, Salem Rubayi Ali and Abdul Fattah Ismail, on a range of
foreign and domestic issues, particularly relations with the Soviet Union
and Saudi Arabia. While Ali advocated a normalisation of relations
with conservative neighbours, diversification of foreign-aid sources and
less dependence on the Soviet Union, Ismail advocated an ideologically
consistent revolutionary approach and close alliance with the socialist
camp, rejecting the moderation of revolutionary principles in exchange
for aid. Each had supporters within the Cabinet and the NF. The
individualistic power-oriented elements tended to coalesce around Ali,
the ideological socialist elements around Ismail, who had a larger
popular following than Ali and was more imposing as a public speaker
and moral figure. The split polarised around the issue of leadership, with
Ali attempting to consolidate power in governmental leadership, and
Ismail attempting to consolidate power in party leadership. A confrontation occurred on 26 June 1978, when a struggle for power between
the forces of Ali and Ismail culminated in Ali's execution and the
consolidation of the ideological faction represented by Ismail. Estimates
of the number of casualties in the twenty-four hour battle range between
600 and 15,000.[60]

The case against Ali, as summarised by Ismail, was based on his deviationist and opportunistic tendencies, revealed principally by the following:

1. Ali's alleged engineering of al-Ghashmi's assassination for the purpose of embroiling North and South Yemen in a war, a strategy designed by the imperialist and reactionary camp to undermine the revolution.

2. Ali's efforts to undermine the transformation of power to collective party leadership and enhance his personal power.

3. Ali's efforts to reduce ties with the Socialist camp and increase ties with the reactionary and imperialist camp.[61]

While it is still too early to assess the meaning of this change, it does not appear to be a point of radical transformation in the PDRY's development. Rather, it appears to signal a consolidation and deepening of the social, economic and political forms of organisation derived from Marxist principles.

The PDRY has proved modestly successful in improving the country's economic prospects in agriculture and industry after the devastation of the services sector by independence and the closure of the Suez Canal. It must constantly be borne in mind that the leaders of the PDRY rule one of the most impoverished states in the world and that their options in foreign and domestic policy are severely curtailed by the fact that the country, most of whose citizens eke out a very precarious subsistence, can not yet support itself. The people are politically volatile, still fundamentally tied to patterns of charismatic leadership and tribal allegiances.

BIOGRAPHY

Abdul Fattah Ismail. Born a peasant in the Hujairah area of North Yemen in 1940, Ismail served as political leader of the Aden guerrillas in the anti-British campaign. In January 1966 he became a member of the NLF leadership. From then on, he has been identified as the ideological mentor and Secretary-general of the National Front, the UPO–NF and the Yemeni Socialist Party, respectively. Following independence he served as Minister of Culture, and subsequently Minister of Information.

Salem Rubayi Ali. Born in the town of Zinjibar near Aden in 1935, Ali served as a leader of guerrillas in the Radsan mountains to the north. A member of the Arab Nationalist Movement in the early 1960s, he supported Ismail's left-wing group in the NLF. Following independence, he held a number of party and ministerial posts. In 1971 he assumed the chairmanship of the Presidential Council, which position he maintained until his execution in 1978.

BASIC FACTS ABOUT THE PDRY

Official name: People's Democratic Republic of Yemen (From 1967 to 1970, known as People's Republic of South Yemen) (Jamhuriyat al-Yaman al-Dimuqratiyah al-Sha'biyah).

Area, by governorate (nos 1–7): 1–7004 sq. km. (2695 sq. miles); 2–12,810 sq. km. (4929 sq. miles); 3 – 21,564 sq. km. (8297 sq. miles); 4 – 74,165 sq. km. (28,536 sq. miles); 5 – 85,744 sq. km. (32,991 sq. miles); 6 – 66,581 sq. km. (25,618 sq. miles); 7–70,175 (27,000 sq. miles); total – 338,043 sq. km. (130,066 sq. miles).

Population, by governorate (nos 1–7) in 1973: 1–291,000; 2–273,000; 3–311,000; 4–162,000; 5–451,000; 6–61,000; 7–41,000; total – 1,590,000 (1 July 1976 census, estimated total – 1,782,803).

Population density (1976): 13·7 per sq. km.

Population distribution: 30 per cent urban, 70 per cent rural.

Ethnic distribution. The formation of Israel in 1948 led to the mass exodus of the 2000-year-old Jewish community of Yemen – 7000 left Aden alone. Independence in 1967 led to the departure of the British administrative and military staff and their dependents as well as much of Aden's cosmopolitan trading community – 80,000 in all – leaving predominantly native Yemenis in the PDRY. Large numbers of Yemenis work in neighbouring Saudi Arabia and Ethiopia. The State religion is Shafie (Sunnite) Islam, with many unorthodox Zaidis (Shiite) in Aden proper.[62]

Major towns: Aden (the capital; pop. 264,326 in 1973); al Mukalla.

Employment, by sector (First Governorate, 1972): Services, 15,564; transport, 9695; commerce, 7943; manufacturing, 6297; agriculture and fishing, 1137; electricity, gas and water, 201; construction, 201; mining and quarrying, 53; miscellaneous, 1239; total, 42,330 [Source: *Middle East and North Africa, 1976–77* (1976) p. 804.]

Total economically active population (1973, sample tabulation of Census returns): 409,742 (333,954 males, 75,788 females); outside the First

Governorate, an estimated 90 per cent of the population are engaged in agriculture. [Source: ibid.]

Agriculture – principal Crops (est.):

	Area (thousand ha.)			Production (thousand tons)		
	1972	1973	1974	1972	1973	1974
Sorghum and Millet	41	42	42	70	72	76
Wheat	14	14	15	15	15	15
Barley	1	1	1	4	4	4
Sesame	4·1	4·1	4·3	3·4	3·8	3·9
Cotton lint Cotton seed	12	12	12	13	15	15

[Source: ibid.]

Foreign trade (aggregate figures, in million SDRs):

	1970	1971	1972	1973	1974
Imports	189·6˙	147·3	134·6	146·0	301·5
Exports	153·8	99·6	98·1	89·7	194·8
Deficity	35·8	47·7	36·5	56·3	106·7

[Source: International Monetary Fund, *Balance of Payments Yearbook*, 1978, p. 676.]

Main imports: clothing, foodstuffs, livestock, manufactured goods.
Main import partners: India, Kuwait, Japan, UK, Iran.
Main exports: petroleum (refined), cotton, fish, rice, coffee, animal skins.
Main export partners: UK, Japan, Australia.
Government finances (million YD) [US$1 = approx 0·345 YD]:

	1971–2	1972–3	1973–4	1974–5
Revenue	15·98	12·05	15·34	13·8
Expenditure	20·74	21·68	22·73	29·4
Deficit	4·76	9·63	7·39	15·6

[Source: International Monetary Fund, *Balance of Payments Yearbook*, 1971–5.]

Education:	Number of students	
	1966–7	*1973–4*
Primary schools	49,928	183,744
Intermediate schools	11,582	23,240
Secondary schools	2,992	6,933
Teacher-training colleges	n.a.	707
Technical institutes	n.a.	499
University of Aden – established 1975		

[Source: PDRY, *The Achievements of Social Development in Democratic Yemen* (1977) pp. 8–14.]

Foreign relations: the PDRY maintains diplomatic relations with 48 states, in four categories (countries in parentheses are those with resident missions in Aden) – (1) all communist states (Albania, Bulgaria, China, Cuba, Czechoslovakia, GDR, Democratic People's Republic of Korea, Romania, USSR, Vietnam); (2) leading and nearby Arab states (Egypt, Libya, Saudi Arabia, Somalia, Sudan); (3) major West European states (France, UK, FRG); (4) major non-aligned states (India, Ethiopia, Philippines). In November 1977 the PDRY re-established diplomatic relations with the USA, severed after the 22 June 1969 'corrective step'. The country has been a member of the UN since 30 November 1967.

NOTES

1. The Kuria Muria Islands, administered by Britain from Aden until 30 November 1967, were awarded to Oman in early 1968 – a decision which further embittered the Yemeni National Liberation Front leadership against Britain and – in conjunction with the Dhofar insurgency – poisoned relations with Oman for the next decade.
2. The odd fact that in Aden it rains in winter while only a few miles inland rain falls only in the summer is thought to be owing to two air currents: a low dry current brings to Aden weather characteristic of the Middle East, while a high wet unstable current originating in Equatorial Africa affects the highlands.
3. W. B. Fisher, 'PDRY (Southern Yemen) Physical and Social Geography', in *The Middle East and North Africa, 1977–78* (1977) p. 798.
4. Muhammad Omar al-Habshi, *Al-Yaman al-Janubi* ('Southern Yemen') (1968) pp. 56–7.
5. See V. Naumkin, 'Southern Yemen: The Road to Progress', *International Affairs (Moscow)* 1978, no. 1, pp. 64–9.
6. E. Rouleau, *Le Monde*, 29 May 1971, p. 5.
7. See.also chart in M. Wenner, 'The People's Republic of South Yemen', in T. Y. Ismael, *Government and Politics of the Contemporary Middle East* (1970) p. 423.

8. Fisher, in *The Middle East and North Africa, 1977–78* p. 8–10. Tom Little, in *South Arabia: Arena of Conflict* (1968), gives a complete and balanced interpretation of the development of political visitations in South Yemen up to independence. Equally useful is the account by the penultimate British High Commissioner, Sir Kennedy Trevaskis, *Shades of Amber* (1967), which interprets from the official British point of view.

9. Wenner, in Ismael, *Government and Politics*, p. 424.

10. Ibid., pp. 412–28.

11. Mansfield, *The Middle East and North Africa: A Political and Economic Survey* (1973) pp. 178–81.

12. The National Liberation Front dropped its middle name after independence, to become the National Front.

13. An official Yemeni source comments: 'Semi feudal land ownership continued to prevail throughout the whole occupation period until the achievement of independence in November 1967. On March 25, 1968, the first agrarian reform law was promulgated by Qahtan al Shaabi. This law, however, did not correspond to the aspirations of the masses of the poor peasantry and could not therefore end semi-feudal landownership, or return the land to its rightful owners. This measure failed for the following reasons:

   (1) the size of the maximum permitted individual holdings enabled those affected by the Law to escape its provisions and keep considerable areas of land.
   (2) the Law did not stipulate how lands confiscated from the sultans or emirs should be worked or make definite regulations for the organization of agriculture.
   (3) the Law permitted individual freehold ownership of land and thus consolidated the fragmentation of agricultural holdings, preventing the development of agricultural cooperatives.'

   See PDRY, Ministry of Information, *Economic Achievements of Democratic Yemen* (1977) p. 10.

14. Some Yemeni sources unaccountably give 22 November 1969 as the date of the 'corrective step'.

15. Interview in *Al-Jundi (Aden)*, 14 Oct 1971, p. 6.

16. Ibid., p. 19.

17. Not, however, the BP Little Aden refinery, oil for which the government could not easily procure by its own efforts. This omission was corrected in 1976, when Saudi Arabia and the United Arab Emerates agreed to provide South Yemen with a guaranteed annual supply of oil. BP was relieved to divest itself of Little Aden, which was no longer a profitable operation.

18. See interview with Deputy Prime Minister for Fiscal and Economic Affairs, Mahmud Ushaysh, *Al-Thawri (Aden)*, 16 Nov 1971, p. 2.

19. See D. MacClintock, 'Constitution of the People's Democratic Republic of Yemen', in *Constitutions of the World*, vol. xv (1976).

20. E. Rouleau, *Le Monde*, 28–9 May 1972, p. 6.

21. The new law reduced the maximum private holdings of irrigated and non-irrigated land to twenty (from twenty-five) and forty (from fifty) feddans, respectively, i.e. by 20 per cent, though most land was parcelled out in considerably smaller lots – five to ten feddans in all.

22. See PDRY, Ministry of Information, *Economic Achievements of Democratic Yemen*, pp. 9–26; also, Naumkin, in *International Affairs*, 1978, no. 1, p. 67. Since the terms may not be clear to all readers, a definition is in order. There are several different types of *collective* (kolkhoz) farms in South Yemen, depending on the level of development of the farmers and the economic possibilities open to them. State farms (soukhozes) are given priority, since they are model facilities for larger production units. Agricultural workers are guaranteed a fixed wage (as in the Soviet prototype) and certain kinds of produce. Concentration of capital permits techniques to be introduced that were not feasible in pre-revolutionary Yemen – innovations in cultivation technique, pesticides plus fertilizer. See *Neue Deutsche Bauerzeitung* (East Berlin), 24 Jan 1975, p. 25.

23. Abdel Fattah Ismail is largely responsible for the form of the State Constitution.

24. See Preamble, articles 1 and 12.

25. Ibid., article 7: the working people shall exercise all political authority in the PDRY. The strong alliance 'between the workers, farmers intelligentsia and petty bourgeoisie' is the invincible political basis of the national democratic revolution in the PDRY.

26. Article 7, clauses 5 and 6 (Note: throughout this section, quotations are from the English text referred to in note 20 above.)

27. See below, concerning Part III, ch. 4.

28. See below, concerning Part III, ch. 1.

29. Article 18.

30. Ibid.

31. Article 14. This slogan is close to Marx's formulation of class relations under socialism (as distinct from communism): from each according to his ability, to each according to his work.

32. Article 18, clause 2.

33. Article 46 posits Islam as the State religion.

34. Article 48.

35. The Prime Minister and Secretary-general of the National Front are *ex officio* members of the Presidential Council. The Chairman of the Council is President of the Republic and head of State.

36. Article 92.

37. Article 101.

38. Article 102.

39. Article 103.

40. Interview, *Rose al-Yusuf* (Cairo), 15 Nov 1971, p. 14.

41. ibid.

42. Ibid.

43. The most recent meeting took place February 1978 in San'a.

44. See also *Manama al-Adwa*, 20 Feb 1975, pp. 10–11, interview with Foreign Minister Muti concerning North-South relations. The Ministry of Information booklet, *programme of 1977*, pp. 59–60, mentions joint efforts on a variety of levels, but does not mention Yemeni political unity as a goal. The Fifth Congress of the UPO-NF made special mention of Yemini unity as a long-term goal.

45. 'In Oman, the regime of Qahbus, the Iranian forces and mercenary military

experts are continuing to launch savage bombing raids against the inhabitants of the liberated regions and the forces of the Popular Front for the Liberation of Oman, in an attempt to bring about the collapse of the armed revolution of liberation and turn Oman into a fortress of aggression and plots against the forces of liberation and progress in the region, particularly the people of Democratic Yemen. However, in spite of these attacks, the people of Oman have persevered under the leadership of their combative vanguard, the Popular Front, and have waged a heroic struggle against the foreign marauders. . . . Since the Iranian marauders invaded their land, they have asserted that they are determined to continue the struggle for liberation until the banner of full national independence is raised over Oman.

'The gravity of the Iranian invasion lies in the context of the notorious appeal to establish the "security of the Gulf". . . . It is obvious that Iran stands at the head of the notorious Gulf security plan [which threatens] the whole Arab nation and will most emphatically serve the interests of the forces antagonistic to the movement of development and progress in the whole area. . . .

'Our Country stresses that it will continue to extend the hand of solidarity and support for this revolution until it attains a victory, the foreign bases are eliminated, and the forces of the Iranian invasion and foreign mercenaries evacuated.' – Speech by Abdel Fattah Ismail before the UPO-NF Central Committee, *Al-Thawri*, 12 June 1976, p. 3.

46. *Arab Record and Review*, 1–15 Apr 1976, p. 351.
47. Ibid., 1977, pp. 222–3.
48. Ibid., 1978, pp. 177–8.
49. Rouleau, *Le Monde* 31 May 1972, p. 3.
50. Ibid.
51. *Aden Radio Transcript*, Aden Domestic Service, 1400 GMT, 1 Oct 1975. Relations on the State level between China and the PDRY remain cordial, as is shown by, for instance, the Foreign Minister's visit to Peking on 3–8 February 1977 to explore relations between the two countries.
52. *October 14* (Aden), 11 July 1975, p. 8.
53. See Naumkin, in *International Affairs*, 1978, no. 1, or V., Gorshkova's 'People's Democratic Republic of Yemen', *Mezhdunarodnays zhisn*, 1971, no. 10, pp. 159–60.
54. *October 14*, 2 Nov 1975, pp. 5–7.
55. National Front, *Al-Thawrah al-Wataniyah al-Dimuqratiyah fi al-Yaman* (Beirut: Dar Ibn Khaldun, Nov 1972) pp. 118–19.
56. Naumkin, in *International Affairs*, 1978, no. 1, p. 66.
57. *Programme of the Unified Political Organization, the National Front for the National Democratic Phase of the Revolution*, (adopted at Unification Congress, Aden, 11–13 Oct 1975) p. 14.
58. Ibid.
59. *Al-Hadaf* (Beirut), x, no. 410, special suppl. 29 Oct 1978) 6.
60. *Guardian*, 10 Sep 1978.
61. See Ismail's address to students, in *October 14* special suppl., 27 Aug 1978; and interview with Presidential Council Chairman, *Al-Hurriyah* (Beirut), 9 July 1978.

62. See Mansfield, *The Middle East*, pp. 169–70.

BIBLIOGRAPHY

See also references in the Notes.

Al-Habshi, Muhammad Omar, *Al-Yaman al-Janubi* ('Southern Yemen') (Beirut: Dar al-Tali'a, 1968).

Halliday, Fred, *Arabia without Sultans* (Harmondsworth: Penguin, 1974).

Hawtmah, Nayif, *Azzmat al-Thawrah fi al-Janub al-Yamani* ('The Crisis of the Revolution in Southern Yemen'). (Beirut: Dar al-Tali'a, June 1968).

Ingrams, Harold, *Arabia and the Isles* (New York: Praeger, 1966).

Ismael, Tareq Y., *Government and Politics of the Contemporary Middle East* (Homewood, IU.: Dorsey, 1970).

Little, Tom, *South Arabia: Arena of Conflict* (New York: Praeger, 1968).

MacClintock, D., 'Constitution of the People's Democratic Republic of Yemen', in *Constitutions of the World*, vol. xv Balustein Flanz (Dobbs Ferry, N.Y.: Oceana Publications, Mar 1976).

National Front, *Kayfa Nafhamu Tajrubat al-Yaman al-Janubiyah al-Sha'biyah?* ('How Do We Understand the Experience of People's Southern Yemen?') (Beirut: Dar al-Tali'a, Apr 1969).

——, *Al-Thawrah al-Wataniyah al-Dimuqratiyah fi al-Yaman* ('The National Democratic Revolution in Yemen') (Beirut: Dar Ibn Khaldun, Nov 1972).

PDRY, *The Achievements of Social Development in Democratic Yemen* (London, 1977).

PDRY, Ministry of Information, *Economic Achievements of Democratic Yemen* (Nottingham: Russell Press, Dec 1977).

Programme of the Unified Political Organization, the National Front for the National Democratic Phase of the Revolution (Aden, 1975).

Trevaskis, Sir Kennedy, *Shades of Amber* (London: Hutchison, 1967).

26 Socialist Federative Republic of Yugoslavia

FRED B. SINGLETON

The first Yugoslav state – the Kingdom of Serbs, Croats and Slovenes – came into existence in 1918. The peoples who joined together to form it did not share a common cultural tradition. Over 80 per cent of the population of 12 million spoke one of the South Slav languages, but there were also significant minorities of non-Slavs, including Magyars, Germans, Romanians, Albanians, Turks, Vlachs, gypsies and Italians.[1] Nowhere in Europe is there an area of comparable size to Yugoslavia[2] which contains such a rich diversity of geographical environments, languages, religions and cultural traditions. Yugoslavia occupies a strategic position in South-eastern Europe, lying across the main routes through the Balkans linking the Danubian lowlands with the Adriatic and Aegean Seas. Central Europe, Alpine Europe and Mediterranean Europe meet in Yugoslavia. Throughout recorded history the South Slav lowlands have been a meeting place for cultural influences from all parts of the European continent and from Western Asia. The present cultural diversity is a legacy from the rich historical experiences of the inhabitants of this area, during the fifteen centuries since the break-up of the Roman Empire. As the first Slav-speaking settlers established themselves, they came under the influence either of the Eastern (Byzantine Greek) tradition or that of the Western (Latin) half of the Empire. The line that divided the two halves of the Roman Empire in the third and fourth centuries approximately coincided with the present division between those Yugoslavs who use the Cyrillic alphabet and have an Orthodox religious background, and those who use the Latin script and derived their Christianity from Rome. The divide runs from the coast near the Albanian border to the confluence of the Sava and the Drina, west of Belgrade. To the west, the Croats and Slovenes have inherited the legacy of Rome, whilst the Serbs and Macedonians to the east are in the Byzantine tradition.

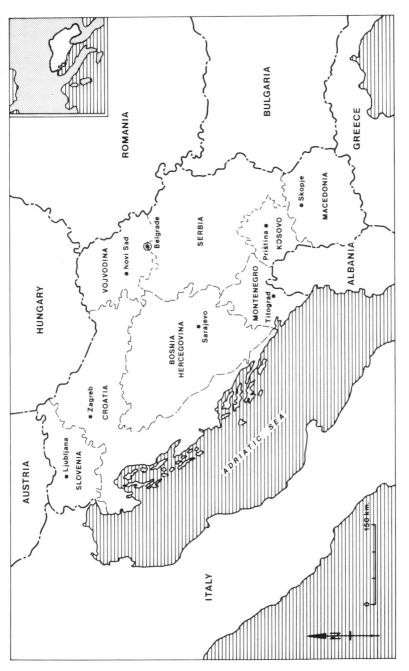

Yugoslavia: boundaries of republics and autonomous provinces.

The incursion of the Turks in the fourteenth century introduced the Islamic faith, especially in Bosnia, where a large number of Christian Slavs embraced the religion of their conquerors. These Christian heretics, the Bogomils, had previously been the victims of persecution at the hands of their fellow Christians. Their conversion to Islam meant that in Bosnia the Turks were able to rule through a local, native-born, Slav-speaking aristocracy. The Turks advanced into the Balkans during the fourteenth and fifteenth centuries. In 1389 they defeated the Serbian prince Lazar at the Battle of Kosovo Polje. During the next century they conquered Bosnia, Hercegovina and Serbia. When Constantinople fell, in 1453, the Ottomans were already in possession of most of the Balkans south of the Danube and Sava rivers. Montenegro resisted, and was never wholly engulfed by the Turks.

The Danube–Sava line forms a boundary of immense significance on the cultural and economic map of present-day Yugoslavia. To the south, where the Turks ruled continuously for five centuries, the Ottoman legacy can still be traced, in both the tangible symbols, such as mosques and Turkish-style bazaars, and in the attitudes of mind of the people and the level of economic development. North of the Sava–Danube line the Turks made inroads into the Danubian lowlands of Hungary and Slavonia, defeating the Hungarians at the Battle of Mohacs (1526). Turkish occupation north of the Danube lasted for a century and a half. By the Treaty of Sremski Karlovci (Carlowitz), in 1699, Hungary and Croatia-Slavonia were surrendered to the Habsburgs, who already held western Croatia and Slovenia.

In 1578, in the face of the growing Turkish threat, the Habsburgs established a defensive zone, known as the Military Frontier (*Militärgrenze*), which survived until 1881. At its greatest extent, the Military Frontier stretched from the northern Adriatic coast, inland along the Sava–Danube line, to the borders of Wallachia and Transylvania.

To encourage settlers to occupy the frontier area, the Habsburgs promised favourable conditions of land tenure in return for military service. Thousands of Serbs who had crossed over from the Turkish-held lands to the south were induced to move in, and their descendants are still there, forming the majority of the inhabitants of some districts along the Croatian–Bosnian border.[3]

During the nineteenth century, Turkish power in the Balkans began to wane. Serbia emerged as an independent principality, and in 1882 was declared to be a kingdom. Serbia's frontiers were enlarged at the expense of the Ottomans, and on the eve of the First World War a large part of

Macedonia was added. Montenegro, never fully subjugated to the Turks, was also undergoing a similar process of growth. Since 1696 Montenegro had been ruled by prince–bishops (vladikas) of the family of Petrović-Njegoš. In 1910 the reigning prince declared himself to be King Nikola I. Between 1878 and 1914 Montenegro almost doubled its area, acquiring a coastal strip and advancing inland to achieve a common frontier with Serbia.[4]

The Treaty of Berlin (1878), at the end of the Russo-Turkish war, placed Bosnia–Hercegovina under Austro-Hungarian occupation, and allowed the Habsburgs to place garrisons in the Turkish-held sanjak (a territorial division) of Novi-Pazar, which separated Serbia and Montenegro. In 1908 the Habsburgs unilaterally annexed Bosnia–Hercegovina.

North of the Sava–Danube line, in Croatia, Slovenia and Vojvodina, a movement for Yugoslav unity began to develop amongst certain groups within the educated middle classes, but there were also particularist tendencies which resisted the idea of pan-Yugoslav unity. The Slovenes under Austrian rule in Carinthia, Carniola and Styria had achieved considerable influence in local government in areas where Slovene speakers were in the majority. The Croats were engaged during the late nineteenth century in a struggle against Hungarian domination, and the Serbs of Vojvodina looked forward to union with the Serbian kingdom.

The circumstances which brought the three main Yugoslav groups together to found an independent state were a direct consequence of the First World War. In 1914 a Bosnian Serb, Gavrilo Princip, shot the heir to the Habsburg throne, during the Archduke's visit to Sarajevo. The Austro-Hungarians accused the Serbian Government of complicity in the crime, and on 28 July, a month after the assassination, declared war on Serbia. A week later, Russia, France and the British Empire were at war on Serbia's side against Austria-Hungary and Germany. Italy joined the Allies in 1915 after promises of territory in Dalmatia had been made.

The Serbian Army was defeated and forced to retreat through Montenegro to the Adriatic, where it was evacuated by the Allies and eventually landed at Salonika with the Anglo-French expedition of 1915. In 1917 the Serbian Government, in exile on British-held Corfu, and a Yugoslav Committee, representing Croats and Slovenes from the Habsburg Empire, drew up the Corfu Declaration, which called for the creation of a Serb–Croat–Slovene kingdom, as 'a constitutional, democratic and parliamentary democracy, with the Karadjordjevic dynasty at its head'. This was proclaimed by the Serbian regent, Alexander, on 1 December 1918.

The new state had the blessing of the Allies (except, perhaps for the Italians, who still had designs on Dalmatia) and was accepted by most Serbs, Croats and Slovenes.[5] The Macedonians were not recognised as a separate national group, and the non-Slavs – Germans, Magyars, Romanians and Albanians – had no choice.

The Vidovdan constitution of 1921 provided for a single-chamber parliament – the Skupština – elected by proportional representation. Local-government councils had limited powers, and real control was retained by the central government. The King had much wider powers than is usual in constitutional monarchies, and he frequently used them.

'Viewed in retrospect, the Constitution of 1921 symbolized the triumph of the unitary, centralist, Serbian tradition over the Austro-Hungarian tradition of ethnic and constitutional complexity.'[7] It clearly did not rest on the consent of important sections of the community. In the session of the Skupština at which it was passed, three groups of deputies were absent in protest against the behaviour of the Serbian-dominated majority – the communists with fifty-eight seats, the Croat Peasants with fifty seats and the Slovene Clericals with twenty-seven seats.

Perhaps because the Constitution satisfied the aspirations of the Greater Serbian nationalists rather than those of the Yugoslav move-ment, its life was short. In January 1929, a few months after the Croat Peasant leader, Radić, had been shot in the Skupština, the King suspended the Constitution and ruled by royal decree. In 1931 he introduced a new and even more centralised constitution, which gave wide powers to the King.

Alexander was murdered in Marseilles in 1934 by a Croat nationalist, and a regency council was established, headed by the King's cousin, Prince Paul, to act until the heir to the throne, the fourteen-year-old Peter, came of age.

By the agreement of 1939 the new regime attempted to reach an accommodation with the Croats, but before it had had a chance to effect a real change in the situation Yugoslavia was engulfed in the Second World War. In 1941 Yugoslavia was virtually encircled by Germany, Italy and their allies.[8] In these circumstances Prince Paul's chief ministers felt that they had no choice but to accede to Hitler's demand that they should sign a pact linking Yugoslavia to the Axis powers. There were widespread protests in Yugoslavia when the news of the pact became known, and a coup, engineered by a group of officers, overthrew the Regency and the government. Hitler's reaction was to order the destruction of Yugoslavia, 'with merciless brutality in a lightning operation'.[9] The Yugoslav Army surrendered after a few days; the Government fled abroad, eventually settling in London. The country was dismembered. Hungary repossessed the Vojvodina; Bulgaria and Italian-occupied Albania divided Macedonia between them; and northern Slovenia was joined to Austria. A so-called independent state of Croatia under a fascist regime was allowed to add most of Bosnia–Hercegovina to its existing Croatian territory. What remained of old Yugoslavia was placed under German or Italian occupation.

A remnant of the defeated Royal Army took to the hills of Šumadija, south of Belgrade, under the leadership of Colonel Draža Mihailović, and formed a resistance group, the Četniks. The Četniks were predominantly Serb, and swore allegiance to the exiled King Peter. Mihailović was later appointed Minister of War in the exiled government in London, although he remained in Yugoslavia until his execution in 1946. In the same area where the Četniks first established a base, another group, the Partisans, led by the communist Tito, also operated. After an abortive attempt at co-operation in the winter of 1941, the two groups became implacable enemies. Mihailović had the narrow aim of restoring the monarchy and recreating a Greater Serbia. The Partisans saw the resistance to the invaders as part of a revolutionary struggle to create a new, socialist Yugoslavia. By 1943 the British had realised that, whereas Tito's Partisans were effectively fighting the enemy and contributing to the Allied war effort, the Četniks were either inactive or were collaborating with the occupiers, against the Partisans.

As the war drew to a close, it was the provisional government led by Tito which was in effective command of the areas liberated from the Germans and their supporters. It was therefore a communist-led government which received recognition by the United Nations as being the rightful government of the Yugoslavs.

The new regime was at first anxious not to offend the Allies, and after a meeting between Churchill and Tito in 1944 it was agreed that some representatives of the royal government, led by Ivan Subasic, should join Tito's provisional administration. For a few months Tito was Premier of a government nominally under the Karadjordjević crown, although the King remained in London.[10] The elections for the Constituent Assembly (Ustavotvorna Skupština) held in 1945 were boycotted by the representatives of the royal government, all of whom had resigned from the provisional government during the previous summer. The Assembly elections were in fact a plebiscite, conducted on the basis of a single list of candidates. The first act of the Assembly when it met on 29 November 1945 was to abolish the monarchy and to establish the Federative People's Republic of Yugoslavia. Two months later it unanimously adopted a new constitution, modelled on the Soviet Constitution of 1936.[11]

THE 1946 CONSTITUTION – DICTATORSHIP OF THE PROLETARIAT

The 1946 constitution provided for a federal structure of government. Six federal republics were established. In order of size they were Serbia, Croatia, Bosnia–Hercegovina, Macedonia, Slovenia and Montenegro. Serbia, the largest of the republics, contained two subordinate units – the Autonomous Province of Vojvodina and the Autonomous Region of Kosovo. The Constitution recognised the right of the Yugoslav *peoples* to secede from the Federation, although it was not clear whether the *republics* had the right to leave.[12] In practical terms, the right of secession was as real as that enjoyed by the Soviet republics. Any attempt to canvass support for separatist policies would certainly have been regarded as a crime, and would have been severely suppressed. Throughout their postwar history, any threat to the 'brotherhood and unity' of the Yugoslav peoples has been regarded as a major political offence. Although the republics are theoretically sovereign bodies, they were left with little real power, it being assumed that they had delegated most of their rights to the Federal Government in Belgrade.

The Constitution provided for the nationalisation of natural resources and means of communication, and divided the economy into three sectors – State, co-operative and private – all of which were granted the protection of the State. The State sector, however, was under 'special protection' as 'the mainstay of the State in the development of the national economy' (article 16), whilst the co-operative sector was given 'assistance and facilities' (article 17) and the private sector was merely guaranteed the right to exist (article 16). In fact, with the nationalisation of resources and communications and the confiscation of the property of aliens and collaborators, the State controlled the 'commanding heights' of the economy in the industrial sector, although most farm land remained in private hands. Subsequent legislation brought almost all manufacturing and distribution of goods outside agriculture into State ownership. The big estates were broken up and, under an agrarian reform law, an upper limit first of thirty-five hectares and later of ten hectares of cultivable land was set for each owner.

The legislature, the Federal Peoples Assembly (Savezna Skupština), was composed of a Federal Council (Savezno Veće), elected by universal adult suffrage, and a Council of Nationalities (Veće Naroda), composed of representatives of the Assemblies of the Republics.[13] The Assembly elected a Presidium of some thirty-five members, which acted as a sort of intermediary organ between the Assembly and the Government'.[14] The republican constitutions copied that of the Federation, except that the republican assemblies did not contain a council of nationalities. At the base of the legislative pyramid were the people's committees (*narodni odbori*) of the communes (*opštine*) and districts (*srezovi*).[15]

The general principle behind the 1946 constitution was the Soviet doctrine of unity of power (*jedinstvo vlasti*), although this was modified to some extent in the Yugoslav version. What the Constitution did not define, however, was the role of the Communist Party, which effectively wielded real power. The Federal Assembly, nominally the supreme representative of the sovereign people, met twice a year, seldom sitting for more than a few days at a time, and its main function was to rubber stamp the resolutions presented to it by the executive. The Presidium, which acted as a collective head of State,[16] and which was composed entirely of prominent members of the Communist Party, was the effective controller of the State machine. At all levels of government, from the Federal ministers in Belgrade to the executive committees (*izvršni odbori*) of the communes, the Party acted as a centralising influence. The lines of command went vertically downwards. In Tito's words, there was 'a high degree of concentration of authority in the central organs of the state, and the direct management of the state mechanism by the Party'.[17] This was the classic Stalinist form of the dictatorship of the proletariat, in which the Party acts in the name of the whole working class. As the Party was itself managed on the basis of 'democratic centralism', real power of decision rested in the hands of a few powerful leaders, the ex-patrisans who had fought under Tito's leadership during the liberation struggle.

The machinery of economic planning was similarly highly centralised along Soviet lines. The First Five-year Plan, launched in 1947, established a cumbersome bureaucracy and led to a sapping of initiative.

Its size bred inefficiency, its authoritarianism sheltered in incompetence and its dogmatism led to arbitrary behaviour by thousands of inexperienced but self-righteous officials, each thinking himself to be the infallible organiser of the world revolution. The economic losses resulting from this system soon became evident, when revolutionary zeal evaporated and the mundane realities of supply, shortages of skilled labour and adequate machinery, began to emerge.[18]

The purpose of this monolith was to organise the industrial revolution which was to thrust Yugoslavia as rapidly as possible into the ranks of the economically developed nations, accomplishing in a generation what Britain require two centuries to achieve. The methods were those of Stalin, the obsession with investment in heavy industry at the expense of the production of food and consumer goods echoed the Stalinist philosophy, and the assumption behind the Plan was that the Yugoslav economy would develop in harmony with those of the other communist countries of Eastern Europe.

THE COMINFORM RESOLUTION OF 1948 AND ITS AFTERMATH

This last hope received a mortal blow when the Yugoslav leaders were denounced by the Cominform in 1948, and all economic links with Eastern Europe were arbitrarily severed. There were signs before 1948 that the system was in danger of self-strangulation in the tangled web of its own built-in inefficiency, but the action of the Soviet-led Cominform countries brought matters prematurely to a head.

Paradoxically, one of the first reactions of the Yugoslavs in the economic field was to intensify the drive to collectivise agriculture, as though to prove the Cominform wrong in its criticisms of Yugoslav agricultural policy. The drive was a dismal failure, and was abandoned in 1951, following a disastrous harvest in the previous year. Peasants were allowed to leave the collectives and the new policy was to create 'general agricultural co-operatives' by consent.[19]

The realisation that Stalin was wrong in his judgement about Yugoslavia – and particularly his crass psychological blunder in belittling the achievements of the Partisans – prompted the Yugoslav leaders to re-examine the whole basis of the doctrines which they had uncritically accepted from their Soviet idol. One result of this was the development of the concept of workers' self-management, in place of the dictatorial methods of factory management which had hitherto prevailed.

WORKERS' SELF-MANAGEMENT

Prior to the passing of the 'Basic Law on the Management of State Economic Enterprises . . . by Working Collectives' there had been some form of advisory worker participation in some factories, but the managers appointed by the State were solely responsible for the carrying out of the orders sent down to them through the economic planning machinery. At first, the new law did little to change this situation, although it did give official status to the workers' councils. Gradually during the 1950s the workers' councils acquired limited powers over the distribution of surplus income and a voice in matters concerned with working conditions, safety and welfare.

The concept of self-management was broadened during the 1960s to include non-productive organisations in the fields of culture, education and welfare, and, finally, in the 1970s, to become the basis of the theory of a self-managed society, in which all social relations are regulated by a form of direct democracy.

Within the sphere of economic production the broadening of the self-management system entailed an increase in the powers of the workers' councils over investment, which involved changes in the banking system.

Implicit in the concept of a self-managed society is the belief in the decentralisation of the apparatus of government. As self-management has developed, the powers of the Federal Government have been devolved to the republics and the communes. In addition, during the 1970s, a complex structure of 'communities of local interest' has been created to provide a machinery for the direct involvement of the people in decisions regarding the provision of social and welfare facilities. A community of local interest concerned with the health service, for example, would contain representatives of the producers of wealth, whose contributions pay for the service; the doctors and nurses, who provide the service; and the patients, who benefit from it.

MARKET SOCIALISM

The evolution of the self-management system took place at a time when the Yugoslav economy was expanding rapidly and at the same time breaking out from the constraints of the autarchy and protectionism which still affected economic policy during the decade following the introduction of workers' councils. In the early 1960s a series of economic reforms were intended to bring Yugoslavia into 'the international division of labour' and to permit market forces, both at home and abroad, to act as regulators of economic performance. The phrase 'market socialism' was used to describe a system in which self-managed enterprises competed with each other and with capitalist enterprises abroad, the 'discipline of the market' being the final arbiter of success. It was hoped that the removal of artificial protective barriers would spur enterprises to greater efficiency. The corollary that 'lame ducks' would have to go to the wall was never rigorously applied, however. The kind of political pressures which led the British Conservative government of Mr Heath to rescue its 'lame ducks', contrary to its declared intentions, have also led the Yugoslav authorities to subsidise rescue operations to prop up ailing enterprises.

Joining the international division of labour meant removing barriers not only to the flow of goods across the frontiers, but also to the flow of people. The number of foreign tourists increased from 1 million in 1961 to over 5·5 million in 1977, and net earnings from tourism rose from under $100 million to over $700 million.[20] An even greater contribution to invisible earnings of hard currency was made by the army of Yugoslav migrant workers which invaded Western Europe after the lifting of frontier restrictions. At its peak, before the recession of the early 1970s, there were over 1 million Yugoslav migrant workers abroad, and their remittances have exceeded $1300 million in all of the last five years. These mass movements of population are accompanied by exchanges of ideas, which may be as important as the flow of currency, although less easily measurable. Yugoslavia is certainly a more open society than is any of the countries in the Soviet sphere, and its citizens have more access to information about the world outside.

The decentralisation of political and economic control which accompanied the reforms of the 1960s tended to accentuate the regional differences in economic development between the republics. The relaxation of party discipline and the generally easier political situation gave an opportunity for these differences to find public expression. In Croatia, the party leadership found itself enjoying an unexpected popularity because it was thought to be expressing the national aspirations of the Croatian people and giving voice to their economic grievances. There were specific economic issues concerning the handing over by the republics of their foreign-currency earnings to the central bank, but behind these were the pent-up frustrations of the new middle classes and the intelligentsia, who felt that their opportunities for advancement were being held back because they were chained to the less developed parts of Yugoslavia. Some romantics seemed to believe that, with one heroic bound, they could leap out of Yugoslavia and find themselves living in an independent national state of Croatia. Others had the more modest objective of greater autonomy, politically and economically, and in the process turning Yugoslavia into a loose confederation of associated states. The 1971 constitutional amendments had probably gone as far along the road towards republican autonomy as was politically possible, but this merely whetted the appetites of some nationalists, who thought that with one more heave they could achieve their objectives.

The ferment in Croatia erupted into street demonstrations. There was an immediate reaction from the leadership of the League of Communists of Yugoslavia (LCY) and from the organs of military and internal security. These federal institutions came together to act in the name of Yugoslav unity, and in opposition to separatist tendencies from all quarters. Although the Croats were the most vociferous, there were nationalists in all republics. It is remarkable, considering the recent history of the Yugoslavs, that nationalism is not a stronger and more disruptive force. It is interesting to note that the call for action in 1971 came first from the LCY, at a special session of its Presidium, and it was the LCY which took the initiative in purging nationalists in Croatia and in other republics. Tito believed that the remedy lay in the revival of the LCY, which had been permeated by opportunists and 'rotten liberals', and had lost its capacity to lead. In September 1972 his famous letter sent in the name of the LCY executive to all its branches set the guidelines for the way ahead. It defined the various forms of deviation against which the comrades should be vigilant – liberalism, nationalism, étatism, bureaucratism, Cominformism. He urged the necessity for a cadre policy, to ensure the political reliability of all candidates appointed to responsible positions in industry, administration, education and public-information services. He also called for a return to the Leninist principles of democratic centralism.

In 1974 a new constitution was introduced which, in Tito's words, made a determined break 'with all the remnants of so-called representative democracy, which suits the bourgeois class'.[21] This was followed in 1976 by a Law on Associated Labour, which provided a new legislative framework for further developments in the system of self-management.

YUGOSLAV CONSTITUTIONS

Considering that the present regime in Yugoslavia has been firmly in power for almost thirty-five years, compared with the prewar royal government's twenty-three years, it is remarkable that there should have been so many constitutional changes. There have been five major constitutional enactments and many lesser amendments. It is understandable that the upheaval which followed the 1948 quarrel with the Cominform should have been followed by the abandonment of the 1946 constitution, which was based on Stalinist principles. In legal theory the Constitutional Law of 1953[22] amended and added to the 1946 constitution, parts of which remained in force; but in fact it was regarded as a new constitution. It was necessary partly because of the need to incorporate into the organic law of the State laws which had already been passed concerning workers' self-management (1950) and the workings of local government (1949 and 1952). The 1953 constitution also made important changes in the structure of the federal legislature. The Council of Nationalities was reduced in importance, and a new second chamber, the Council of Producers (Veće Proizvodjača) was introduced. This was indirectly elected by the producers' councils of the communes, and those chosen represented occupational groups, such as industry, commerce and agriculture. In addition, the post of President of the Republic was introduced, the only holder of which to date has been President Tito.

In 1963 a new constitution extended the concept of workers' self-management to that of 'social self-management'. There was a further degree of devolution, and the assemblies of the municipalities were given an important voice in the selection of deputies to the Federal Chamber (Savezno Veće). Seventy of the 120 deputies in the Federal Chamber were elected by the republican assemblies and could meet separately as a Chamber of Nationalities. The Council of Producers was replaced by four chambers, representing various economic and social interests. The principle of rotation of office was introduced, and it was forbidden for persons other than Tito to hold high office simultaneously in both State and party. These provisions were intended to make it easier for new faces to appear at the top table. The small group of ex-partisans who had held the reins of power since the war was aging, and an influx of fresh blood was needed. The 1963 constitution established a constitutional court to preserve 'socialist legality' and to interpret the constitution, and also to protect individuals against the violation of their rights. Yugoslavia was the first socialist country to introduce a court of this type. Another innovation was the establishment of a Council of the Federation (Savet Federacija), chosen by the President as a kind of privy council, with advisory and consultative functions but without executive power. It has consisted mainly of distinguished war veterans, ex-ministers and elderly intellectuals, who are honoured for their public services.

In 1967 the new constitution was amended to give wider powers to the Chamber of Nationalities and to the republics. These changes were made in response to pressure from the republics, some of which had shown some restiveness over their relations with the Federation. Having won a few concessions, the republics began to press for more. National feelings were growing and were expressing themselves in both economic and cultural manifestations. President Tito took the initiative in calling for new constitutional arrangements to cope with 'the very grave crisis that might face Yugoslavia' if he died before a new social contract had been worked out. The immediate question was that of the succession; but there were others concerning the relationship of the republics to each other and to the federal institutions; and there were also problems concerning the further development of the system of self-management. All three sets of problems were closely interlinked. In 1971, twenty-three amendments to the Constitution were enacted. Amendment xxxv provided for the establishment of a collective presidency, composed of three members from each republic and two from each autonomous province. The twenty-two members of the Presidency are elected by the republican assemblies for terms of five years. The members then elect annually their own president and vice-president, according to a predetermined order of rotation. Amendment xxxvi exempted Tito from the principle of rotation.

In the economic sphere, workers' councils were given increased powers over investment, and there were changes in the banking system, designed to prevent the emergence of a capital market.

Throughout the amendments relating to the economy runs the principle of decentralisation. Enterprises were given greater power at the expense of republican and federal government agencies, and the Federation lost powers to the republics. Certain basic unifying principles, however, were maintained. The unified market remained. Republics were not able to erect barriers between themselves to obstruct the free flow of capital, labour and goods. A common currency, common laws regarding foreign trade, customs duties, and so on, were also retained. The basic principles of self-management and of the socialist economic and political system were also held to be common to all republics. The Federal Government was charged with responsibility for national defence and foreign policy and for assisting the economically backward regions, and was empowered to raise taxes to pay for these services. A complicated system of checks and balances was established, which required the agreement of the republics to any extension of federal power.

The new arrangements were based on the assumption that the open recognition of differences between the nationalities and the provision of constitutional machinery to reconcile these differences, would lead to a voluntary acceptance of common interests, and a willingness to work together. There was some improvement, but deadlock remained over such matters as the allocation of funds to the less developed republics, until either the federal authorities or the LCY intervened.

The Croatian outburst of November 1971 was the last straw. Tito and the LCY, with the loyalty of the Army underpinning their authority, acted swiftly and decisively. The Tenth Congress of the LCY in 1974 set the seal on the purge which had been conducted during 1972 and 1973, and reaffirmed the leading role of communists in Yugoslav society. In the same year a new constitution was promulgated, which, whilst apparently decentralising even further the machinery of economic decision-making, at the same time ensured that the political diversity and even incoherence of the previous decade would give way to a greater degree of uniformity.

The 1974 constitution established as the norm a system of election to the various legislative assemblies based on delegations drawn from occupational and interest groups. The members of these delegations who sit in the legislative chambers of the assemblies are subject to immediate recall and replacement by another member, should they act against the wishes of the delegation which sent them. The delegations are formed at local level from six groupings (see Figure 26.1).

1. *Workers in the social sector.* These delegations represent members of 'organisations of associated labour' and 'work units'. These are in effect the workers within self-managed enterprises, of whom there are 5·3 million, in 21,000 organisations.
2. *peasants and farm workers:* 3·9 million active individual peasants.
3. *liberal professions:* 300,000 doctors, dentists, lawyers, and so on.
4. *State and LCY officials and soldiers.* These delegations are formed from workers in the civil service, the socio-political organisations, and civilian employees of the armed forces as well as military personnel.

THE 1974 CONSTITUTION

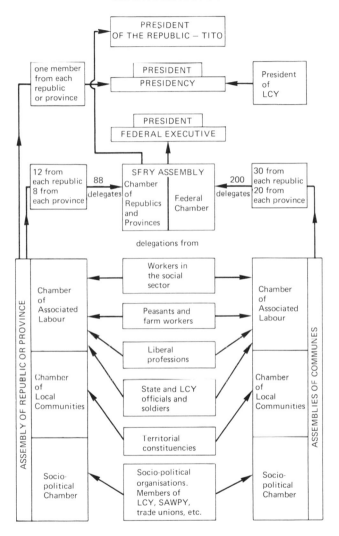

FIGURE 26.1 The government of Yugoslavia, 1974

Source: F. B. Singleton, *Twentieth-century Yugoslavia* (London: Macmillan, 1976).

The above four groups send their delegates to the Chambers of Associated Labour (veće udruženog rada) of both the communal and the republican assemblies.

5. *Territorial constituencies.* Within each commune there are 'local communities' of citizens resident in the area. The 520 communes contain approximately 10,000 such units. They send delegates to the chambers of local communities within both the communal and republican assemblies.

6. *Social-political organisations.* The delegations mentioned under (4) above include only the paid officials of the socio-political organisations. The rank-and-file members also have a separate voice, through the delegates whom they send to the socio-political chambers of both republican and communal assemblies.

The collective presidency was retained, but with reduced numbers and increased powers. For the first time since the war, both the LCY and the Army had their roles in the legislative process written into the Constitution at federal, republican and local levels. The Army's role in Yugoslav society has been greatly enhanced in recent years, both through the constitutional provision which enables soldiers to elect delegates to the chambers of associated labour, and by the changes in the statutes of the LCY, which have increased the number of Army officers in the governing bodies of the party. It is also significant that the new public prosecutor is General Vuko Goce-Gučetić. Since 1971 Tito has often spoken of the role of the Army in defending Yugoslav unity. In the afrermath of the Croat troubles, he emphasised the readiness of the Army to 'defend the achievements of our revolution, if necessary from internal enemies. This should be known!' As both the LCY and the Army are all-Yugoslav agencies, the strengthening of the role of these two powerful forces ensures that there are strong pressures against any centrifugal tendencies.

The 1974 constitution was complemented in 1976 by a new Law on Associated Labour, which regulates the relationships between self-managed enterprises and defines their role in the community.

The Law provides for a decentralisation of decision-making within an enterprise or work organisation (*radna organizacija*) from the central workers' council down to the 'basic organisation of associated labour' (BOAL). The basic organisations are the smallest intelligible units into which the work force can be divided without impairing the operational efficiency of the enterprise. They may number as few as five or six workers in one workshop, or as many as several hundred workers in a large assembly plant. The BOALs send delegates to the higher levels of self-management within the enterprise. Above the enterprise there may be a body known as a 'complex organisation of associated labour' (COAL), which integrates the activities of several BOALs working in related fields (for instance, industrial combines formed by the amalgamation of several enterprises).

There is a complicated relationship between the State, the self-management bodies and the market. In the 1960s, when enthusiasm for 'market socialism' was at its height, the 'rationality' of the market was the yardstick by which the success of an enterprise, or of the economy as a whole, was measured. In fact, there was never an unregulated free market, as the State frequently intervened – often in a piecemeal, sporadic and ineffective way. The new system envisages a decline in direct State intervention and an increase in the regulation of the market by the organs of the self-management system, including the following.

1. *Self-management agreements* (*samoupravni sporazumi*). These are legally binding agreements between enterprises, basiç organisations and COALs, regulating a whole range of activities, including pricing and incomes strategies and co-operation in marketing, advertising and commerce. They are also made between producers and distributors, and between producers and financial institutions.
2. *Social compacts* (*društveni dogovori*) are of more general significance, regulating matters of 'wider social concern' – for instance, planning, economic policy, and prices and incomes policy.

Although in theory the system of self-management has created a direct democracy in which workers 'can participate every day in the management of the economy and the political, state and other public affairs',[23] in practice this ideal has not been achieved. The fact that strikes[24] and other forms of conflict occur indicates that there are many workers who do not feel that the official channels are adequate for the settlement of grievances. As recently as November 1978, Tito, in a frank talk to trade unionists in Belgrade, warned that 'economic technocrats and political bureaucrats' were usurping the democratic rights of workers.[25] The official machinery for protecting workers' rights includes self-management courts, which can adjudicate in disputes between a workers' council and its management, and 'social attorneys for self-management', who act as industrial ombudsmen. Nevertheless, many disputes are settled by the intervention of the LCY.

THE RISE OF THE COMMUNIST PARTY IN YUGOSLAVIA

The LCY has been described by Tito as the 'connective tissue which binds multinational Yugoslavia together'. The transformation of the Communist Party in Yugoslavia from a small band of Comintern agents, operating illegally in royal Yugoslavia, to the ruling party, exercising a monopoly of power, occurred during the four years (1941– 5) during which Yugoslavia was involved in the Second World War.

The Party was founded in 1919, as the Socialist Workers' Party of Yugoslavia (Communist), its birth coinciding with the victory of Bela Kun in Hungary, when the prospects for communism in eastern Europe seemed reasonably bright. One of the Party's first acts was to organise a general strike in July 1919, which probably 'prevented Yugoslavia from participating in the march on Budapest' by Romanian and Czechoslovak forces which led to the overthrow of Bela Kun's regime.[26] At the Party's Second Congress, in 1920, the name Communist Party of Yugoslavia (CPY) was adopted, and the pro-Bolshevik left wing gained control of the Central Committee. The expulsion of a number of former socialists soon followed. In the municipal elections in the spring and summer of 1920, CPY candidates gained control of several large towns, and in the elections to the Constituent Assembly in November 1920 they emerged as the third largest party, with fifty-eight seats out of 419, and a popular vote of almost 200,000. Their greatest successes were in Macedonia and Montenegro, but they shared with the Democrats the distinction of winning seats in every province of the country. The other main parties – the (Serbian) Radicals and the Croat Peasant Party – had little appeal outside their own national groups.

Despite these initial successes, the communists were soon driven from public life, after the murder in 1921 of a former Minister of the Interior by a Bosnian communist. The Skupština passed a Law for the Protection of the State, which forbade communists to hold public office and even made it possible for courts to pass the death sentence[27] on those convicted of propagating communism. For a few years it was possible for communists to operate semi-legally through nominally independent trade unions, youth organisations, and cultural societies. They spent much of their time in factional disputes amongst themselves and within the Comintern, where it was alleged that, if you had two Yugoslavs, you got three factions. Shortly before January 1929, when King Alexander overthrew the Vidovdan constitution and instituted his personal dictatorship, the Party had been engaged on a thorough reorganisation, under Comintern guidance. In this process, Josip Broz (later known as Tito) emerged as secretary of the Party Committee in Zagreb, and received the praise of the Comintern for his activities amongst industrial workers there. Police activity against communists increased after the royal coup of 1929, which dissolved the Skupština and made all political parties illegal. The independent trade unions, in which the communists had been able to operate, were banned. The communists replied by issuing a call to workers and peasants to rise in an armed insurrection. This was a dismal failure, resulting only in the deaths of several leaders in street forays with the police, and in the imprisonment of many others, including Tito, who was arrested in 1928 and sentenced to five years' imprisonment. In 1930 the surviving remnant of the leadership fled abroad. In Tito's words, the Party was 'decimated and broken, rendered incapable of work'.[28]

A revival occurred during the mid 1930s, when the Party abandoned its policy of armed insurrection and began to work through the 'reformist and reactionary trade unions'.[29] It also accepted the Comintern's popular-front tactics and began to recruit Yugoslavs for service in the Spanish Civil War. Many of these so-called 'Spaniards' returned to Yugoslavia with the kind of experience which proved useful later during the partisan struggles of the Second World War.

In 1937, Gorkić, the Secretary-general of the CPY was summoned to Moscow and was never seen again. Along with over a hundred other Yugoslav communists,[30] he was probably liquidated in the bloodbath which Stalin had prepared for those comrades who displeased him. The successor named by the Comintern was Josip Broz Tito.

The new leadership, according to Tito's own account, decided completely to halt political emigration, and that 'the leadership of the Party shall be in the country together with the whole Party . . . and that it shall turn towards the problems of the country.'[31]

During the next few years, Tito, with Comintern support, got rid of many of the older leaders who had been involved in the futile faction fights of the previous decade, and replaced them with younger men, many of whom (such as Djilas, Koča Popović, Ivo Lola Ribar and Olga Ninčić) were intellectuals from bourgeois backgrounds. The Party machinery was overhauled and a recruiting drive launched. Party membership rose from 1300 in 1937 to 8000 in 1941.[32] In conformity with the popular-front tactics advocated by the Comintern, the CPY worked through a number of other political, cultural and youth organisations, and strengthened its influence in the trade unions.

In common with other communist parties, the CPY found no

difficulty in accepting the Nazi-Soviet Pact of August 1939, although it meant a complete reversal of the popular-front policy. Any ambiguities in the policy towards the Nazi–Soviet Pact were resolved when, in 1941, Germany invaded Yugoslavia in April and the USSR in June. Overnight the imperialist bloodbath had become a war for the liberation of the workers. The Central Committee of the CPY issued a declaration on 4 July calling for an armed uprising against the invaders. In August Tito left Belgrade for the Šumadija, and began to organise the first Partisan detachments. In the same area of Serbia, Colonel Mihailović of the Royal Army was organising his Četniks, and for a time there was some contact between the two groups, but by November their paths had diverged. Mihailović was not prepared to risk the appalling reprisals which guerrilla activities against the Germans brought upon the heads of the Serbian population. Tito and the communists realised that the German atrocities would drive the civilian population into the ranks of the resistance movement. The communists saw the war as an opportunity to achieve their aim of social revolution. They were confident that the Soviet Union would be victorious and that they would be able to introduce a Soviet-style regime after the war. The strategy proved to be successful. The communist-led partisans drew to their side people from all walks of life and all regions of Yugoslavia. By early 1944 the People's Liberation Army numbered 300,000.[33] In areas occupied by the Partisans, a civil administration based on local peoples' committees was established. In November 1943 a provisional government was inaugurated at Jajce, and a year later a combined force of Partisans and Soviet troops entered Belgrade.

Relations between the Soviet and Yugoslav communists had not always been happy during the war. The Comintern had been disbanded in June 1943, and Stalin was critical of what he regarded as the Yugoslav comrades' sectarianism in forming proletarian brigades and using the red-star emblem. He was anxious not to offend the Western Allies by appearing to support Tito against the Četniks.[34] The Yugoslavs got little material help from the Soviet Union, but the Party remained loyal to Stalin until 1948.

THE COMINFORM DISPUTE AND ITS AFTERMATH

It is possible with hindsight to discern some of the seeds of conflict between the Yugoslav and Soviet parties long before 1948. Communism came to Yugoslavia as a result of the actions of its own people. It was not, as in other East European countries, an import from Moscow. In the other countries there was no broad partisan movement of national liberation led by communists. The Yugoslavs believed that their form of people's democracy was already socialist in 1946, whilst the Soviet line was that the peoples' democracies were merely 'paving the way for entry on to the path of socialist development'.[35] Another important divergence between Soviet and Yugoslav attitudes concerned the role of the peasantry. The Partisan movement had drawn much support from the peasants, and the Yugoslav leaders talked of building socialism on the basis of a peasant–worker alliance. To the Soviets this was a denial of Leninist teaching on the role of proletariat. There were also differences of opinion regarding the economic development of Yugoslavia, Russo–Yugoslav trade relations and the reorganisation of the Yugoslav Army. The Yugoslavs afterwards alleged that the Soviet Union was trying to exploit their economy, placing Yugoslavia in the position of a colonial dependency.[36]

The exchange of views which preceded the open break with the Cominform in June 1948 began earlier that year, with the withdrawal of Soviet military advisers. On 27 March Stalin complained that his representatives were shadowed and spied on by Yugoslav agents and publicly insulted by members of the Central Committee of the CPY. Djilas is said to have alleged that 'the Soviet officers were, from a moral standpoint, inferior to the officers of the British army'.[37] There was also a hint of Yugoslav criticisms of a more serious kind, concerning the development of socialism in the USSR. Stalin refers to 'anti-Soviet rumours' circulating amongst 'the leading comrades in Yugoslavia' to the effect that 'the CPSU is degenerate', and that 'socialism in the Soviet Union has ceased to be revolutionary'.[38]

Between March and June charges and counter-charges flew backwards and forwards between Moscow and Belgrade, as the Yugoslavs tried to defend themselves against Stalin's accusations. On 28 June, less than a year after communism had been established in Belgrade, a Cominform meeting in Bucharest expelled the Yugoslavs, and called upon 'healthy elements' to replace its leaders. Apart from the charges that the Yugoslav leaders were anti-Soviet, it was alleged that they were encouraging kulaks in the villages; being over-hasty in passing 'leftist laws' on the nationalisation of 'medium industry and trade'; stifling 'inner Party democracy'; and submerging the identity of the Party in the People's Front, 'a non-Party mass organisation'.

The Fifth Congress of the CPY, held a few weeks after the Cominform onslaught, reaffirmed the support of the CPY for Tito's stand[39] whilst at the same time hoping for a healing of the breach. Tito's report to the Congress ended with the cry 'Long live Stalin!' It was not until a year later that the Yugoslavs finally accepted that, as long as Stalin lived, there was no hope of reconciliation.

The Cominform blockade forced Yugoslavia to turn elsewhere for trade partners, and to adjust its foreign policy to meet the practical necessities of the situation, but there was no immediate abandonment of 'Stalinist' domestic policies. Djilas made it clear in an interview in October 1948 that the CPY still adhered to the concept of the dictatorship of the proletariat.[40] There was even an acceleration of the drive to collectivise agriculture.

The shock of the Cominform resolution did eventually bring about a re-examination of the CPY's position. Moša Pijade told the Fifth Congress that the Party had been too busy with the mechanics of running the State to pay attention to theoretical questions.[41] It is apparent that many Party leaders only knew of Marxism and Leninism through the writings of Stalin and other Soviet writers, and had not studied 'scientific socialism' from the original words of the founding fathers. Nor had they attempted to relate theory to practice in the context of the reality of the Yugoslav situation.

When they began to do this, they began to evolve a set of policies which might be called 'the Yugoslav road to socialism'. These involved

(1) the introduction of workers' self-management;
(2) the decentralisation of decision-making;
(3) the withdrawal of the Party from direct control over all aspects of administration;
(4) the utilisation of broad front organisations under the control of communists;
(5) the introduction of 'market socialism'; and
(6) the adoption of a foreign policy based on non-alignment.

At the Sixth Congress, in 1952, the Party changed its name to the League of Communists of Yugoslavia, and stated that the League 'is not and cannot be the direct operative manager and commander in economic, State or social life'. In 1953 the People's Front changed its name to the Socialist Alliance of the Working People of Yugoslavia (SAWPY).[42] This body, which by 1963 had over 7·5 million members – almost 60 per cent of the population over fifteen years – was formed by the affiliation of other mass organisations, such as the trade unions and the League of Youth.

The opening up of discussion on the role of communists in Yugoslav society soon produced a serious controversy at the top level. Milovan Djilas, once a fervent dogmatist himself, wrote a series of articles in *Borba* between October 1953 and January 1954. In these he pleaded for an abandonment of Stalinist dogmatism and for 'more democracy, freer discussion, freer elections to social, State and economic organs, stricter adherence to the law'.[43] At first it seemed that Djilas was flying a kite for Tito, and many LCY members wrote letters of approval, in the belief that the articles were officially sanctioned. However, behind the scenes Kardelj and others were attempting to silence the stubborn Montenegrin. The last straw came when the journal *Nova misao* published on 1 January 1954 a bitter satire on the social pretensions of the men and women – especially the women – who formed the inner circle of the LCY establishment. A special plenum of the Central Committee was called to examine the Djilas case. He was expelled from all public offices,[44] and shortly afterwards he resigned from the League. The manner in which he was dismissed from public office, without legal process, on the initiative of the Central Committee, confirmed some of his criticisms of the arbitrariness of communist justice. Djilas was later tried and imprisoned for publishing articles and books in the West, which were judged to be 'hostile propaganda'. In all, he spent almost nine years in prison.

At the Seventh Congress, in 1958, the Yugoslav critique of Stalinism was further elaborated, to the anger of *Pravda*, which denounced Yugoslav 'revisionism' as 'contrary to the principles of Marxism–Leninism'. The Chinese also denounced the Seventh Congress in even stronger terms than the Russians. The LCY programme recognised the necessity for a temporary phase of the dictatorship of the proletariat, in order to consolidate the revolution, but recognised the danger that

the state may turn into a factor of stagnation, into a fetter of social development. . . . Our experience has shown that the management of the economy and of the whole of social life exclusively through the state apparatus inevitably leads to greater centralisation of power, to an ever closer merging of the State and Party apparatus, strengthening them to the point where they tend to become independent and impose themselves as a force over and above society.[45]

These 'bureaucratic-etatist deformities' can lead to personality cults, and to the betrayal of the revolution. The way out of this cul-de-sac is to initiate, as soon as possible, forms of direct democracy. Gradually the

State will begin to wither away, as socialist consciousness develops and as new forms of social and economic organisation evolve. The evolutionary process will be a long one, however, and during the transitional period the State will still have vital functions to perform. 'It will be less an instrument of force, and more and more an instrument of social self-government, based on the consciousness of the common material interests of working people and on the concrete needs of their producing organisations.' The task of the LCY is 'to give ideological guidance in the process of socialist development; in doing so it is in the vanguard. . . . But this does not confer any special prerogatives or privileges on the members of the League'.[46]

During the 1960s the LCY seemed to have lost its way ideologically. Attempts to justify 'market socialism' sounded like apologias for the return of capitalism. The leaders of the LCY have never been great ideologues. They are men of action, grappling with day-to-day problems of political and economic survival for their country. They tend to use Marxist phraseology to justify policies which have been arrived at pragmatically. At the political level, the conflicts amongst the leadership were based on such specific questions as the degree of decentralisation which could safely be permitted without releasing the centrifugal forces of nationalism; on the role of market forces in the economy; and on the forms in which the LCY was to exercise its function as 'the connective tissue which binds multinational Yugoslavia together'.[47] Thus, in 1966, Ranković was expelled for misuse of power rather than for any ideological deviation, although he was suspected of 'étatist' tendencies. The debate about ideology was conducted amongst academics, in the pages of such journals as *Filosofija* and *Praxis*. The latter voiced the opinions of a group of Marxist humanists who pointed out that the objectives of the 1958 programme were not being fulfilled in practice. They called for an end to the privileges of the newly enriched 'red bourgeoisie', and for a 'greatly transformed and integrated system of self-management'. *Praxis* was forced out of publication in 1975 and eight of its contributors were stopped from teaching students in Belgrade University.

The demonstrations of November 1971 in Croatia were only one sign of a widespread malaise. A resolution of an LCY conference in December 1972 referred to 'the penetration of bourgeois . . . concepts into the ranks of young people; a strengthening of the influence of anarcho-liberalism; spurious left-wing behaviour and demagogic ultra-nationalism; and a spread of nationalism'.

At the Tenth Congress (1974) the purged and chastened LCY asserted its role as a vanguard of the working classes, operating through the Leninist principles of democratic centralism. There has not been a return to the old administrative methods, but the loose and easy-going ways of the 1960s have been abandoned, along with the mixed bag of 'rotten liberals', opportunists, nationalists and 'étatists' who were thrown out in the early 1970s.

TABLE 26.1 Membership of the LCY, 1941–78

Year	Membership
1941	12,000
1945	161,880
1946	258,303
1947	285,147
1948	482,938
1949	530,812
1950	607,443
1951	704,617
1952	772,920
1953	700,030
1954	654,669
1955	624,806
1956	648,616
1957	755,066
1958	829,953
1959	935,856
1960	1,006,285
1961	1,035,003
1962	1,018,331
1963	1,019,013
1964	1,031,634
1965	1,046,202
1966	1,046,018
1967	1,013,500
1968	1,146,084
1969	1,111,682
1970	1,049,184
1971	1,025,476
1972	1,009,947
1973	1,076,711
1974	1,192,466
1975	1,302,843
1977	1,400,000
1978	1,629,082

Source: Jugoslovenski pregled, Dec 1976, p. 121;
Borba, 30 Mar 1977 and 10 Feb 1978.

The 1974 constitution gives a greater opportunity for communists to exercise their integrative functions throughout Yugoslav society, from the Federal Government level to the basic organs of self-management. One of the purposes of the revitalisation of the LCY (see Tables 26.1– 26.5 for data on the League and the Socio-political organisations) is to ensure that its influence will be more effectively brought to bear when Yugoslavia has to face the inevitable strains which will follow the departure of Tito.

TABLE 26.2 Social composition of the LCY, 1976

Social group	No.	%
White-collar workers	542,248	41·8
Blue-collar workers	366,272	28·1
Private peasants	65,910	5·1
Students and pupils	96,139	7·5
Others	232,274	17·5

Source: *Večernje novosti*, 12 June 1976.

TABLE 26.3 Membership of the LCY by republic, 1976

Republic	Numerical strength	Percentage of total LCY membership
Serbia	575,713	47·09
Serbia proper	370,088	30·27
Vojvodina	147,455	12·06
Kosovo	58,170	4·76
Croatia	237,977	19·46
Bosnia-Herzegovina	192,263	15·72
Macedonia	84,250	6·89
Slovenia	83,657	6·84
Montenegro	48,930	4·00

Source: Jugoslovenski pregled, Dec 1976, p. 126.

TABLE 26.4 Members of the Presidium of the Central Committee of the LCY, 1978

Name	Age	Republic or province	State post	Party post
Josip Broz Tito	86		President of Yugoslavia	President of the LCY
Edvard Kardelj	68	Slovenia		
Stane Dolanc	53	Slovenia		
Franc Popit	57	Slovenia		President of Slovenian CC
Petar Stambolić	66	Serbia		
Miloš Minić	64	Serbia		
Tihomir Vlaškalić	55	Serbia		President of Serbian CC
Vidoje Žarković	51	Montenegro		
Veselin Djuranović	53	Montenegro	Prime Minister of Yugoslavia	
Vojo Srzentić	44	Montenegro		President of Montenegrin CC
Lazar Koliševski	64	Macedonia		
Aleksandar Grličkov	55	Macedonia		
Angel Čemerski	55	Macedonia		President of Macedonian CC
Vladimir Bakarić	66	Croatia		
Dušan Dragosavac	59	Croatia		
Milka Planinc (Mrs)	54	Croatia		President of Croatian CC
Branko Mikulić	50	Bosnia–Hercegovina		
Cvijetin Mijatović	65	Bosnia–Hercegovina		President of Bosnia-Hercegovina CC
Nikola Stojanović	45	Bosnia–Hercegovina		
Stevan Doronjski	59	Vojvodina		
Dušan Alimpić	57	Vojvodina		President of Vojvodina PC
Fadilj Hodža	68	Kosovo		
Mahmut Bakalli	42	Kosovo		President of Kosovo PC
Nikola Ljubičić (General)	64		Minister of Defence	

CC = Central Committee; PC = Provincial Committee.

TABLE 26.5 Membership of socio-political organisations in Yugoslavia, 1976

	LCY	SAWPY	Trade unions
All Yugoslavia	1,460,000	12,555,000	4,511,000
Bosnia–Hercegovina	222,000	1,512,000[a]	670,000
Montenegro	53,000	315,000	93,000
Croatia	261,000	2,700,000	1,079,000
Macedonia	95,000	730,000	321,000
Slovenia	93,000	1,225,000	684,000
Serbia	635,000	6,073,000	1,663,000
Serbia proper	407,000	4,094,000	1,164,000
Kosovo	65,000	473,000	105,000
Vojvodina	163,000	1,506,000	394,000

[a] 1969 figures.

Source: *Statistički Godišnjak*, 1978.

BIOGRAPHIES

Josip Broz Tito, President of the Republic, was born 1892 in Kumrovec, near Zagreb, of a Croatian father and a Slovene mother. Apprenticed as a metal worker, at eighteen years of age he joined the metal workers' union and the Social Democratic Party. In the First World War he served as a non-commissioned officer in the Austrian Army and in 1915 he was captured by Russians. As a result, he was in Russia during the revolution. He returned to Yugoslavia in 1920 and was a founder member of the Communist Party in Yugoslavia. From 1920 to 1927 he worked as mechanic, and was active in trade-union and political work. In 1928 he became secretary of the Party committee in Zagreb. Sentenced to five years' imprisonment for political activities, he was released in 1934, in which year he began to use the code name Tito. He attended the Seventh Congress of the Comintern (Moscow, 1935) as a member of the Yugoslav delegation. In 1936 he returned, illegally, to Yugoslavia, and in 1937 he was appointed Secretary-general of the CPY, on Comintern orders, after the removal of Gorkić. He worked underground until he left Belgrade, in July 1941, to lead the resistance. At the Anti-Fascist Council for the National Liberation of Yugoslavia (AVNOJ) meeting in Jajce in 1943 he was nominated leader of the provisional government and Marshal of Yugoslavia. From 1945 to 1953, when he became President of Yugoslavia, he served as Prime Minister and Minister of Defence. He became Life President of the Republic in 1971 and is also Life President of the LCY.

Dr Vladimir Bakarić was born in Zagreb in 1912 and obtained his doctorate in law from Zagreb University in 1937. In 1933 he joined the CPY, and in 1935 he became secretary of the student communist organisation in Zagreb. Subsequently he went on to become a member of the Croatian Central Committee (1940); Political Commissar of the National Liberation Army in Croatia; President of the Croatian Republican Government (1945–53); a member of the Central Committee of the LCY (1952–66); and a member of the Presidency of the LCY (since 1966). He is author of books on rural social and economic problems.

Stane Dolanc was born in Hrastnik, Slovenia, in 1925 and is a law graduate. He joined the CPY in 1944 and was in military service until 1960. He has held the following positions: secretary of the LCY in Ljubljana University; member of the Secretariat of the Slovene Central Committee; and delegate to the Federal Assembly. He emerged as a national figure during the 1971 crisis and is now Secretary of the Executive Committee of the LCY Presidium.

Edvard Kardelj was born in Ljubljana in 1910 and joined the Communist Youth Organisation in 1926 and the CPY in 1928. He graduated from teacher-training college in 1929 and that same year became secretary of the Communist Youth Organisation in Slovenia. During the 1930s he was imprisoned for illegal political activities. He studied in the Lenin School, Moscow, and lectured at the Communist University for National Minorities; joined the Central Committee of the CPY when Tito became Secretary-general; and has remained a member of the Committee ever since. He was a founder member of Slovene Liberation Front in 1941 and a member of the Supreme Command of the National Liberation Army. He served as Vice-president of the Federal Government from 1946 to 1953; as Foreign Minister, from 1948 to 1953; and in other high government posts, from 1953 to 1967. Until his death on 11 Feb 1979 he was a Member of the Federal Presidency. Kardelj was the author of books on self-management and ideological and con-stitutional questions.

BASIC FACTS ABOUT YUGOSLAVIA

Official name: Socialist Federative Republic of Yugoslavia (Socijalistička Federativna Republika Jugoslavija).

Area, by republic: Bosnia–Hercegovina, 51,129 sq. km. (19,673 sq. miles); Croatia, 56, 538 sq. km. (21,754 sq. miles); Macedonia, 25,713 sq.km. (9893 sq. miles); Montenegro, 13,812 sq. km. (5314 sq. miles); Serbia, 88,361 sq. km. (33,998 sq. miles), made up of Serbia Proper 55,968 sq. km. (21,534 sq. miles), Kosovo 10,887 sq. km. (4189 sq. miles) and Vojvodina 21,506 sq. km. (8275 sq. miles); Slovenia 20,251 sq. km. (7792 sq. miles); total, 255,804 sq. km. (98,424 sq. miles).

Population, by republic (1977 est.): Bosnia–Hercegovina, 4,082,000; Croatia, 4,551,000; Macedonia, 1,811,000; Montenegro, 572,000; Serbia, 8,945,000, made up of Serbia Proper 5,467,000, Kosovo, 1,486,000 and Vojvodina, 1,992,000; Slovenia, 1,806,000; total, 21,767,000.

Population density: 85 per sq. km.

Membership of the LCY (Savez Komunista Jugoslavije) in 1978: 1,629,082.

Administrative division: 6 socialist republics, i.e. Bosnia–Hercegovina (Bosna i Hercegovina), Croatia (Hrvatska), Macedonia (Makedonija), Montenegro (Crnagora), Serbia (Srbija) and Slovenia (Slovenija); 2 socialist autonomous provinces, i.e. Kosovo and Vojvodina; 512 communes (*opština*); 11,673 local communities (*Mestni zajednice*).

Ethnic nationalities (1971): Serbs, 8,143,246 (6,016,811 in Serbia); Croats, 4,526,782 (3,513,647 in Croatia); ethnic Moslems, 1,729,932 (1,482,430 in Bosnia–Hercegovina); Slovenes, 1,678,032 (1,624,029 in Slovenia); Albanians, 1,309,523 (916,168 in Kosovo); Macedonians, 1,194,784 (1,142,375 in Macedonia); Montenegrins, 508,843 (355,632 in Montenegro); Hungarians, 477,374 (430,314 in Vojvodina); Turks, 127,920 (108,552 in Macedonia); Slovaks, 83,656 (76,733 in Vojvodina); Bulgarians, 58,627 (53,800 in Serbia Proper); Romanians, 58,570 (57,419 in Vojvodina); 'Yugoslavs' 273,077 (123,824 in Serbia).

Population of towns with over 100,000 inhabitants (1976 est.; figures refer to municipality only, not conurbation): Belgrade (Beograd, capital of the Republic and of Serbia) 746,000; Zagreb (capital of Croatia) 566,000; Skopje (capital of Macedonia) 313,000; Sarajevo (capital of Bosnia–Hercegovina) 244,000; Ljubljana (capital of Slovenia) 174,000; Split (Dalmatian seaport) 153,000; Novi Sad (capital of Vojvodina) 141,000; Rijeka (north Adriatic seaport) 132,000; Niš (in Serbia Proper) 128,000.

National income by sector (1977, with 1947 figures in parentheses): industry, 37·2 (18·2) per cent; agriculture, 15·7 (39·7) per cent;

forestry, 0·9 (4·9) per cent; construction, 10·7 (13·3) per cent; transport and communications, 8·3 (5·1) per cent; trade and catering, 21·1 (12·8) per cent; trades, 5·7 (6·0) per cent; communal activities, 0·4 (−) per cent.

Main natural resources: iron, bauxite, copper, lead, zinc and nickel, plus hydroelectric power and coal (low grade).

Foreign Trade (1977): exports, 95,927 million dinars; imports, 175,796 million dinars; total, 271,723 million dinars. ($1 = 18·25 dinars.)

Main trading partners, by total value of exports and imports (1977): USSR, 44,520 million dinars; FRG, 35,805 million dinars; Italy, 30,905 million dinars; USA, 15,372 million dinars; Iraq, 11,851 million dinars; France, 11,587 million dinars.

Rail network (1976): 9967 km. (2649 km electrified).

Road network (1976): 101,000 km. (41,100 km metalled).

University students (1976–7): 272,439.

Foreign relations (1977): 79 diplomatic missions in Belgrade (78 states, plus Palestine Liberation Organisation); member of the UN, the Conference of Non-aligned Nations and the General Agreement on Trade and Tariffs; associated with Comecon.

NOTES

1. The first census of the Kingdom, in 1921, recorded the following; Serbs and Croats, 8·9 million; Slovenes, 1·0 million; Germans, 0·5 million; Magyars, 0·47 million; Albanians, 0·44 million; Romanians, 0·23 million; Turks, 0·15 million; and Czechoslovaks, 0·11 million.
2. Yugoslavia's present area is nearly 256,000 sq. km., slightly larger than that of the UK (244,000 sq. km.) and the FRG (249,000 sq. km.).
3. Some villages in Bosanska Krajina, Lika, Kordun and Banija recorded over 60 per cent Serbs in the census of 1971. Examples of the percentage of Serbs in places in the Croatian border areas are as follows: Obrovac, 60 per cent; Kostajnica, 63·5 per cent; Titova Korenica, 75·9 per cent; Vrgin Most, 75·9 per cent; Gračac, 76·1 per cent; and Dvor, 88·4 per cent.
4. In 1878, after the Treaty of Berlin, Montenegro's area was 9564 sq. km. (3680 sq. miles). In 1914 it had grown to 16,243 sq. km. (6250 sq. miles). Its present area is 13,812 sq. km. (5314 sq. miles).
5. The Slovenes joined more from fear of the Italians than from love of the Serbs and Croats.
6. Vidovdan, 29 June, is Serbia's national day. On that day in 1389 the Serbs suffered their defeat at the hands of the Turks at the Battle of Kosovo Polje. On Vidovdan in 1914 the Archduke was assassinated in Sarajevo. On Vidovdan in 1921 the new constitution was promulgated. It is significant that the new regime chose 29 November for Republic Day – the anniversary of the Jajce Declaration of 1943, establishing the new provisional government.

7. S. K. Pavlowitch, *Yugoslavia* (London, 1971) p. 64.
8. The Austro-German *Anschluss* of 1938 brought German troops to the Carinthian and Styrian borders. Mussolini's Italy, already an ally of Germany, occupied Albania in 1939. Bulgaria, Hungary and Romania were all under some degree of German influence before 1941 and all eventually became allies of the Axis powers.
9. H. Trevor-Roper, *Hitler's War Directives* (London, 1964) p. 62.
10. The title Democratic Federal Yugoslavia was used by the provisional government.
11. Edvard Kardelj is quoted as stating, 'For us the model was the Soviet Constitution, since the Soviet federation is the most positive example of the solution of relations between peoples in the history of mankind' – in F. W. Hondius, *The Yugoslav Community of Nations* (The Hague, 1968) p. 137.
12. See ibid., p. 141.
13. The Council of Nationalities had thirty deputies from each of the six republics, with twenty from the autonomous province of Vojvodina and fifteen from the autonomous region of Kosovo.
14. E. Kardelj, *The New Fundamental Law of Yugoslavia* (Belgrade, 1953) p. 35.
15. The district (*srez*) was gradually phased out, disappearing altogether in the late 1960s.
16. The post of President of the Republic was not created until 1953. Its only holder has been President Tito, who in 1971 was declared to be Life President.
17. J. B. Tito, *Forty Years of Revolutionary Struggle of the Communist Party of Yugoslavia* (Belgrade, 1959) p. 32.
18. R. Bičanić, *Economic Policy in Socialist Yugoslavia* (Cambridge, 1973) p. 64.
19. In 1973 only six collectives of the Soviet type – peasant work collectives (*seljačke radne zadruge*) – remained, with a total of 810 members. There were some 2000 other types of socialist farms, involving a further 250,000 peasants. The whole socialist sector accounted for one-seventh of the land area, the remainder being in private ownership. Source: *Statistički godišnjak*, 1976 (Belgrade, annual), Tables 102.11, 107.4 and 108.32.
20. Numbers of tourists taken from *Statistički godišnjak*; value of earnings from *OECD Economic Survey* (Geneva, 1978), Table M.
21. J. B. Tito, *Socialist Thought and Practice*, vol. vi–vii (1974) p. 46.
22. Its full title was 'Constitutional Law on the Bases of the Social and Political Structure of the SFRY and on the Federal Organs of Power' (*Ustavni Zakon o osnovnama društvenog i političnog uredjenja FNRJ i saveznim organima vlasti*).
23. *Yugoslavia's Way: Programme of the League of Communists* (New York: 1958) p. 162.
24. Over 3000 have been recorded since their existence was first admitted in the early 1960s.
25. Report of Tito's speech in BBC, *Summary of World Broadcasts*, 23 Nov 1978.
26. I. Avakumović, *The Communist Party of Yugoslavia* (Aberdeen, 1964) p. 37.
27. Between 1921 and 1941 only three communists were in fact executed for political offences, but in all cases there were other charges – two of murder

and one of incitement to mutiny. Many others were killed in street battles with the police.
28. Quoted in Avakumović, *The CPY*, p. 97.
29. C. Djurdjević, *Komunistička Partija Jugoslavije 1919–37* (Belgrade, 1959), p. 29.
30. Tito *Forty Years*, p. 16 ('during Stalin's "purges" in the Soviet Union, . . . over a hundred of our Communists perished').
31. Ibid., p. 17.
32. The figure of 8000 at the beginning of 1941 is quoted in Avakumović, *The CPY*, appendix A, p. 185. Tito (*Forty Years*, p. 20) states that 'Our Party entered the Liberation War with about 12,000 members and about 30,000 members of the Young Communist League'.
33. Ibid., p. 23.
34. See Documents 42 (p. 139) and 62 (p. 145) in S. Clissold (ed.), *Yugoslavia and the Soviet Union 1939–1973* (London, 1975).
35. A. Zhdanov, *O mezhdunarodnom polozhenii* (Moscow, 1947) p. 8.
36. Clissold, *Yugoslavia and the Soviet Union*, p. 230.
37. Ibid., P. 171.
38. Ibid., p. 172.
39. According to Ranković, it was necessary to punish some 11,000 Party members who were Cominform supporters. In his report to the Sixth Party Congress (1950) he spoke of 8400 who were imprisoned. Only a handful of leading members were involved.
40. 'Odgovor druga Djilasa . . .', *Vojno-politički glasnik*, no. 3 (Sept–Oct 1948) pp. 17–22.
41. M. Pijade, *Izabrani govori i članci 1948–49* (Zagreb, 1950) pp. 51–2.
42. Socialistički Savez Radnog Naroda Jugoslavije.
43. *Borba*, 20 Dec 1953.
44. On 25 December 1953 he had been elected President of the Federal Assembly. He was also deputy for a Montenegrin constituency and a member of the Central Committee.
45. *Draft Programme of the League of Communists of Yugoslavia* (Belgrade, 1958) p. 326.
46. Tito's speech to the Congress of the SAWPY, reported in *Borba*, 23 Mar 1960.
47. Tito interviewed by *Vjesnik*, 10 Oct 1972.

BIBLIOGRAPHY

Political and economic geography

Fisher, J. C., *Yugoslavia, a Multinational State: Regional Differences and Administrative Response* (San Francisco: Chandler, 1966).
Hamilton, F. E. I., *Yugoslavia: Patterns of Economic Activity* (London: Bell, 1968).
Melik, A., *Yugoslavia's Natural Resources* (Belgrade: Jugoslavija Publishing House, 1952).
Moodie, A. E., *The Italo-Yugoslav Boundary* (London: Phillip, 1945).

History

GENERAL
Babić, V., Grafenauer, B., Perović, D. and Sidak, J. (eds), *Historija Naroda Jugoslavije*, 2 vols (Zagreb: Školska Knjiga 1953, 1959).
Clissold, S. (ed.), *Short History of Yugoslavia from Early Times to 1966* (Cambridge: Cambridge University Press, 1968).

THE BYZANTINE PERIOD
Obolensky, D., *The Bogomils: A Study in Balkan Neo-Manichaeism* (Cambridge: Cambridge University Press, 1948).

THE SOUTH SLAVS UNDER OTTOMAN RULE
Coles, P. H., *The Ottoman Impact on Europe* (London: Thames and Hudson, 1968).

THE SOUTH SLAVS UNDER HABSBURG RULE
Seton-Watson, R. W., *The Southern Slav Question and the Habsburg Monarchy* (New York: H. Fertig, 1969).
Taylor, A. J. P., *The Habsburg Monarchy, 1809–1918* (London: Hamilton, 1948).
Zwitter, Fran., *Nacionalni Problemi v Habsburski Monarhii* (in Slovene) (Ljubljana: Slovenska Matica, 1962).

THE NINETEENTH CENTURY
Wilson, Sir D., *The Life and Times of Vuk Stafanovic Karadžić* (Oxford: Oxford University Press, 1970).

FROM SARAJEVO TO VERSAILLES
Dedijer, V., *The Road to Sarajevo* (London: MacGibbon and Kee, 1967).

THE YUGOSLAV KINGDOM, 1918–1941
Bogdanov, V., *Historija Polticnih stranaka u Hrvatskoj* (Zagreb: Novinarska izdavačko poduzeće, 1958).
Hoptner, J. B., *Yugoslavia in Crisis, 1954–1941* (New York: Columbia University Press, 1962).
Maček, V., *In the Struggle for Freedom* (New York: Pennsylvania State University Press, 1957).
Ristić, D. N., *Yugoslavia's Revolution of 1941* (University Park, Pennsylvania: State University Press, Penn, 1966).

MISCELLANEOUS
Rothenberg, G. E., *The Austrian Military Border in Croatia, 1522–1747* (Chicago: University of Chicago Press, 1966).
——, *The Military Border in Croatia, 1740–1881* (Chicago: University of Chicago Press, 1966).
Barker, E., *Macedonia – Its Place in Balkan Power Politics* (London, 1950).
Čašule, V. (ed.), *From Recognition to Repudiation: Bulgarian Attitudes on the Macedonian Question* (Skopje: Kultura 1972).
Morison, W. A., *The Revolt of the Serbs Against the Turks, 1804–1813* (Cambridge: Cambridge University Press, 1942).

SECOND WORLD WAR
Deakin, F. W., *The Embattled Mountain* (Oxford: Oxford University Press, 1971).
Dedijer, V., *With Tito Through the War – Partisan Diary 1941–44* (London, 1951).

Postwar Yugoslavia

Djilas, M., *The New Class: An Analysis of the Communist System* (London: Allen and Unwin, 1957).
Hondius, Frits W., *The Yugoslav Community of Nations* (The Hague: Mouton, 1968).
Praxis, Smisao i Perspektive Social Socijalizam (Zagreb, 1965).
Zukin, Sharon, *Beyond Marx and Tito: Theory and Practice in Yugoslav Socialism* (London and New York: Cambridge University Press, 1965).

ENGLISH TEXTS OF CONSTITUTIONS
The Constitution of the SFRY: Constitutional Amendments (Belgrade: Secretariat of Information, 1969).
The Constitution of the SFRY (Belgrade: Secretariat of the Federal Assembly Information Service, 1974).
Kardelj, E., *The New Fundamental Law of Yugoslavia* (Belgrade, 1953).

COMMUNIST PARTY
Avakumović, I., *History of the Communist Party of Yugoslavia,* vol. 1 (Aberdeen: University of Aberdeen Press, 1964).
Draft Programme of the League of Communists of Yugoslavia (Belgrade, 1968).
Johnson, A. Ross, *The Transformation of Communist ideology: The Yugoslav Case 1945–53* (Cambridge, Mass. and London: MIT Press, 1972).
Marković, M., *The Contemporary Marx: essays on humanist Communism* (Nottingham: Spokesman, 1974).
Tito, J. B., *Political Report of the Central Committee of the CPY* (Belgrade, 1948).
Tito, J. B., *Forty Years of Revolutionary Struggle of the Communist Party of Yugoslavia* (Belgrade, Yugoslavija, 1959).

YUGOSLAVIA, THE COMINFORM AND THE USSR
Clissold, S. C. (ed.), *Yugoslavia and the Soviet Union 1939–1973* (London: Oxford University Press, 1975).
Dedijer, V., *Tito Speaks: His Self Portrait and Struggle with Stalin* (London: Weidenfield and Nicolson, 1953).
Dedijer, V., *Izgubljena Bitka J. V. Stalina* (Sarajevo, 1969).
Djilas, M., *Conversations with Stalin* (London: Hart Davis, 1962).
Pijade, M. S., *About the Legend that the Yugoslav Uprising Owed Its Existence to Soviet Assistance* (London, 1950).

FOREIGN RELATIONS
Rubinstein, A. A., *Yugoslavia and the Non-aligned World* (Oxford: Oxford University Press, 1970).

820 Marxist Governments

ECONOMICS AND SOCIOLOGY
Bićanić, R., *Economic Policy in Socialist Yugoslavia* (Cambridge: Cambridge University Press, 1973).
Dirlam, J. and Plummer, J., *An Introduction to the Yugoslav Economy* (Columbus, Ohio: Charles E. Merrill, 1973).

ECONOMIC PLANNING
Meneghello-Dincic, K., *Les Experiences Yugoslaves d'Industrialisation et Planification* (Paris: Editions Ciyas, 1970).
Milenkovitch, B., *Plan and Market in Yugoslav Economic Thought* (New Haven, Conn.: Yale University Press, 1971).
Sirc, L., *Economic Devolution in Eastern Europe* (London: Longman, 1969).

SELF-MANAGEMENT
Adizes, Ichak and Borgese, E. M. (eds), *Self-Management: New Dimensions to Democracy. Alternatives for a New Society* (Santa Barbara, California and Oxford: ABC-Clio, 1975).
Broekmeyer, M. J. (ed.), *Yugoslav Workers' Self-Management* (Dordrecht: Reidel, 1970).
First International Conference on Participation and Self-Management Dubrovnik, 13–17 December, 1972. Reports, 2 vols (Zagreb, 1972).
Moore, R., *Self-management in Yugoslavia* (London: Fabian Society, 1970).
Singleton, F. B. and Topham, A. J., *Workers' Control in Yugoslavia* (London: Fabian Society, 1963).
Vanek, J., *The Economics of Workers' Management: A Yugoslav Case Study* (London: Allen and Unwin, 1972).

REGIONAL ECONOMIC PROBLEMS
Mihailović, K., *Regional Aspects of Economic Development* (New York, 1972).

AGRICULTURE AND RURAL SOCIETY
Tomasevich, J., *Peasants, Politics and Economic Change in Yugoslavia* (Stanford, Calif.: Stanford University Press, 1955).

RELATIONS BETWEEN THE NATIONALITIES
Jončić, K., *The Relations between the Nationalities in Yugoslavia* (Belgrade: Medjunarodua Politika, 1967).
Palmer, S. E. and King, R. R., *Yugoslav communism and the Macedonian Question* (London: Archon Books, 1971).
Shoup, P., *Communism and the Yugoslav National Question* (New York: Columbia University Press, 1968).

Biographies

Auty, P., *Tito: A Biography* (London: Penguin Books, 1970).
Maclean, Sir F., *Disputed Barricade – The Life and Times of Josip Broz-Tito, Marshal of Yugoslavia* (London: Cape, 1957).
Zilliacus, K., *Tito of Yugoslavia* (London: Cape, 1952).

AUTOBIOGRAPHIES
Čolaković, R., *Winning Freedom* (London: Lincolus-Praeger, 1962).
Dedijer, V., *Beloved Land* (London:MacGibbon and Kee, 1961).

Djilas, M., *Land without Justice* (London: Methuen, 1958).
——, *Parts of a Lifetime* (New York, London: Harcourt Brace Jovanovich, 1958).
Vukmanović, S. (Tempo), *Revolucija Koja Teče: Memoari* (Belgrade, 1971).

General works

Burks, R. V., *The Dynamics of Communism in Eastern Europe* (Oxford: Oxford University Press, 1961).
Heppell, M. and Singleton, F. B., *Yugoslavia* (London: Benn, 1961).
Pavlowitch, S., *Yugoslavia* (London: Benn, 1971).
Seton-Watson, H., *East European Revolution*, 3rd ed. (London: Methuen, 1956).
Singleton, F. B., *Background to Eastern Europe* (Oxford: Pergamon, 1965).
——, *Twentieth Century Yugoslavia* (New York, London: Macmillan, 1976).

Glossary

aktiv	leading cadre (USSR)
aktyw	leading cadre (Poland)
aldeamento	fortified village (Mozambique)
aldeia communal	communal village (Mozambique)
apparatchik	government official
centro de descolonização	
mental	mental decolonisation centre (Mozambique)
Četnik	Serbian resistance soldier in World War II
circulo	party group (Mozambique)
društveni dogovorii	social compacts (Yugoslavia)
grupo dinamizador	dynamising group (Mozambique)
izvršni odbor	commune executive committees (Yugoslavia)
Jaalle	comrade, friend (Somalia)
knez	prince (Serbia)
kolkhoz	collective farm (USSR)
krai	territory (USSR)
kulak	rich peasant
Narodni Odbori	People's Committees (Yugoslavia)
oblast	province (USSR)
opština	commune (Yugoslavia)
Ostpolitik	Eastern policy (FRG)
radna organizacija	work organisation (Yugoslavia)
samizdat	underground publication
samoupravni sporazumi	self-management agreements (Yugoslavia)
Savet Federacija	Council of the Federation (Yugoslavia)
Savezna Skupština	People's Assembly (Yugoslavia)
Savezno Veće	Federal Council (Yugoslavia)
Sejm	National Assembly (Poland)
Skupština	Parliament (Yugoslavia 1921)
srezov	district (Yugoslavia)
ustavotvorna skupština	constituent assembly (Yugoslavia)
veće naroda	council of nationalities (Yugoslavia)
veća udruženog rada	chambers of associated labour
vladika	prince-bishop (Montenegro)
Znak	The Sign: a Catholic group (Poland)

Index

Cumulative Index for Volumes 1–3

Somalia, 311, 645
Soviet Union, 293, 311
United States, 293
Yemen, People's Democratic
    Republic, 311, 772
'Ethiopia Tikdem' (Ethiopia First),
    299–300
Ethiopian Democratic Union (EDU),
    299, 302, 306
Ethiopian National Democratic
    Revolution Programme
    (ENDRP), 305, 307
    and Eritrea, 311
Ethiopian Orthodox Church, 295
Ethiopian People's Revolutionary
    Party, 308
Ethnic groups:
    Ethiopia, 293, 295
    Mozambique, 527–9
    Vietnam, 715, 727, 735–6, 746
    Yemen, PDR, 762, 777
    see also Tribal rivalries
Ethnic minorities:
    Angola, 64
    Benin, 87, 89, 111
    Congo, 214, 222
    Hungary, 385
    Laos, 471, 477, 479
    see also Minorities; Nationalities
Eurocommunism, 345, 578, 625
    Hungarian attitude to, 403
Europe and Soviet Union, 661, 663
European Economic Community
    and:
    Benin, 103
    Congo, 229
    German Democratic Republic, 348
    Hungary, 402
    Romania, 626
European residents, Mozambique,
    529
Examinations (China), 181
Executive Committee, Partido
    Africano de Independência de
    Guiné e Cabo Verde, 373
Exiles (Congo), 222
    see also Emigré groups
Expatriates, Congo, 214, 215, 226
'Export of revolution', Cuba, 253

Exports:
    Benin, 104–5
    Congo, Mozambique, 226, 540
    Mozambique, 540
    see also Foreign trade
Expulsion from ruling party:
    Albania, 46
    Poland, 562, 564
    Soviet Union, 669, 671
External affairs:
    Albania, 56
    Angola, 81
    Benin, 108
    Bulgaria, 138–9
    China, 169
    Congo, 229, 231
    Cuba, 353–4
    Czechoslovakia, 282–3
    German Democratic Republic, 349
        and developing countries, 351
        proletarian internationalism, 351
        socialist internationalism, 350–1
    Guinea-Bissau and Cape Verde,
        377–8
    Hungary, 402–3
    Kampuchea, 426–8
    see also Kampuchea (since 7
        January 1979), diplomatic re-
        cognition; National United
        Front for the Salvation of
        Kampuchea, programme
    Korea, DPR, 454–6
    Laos, 482–5
    Mongolia, 519
    Mozambique, 543–5
    Poland, 578–9
    Romania, 624–7
    Somalia, 653–7
    Soviet Union, 687ff., 697
    Vietnam, 739–42
    Yemen, PDR, 769–72
    Horn of Africa, 772

Farmers' organisations:
    Cuba, 249, 250–1
    Ethiopia, 302
    German Democratic Republic,
        334
Fatherland Front (Vietnam), 734

Polish United Workers' Party, 564–70
see also Poland, Polish United Workers' Party
Political Bureau:
  Bulgarian Communist Party, 124, 126, 127, 129, 136
  Communist Party of China, 145
  Communist Party of Cuba, 245
  Communist Party of the Soviet Union, 669–70, 673
  meetings, 669
  membership, 669
  planning, 675
  Congolese Party of Labour, 217, 218–19
  Ethiopia, see Provisional office for Mass Organisational Affairs
  Frelimo, see Permanent Bureau
  Hungarian Socialist Workers' Party, 394
  Kampuchea, see Standing Committee of the Central Committee of the Communist Party of Kampuchea
  Korean Workers' Party, see Political Committee
  Mongolian People's Revolutionary Party, 507
  MPLA – Party of Labour, of Angola, 72, 74, 78–9
  Party of Labour of Albania, 45, 49, 51
  People's Revolutionary Party of Benin, 94
  Polish United Workers' Party, 566
  Polish Workers' Party, 557–9
  see also Polish Socialist Party
  Romanian Communist Party, 610
  Socialist Unity Party, 330
  Somali Socialist Revolutionary Party, 650
  Vietnam Communist Party, 721, 723, 724, 725, 726, 744, 745
  membership, 731–2
  see also Presidium of Central Committee; Permanent Political Committee, Permanent Bureau; Standing Presidium

Political Committee, Korean Workers' Party, 460, 461, 463
Political consciousness (Soviet Union), 684
Political education (Soviet Union), 682
Political parties (non-ruling):
  Bulgaria, see Bulgarian Agrarian Union
  Czechoslovakia, see Czech Socialist Party; People's Party; Slovak Freedom Party; Slovak Revival Party
  Ethiopia, see All Ethiopian Socialist Movement; Marxist–Leninist Revolutionary Organisation; Revolutionary Seded Labour League; Revolutionary Struggle of the Oppressed Peoples of Ethiopia
  German Democratic Republic, see Christian Democratic Union; Democratic Farmers' Party; Liberal Democratic Party of Germany; National Democratic Party
  Korea, DPR, see Korean Democratic Party; Chŏngu Party
  Poland, see Democratic Party; United Peasant Party
  Romania, outlawed, 598
  Vietnam, 734
  Yugoslavia, 788, 789, 802
Political trials (Czechoslovakia), 264, 270
Polycentrism, 690
Popović, Koča, 803
Popular Front for the Liberation of Oman, 762, 771–2
Popular Movement for the Liberation of Angola (MPLA), 65ff., 543
  see also MPLA – Party of Labour
Popular Socialist Party (Cuba), 239, 240, 241, 242
  M 26/7 relations with, 240
  see also Communist Party of Cuba; Revolutionary Communist Union

DATE DUE

GAYLORD			PRINTED IN U.S.A.